WORLD YEARBOOK
OF EDUCATION 1984

World Yearbook of Education 1984

Women and Education

Edited by **Sandra Acker** *(Guest Editor)*
Jacquetta Megarry *(Series Editor)*
Stanley Nisbet *(Associate Editor)*
and **Eric Hoyle** *(Consultant Editor)*

**Kogan Page, London/Nichols Publishing
Company, New York**

Previous titles in this series

World Yearbook of Education 1980
Professional Development of Teachers
Edited by Eric Hoyle and Jacquetta Megarry
US Consultant Editor: Myron Atkin

World Yearbook of Education 1981
Education of Minorities
Edited by Jacquetta Megarry, Stanley Nisbet
and Eric Hoyle
Subject Adviser: Ken Eltis

World Yearbook of Education 1982/83
Computers and Education
Edited by Jacquetta Megarry, David R F Walker,
Stanley Nisbet and Eric Hoyle

WIDENER UNIVERSITY
WOLFGRAM
LIBRARY
CHESTER, PA

DISCARDED

WIDENER UNIVERSITY

First published in Great Britain in 1984 by Kogan Page Limited
120 Pentonville Road, London N1 9JN

Copyright © 1984 Kogan Page Limited and contributors
All rights reserved

British Library Cataloguing in Publication Data

World Yearbook of Education. — 1984
    1. Education — Periodicals
    I. Title
    370'.5 L16

ISBN 0-85038-763-9
ISSN 0084-2508

First published in the USA 1984
by Nichols Publishing Company
PO Box 96, New York, NY 10024

ISBN 0-89397-176-6

Printed and bound in Great Britain by
Billing & Sons Ltd, Worcester

Contents

Acknowledgements

The editors would like to thank the following people who made valuable comments on our many draft contents lists and helped us to locate suitable contributors: Madeleine Arnot, Loulou Brown, Miriam David, Alison Kelly, Gail Kelly, Renate Duelli Klein, Lyn Yates.

List of contributors

Preface

Margaret Sutherland

UNESCO declared 1975 International Women's Year: but in education progress towards equality for women had already begun. During the preceding ten to fifteen years there had been marked improvement in the access of females to education throughout the world. In countries where formerly the participation of girls in primary education had been limited, a higher percentage of girls was now found in primary schools. In countries where girls had been less well represented in secondary education, in many cases the statistics began to show equal proportions of girls and boys at this level. In higher education, where females had been under-represented in all countries, there was an upsurge in numbers of female students so that in the most developed educational systems equality came nearer at this level too. During the ensuing, and now nearly ending, Decade for Women announced by UNESCO, the rate of improvement has been less dramatic but improvement has continued in many countries. There has also been a tremendous growth in books and articles about women and education. Much research has analysed the influence of gender in education, including the subtler effects of materials used in teaching, of school practices and teachers' attitudes. Women have contributed greatly to this writing and research. In the curriculum of schools and higher institutions in many countries a new element — or indeed a re-thinking of the whole content — has been introduced by the development of Women's Studies. Even language usages have been affected: there is now a much greater probability that statements will be made in a form indicating explicitly that both females and males are referred to. In English, 'he or she', despite protests about awkwardness, is a wording much more often heard or read now than in the past. So it seems appropriate to do some stock-taking now. How far has equality in fact been achieved? What problems still remain to be solved? Is there a continuing need for further studies of the situation of women in education?

The 1984 *World Yearbook: Women and Education* helps us to answer such questions: further studies and further thought are certainly needed. In many educational systems women are still under-represented in higher education, most notably at the level of masterships, doctorates and university teaching. In some systems girls still have less secondary education than boys, and there are still some systems in which girls are under-represented in primary education. At one level, these patterns are consequences of individual and family decisions. For example, in countries where education is not compulsory or free, families may be more likely to think that educating boys is more important and a more profitable investment. At another level, differential enrolment reflects decisions by governments as to what kinds and amounts of education are to be provided for girls. Furthermore, all education systems at some stage offer options within and between courses which lead to different vocational and career prospects. Insidiously, adolescent choices tend to follow traditional patterns and expectations of male and female, so that options end by reinforcing inequality in career prospects, pay and prestige. Education leads on to work in the larger society. If that society does not offer equal chances in employment then the efforts of educators to provide fairly for all pupils, irrespective of gender, will be fruitless. Perceptions of the practices and attitudes of society will determine the reaction of both girls and boys to such education as is offered in schools and higher institutions.

Moreover, many people remain convinced that the natural abilities of males and females do indeed differ significantly and that from this must follow differences in the kind of life-pattern most appropriate to them. Such beliefs are often used to support an elaborate edifice based on allegedly sex-specific abilities, though in fact any observed and measured differences may be slight, showing greater differences within groups than between groups. Almost complete dichotomies of subject-studies, careers and ways of life may be founded on this slight base. Higher spatial ability, for example, is not, one would judge, necessarily associated with inability to use a vacuum cleaner or inability to get up in the night to attend to a crying child — yet at times it would almost appear that some such associations are assumed.

Action evokes reaction. In a number of countries there is evidence of a backlash against claims for the improvement of women's situation and against claims for recognition of the important contribution women make to education, both formal and informal. In the USA, the proposed Equal Rights Amendment to the constitution — 'Equality of rights under the law shall not be denied or abridged by the United States or any state on account of sex' — has failed to gain approval by the required number of states. Elsewhere, legislation originally intended to help the employment chances of women has been interpreted in a way that effectively reduces these chances. There are many expressions of hostility towards 'feminists', a hostility often based on misunderstanding of the feminist arguments and on ignorance of the problems which feminist movements are striving to solve. All these reactions reveal a continuing likelihood that inequality in education and society will be sustained.

Particularly strong reactionary trends are evident in the definitions of women's education and status provided by some exponents of Islamic religion. Not all Muslim states and groups interpret the teachings of their religion in the same way as, for example, Iran at present, but there are certain conflicts of principle which have to be recognized and judged between societies offering equal rights to females and males and those determining life-style and education on the basis of gender. The effects of the teachings of various religions on male and female roles have often been to limit the access of women to education: thus the influence of religion on educational opportunity continues to merit attention.

Given this present complex of forces working for and against women's access to and benefit from education, the present *World Yearbook*'s systematic review of the position is indeed essential. We need to know what is happening in a number of countries and what principles seem to be deciding educational practice. Present practices cannot be understood without reference to historical and sociological factors. Links between employment and education are decisive, as are the links between what is provided as education in schools and what the family teaches: the interpretation of roles in the family must affect the course of education for individuals. This *World Yearbook* includes discussion of these matters of wider principle, together with reports on the actual situation of the education of girls and women in different countries.

If we are concerned about equality, there is a further question which has to be thought about today. Is the progress which has been made in the education of women going to be maintained? Is there the possibility or probability of regression, a regression strengthened by the problems of economic recession in so many countries? At different points in history we can trace upsurges of improvement in the position of women in education and in society, followed all too often by reversion to an inferior state or to the *status quo*. One of the late nineteenth and early twentieth century victories in the Western world, for example, was the opening of universities to female students. But what happened after the initial enthusiasm and liberalization? The proportion of women students remained relatively small, women were a minority group among university students until the sudden renewal of progress in the 1960s and 1970s of this century. Looking at such fluctuations, we must wonder whether the line of progress, having recently reached a peak, is now going on to re-descend into a trough, possibly sustained by some of the recent gains but still falling lower than in the best years.

Is this too pessimistic a view? Surely, it can be argued, the position of girls and women in education is now firmly secured by relevant legislation? So, too, in many societies, is the general position of women secured by equal opportunities acts, by acts against discrimination on the grounds of sex as well as of race and religion. This, one would hope, is so. Legislation does offer important safeguards, even if there remains much work to be done in ensuring that legislation is respected and works in practice as it was intended to work in principle. Some students of the situation would indeed assert that legislation, in the most advanced countries at least, has afforded all possible provision and safeguarding. Yet we cannot assume that the situation is therefore now satisfactory.

As many of the contributions to this book show, the attainment of equality in education is still far from complete; despite legislation, we still have to cope with attitudes which are long-lived, deeply-rooted and not simply to be altered by laws. Such attitudes, expressed through formal and informal education, may, for example, be producing reluctance in women to take a full part in the political life of their country, for women are still very much in a minority in governments all over the world, even where women's right to vote has long since been recognized. Legislation cannot ensure changes in the way people think and feel: hence impediments to the progress of reform remain.

At present, therefore, concern for women's education must impose a two-fold task — to guard against regression and to modify attitudes. For both divisions of the task it is important to be well informed and be kept well informed. Past regressions have taken place in response to various social and economic forces operating unperceived, with little comment or awareness at the time: they have been fostered by complacency about, and ignorance of, the actual situations. This present review of women and education serves to dispel complacency and ignorance. Many chapters here show the need to work for further improvement and indicate the ways in which further improvement might be made. Regression should not pass unobserved.

However, modification of attitudes is a difficult process. Some educational systems are recognizing the problem by including discussion of sex roles and sex stereotypes in their curricula even if, in so doing, they are aware that the views put forward in school may run counter to some parents' strongly held beliefs. Some systems are studying (as, for example, the Finnish system) how a national policy on promoting equality between the sexes can be implemented by teaching about equality through school subjects. It remains to be seen whether these methods will succeed or others must be found. Which educational system will prove most effective not only in offering equal and apparently open access to all children and all members of society but also in educating people so that the older and less rational beliefs about gender and associated life-styles and employment are eradicated? Some of the present *World Yearbook* contributors throw light on this problem.

In the formation and modification of attitudes, information also has a part to play. Reasonable people find that their attitudes are affected by the study of relevant information. Similarly, those who wish to improve the understanding of others — friends, acquaintances, pupils or students — who have unthinkingly adopted current prejudices will find valuable ammunition here.

Thus, on all counts, the present publication is to be most warmly welcomed. *Women and Education* offers evidence as to the situation of girls and women in different educational systems, including Third World as well as 'developed' countries. It illuminates their position with insights from philosophy, psychology, sociology and sociolinguistics in Part 1. Part 2 presents case studies with empirical evidence from five continents.

Part 3 sets the education of women into the wider context of the family, the labour market, religious tradition and technological change, while Part 4 illustrates some policies and strategies for change as pursued in different parts of the world. So this volume provides a firm base for the formulation of policies for further development, an overview of what has so far been achieved and what remains to be achieved: in all, an inspiration as to what should be done in women's education in future.

1. Introduction: sex, gender and education

Jacquetta Megarry

Summary: All over the world women encounter special problems as consumers and providers of education. By comparison with their male counterparts, they under-participate in formal education, tend to under-achieve in post-primary education (especially in science and technology-related subjects) and are under-represented in senior and promoted posts in the education service, whose decision-making bodies tend to suffer from the 'man-as-the-norm' syndrome. Until recently, these problems had been neglected for reasons which include (i) persistent confusion between sex and gender; (ii) the prevailing power of traditional assumptions; (iii) the 'invisibility' of important evidence and (iv) the subtlety and pervasiveness of gender-typing.

Empirical studies of sex differences in aptitude have been inconclusive, and rife with methodological difficulties. A more pressing question than the origins of sex differences in aptitude — insofar as they do exist — is how the education system should respond to them. There is widespread evidence that the content, process and organization of formal education all tend to reinforce, rather than counteract, the gender-typing tendencies of society, the world of work and family life. Combining an awareness of the problems with a willingness to learn from successful experiments in different parts of the world, education systems can overcome many of women's difficulties hitherto regarded as intractable.

In her preface, Margaret Sutherland poses a number of questions which she believes this book will help to answer. This chapter provides an introductory background to her questions and indicates the framework in which the various contributions are placed.

The choice of 'Women and Education' as a *World Yearbook* theme will seem long overdue to some readers — yet others will find it surprising and perhaps feel that it requires justification. Why, the sceptic might ask, is 'Women and Education' a theme while 'Men and Education' self-evidently is not? Are not all *World Yearbooks* relevant to the education both of men *and* of women? Is there, in fact, a problem about women as consumers and providers of education?

This chapter starts by summarizing the evidence that a problem does indeed exist, and tries to explain why it has been neglected for so long. It then considers the relationship between gender, aptitude and achievement; looks briefly at gender and schooling and problems of unequal access; and discusses some of the remedies proposed by later chapters.

What is the problem?

Under-participation

Nowhere in the world do women participate equally with men in formal education. Chapter 6 in this volume shows how in the Third World, where universal primary education is the exception rather than the norm, male enrolments outnumber female by a factor of two to three times; later on, the gap between enrolments for each sex 'grows exponentially for each year of education' according to Kelly. In countries where schooling is compulsory, the earlier it ends, the greater the disparity between the sexes. As soon as students are legally allowed to opt out of formal education (and in some cases sooner), girls drop out to a greater extent than boys. The reasons may be varied: a shortage of available and accessible places in schools or colleges, pressures of current domestic duties, anticipation of impending housewifery and maternity, or the difficulty of reconciling society's idealized notions of femininity with the pursuit of qualifications and job satisfaction.

Despite a worldwide increase in women's participation in higher education, the total number of women continues to lag behind that of men, especially in the university sector. Throughout post-school education, too, there is a striking difference between the types of courses studied by men and women; the vast majority of women are concentrated in the arts, social sciences and teacher education.

Under-achievement

Where primary education is universal and free, girls tend to do as well as boys and sometimes better. However, once out of the primary school environment, females under-achieve in a variety of subjects, especially in physical sciences, engineering and technology-related subjects. This is true during the secondary years, and becomes more pronounced in higher education. The term 'under-achievement' does not simply refer to the low numbers of female achievers as measured by examination passes in such subjects. It also emphasizes the way in which early promise shown by many girls (as measured by standardized aptitude tests) fails to materialize in later success.

A massive international study of science achievement in 19 countries found that boys consistently out-performed girls; the gap was largest in physics, smaller in biology, with chemistry intermediate (Comber and Keeves, 1973). Interestingly, sex differences were smallest among ten-year-olds (but still marked for physics) and much greater at pre-university level. A detailed examination of the 14-year-old stratified sample in 14 developed countries suggested that the girls were handicapped by holding less favourable attitudes to science (Kelly, 1978). The masculine image of science as presented in schools made physics a particularly difficult choice for adolescent girls who were striving to achieve a feminine identity. Once girls have fallen behind, feedback loops within the school tend to increase the boys' lead.

Under-representation

Women are under-represented in the decision-making bodies in education, but they are strongly represented in the teaching workforce, especially in the West and especially among those teaching younger children. Indeed, as Cunningham observes in Chapter 14, teacher training has traditionally been a principal avenue of higher education for women — an avenue which recent cutbacks in Britain have drastically narrowed (Bone, 1980). Likewise teaching, especially part-time, has been one of the few jobs whose hours make it compatible with full-time responsibility for school-age children.

Above the level of primary schools, however, women are present in progressively smaller numbers at higher levels of work and in higher-status institutions. In Chapter 5, Acker contrasts the percentage of primary teachers (77 per cent) who are women with that of university lecturers (13 per cent). Women predominate only at the lowest ranks of school teaching; the higher the promotion level, the smaller the percentage of women.

These figures do not in themselves demonstrate any kind of discrimination in the sense of women applicants being unfairly treated. To examine that claim would require comparison of the numbers of women who apply, are short-listed and succeed at each job level. Such figures are difficult to obtain, and the main direct evidence of discriminatory attitudes rests on allegations of improper questions being put at interviews (National Union of Teachers, 1980: 48).

In colleges and universities, educational administration and curriculum advisory bodies, women are grossly under-represented in most countries. It is hardly surprising that the curriculum represents a distillation of what knowledge males consider worth having. Does this matter?

In Chapter 23, Duelli Klein argues that education is flawed in that it purveys man-made knowledge. The Women's Studies catechism of questions (page 293) deserves serious attention. *Does* the education system perceive women only in relation to men — the 'man-as-the-norm' syndrome? Some readers will find this charge justified; others will reject it or think it 'not proven'. In any event, there is scope for debate about the remedy. Could institutionalized Women's Studies really provide 'a feminist power base' from which to challenge androcentric educational thought? Or will Women's Studies lack teeth precisely because it is by-passed by mainstream academics who retain the real power to control the system?

Why has the problem been so neglected?

If there is really so much evidence of inequality, why has there not been more public concern or demand for redress? Why, until the last decade or so, has there been little published research and still less effective action? This section looks at four reasons why people commonly underestimate the problem.

Confusion between sex and gender

Gender refers to the set of meanings, expectations and roles that a particular society ascribes to sex. Differences due to sex should be stable and appear in all cultures if they are genuinely biologically determined. Gender differences, on the other hand, vary widely from one culture to another; they may reflect, exaggerate or be quite independent of sex differences.

For example, gender differences in retirement age are the *reverse* of sex differences in life expectation: for children born in Britain in 1971, females had a life expectation of 74.9 years, 6.3 years longer than males. Yet the gender difference in age of retirement on full pension is almost the exact opposite, allowing women to retire five years earlier.

Gender differences in employment patterns are often assumed to be based on sex differences in physical strength — but they magnify these out of all proportion. Indeed, in many Western countries gender-typing in employment is most marked in manufacturing and distribution sectors where mechanical and electrical aids greatly reduce the need for muscle-power. Men often have a near-monopoly of jobs which involve the handling of heavy materials; meanwhile women frequently do sustained heavy physical work in the everyday course of housework and infant care.

It is difficult to distance oneself from the culture in which one is immersed, just as it would be hard for a fish to examine critically the water it swims in. Cross-cultural studies suggest that nearly all cultures seem to differentiate the roles of male and female to a greater or lesser extent; traits like aggression and patience are gender-typed. But *different* traits are gender-typed in different societies, and sometimes the same traits are gender-typed in opposite directions. This casts serious doubt on the ready assumption that large discrepancies between the achievements of males and females in, say, engineering subjects, are in any sense 'natural'. Even if there is a greater reservoir of spatial/mechanical aptitude among boys than girls (and the evidence is by no means conclusive), this might account for a sex balance of perhaps 60/40 among adult engineers. But only in the USSR does the proportion of female engineers even approach 30 per cent. In Poland it is 11 per cent, in France just 2 per cent — and in Britain, almost incredibly, only 0.5 per cent. The gender difference may be in the same direction as a small sex difference, but it is enormously exaggerated, and the magnification factor itself varies widely between different countries.

The power of traditional assumptions

Other difficulties of thinking clearly about gender and education are the almost insidious power of lifelong assumptions and the deeply ingrained effects of early training. 'Everyone knows' that women talk more than men, but only comparatively recently have researchers made serious efforts to test this belief empirically. My own small experiments were prompted by incredulity at Spender's evidence of the extent to which males out-talked and interrupted females (Spender, 1980). I recorded and timed student teachers participating in mixed-sex seminar groups on general educational topics — and found the results astonishing. The sex ratio was 50/50 (to eliminate possible distorting effects from one sex being in a strong majority), but the percentage of male talk was 88 per cent — that is, males out-talked females by a factor of over 7 to 1. This result was stable over the four weeks of seminar meetings which were recorded.

Even more striking was the extent to which no one present was *aware* of this disproportion. The students underestimated the percentage of male talk (average estimate 62 per cent), but not as seriously as the tutor, whose 52 per cent estimate revealed that he was quite unconscious of male domination of the group's talk. This is no criticism of the tutor, who was both skilled and experienced in group work, and also sensitive to the problem of sex bias in education (although by mutual agreement not made fully aware of the exact purpose of the recording experiment in advance). All groups showed over-representation of male talk, irrespective of the sex of tutor.

The terms 'under-represented' and 'imbalance' are intended here in a statistical sense, but may also suggest a value judgement. Nothing in the recordings (which I spent many hours listening to) suggested that the female contributions were of lower quality than the male; nothing about the students suggested that the women had less interesting things to say. Once the groups were told the results, both sexes generally felt that the ratio was unfair and expressed some interest in changing it. I do not suggest that the male students were in any deliberate or conscious way excluding the females, nor that the female students were oppressed by their male peers. However, I contend that the general lack of awareness of the disparity requires explanation and remedy.

This small-scale experiment (Megarry, 1981) receives support from the more systematic research conducted and cited by French and French in Chapter 4. Such studies raise far-reaching questions: how widespread is this imbalance in other colleges, in schools, in other countries? What are its long-term effects? How easily can the tutor or students redress or reverse the imbalance if they are made aware of it? Since the problem occurs only in mixed-sex groups, does it suggest a role for single-sex groups or even for single-sex education? These and other issues are explored further in *Man Made Language* (Spender, 1980).

'Invisible' evidence

Only recently have empirical studies like those reported above been conducted on any scale, and most of the studies have been done by women. Because academic research is dominated by men (statistically, and perhaps in others ways as well), the questions pursued have naturally reflected 'male' concerns, among which possible under-achievement by women has not figured largely. Paradoxically, sex differences in personality, aptitude and cognition have interested psychologists of both sexes to a degree which may even have been self-defeating (see below).

The difficulties presented by the sheer lack of evidence in educational studies are compounded by a basic lack of statistical evidence. Women have been so often absent from official thinking that they frequently do not figure in statistical tables at all. Even recent publications (for example, Weir and Nolan, 1977) confine themselves to the male half of the age-group without apparent awareness of this important limitation. Readers are often left to infer that 'children' actually means 'sons'; the omission of daughters is not even thought to be worth mentioning.

Gender-typing is subtle and pervasive

Even people who regard themselves as enlightened and sensitive about sex roles often underestimate the prevalence of gender-typing. It is embedded in our very language and the concepts that we use to organize our perceptions of society. For example, many Western countries define the family in relation to its male members; a man is automatically assumed to be the head of household and families are said to 'die out' if there are no male heirs. Countries which preserve the mother's surname are unusual. Again, sociologists are fond of categorizing people according to their social class, and, as Acker points out in Chapter 5, traditional sociology has been preoccupied with this source of inequality to the exclusion of gender inequality. Sociologists define social class operationally in terms of the head of household's paid employment, so many women are categorized only through their relationship with men — often taking on the social class of their husbands or fathers. This practice subtly perpetuates the assumption of man-as-the-norm.

Modern linguistics has drawn attention to the importance of language in shaping and organizing our perceptions of the world. The Sapir-Whorf hypothesis suggests that a speaker's native language sets up a series of categories which influence his or her perception of the world (Trudgill, 1974). If language influences society through its effect on the world-view of its speakers and writers, what might be the effect of noun and pronoun gender on sex roles? Conventional wisdom on the English language asserts that 'he' includes 'she', that 'man' means 'man and woman' and that 'mankind', 'man-made' and their like are generic not genderized.

Empirical studies have challenged the validity of these comfortable assumptions. A majority of students interpret 'man' to mean 'male people' in phrases like 'man needs food' and 'the evolution of man' (Nilsen, 1973; Harrison, 1975). Other experiments have invited college students to select appropriate illustrations for phrases like 'industrial man' and 'political man', and contrasted their selection with those chosen for 'industrial life' or 'political behaviour'. The results demonstrated conclusively that students of both sexes tended to interpret 'man' in terms of male images, with the more generic terms like 'life' evoking less masculine images (Schneider and Hacker, 1972).

If sophisticated adults have difficulty in interpreting the ambiguity of whether 'man' is meant in the inclusive or exclusive sense, this suggests that children may be even more confused by such usage. A common rationalization for using 'man' is that it is poetic and economical: witness Alexander Pope's much-quoted line about 'the proper study of mankind is man'. Unfortunately for those who argue that he meant women too, later in the same *Essay on Man* he refers to 'thy dog, thy bottle and thy wife'. The lesson is surely to avoid the ambiguity wherever possible.

Gender, aptitude and achievement

There is widespread controversy over the evidence about sex differences in ability. A huge field of research has grown up, known as the Psychology of Sex Differences, and vast numbers of studies have been conducted seeking to demonstrate how sex is linked to mental differences. For example, Maccoby and Jacklin's (1975) book summarizes over 1400 research studies (some of them very large-scale) conducted between 1965 and 1975. They conclude that environmental differences play an overwhelmingly important role in the development of sex differences.

Maccoby and Jacklin have been criticized for this conclusion, and more research has been called for. After more than half a century of such studies, however, it is worth drawing attention to some methodological difficulties. Researchers have repeatedly claimed that boys are superior on spatial and mechanical tasks, girls on verbal ones. This belief has motivated thousands of studies, of which a number have alleged that there were significant sex differences. However:

(a) The differences have usually been very slight, with tremendous overlap between the sexes. The large numbers of subjects allowed these slight differences to achieve *statistical* significance, although their *educational* significance is far from clear.

(b) We do not know how many studies found no significant difference but were never reported or published. Those null results which have been published may be the tip of an iceberg, as they are usually considered less interesting by authors and editors. Even if there were no sex differences at all, about one study in 20 would *appear* to find them on the usual 5 per cent criterion for statistical significance.

(c) No tests exist for 'pure' aptitude; we can only infer aptitude from performance. By the time that girls are old enough to be tested, their lack of experience with mechanical toys, gears and construction kits as compared with boys may account for lower performance on tests which employ or portray such things.

Macaulay's (1978) article called 'The myth of female superiority in language' exposed how many investigators appear to have been biased by their prior convictions. One can only speculate about why these prior convictions should be so widespread, and whether a similar process is responsible for the general belief in male superiority on spatial/ mechanical tasks. Whether or not there is a genetic component, there is evidence of a cultural component at work; Maccoby and Jacklin (1975) report that apparent male superiority seems to be linked to cultures in which child-rearing practices give boys greater autonomy and a larger radius of independence.

The evidence for cultural effects gets stronger as young people get older. In general, minor differences in measured aptitude lead to major sex differences in attainment, notably in subjects like physical sciences and mathematics, which in turn lead to yawning chasms in higher education and vocational choices. Thus the evidence on sex differences is ambiguous, fraught with methodological problems, and capable of a variety of different explanations.

Great ingenuity and effort has been expended on accounting for these supposed sex differences, as Sayers demonstrates (Chapter 3). Biological theories have been varied. Some have invoked a sex-linked recessive gene; others have singled out hormones; others again have linked them with differences in brain lateralization, suggesting that the two halves of the brain specialize later and more completely in boys than in girls. Sayers catalogues the difficulties this theory has in explaining the evidence.

Environmental theories tend to attribute sex differences to consistently different treatment in early upbringing, different pressures and expectations from the family and peer group, and the effects of sex-stereotyping in society at large. Experimental evidence shows that parents respond differently to boy and girl babies from the earliest age, so it would be difficult to disentangle the contribution of different factors. Sayers' critique of social-learning theories, cognitive-developmental theories and psychoanalytic perspectives is of great interest, not least because of the way she reminds us of the discrepancies which they fail to explain.

In some ways, however, the search for the origins of sex differences may be less rewarding than consideration of what, if anything, the education system should do about them. If a child is having trouble learning to read and write (a problem slightly more likely to affect boys than girls), his parents may be less interested in whether it is caused by brain lateralization or early learning, and more likely to want remedial teaching for him. Similarly, should not those who have trouble with spatial/ mechanical tasks (a problem slightly more likely to affect girls than boys) have access to remedial tuition? This seems a more pressing question than whether the learning difficulty results from some genetic weakness or from a lack of suitable early experience.

Irrespective of the origins of sex differences, the important question is surely how the education system should react. Figure 1 illustrates two options: the system can exaggerate the differences, or it can minimize them. A third possibility (not illustrated) is that it should simply reflect them.

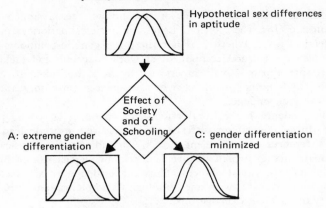

Figure 1. *Possible effects of society and schooling*
upon hypothetical sex differences in aptitude

Gender and schooling

There is evidence from all over the world that education systems exaggerate the effects of sex differences, and do so in ways which limit the
educational opportunities of females in particular. Gender-typing recurs
in the official curriculum, teaching materials and organization of subject
choice, in teacher behaviour both inside and outside the classroom, and in
the hidden curriculum of traditional assumptions, unquestioned expectations and codes of behaviour.

Stereotyping in children's reading books has been extensively documented over the last decade in various countries. It is ten years since
Lobban conducted a detailed analysis of six reading schemes and concluded that: 'they showed a "real" world peopled by women and girls
who were almost solely involved with domestic activity . . . The world
they depicted was not only sexist, it was more sexist than present reality'
(Lobban, 1974: 41-42). Yet most of these readers were still in widespread
use in Britain at the time of writing, and seem likely to remain so.

Nevertheless, such palpable and quantifiable stereotyping is easy to
identify and comparatively easy to combat if the resources are made
available. In Chapter 7, Evans illustrates a more elusive form of sexism in
Australian primary schools. Stereotypes are transmitted through the
unspoken assumptions which govern teacher behaviour and transactions
in the classroom. That Pinewood and Walkwood teachers interacted two
to three times more frequently with boys than with girls is a remarkable
finding. It is reinforced by classroom interaction research cited by Acker
(Chapter 5). Like the mixed-sex seminar results mentioned earlier, these
findings raise formidable questions for teacher education.

In secondary schools, it is even easier to point to measurable inequality
and discriminatory practices, whereby there is encouragement only for
boys to take technical subjects or (more subtly unfair) the enforcement of

equal numbers of boys and girls in groups supposedly selected for ability. Such practices have for some time been illegal in many Western countries (and persist in some schools nonetheless). Enlightened practice has tended to lag behind legislation. But teacher attitudes cannot be legislated. Buswell's fieldwork (Chapter 8) shows how subtle interpersonal messages reinforce and reproduce dependency relations. Her case studies of a sponsored boy, a nurtured girl, an acquiescent girl and an 'invisible' girl are evocative, leading to a different kind of understanding from the harder statistical evidence elsewhere.

Hamilton and Leo-Rhynie illustrate the persistence of familiar stereotypes in Jamaican secondary schools (Chapter 10). The images of the active, independent, confident male and the passive, dependent, anxious female seem too powerful to be swept aside by the strong similarities between the sexes in motivation and achievement. Chapter 5 summarizes the way gender provides a powerful and pervasive basis for differentiation throughout British school life: 'The school works on the side of tradition; it is even more traditional than the outside world.'

Sex-stereotypes also pervade higher education, but their effects are overlaid by issues of access. Once the years of compulsory education are over, females become especially vulnerable to social and domestic pressures. Self-selection permits, and even encourages, large numbers of females to opt out (Sutherland, 1981). The next section looks at problems of access more generally.

Gender and access

Educational delivery systems have largely been devised by men; it is hardly surprising that they suit typically male patterns of education and working-life fairly well, and typically female patterns rather poorly.

Pre-school provision has received very low priority in official thinking, yet unrelieved responsibility for young children is an enormous obstacle to self-determination and self-fulfilment for women. The fact that it may also be a source of great joy and interest is beside the point: fathers are parents too, but no-one expects fatherhood to represent total fulfilment for men, 24 hours a day. Many women want to be mothers *and* to be people with interests and sources of fulfilment unrelated to motherhood, whether in full-time or part-time employment, formal or informal education, voluntary work or leisure activity. This is made extremely difficult for mothers of pre-school children. In the West, those who live in extended families or can afford to pay for child care are in a privileged minority. David demonstrates how unquestioningly the organization of schooling, pre-school care and welfare services relies on the 'voluntary' (unpaid) work of mothers; she contrasts official rhetoric about the educational value of involving parents in their children's schooling with the reality of dependence on unpaid mothers to fill the gaps left by public spending cuts (Chapter 15). Thus the school system and stage agencies reinforce the notion of sexual division of responsibilities in the home. Even in socialist countries, which have given higher priority to state nursery provision, powerful attitude barriers have sustained continuing disparity between the sexes, as McAuley (Chapter 16) and Molyneux (Chapter 21) demonstrate.

Some countries still operate unequal durations of compulsory schooling. Other countries may have the same official leaving age for both sexes, but such inefficient enforcement that in practice girls may stop attending earlier. In Britain, for example, there is some evidence of a dual standard — especially in working-class families — which takes teenage girls away from school for domestic purposes like child-minding. On a sustained basis this can amount to premature leaving (Byrne, 1978).

Adolescent girls are especially vulnerable to peer group and societal pressures which suggest implicitly but powerfully that femininity and career ambitions will conflict. The dilemma is greater where access to higher education demands a move away from home for several years. Explaining why so few women go on to higher education in Britain, one polytechnic principal commented 'the norms of our higher education policies and system are the norms of the bachelor boy student' (Robinson, 1980). Even where post-school education does not entail a major discontinuity, like a move away from home, its institutions are often inflexible in their organization and make it unnecessarily difficult for people to combine attendance with major domestic responsibilities.

In post-school education, open and distance learning techniques could make a major contribution to expanding educational opportunities. A previous World Yearbook — Recurrent Education and Lifelong Learning — (Schuller and Megarry, 1979) argued the case for lifelong learning on other grounds as well. Adolescence may not be the best time for a single dose of education for either sex, and, even if it were, we no longer live in a world in which single doses are adequate (if indeed we ever did). Education is a lifelong need, not only because of changing individual needs, but also because of the need for vocational retraining consequent on profound changes to the structure and nature of employment.

The new technology could be used to create educational delivery systems which help those who are housebound, or to encourage flexibility in the administrative practices of providing institutions. But women are in danger of remaining estranged from new technology, both in education and in employment. To take a common example, the introduction of word processing primarily affects female workers. However, far from upgrading their typing skills, it may be accompanied by a specialization of function which destroys job satisfaction (Communications Studies and Planning Ltd, 1980). Berner provides a case study of the way in which the introduction of new technology threatened to de-skill female workers, and of the union's efforts to resist this (Chapter 18).

The paradox is that computers are potentially an excellent medium for distance education (Hooper, 1983), and could be used to make highly interactive education of good quality easily available in people's homes. Britain has pioneered a variety of distance-learning initiatives, has taken a lead in telesoftware by broadcast and telephone, and has the highest *per capita* rate of personal computer ownership in the world. But the owners and users are predominantly male. Unless something profoundly alters the traditional patterns and attitudes, home-based education may paradoxically be *less* accessible to women than institution-based provision, which at least allows and requires them to escape from domestic roles for the duration of the classes.

What can be done?

Although this book contains abundant evidence of disadvantage, it also offers considerable grounds for optimism. For example, Elliott documents a wealth of positive ideas for promoting educational opportunities for females in India (Chapter 19). She explains how adult education centres have had much greater success in reaching Indian women than formal education, how community involvement has assisted programmes for tribal women in South India and night classes for pre-adolescent girls in Maharashtra, and how education for girls can be encouraged by a combination of positive incentives, organizational flexibility and appropriate curricula.

In Chapter 6, Kelly provides ammunition against defeatism about the social, cultural and religious pressures. She demonstrates that the most important single factor influencing women's access to schooling is whether suitable schooling is made available and accessible. Since that is a matter of public policy, it can be changed if the will is there. In Chapter 9, Hamid Don documents the tremendous increase in educational opportunities for girls in Malaysia since the expansion of the system following independence.

In higher education, controversial remedies like positive discrimination and the use of quotas are often proposed; Lindsay touches on the legal admissibility of race and sex as admission criteria in the US (Chapter 11). She advances affirmative action on the basis not of *lowering* standards for a particular group but of *re-examining* traditional entry requirements to see whether they are really justifiable — or whether they needlessly exclude or discourage that group. Many countries which have already legislated against direct discrimination have yet to tackle the problem of *indirect* discrimination — conditions applied to admission, employment or promotion which cannot be justified. Traditional rules about examination passes, age limits and types of prerequisite experience need careful re-examination.

Several chapters in Part 4 report further positive strategies to redress the balance. In Chapter 22 Yates provides a survey of Australian initiatives, from legal and formal safeguards, to attempts to reform the processes of teaching, and curriculum re-examination. The final Chapter (23) is devoted to the most radical and controversial strategy of all. Duelli Klein charts the attempts of Women's Studies to become institutionalized in various parts of the world. Whether Women's Studies is a new discipline, a minority way of life or a serviceable umbrella, it has provided a valuable focus for feminist research, a pivot for exerting pressure on traditional thinking and a seed-crystal for the establishment of feminist periodicals, conferences and contact networks. Even those who believe that the attempt to institutionalize Women's Studies as a separate discipline is misconceived will recognize its achievements in raising the general level of awareness of the issues.

Unquestionably, the most important barrier to women's advancement is that of shifting the attitudes of men and women who have accepted the *status quo* for too long. In this respect, sexism resembles ethnocentrism. In a previous *World Yearbook* I argued for a Copernican shift in world view for ethnic and linguistic minorities (Megarry *et al,* 1981: 10). Just as the multicultural ideal demands that majority culture should accommodate to that of minorities, not merely seek to assimilate them, so the message of this *World Yearbook* is that man-made education can benefit from greater participation by women — as consumers, providers and decision-makers. Martin expands this notion when she argues for a gender-sensitive educational ideal. Its implications are not only the Platonic attempt to build into women's education those traits gender-typed in favour of males, but also the more revolutionary task of building into *everyone's* education those traits gender-typed in favour of females (Chapter 2). Duelli Klein pursues a similar line when she criticizes the 'add-women-and-stir' approach; she contends that the nature of knowledge and knowledge-making require fundamental reassessment (Chapter 23).

Even if educators were to tackle this task with energy and determination, it is important to recognize the limitations to what education on its own can achieve. Educational practice is persistently affected by wider social forces, especially the world of work. For example, in Chapter 13 Danylewycz and Prentice trace the influences — past and present — of labour market segregation on the struggle for equality by schoolmistresses in Quebec and Ontario. In another context, Scott comments on the pressure on Swedish schools to fit young people for working life as it is; the labour market is not only strongly sex-segregated but also contracting in those sectors where women have traditionally found jobs (Chapter 20).

Many of women's problems stem from traditional patterns of working days and years which mean that too often they are forced to choose between building a satisfying career and preparing to raise a family; the ripple effects of this incompatibility spread to adolescent girls, to childless women, and even to women nearing retirement age. At the root of the problem is the assumption that permanent satisfying employment must be 'full-time' and continuous. There is a strong historical association between part-time work, a female workforce and a syndrome of low status, poor promotion prospects and scarce training opportunities. This is not merely a middle-class problem; it has a strong knock-on effect on participation in apprenticeships, vocational training and further education, as Blunden shows in Chapter 12. Alternative patterns like job-sharing challenge the all-or-nothing model of full-time work, which has little logic in societies in which *all* employment is part-time by the standards of the last century. But unless job-sharing is embraced by men, as well as women, it will suffer from the same status problems as beset part-time work.

The range of problems dealt with in the chapters which follow is incredibly wide. In Western countries, for instance, concern is often expressed about the scarcity of women in academic life. In countries like India, as Elliott reminds us, the problem is very much more basic: there are over 200 million illiterate adult women, and secondary education for girls is largely confined to the urban middle classes and wealthy rural families (Chapter 19). In Islamic countries the basic question of whether education is as necessary for women as for men is controversially entangled with the traditional Islamic conception of women's status; Nelson's study of the tensions in Egypt between alternative Islam and secular education for women exposes quite different problems than — for example — arise in the socialist countries studied by Molyneux and McAuley.

Common to all parts of the globe, however, is the marginal status of 'women and education' as a field of study. It is symptomatic that few men write or research in this field. Indeed, male contributors to this volume are as scarce as were female authors in the previous *World Yearbook — Computers and Education* (1983). *World Yearbook* authors tend to reflect the sex ratio of those who are eminent in their field, since it is not the policy of the editorial team (two male, two female) to practise positive discrimination in favour of either sex.

However, if this book is read only by women it will have failed in its purpose. Men overwhelmingly control the decision-making bodies in educational systems throughout the world. It is as partners — *equal* partners — that women wish to join with them in improving education for both sexes.

References

Bone, A (1980) *The Effect on Women's Opportunities of Teacher Training Cuts* Equal Opportunities Commission: London

Byrne, E M (1978) *Women and Education* Tavistock Publications: London

Comber, L C and Keeves, J P (1973) *Science Education in Nineteen Countries* Almqvist and Wiksell: Stockholm

Communications Studies and Planning Limited (1980) *Information Technology in the Office: the Impact on Women's Jobs* Equal Opportunities Commission: Manchester

Harrison, L (1975) Cro-Magnon woman in eclipse *The Science Teacher* April: 8-11

Hooper, R (1983) The computer as a medium for distance education *in* Megarry *et al* eds

Kelly, A (1978) *Girls and Science* (IEA Monograph no 9) Almqvist and Wiksell: Stockholm

Lobban, G (1974) Sex-roles in reading schemes *Forum — for the Discussion of New Trends in Education* **16** 2

Macaulay, R K S (1978) The myth of female superiority in language *Journal of Child Language* 5: 353-63

Maccoby, E and Jacklin, C (1975) *The Psychology of Sex Differences* Oxford University Press: Oxford

Megarry, J (1981) *Sex, Gender and Education* Jordanhill College of Education: Glasgow

Megarry, J (1981) Preface *in* Megarry, Nisbet and Hoyle *eds World Yearbook of Education 1981: Education of Minorities* Kogan Page: London

Megarry, J, Nisbet, S and Hoyle, E *eds* (1981) *World Yearbook of Education 1981: Education of Minorities* Kogan Page: London

Megarry, J, Walker, D R F, Nisbet, S and Hoyle, E (1983) *World Yearbook of Education 1982/83: Computers and Education* Kogan Page: London

Nilsen, A P (1973) Grammatical gender and its relationship to the equal treatment of males and females in children's books PhD thesis submitted to the University of Iowa

National Union of Teachers (1980) *Promotion and the Woman Teacher* National Union of Teachers/Equal Opportunities Commission: Manchester

Robinson, E (1980) Address to SRHE/EOC Conference in Manchester Polytechnic, 6 March 1980

Schneider, J W and Hacker, S L (1972) Sex role imagery and the use of the generic 'man' in introductory texts Paper presented at the American Sociological Association Annual Meeting in New Orleans

Schuller, T and Megarry, J *eds* (1979) *World Yearbook of Education 1979: Recurrent Education and Lifelong Learning* Kogan Page: London

Spender, D (1980) *Man Made Language* Routledge and Kegan Paul: London

Sutherland, M (1981) *Sex Bias in Education* Basil Blackwell: Oxford

Trudgill, P (1974) *Sociolinguistics* Penguin: Harmondsworth

Weir, D and Nolan, F (1977) *Glad to be Out: a Study of School-leavers* Scottish Council for Research in Education: Edinburgh

Part 1:
Theoretical perspectives

2. Philosophy, gender and education

Jane Roland Martin

Summary: Women have received little attention in the history of educational thought. As a consequence, they have been denied the opportunity to understand and evaluate the range of ideals that educational thinkers of the past have held up for them. Two examples of the kind of illumination that can be gained from the inclusion of women in the subject matter of the history of educational thought emerge from a comparative study of Rousseau's *Emile* and Plato's *Republic*. The first is derived from Rousseau's insight that neither the girl Sophie by herself nor the boy Emile by himself can be a complete moral person; that Emile's education, modelled on that of the guardians of Plato's 'Just State', is only plausible given the very different one Rousseau prescribes for Sophie. The second is derived both from Plato's insight that sex is of no consequence in determining the rulers of a state and from Rousseau's insistence, against Plato, that traits and gender are, nonetheless, related to one another in ways significant for education. Both examples indicate that a *gender-sensitive* educational ideal is required for women. Taking gender into account when it makes a difference to education and ignoring it when it does not, a gender-sensitive ideal would neither imprison women in gender, as Rousseau's explicitly gender-bound ideal for Sophie does, nor make women the victims of a mistaken gender blindness, as does Plato's supposedly gender-free ideal for his female guardians.

Absent women

In Book V of the *Republic*, Plato argues that women as well as men can be rulers of the 'Just State' and, on the grounds that identical roles require identical education, he makes the radical proposal that the female guardians of the state be given the same education as their male counterparts, indeed that the two sexes be educated together (1974: 113-19). In Book V of *Emile*, Rousseau prescribes for the girl Sophie — who represents Everygirl, just as the boy Emile, whose wife she is to be, represents Everyboy — an education separate and different from Emile's (1979).

Plato and Rousseau are two of the greatest educational philosophers in the Western tradition. The standard English-language texts in the history of Western educational thought discuss their ideas at length (for example, Ulich, 1945; Brumbaugh and Lawrence, 1963; Nash *et al*, 1965; Rusk,

1965); the standard anthologies all include selections from the *Republic* and *Emile* (for example, Ulich, 1948; Price, 1967; Nash, 1968; Cahn, 1970). The theories of Plato and Rousseau on the education of girls and women, however, are neglected. Many texts and anthologies omit all reference to the *Republic* Book V, and those which mention Plato's views on women do so in passing or with significant distortion. Similarly, the texts and anthologies either ignore Sophie altogether or treat Rousseau's discussion of her education as some kind of aberration.

As a systematic philosopher, John Heinrich Pestalozzi is not the equal of Plato or Rousseau, but he is considered to be an important educational thinker and is represented in most of the standard texts and anthologies in the field. In his classic pedagogical novel, *Leonard and Gertrude* (1885), Pestalozzi presents Gertrude as the model of a good educator and proposes an ideal school based on principles extracted from Gertrude's child-rearing practices. For Pestalozzi, Gertrude's maternal character and her activities in the home set the example for a new order, yet the history of educational thought has not seen fit to preserve his insight that mothers are educators of their children.

In general, women have been invisible both as the objects and subjects of educational thought: their own education has been ignored and their childrearing activities neglected; furthermore, their theoretical writings about education have been overlooked (Martin, 1982a). There is no mention of Catherine Macauley's *Letters on Education* (1974), Mary Wollstonecraft's *A Vindication of the Rights of Woman* (1967), or Catharine Beecher's *A Treatise on Domestic Economy* (1977) in the texts and anthologies of the field. Maria Montessori's theoretical works on the education of children are discussed by Rusk (1965), but by few others.

How is the exclusion of women from the history of educational thought to be explained? Lorenne Clark (1976) has shown that the reproductive processes of society, defined broadly to include not just creation and birth but the rearing of children to maturity, are effectively excluded from the political domain, which is defined in relation to the public world of productive processes. Since reproductive processes have traditionally been assigned to women and have taken place within the family, women and the family have thus been excluded from the very subject matter of politics and political theory. The analogy with education is striking. Society's reproductive processes are largely devoted to childrearing and thus include the transmission of skills, beliefs, feelings, emotions, values and even world views. Nevertheless, such processes are not considered to belong to the educational domain. Like the political realm, the educational is defined solely in relation to the productive processes of society.

The exclusion of women from the history of educational thought is thus not a matter of individual whim, but a systematic consequence of the way that the subject matter of educational theory and philosophy is defined. Since Sophie's training is intended to prepare her to carry on the reproductive, not the productive, processes of society, by definition it falls outside the educational realm. Since Gertrude's teaching takes place in the context of childrearing in the heart of the family, this activity of hers falls outside it, too. And since Wollstonecraft writes about the appropriate upbringing for Sophie and Gertrude, her work is not even perceived as educational philosophy.

The question remains as to whether the exclusion of women from the history of educational thought matters. So long as women can enter the educational realm in practice — as they increasingly can and do today — what difference does it make if women have heretofore been excluded from it in theory?

The exclusion of Gertrude, Sophie, Plato's female guardians, Macauley, Wollstonecraft and Beecher matters for many reasons, perhaps the most serious of which is that both sexes are thereby denied the opportunity to understand and evaluate the range of ideals that the great educational thinkers of the past have held up for women. Such opportunity is essential if adequate ideals are to be developed and the mistakes of earlier generations are not simply to be repeated. Even historical views like Rousseau's, that seem most inimical to the interests of women, need to be studied for the kernels of truth they may contain. Even theories like Plato's and Wollstonecraft's, that seem most consonant with women's goals today, need to be subjected to critical analysis lest their problematic aspects be incorporated into our own constructs.

Incomplete people

For two examples of the kind of illumination the inclusion of women in the subject matter of educational thought can yield, I turn to Book V of *Emile* in which Rousseau engages in what amounts to a dialogue with Plato about women's place and women's education. He embraces Plato's assumption that the function of education is to prepare people to carry out their predestined societal roles, but replaces the Platonic vision of a society in which men and women rule together by one in which the two sexes are assigned very different tasks and functions. Thus, the education Rousseau designs for the boy Emile is intended to produce the type of citizen described in *The Social Contract*: a rational self-governing individual whose judgements are objective and whose beliefs are formed independently of others. The education he designs for the girl Sophie, on the other hand, is intended to produce a traditional wife/mother: a woman who will bear and raise many children, govern her husband's household, oversee his garden, act as his hostess, care for his reputation, and, above all, please him (Martin, 1981a).

To understand fully Rousseau's reasons for prescribing for Sophie the education he does, one needs to know that in *Emile* V he is addressing what he takes to be two fundamental mistakes contained in *Republic* V. In the latter, Plato abolishes the institutions of private marriage, home, family and childrearing for the guardians of the Just State. There he also argues that sex is a difference that makes *no* difference in determining whether a person is suited by nature to rule, and hence no difference in determining a person's education. Against Plato, Rousseau maintains that private marriage, home, family and childrearing are required by the ideal state and, furthermore, that sex is a difference that makes *all* the difference. Rousseau, indeed, divides up everything according to sex: societal tasks, the knowledge and skill he considers essential to their performance, and the personal qualities and traits of character he associates with them.

Writing nearly 200 years ago, Wollstonecraft argued with passion and cogency that Sophie's docility and 'spaniel-like affection' makes her the 'toy of man, his rattle' (1967: 68). As such, Sophie cannot be the kind of wife Rousseau intended for Emile or the kind of mother he envisioned for Emile's children. 'Meek wives', Wollstonecraft said, 'are in general, foolish mothers' (1967: 227). 'If women be educated for dependence; that is, to act according to the will of another fallible being', she asked, 'where are we to stop?' (1967: 87). Will they not, in turn, make their children endure *their* tyrranical oppression?

Wollstonecraft's critique of Sophie's education and character remains compelling today, but her assumption that the educational ideal which Rousseau holds up for Emile is the proper one for both sexes (1967: 52) ought to be questioned; yet in fact it has been taken on trust. Wollstonecraft's appropriation for her daughters of the educational goals posited for Emile has indeed been echoed throughout history by many of those most concerned with the education of women. This acceptance is quite understandable. Rousseau's misogyny in *Emile* V is sufficient in itself to cause readers to overlook Sophie's positive qualities. Furthermore, his fundamental insight about education is lost to view unless Books I-IV of *Emile* are read together with Book V, and Book V is, in turn, read in conjunction with Book V of Plato's *Republic*. Since women have been absent from the history of educational thought, it has been all but impossibly difficult to undertake these comparative studies.

Study of Rousseau's text shows that Sophie is passive and full of guile; she is also the one with the patience, gentleness, zeal and affection necessary for raising children. Furthermore, she is the one with the tenderness and care 'required to maintain the union of the whole family' and the one who is willing and able to make the lives of her loved ones agreeable and sweet (Rousseau, 1979: 361, 365). Because Sophie acquires, through her education, the attributes so necessary for carrying out the reproductive processes of society, and because Rousseau advocates a strict division of roles according to sex, there is perhaps a *prima facie* case for Emile not to acquire these. However, as Sophie's husband, father of her children, and head of the family, one would hope that he, too, would be tender and caring and disposed to make the lives of his loved ones agreeable and sweet. Be that as it may, it makes no sense at all to advocate Emile's *and only* Emile's education for either sex, once traditional sex roles are rejected, let alone to advocate it for both sexes.

Rousseau's fundamental insight in *Emile* is that the plausibility of Emile's education is due to the existence of Sophie. This insight is lost to view when Sophie is excluded from the history of educational thought, for it is in Book V of *Emile* that Rousseau makes it very clear not only that Sophie will carry on the reproductive processes of childrearing and maintaining home and family for Emile (and is to be educated in the qualities necessary for doing so) but also that the man Emile, even when educated according to plan, *is not and cannot be a complete moral person*. Only in partnership, says Rousseau, can Sophie and Emile be completely moral, and, even then, neither individual alone is a complete moral person, but rather the *union* of Sophie and Emile constitutes a complete moral entity.

It is easy to be blinded to Sophie's virtues and dazzled by Emile's upon reading *Emile*, for Rousseau himself tends to concentrate on what Wollstonecraft correctly diagnoses as Sophie's vices. However, once the education of Sophie and Emile is considered in relation to that of Plato's guardians, one begins to realize just how problematic it is to extend to women the educational ideal Rousseau holds up for males without first transforming it. Rousseau models the ideal guiding Emile's education on Plato's ideal for the guardians of his 'Just State'. Granted, Plato himself extends this ideal to both sexes, but it must not be forgotten that in the 'Just State', whatever reproductive processes the guardians require (for example, childrearing) will be carried on by others. It can plausibly be argued, therefore, that Plato's guardians do not need to possess Sophie's virtues, although in the final analysis this fails to convince (Martin, in press).

Unlike most modern commentators on the *Republic* (Pierce, 1973), Rousseau read the *Republic* Book V carefully and took its social programmes concerning women, children and the family seriously. He saw, as few others have, that Plato's philosophy of education is incomplete. It specifies the education of those with responsibility for the productive processes of society — or, at least, for the processes of defending and ruling the state — but is silent about those with responsibility for society's reproductive processes. Rousseau thus understood that, having rejected Plato's social programme, he could not embrace Plato's philosophy of education without modifying it significantly; he understood that he would have to make sure in his own philosophy that *someone* was educated to perform the tasks and functions to be carried on in Emile's home. In principle, Rousseau could have chosen Emile for this role or he could have rejected a sex-based division of labour altogether. Not surprisingly, however, Rousseau chose Sophie for it. Having done so, and having designed Sophie's education accordingly, he felt free to retain for Emile the educational ideal Plato holds up for his male and female guardians. Just as Plato had removed all responsibility for carrying on the reproductive processes of society from the guardians' lives, so Rousseau had removed it from Emile's.

We may reject Sophie and the sex-based division of labour in which her education is grounded but we have much to learn from Rousseau's reaction to Plato. For, unless women want to drop from their lives responsibility for society's reproductive processes, they must acknowledge, as does Rousseau, that the educational ideal Plato holds up for his guardians of both sexes is incomplete, as is the one Rousseau holds up for Emile. Recognizing Rousseau's insight does not entail endorsing prescriptions for a patriarchal society in which only males can be citizens, nor endorsing a patriarchal family in which wives must endure their husbands' wrongs without complaining. Nor does it require one to support a two-track educational system and a division of labour based on sex. It does, however, require that we take Sophie's virtues seriously and seek ways of incorporating them into the ideals we develop to guide women's own education and that of the men who share with them responsibility for the reproductive processes of society.

The difference of sex

The exclusion of any preparation for society's reproductive processes from the education of Plato's guardians argues against the acceptance of his educational ideal today. Plato's assumption that, when they are to perform the same societal roles, males and females must receive the same education argues against it also. By all means let us side with Plato against Rousseau in extending the duties, tasks and privileges of citizenship to women. But let us not, therefore, suppose that Plato is correct in judging gender to be irrelevant to education.

People with similar talents who might be expected to perform the same tasks with equal proficiency often learn in different ways, thereby benefiting from different modes of instruction. Furthermore, some start with handicaps, which have nothing to do with natural aptitude, and these must be overcome if a given end is to be achieved. In either case, it is a mistake to assume that an identical education will yield identical results in all instances. The question is whether differences in learning styles and learning readiness are systematically related to gender. Merely to ask this question is not in itself to raise the spectre of biological determinism. Some aspiring female tennis players face difficulties their male counterparts do not so frequently encounter in acquiring an adequate serve, not because of their biological make-up, but because they have had less practice in throwing a ball. Similarly, some female students of mathematics experience an anxiety their male counterparts are spared, not because of their genetic constitution, but because of their early socialization. To insist that these females must receive an education identical to that of males is to court failure.

These two examples show that one can reject Plato's assumption that gender makes no difference to education without being committed to the existence of *innate* sex differences. They do not in themselves settle the issue of the relevance of gender to learning generally. They do, however, point to the need for those committed to the ideal of sex equality to remember that whether or not identical *results* require identical educational *treatment* is an empirical question. Until the necessary research on gender and learning is done, a healthy scepticism must be maintained toward Plato's dictum that the same role requires the same education (Martin, 1982b).

Given the ease with which any recognition of the difference of sex can be turned against women, it is tempting to adopt the Platonic strategy of ignoring it entirely. Yet the familiar phenomenon of what may be called 'trait genderization' lends strong support to the hypothesis that gender is indeed a significant educational category (Martin, 1981b; 1982b). That many traits are genderized — that is, they are appraised differently by a given culture or society when possessed by males rather than females, and *vice versa* — cannot be doubted. Aggressiveness, for example, is judged in North America to be a desirable trait for males, but not for females (Beardsley, 1977; Bloom *et al*, 1975). Likewise, a highly developed capacity for abstract reasoning, a self-control in which feeling and emotion are subordinated to the rule of reason, and an independent spirit — all these are qualities for which men are praised and women are regarded with suspicion if not downright disdain. Yet these last are the very traits incorporated into the educational ideal Plato holds up for his guardians, Rousseau holds up for Emile, and philosophers today hold up for both sexes (Martin, 1981b).

Once it is understood that an ideal guiding the education of women is likely to embody traits genderized in favour of males, Plato's thesis that sex is a difference of no consequence to education loses all credibility. If females are educated in traits for which they tend to be denigrated, one must assume that this negative evaluation will reverberate in the way and the extent to which the traits are acquired. Because Plato does not realize this, he leaves no room in his philosophy for the educational problems his female guardians will encounter when they are asked to conform to an ideal embodying traits genderized 'against' them. If we take the ideal of sex equality seriously, however, we must leave room for these problems in our philosophy.

Rousseau needs no room for the problems generated by genderized traits in his philosophy, since Sophie is to be denied all access to education in traits evaluated positively in males but negatively in females in her own society. No one who has read Wollstonecraft's arguments in favour of the education of female reason could possibly want to follow Rousseau in sealing off the ideal guiding women's education from every trait genderized in favour of males. Yet, in rejecting theories such as Rousseau's which try to project on to our education the cultural stereotype of a female, we must not lose sight of his insight that traits and gender are related to one another. Rather, we must find a way to resist Rousseau's efforts to imprison Sophie in gender without adopting Plato's untenable alternative of denying the relevance of sex to education altogether.

A gender-sensitive ideal

The history of educational thought will never yield pat solutions to contemporary problems, but when women are included in its subject matter there is, at least, the possibility of our avoiding the mistakes of earlier generations. Such mistakes include both Rousseau's gender-bound educational ideals for Sophie and Emile and Plato's attempt at constructing a gender-free ideal for the guardians of his 'Just State'. As long as women's education is designed to develop traits genderized in favour of males and ignores sex differences related to learning (if such there be) the gender-freedom envisioned by Plato will be illusory. In the name of identical educational treatment, females may experience difficulties and suffer hardships their male counterparts will never know.

Fortunately, it is not necessary to choose between an educational ideal bound explicitly to gender, as Rousseau's is, or implicitly to gender, as Plato's is. Another possibility is open to us: joining Rousseau's insight that traits and gender are connected to Plato's insight that roles and gender are not fixed by nature, we can opt for a *gender-sensitive* ideal (Martin, 1981b). Taking gender into account when it makes a difference, and ignoring it when it does not, such an ideal allows us to build — into curricula, instructional methods and learning environments — ways of dealing with trait genderization and with the many and various other gender-related phenomena (for example, the portrayal of women in the subject matter of the curriculum) which impinge on education today.

In acknowledging the difference of sex without making us prisoners of gender, a gender-sensitive ideal allows one not only to continue the Platonic project of building into the education of females traits genderized in favour of males, but also to undertake the new and even more revolutionary project of building into everyone's education traits genderized in favour of females. It must be understood that Sophie's virtues tend to be evaluated *positively* in females, but *negatively* in males. We must, then, anticipate that boys and men will encounter problems in acquiring them, just as girls and women encounter problems acquiring Emile's virtues. We must also anticipate problems in their being incorporated into an ideal guiding education, for the very fact that they are *Sophie's* virtues will very likely make them suspect in the eyes of many. Yet, if our philosophy of education is to be complete, it must include those virtues of Sophie which are related to the successful performance of the reproductive processes of society. If males and females are to be complete people, they must, regardless of sex, acquire Sophie's virtues.

References

Beardsley, E (1977) Traits and genderization *in* Vetterling-Braggin *et al*
Beecher, C (1977) *A Treatise on Domestic Economy* Schocken: New York
Bloom, L Z, Coburn, K and Pearlman, J (1975) *The New Assertive Woman* Delacorte: New York

Brumbaugh, R S and Lawrence, N M (1963) *Philosophers on Education: Six Essays on the Foundations of Western Thought* Houghton Mifflin: Boston

Cahn, S M *ed* (1970) *The Philosophical Foundations of Education* Harper and Row: New York

Clark, L (1976) The rights of women: the theory and practice of the ideology of male supremacy *in* Shea and King-Farlow

Macauley, C (1974) *Letters on Education* Luria, G *ed* Garland: New York

Martin, J R (1981a) Sophie and Emile: a case study of sex bias in the history of educational thought *Harvard Educational Review* **51**: 357-72

Martin, J R (1981b) The ideal of the educated person *Educational Theory* **31**: 97-109

Martin, J R (1982a) Excluding women from the educational realm *Harvard Educational Review* **52**: 133-48

Martin, J R (1982b) Sex equality and education: a case study *in* Vetterling-Braggin

Martin, J R (in press) *Ideals of the Educated Woman* Rowman and Allenheld: Totowa, New Jersey

Nash, P (1968) *Models of Man: Explorations in the Western Educational Tradition* Wiley: New York

Nash, P, Kazemias, A M and Perkinson, H J *eds* (1965) *The Educated Man: Studies in the History of Educational Thought* Wiley: New York

Pestalozzi, J H (1885) *Leonard and Gertrude* Channing, E *trans* Heath: Boston

Pierce, C (1973) Equality: *Republic V The Monist* **57**: 1-11

Plato (1974) *Republic* Grube, G M A *trans* Hackett: Indianapolis

Price, K *ed* (1967) *Education and Philosophical Thought* Allyn and Bacon: Boston

Rousseau, J-J (1979) *Emile* Bloom, A *trans* Basic Books: New York

Rusk, R R *ed* (1965) *The Doctrines of the Great Educators* St Martins: New York

Shea, W R and King-Farlow, J *eds* (1976) *Contemporary Issues in Political Philosophy* Science History Publications: New York

Ulich, R (1945) *History of Educational Thought* American Books: New York

Ulich, R *ed* (1948) *Three Thousand Years of Educational Wisdom* Harvard University Press: Cambridge, Mass

Vetterling-Braggin, M *ed* (1982) *'Femininity', 'Masculinity' and 'Androgyny'* Littlefield, Adams: Totowa, New Jersey

Vetterling-Braggin, M, Elliston, F A and English, J *eds* (1977) *Feminism and Philosophy* Littlefield, Adams: Totowa, New Jersey

Wollstonecraft, M (1967) *A Vindication of the Rights of Woman* Norton: New York

3. Psychology and gender divisions

Janet Sayers

Summary: This chapter presents a critical survey of biological determinist, social learning, cognitive-developmental, and psychoanalytic accounts of the development of psychological sex differences. Determinist and functionalist accounts explain these differences as a result of fitting individuals psychologically for existing sexual divisions in society, but these are rejected. Instead it is argued that what is needed is a theory of gender development that takes account of how individuals psychologically resist, as well as acquiesce in, these divisions. It must also take into account the biological and historical bases of the current structuring of social relations by sex so as to explain the centrality of sex and gender in psychological development.

Introduction

Sociologists (Barrett, 1980) and biologists (Wilson, 1978) have variously sought the historical and biological determinants of current sexual divisions in society. Psychologists, in contrast, have been less concerned with the determinants of these divisions, than with how individuals come to be located psychologically in relation to them. Some have been strongly influenced by biological determinism, others variously by social-learning, cognitive-developmental and psychoanalytic theory. This chapter evaluates these approaches and proposes a missing element in them all.

Biological determinism

Any adequate explanation of psychological sex differences must take into account the fact that the sexes differ biologically from each other. One way of doing this is to argue that biology directly determines these psychological differences. It has been argued, for instance, that the 'female' hormone oxytocin makes women more nurturant and therefore better equipped psychologically than men to look after children (Rossi, 1977). Others have claimed that boys are more aggressive than girls, and that this psychological sex difference is determined by the higher levels of circulating androgens in boys which, it is claimed, fits them as men for the competitive struggles of occupational life (Goldberg, 1977; Wilson, 1978).

One problem with the above arguments is that the evidence for sex differences in nurturance and in aggression is not conclusive (see Maccoby and Jacklin, 1974, and Tieger, 1980, respectively). Rossi's argument is also flawed because it rests on the dubious assumption that because oxytocin stimulates nipple erection preparatory to breast feeding it thereby makes women nurturant. The argument that aggression facilitates occupational success is similarly flawed. Aggressive individuals are indeed more often marked by their occupational failure than by their occupational success (See Sayers, 1982, for a more extended discussion of these arguments.)

A biological determinist account of psychological sex differences that is gaining currency in education concerns girls' relative lack of science attainment. This sex difference has been linked to the oft-repeated finding (Orsini et al, 1982) that, on average, girls perform less well than boys on psychological tests of visuo-spatial ability (Gray, 1981). In turn, this difference has been linked to the fact that boys' brains seem to be more specialized than girls' for visuo-spatial function (Levy, 1972; Jones and Anuza, 1972; de Lacoste-Utamsing and Holloway, 1982). Selection for this biological sex difference, it is suggested, occurred over the course of human evolution because it aided species survival by fitting men for territorial defence and hunting thus protecting women and leaving them free to care for children (Gray, 1981).

Whatever the virtues of this evolutionary and functionalist account of existing sex differences in visuo-spatial ability, it cannot adequately explain the current under-achievement of girls in science. In the first place, there is no evidence that specialization of spatial function within one hemisphere of the brain is causally related to spatial ability (Jacklin, 1979). Second, there is no evidence that the ability measured by visuo-spatial tests is necessary to science achievement (Saraga and Griffiths, 1981). Third, sex differences on these tests are minuscule by comparison with the large differences between boys and girls in their attainments in science. Last, the research on sex differences in the science attainment of 14-year-old boys and girls on which Gray bases his argument did not control for the number of science-based subjects currently being taken by these teenagers. Where such controls are introduced, as in a related study of sex differences in mathematical ability (Fennema, 1980), few sex-related differences emerge. It has accordingly been suggested that sex differences in mathematics and science attainment might be related more to social than to biological factors — to the apparent irrelevance to girls of science and mathematics for their anticipated roles as women in our society, so that they feel less enthusiastic about, and less eager to opt for, courses in these subjects (Fennema, 1980; Saraga and Griffiths, 1981).

The general inadequacy of existing biological determinist hypotheses concerning the psychological correlates of sexual divisions in society has led many psychologists and feminists to favour a socialization account, and in particular a social-learning explanation of psychological sex differences.

Social-learning theory

According to social-learning theory, the child acquires his or her know-ledge and repertoire of sex-typed behaviours on the basis of observation. He or she observes the behaviour modelled by parents, teachers, other children, etc (Raskin and Israel, 1981), and on the basis of the sex-typing of behaviours depicted, for instance, in picture books (Weitzman *et al*, 1972; Ashton, 1983), television (McGhee and Frueh, 1980), reading schemes (Sharpe, 1976), and in school subjects such as history and geography (Scott, 1980).

Whether the child actually imitates these behaviours depends on whether or not he or she has observed that rewards are experienced when the behaviour is performed by someone of his or her sex (Mischel, 1966). Evidence that children are quickly given the chance to learn the sex-linked rewards of particular behaviours comes, for instance, from research indicating that parents show approval of their children's sex-appropriate and disapproval of their sex-inappropriate behaviour; that three- and four-year-old children criticize, and are less willing to play with, other children who indulge in activities associated with the opposite sex, and from the finding that nursery school teachers criticize their pupils for playing with opposite sex-typed toys (Archer and Lloyd, 1982). Mischel also suggests that children learn the sex-linked rewards of particular activities in the process of learning about sex-role stereotyping; that is, through learning that such activities are socially labelled as appropriate for one sex but not the other.

The stereotyping of school subjects as male (for example, science) might explain reported differences between girls and boys in their explan-ations of their school successes and failures. Girls, it is said, typically attribute their failures to lack of ability, boys to lack of effort (Etaugh and Hadley, 1977; but see Frieze *et al*, 1982). Furthermore, teachers appear to contribute to this process through their assumption that, unlike boys, girls are well-behaved and work hard at school, so that girls are made to feel that errors in their school work reflect lack of ability rather than lack of effort (Dweck, 1978). As one teacher expressed this attitude: 'On the whole you can generally say that the boys are more capable of learning . . . Although the girls tend to be good at most things, in the end you find it's going to be a boy who's your most brilliant pupil' (Clarri-coates, 1980: 33). Parents convey a similar message to their children, viewing their daughters as having to work harder than boys to reach the same level of attainment in mathematics (Parsons *et al*, 1982). The general message seems to be that boys have a natural aptitude for mathematics which girls can only equal through hard work. And this is reinforced by the attitude that attributes girls' mathematical successes, unlike boys', to rule-following rather than to reasoning ability (Walkerdine, 1982). There is an interesting parallel here with racial divisions in society, where one finds some educationalists (Jensen, 1969) viewing school work among Blacks as properly a matter of rote-learning, and among Whites as a matter of intelligence!

Perhaps the differences in the attributions that parents, teachers and children make about the school successes and failures of boys and girls reflects the male-typing of the intellectual processes involved in education. However, although social-learning theory draws attention to the importance to child development of the sex-typing of activities such as school work, it does not address the source of this sex-typing. One possible source lies in the fact that reason and education have for many centuries been regarded as irrelevant, or even as downright harmful to girls' future roles as wives and mothers (Walkerdine, 1982; Walden and Walkerdine, 1982), so that they have come to be viewed as men's natural sphere — one in which girls can hope to succeed only through hard work. The extreme male-typing of subjects such as science might then be due to their particularly strong association with social production (Rose, 1982) — a sphere that has come to be regarded as a male preserve as it has become progressively divorced from social reproduction within the home.

Social-learning theorists (Bem, 1981) have typically not addressed themselves to the origins of sex-typing nor how it is that particular activities have come to be viewed as male- or female-typed. However, as I shall indicate later, this is crucial to the explanation of patterns of gender development, and the psychological centrality of sex in child development. The more usual objections raised against social-learning theory are: first, that parents do not reward their children differentially according to sex to the degree anticipated by the theory; and, second, that children's sex-role concepts and behaviour are not an exact model of those around them (Maccoby and Jacklin, 1974; Constantinople, 1979). These two objections are avoided by cognitive-developmental theory which provides another, equally influential, framework for current psychological research on gender development.

Cognitive-developmental theory

According to cognitive-developmental theory, it is neither biology nor society but their conceptualization by the child that determines gender development. This development, as the Piagetian psychologist Lawrence Kohlberg (1966) has argued, is initiated by the child's ability to correctly categorize itself as either a boy or a girl — an ability that is normally acquired by the age of three years (Thompson, 1975). Having correctly categorized itself by sex, the three-year-old's egocentrism leads it to value the objects and activities associated with its sex. Evidence on this point, and on the linkage of gender identity with sex-role stereotyping in pre-school children comes, for instance, from Albert and Porter (1983) and Kuhn et al (1978).

Kohlberg accounts for young children's avoidance of sex-inappropriate behaviour, not in terms of reinforcement contingencies but in terms of Piaget's account of the development of object constancy. Conservation experiments reveal that the nursery and infant school child lacks a stable

sense of object constancy, and that, at this age, the child wrongly thinks
that the volume of a liquid expands when it is poured from a fat into a
thin glass because its level is now higher up the glass. Similar evidence
shows that children of this age can wrongly believe that if a child dresses
or plays in a sex-inappropriate way its sex thereby changes (Emmerich
et al, 1977). According to cognitive-developmental theory, the child's
cognitive need to maintain a stable gender identity leads it to vigorously
avoid cross-sex behaviour and to condemn such behaviour in other
children (Damon, 1977) until gender constancy is firmly established at
about five or six years of age (Marcus and Overton, 1978). It is in these
terms that this theory explains the peaking of sexism at this age – a sexism
that contrasts with the generally more liberal sex-role attitudes of older
children, parents, and teachers (Garrett *et al*, 1977; Meyer, 1980; Urberg,
1982).

Kohlberg maintains that, consistent with the concrete-operational level
of the five- and six-year-old's conceptual structures, it is found that the
sex-role concepts of children at this age are based on obvious physical
differences between the sexes. Since men are clearly bigger than women
they are viewed by young children as more powerful and older, and
therefore as more intelligent than women. And, just as the child of this
age regards moral and social rules as absolute and God-given (Piaget,
1932), so the child of this age also regards sex-role norms as absolute;
the ten-year-old child, in contrast, tends to view them as more a matter of
social convention than of biological imperative; whilst the teenager, just
as he judges social conventions in terms of their correspondence with
general principles of equity and justice (Piaget, 1932), likewise assesses
and questions sex-role norms in these terms (Kohlberg and Ullian, 1974;
Ullian, 1976).

Although cognitive-developmental theory avoids some of the problems
of social-learning theory, it raises other problems. It has been pointed out,
for instance, that even if boys come to make moral judgements in terms
of justice and natural rights, girls come to make these judgements in terms
of their bearing on relations between people and not in terms of abstract
rights (Gilligan, 1982). If this is the case, and sex-role development
parallels moral development (as Kohlberg claims) then it is unlikely that
girls' sex-role development proceeds in the way described by Kohlberg and
Ullian. Others (for example, Mischel, 1966) have objected to Kohlberg's
theory in that it fails to explain individual differences in gender development (except tendentiously in terms of individual differences in IQ – see
Kohlberg and Zigler, 1967). Nor can Kohlberg explain the very early
appearance of sex-typed behaviour as evidenced, for instance, by the fact
that babies look more at pictures of other infants of the same than of the
opposite sex (Lewis and Brooks-Gunn, 1979) for he assumes that such
sex-typing depends for its appearance on the acquisition of gender identity
at three years of age. Lastly, Kohlberg does not explain the acquisition
of gender identity, nor why it becomes so crucial in the child's subsequent
development. Recent attempts to make good this flaw in cognitive-

developmental, as in social-learning theory, have suggested that the centrality of sex as a basis of social classification and hence its centrality to child development derives from the obviousness of sex difference (Lewis and Weinraub, 1979; Martin and Halverson, 1981). But this does not explain why this physical difference becomes crucial whilst other obvious physical differences (such as hair colour) do not become crucial in psychological development. Freudian psychoanalysis, on the other hand, does address this problem.

Psychoanalytic perspectives

Freud argued that psychological differentiation between the sexes is initiated by the three- and four-year-old's interpretation of genital sex difference in terms of castration and lack. Prior to this, he claimed, boys and girls are equally masculine and feminine in their attitudes and behaviour; they both equally entertain active as well as passive oral, anal, and genital strivings toward their primary care-giver, the mother. It is, he said, the genital eroticism of the phallic phase, and the significance that the child places on genital sex difference on account of this eroticism, that leads boys to become primarily masculine, and girls primarily feminine, in their subsequent behaviour.

The dawning of genital eroticism, at around age 4 says Freud, leads the boy to desire his mother genitally, thus bringing him into direct rivalry with his father. The boy dreads that his father will retaliate against his genital desire for the mother by castrating him. This dread now gives the genital difference between the sexes — previously ignored or denied — a new significance. Girls, it now seems to the boys, literally have been castrated. This interpretation fuels his castration anxiety and leads to the destruction or repression of his Oedipus complex, and to his identifying with the father and the masculine values he represents (Freud, 1977).

In girls, too, argues Freud, genital eroticism leads to their putting a new construction on the genital difference between the sexes. The penis, says Freud, 'strikingly visible and of large proportions', now seems on this account to be 'the superior counterpart of their small and inconspicuous organ'. Girls, claims Freud, accordingly 'fall a victim to envy for the penis' to which they respond either by giving up their phallic activity and their sexuality in general, or by clinging to the phantasy of being a man (that is, developing a 'masculinity complex'), or by following the 'very circuitous' path of 'normal' femininity in which they blame the mother for their genital lack and — drawing on the passive (feminine) trends of their bisexual constitution — turn instead to the father (Freud, 1977).

Feminists have generally objected on ideological grounds to Freud's argument that psychological sex differences originate in the child's erotically determined construction of the penis as superior to the clitoris. Instead, they have argued that this construction is socially, not biologically, determined (de Beauvoir, 1972; Friedan, 1965); for instance, that the construction is determined by the centrality given the phallus within male-dominated societies (Mitchell, 1974; Rubin, 1975). A more telling empirical objection to Freud's account of the development of psychological sex differences is that these differences appear well before the age at which Freud locates the first appearance of phallic eroticism and the castration complex. Nevertheless, there are some feminists who remain sympathetic to psychoanalysis, because its account of the unconscious and of the infantile roots of behaviour, unlike social-learning theory, seems to address the deep-rootedness of women's and men's psychological acquiescence in existing sexual divisions in society. Given the inadequacy of Freud's explanation of psychological sex differences in terms of the Oedipus complex, they have sought instead an explanation of these differences in terms of psychoanalytic accounts of the pre-Oedipal phase of development.

Post-Freudian accounts of this phase stress that it is initially marked by a sense of psychological fusion between mother and infant out of which mother and infant gradually come to individuate themselves as infancy progresses. Mothers, says Nancy Chodorow (1978), being the same sex as their daughters, tend on this account to merge more with them and therefore to prolong in them the experience of personal relations in terms of fusion. On the other hand, being the opposite sex from their sons, mothers tend to relate to them as separate and different, and hence propel them relatively early into the individuation process. As a result, claims Chodorow, boys and girls grow up with differing relational capacities: boys with the sense of separateness in personal relations that fits them for the impersonal demands of the labour market; girls with the sense of mergence and empathy in personal relations that fits them for the demands of childcare. In effect, Chodorow, unlike Freud argues that psychological sex differences are initiated in infancy by the mother's, rather than by the child's, psychological response to the fact of biological sex similarity and difference.

The subtle sex differences in emotional dynamics between mother and infant postulated by Chodorow are neither addressed nor easily handled by social-learning or cognitive-developmental theory (Ingleby, 1981). Nevertheless, there is now considerable evidence for the early appearance of differences in the way women handle girl and boy babies (Moss, 1967; Smith and Lloyd, 1978). It might well be that one reason girls do so well in primary, as compared to secondary, schools is that the former are mainly staffed by women teachers who, like mothers, identify more on grounds of sex with girls, thus facilitating their school progress.

Chodorow's account of psychological sex differences, however, raises a recurrent problem with psychological perspectives on sexual divisions in society. Like biological determinist and social learning theorists, Chodorow assumes that psychological sex differences smoothly fit men and women for existing sexual divisions in society. And this assumption is equally made by those who assume that education effectively functions to socialize girls and boys for the roles allotted to them as women and men by our society. But the very existence of the women's movement attests to the fact that neither psychology nor education smoothly conditions women into a primarily maternal and domestic role: women are even now vigorously protesting their discontent with this role. Neither biological determinist, nor social-learning, nor Chodorow's perspectives on psychological sex differences address the fact of resistance to existing sexual divisions. In contrast, Freud (1973), in his account of everyday errors and neurotic symptoms, drew attention to the way individuals both conform with and resist social, including sex-role, conventions. His theory of the unconscious, by which he explained these phenomena, provides a means of conceptualizing the contradiction between women's and men's psychological resistance to, and simultaneous acquiescence in, existing sexual divisions (Sayers, 1983) — something that is not provided by any of the other theories of gender development considered above.

Sex, society and gender development

I have sought to provide a critical, albeit brief, introduction to perspectives currently guiding research on the way individuals come to be situated psychologically in terms of existing sexual divisions in society. None of the theories outlined above is concerned with the origins of these divisions. This is not seen as problematic by those who adhere to biological determinism; they assume that gender development is directly determined by biology unmediated either by the child's construction of its gender identity, or by behavioural sex differences. Nor is it a problem for Freudian theorists who explain the acquisition of gender identity, and its centrality to the development of these differences, as an effect of the development of genital eroticism and the child's construction of genital sex difference.

However, as I have indicated, neither of these two theories adequately explains gender development. By contrast, social-learning and cognitive-developmental theorists, and Chodorow's use of post-Freudian psychoanalytic theory, assume, but do not explain, the psychological salience of biological sex to parents and children. Chodorow, as we have seen, assumes that mothers relate differently to boy and girl children because of the significance they attach to biological sex similarity and difference. Similarly, social-learning theorists assume that children quickly come to classify behaviours by sex, and to imitate these behaviours in accord with their own self-categorization by sex. Likewise, cognitive-developmental theorists assume, but do not explain, the acquisition of gender identity by the three-year-old, and the centrality of this acquisition to the child's subsequent psychological development.

This centrality can only be explained by examining the way that social relations have come to be structured historically by sex. It is here that biology is important. Biology does not directly determine sexual divisions. It does not entail, as some suggest (Firestone, 1970), that women be

primarily tied to the home and dependent on a male breadwinner. The
biological fact that women bear babies does not prevent them from
participating substantially in 'breadwinning' activity, either in industrial
or non-industrial societies (Slocum, 1975; Land, 1975). However, the way
in which the biological fact of women's childbearing has interacted with
forms of social and economic organization has had a significant impact
on sexual divisions in society. The social and historical elaboration of this
biological fact has resulted in a particular family household system that
structures sexual divisions in social and educational institutions, and
determines the direction of the sex-typing of educational and occupational
activities (Coote and Campbell, 1982). It is because of the all-pervasive
dichotomizing of social relations in these terms that sex is psychologically
so salient to parents, teachers, and children, and hence is so central to
psychological development (Bem, 1981). Any psychological theory
must accordingly take into account the historical development of existing
gender divisions if it is adequately to explain the psychological importance
of sex in child development, and the current patterning of sex role
stereotypes.

References

Albert, A A and Porter, J R (1983) Age patterns in the development of children's
    gender-role stereotypes *Sex Roles* **9**: 59-67
Archer, J and Lloyd, B (1982) *Sex and Gender* Penguin: Harmondsworth
Ashton, E (1983) Measures of play behavior: the influence of sex-role stereotyped
    children's books *Sex Roles* **9**: 43-47
Barrett, M (1980) *Women's Oppression Today* Verso: London
Bem, S L (1981) Gender schema theory: a cognitive account of sex typing *Psycho-
    logical Review* **88**: 354-64
Chodorow, N (1978) *The Reproduction of Mothering* University of California
    Press: Berkeley
Clarricoates, K (1980) The importance of being Ernest . . . Emma . . . Tom . . . Jane.
    The perception and categorization of gender conformity and gender deviation
    in primary schools *in* Deem, R ed *Schooling for Women's Work* Routledge and
    Kegan Paul: London
Constantinople, A (1979) Sex-role acquisition: in search of the elephant. *Sex Roles*
    5: 121-33
Coote, A and Campbell, B (1982) *Sweet Freedom: The Struggle for Women's Liber-
    ation* Picador: London
Damon, W (1977) *The Social World of the Child* Jossey-Bass: San Francisco
de Beauvoir, S (1972) *The Second Sex* Penguin: Harmondsworth
Deem, R ed (1980) *Schooling for Women's Work* Routledge and Kegan Paul:
    London
de Lacoste-Utamsing, C and Holloway, R L (1982) Sexual dimorphism in the human
    corpus callosum *Science* **216**: 1431-32
Dweck, C S (1978) Achievement *in* Lamb, M E ed *Social and Personality Develop-
    ment* Holt, Rinehart and Winston: New York
Emmerich, W, Goldman, S, Kirsh, B and Sharabany, R (1977) Evidence for a trans-
    itional phase in the development of gender constancy *Child Development* **48**:
    930-6
Etaugh, C and Hadley, T (1977) Causal attributions of male and female performance
    by young children *Psychology of Women Quarterly* **2**: 16-23

Fennema, E (1980) Sex-related difference in mathematics achievement: where and why *in* Fox, L H *et al eds Women and the Mathematical Mystique* John Hopkins University Press: Baltimore

Firestone, S (1970) *The Dialectic of Sex* Morrow: New York

Fox, L H, Brody, L and Tobin, D *eds* (1980) *Women and the Mathematical Mystique* John Hopkins University Press: Baltimore

Freud, S (1973) *Introductory Lectures on Psycho-Analysis* Penguin: Harmondsworth

Freud, S (1977) The dissolution of the Oedipus complex *in On Sexuality* Penguin: Harmondsworth

Freud, S (1977) Female sexuality *in On Sexuality* Penguin: Harmondsworth

Freud, S (1977) *On Sexuality* Penguin: Harmondsworth

Friedan, B (1965) *The Feminine Mystique* Penguin: Harmondsworth

Friedman, R C, Richart, R M and Van de Wiele, R L *eds* (1974) *Sex Difficulties in Behaviour* Wiley: New York

Frieze, I H, Whiteley, B E, Hanusa, B H and McHugh, M C (1982) Assessing the theoretical models for sex differences in causal attributions for success and failure *Sex Roles* 8: 333-43

Garrett, C S, Ein, P L and Tremaine, L (1977) The development of gender stereotyping of adult occupations by elementary school children *Child Development* 48: 507-12

Gilligan, C (1982) *In a Different Voice: Psychological Theory and Women's Development* Harvard University Press: Cambridge, Mass

Goldberg, S (1977) *The Inevitability of Patriarchy* Temple Smith: London

Gray, J A (1981) A biological basis for the sex differences in achievement in science? *in* Kelly, A *ed The Missing Half: Girls and Science Education* Manchester University Press: Manchester

Ingleby, D (1981) The politics of psychology: review of a decade *Psychology and Social Issues* No 2: 4-18

Jacklin, C N (1979) Epilogue *in* Wittig, M A and Petersen, A C *eds Sex-Related Differences in Cognitive Functioning* Academic Press: New York

Jensen, A (1969) How much can we boost IQ and scholastic achievement? *Harvard Educational Review* 39: 1-123

Jones, B and Anuza, T (1982) Sex differences in cerebral lateralization in 3- and 4-year old children *Neuropsychologia* 20: 347-50

Kelly, A *ed* (1981) *The Missing Half: Girls and Science Education* Manchester University Press: Manchester

Kiger, J A *ed* (1972) *The Biology of Behaviour* Oregon Univerity Press: Corvallis, Oregon

Kohlberg, L (1966) A cognitive-developmental analysis of children's sex-role concepts and attitudes *in* Maccoby, E E *ed The Development of Sex Differences* Stanford University Press: Stanford

Kohlberg, L and Ullian, D (1974) Stages in the development of psychosexual concepts and attitudes *in* Friedman, R *et al eds Sex Differences in Behavior* Wiley: New York

Kohlberg, L and Zigler, E (1967) The impact of cognitive maturity on the development of sex role attitudes in the years four to eight *Genetic Psychology Monographs* 75: 89-165

Kuhn, D, Nash, S C and Bruchen, L (1978) Sex role concepts of two- and three-year-olds *Child Development* 49: 445-51

Lamb, M E *ed* (1978) *Social and Personality Development* Holt, Rinehart and Winston: New York

Land, H (1975) The myth of the male breadwinner *New Society* 9 10 75; 71-73

Levy, J (1972) Lateral specialization of the human brain: behavioral manifestations and possible evolutionary basis *in* Kiger, J A *ed The Biology of Behavior* Oregon University Press: Corvallis, Oregon

Lewis, M and Brooks-Gunn, J (1979) *Social Cognition and the Acquisition of Self* Plenum: New York

Lewis, M and Weinraub, M (1979) Origins of early sex-role development *Sex Roles* **5**: 135-53

Lloyd, B and Archer, A eds (1976) *Exploring Sex Differences* Academic Press: London

Maccoby, E E ed (1966) *The Development of Sex Differences* Stanford University Press: Stanford

Maccoby, E E and Jacklin, C N (1974) *The Psychology of Sex Differences* Stanford University Press: Stanford

McGhee, P E and Frueh, T (1980) Television viewing and the learning of sex-role stereotypes *Sex Roles* **6**: 179-88

Marcus, D E and Overton, W F (1978) The development of cognitive gender constancy and sex role preferences *Child Development* **49**: 434-44

Martin, C L and Halverson, C F (1981) A schematic processing model of sex typing and stereotyping in children *Child Development* **52**: 1119-34

Meyer, B (1980) The development of girls' sex-role attitudes *Child Development* **51**: 508-14

Mischel, W (1966) A social-learning view of sex differences in behavior *in* Maccoby, E E ed *The Development of Sex Differences* Stanford University Press: Stanford

Mitchell, J (1974) *Psychoanalysis and Feminism* Allen Lane: London

Moss, H A (1967) Sex, age, and state as determinants of mother-infant interaction *Merrill-Palmer Quarterly* **13**: 19-36

Orsini, A, Schiappa, O, Chiacchio, L and Grossi, D (1982) Sex differences in a children's spatial serial-learning task *Journal of Psychology* **111**: 67-71

Parsons, J E, Adler, T F and Kaczala, C M (1982) Socialization of achievement attitudes and beliefs: parental influences *Child Development* **53**: 310-21

Piaget, J (1932) *The Moral Judgment of the Child* Routledge and Kegan Paul: London

Raskin, P and Israel, A (1981) Sex-role imitation in children: effects of sex of child, sex of model, and sex-role appropriateness of modeled behavior *Sex Roles* **7**: 1067-77

Reiter, R R ed (1975) *Toward an Anthropology of Woman* Monthly Review Press: New York

Rose, H (1982) Making science feminist *in* Whitelegg, E et al eds *The Changing Experience of Women* Martin Robertson: Oxford

Rossi, A (1977) A biosocial perspective on parenting *Daedalus* **106**: 1-32

Rubin, G (1975) The traffic in women: notes on the 'political economy' of sex *in* Reiter, R R ed *Toward an Anthropology of Women* Monthly Review Press: New York

Saraga, E and Griffiths, D (1981) Biological inevitabilities or political choices? The future for girls in science *in* Kelly, A ed *The Missing Half: Girls and Science Education* Manchester University Press: Manchester

Sayers, J (1982) *Biological Politics: Feminist and Anti-Feminist Perspectives* Tavistock: London

Sayers, J (1983) Is the personal political? Psychoanalysis and feminism revisited *International Journal of Women's Studies* **6**: 71-86

Scott, M (1980) Teach her a lesson: sexist curriculum in patriarchal education *in* Spender, D and Sarah, E eds *Learning to Lose* Women's Press: London

Sharpe, S (1976) *Just Like a Girl* Penguin: Harmondsworth

Slocum, S (1975) Woman the gatherer: male bias in anthropology *in* Reiter, R R ed *Toward an Anthropology of Women* Monthly Review Press: New York

Smith, C and Lloyd, B B (1978) Maternal behaviour and perceived sex of infant *Child Development* **49**: 1263-65

Spender, D and Sarah E eds (1980) *Learning to Lose: Sexism and Education* The Woman's Press: London

Thompson, S K (1975) Gender labels and early sex role development *Child Development* **46**: 339-47

Tieger, T (1980) On the biological basis of sex differences in aggression *Child Development* **51**: 943-63

Ullian, D Z (1976) The development of conceptions of masculinity and femininity *in* Lloyd, B and Archer, J eds *Exploring Sex Differences* Academic Press: London

Urberg, K A (1982) The development of the concepts of masculinity and femininity in young children *Sex Roles* **8**: 659-68

Walden, R and Walkerdine, V (1982) *Girls and Mathematics: The Early Years. Bedford way Papers 8* University of London Institute of Education: London

Walkerdine, V (1982) Gender and the production of rationality in the family and at school. Paper given in Manchester at the British Sociological Association Annual Conference, 'Gender and Society'

Weitzman, L J, Eifler, D, Hokada, E, Ross, C (1972) Sex-role socialization in picture books for preschool children *American Journal of Sociology* **77**: 1125-50

Whitelegg, E *et al* eds (1982) *The Changing Experience of Women* Martin Robertson; Oxford

Wittig, M A and Petersen, A C eds (1979) *Sex-Related Differences in Cognitive Functioning* Academic Press: New York

Wilson, E O (1978) *On Human Nature* Harvard University Press: Cambridge

Acknowledgements

I would like to thank Valerie Walkerdine for helpful discussions she had with me while I was writing this chapter, and Sean Sayers for his supportive and useful comments on it.

4. Sociolinguistics and gender divisions

Jane French and Peter French

Summary: The chapter discusses a selection of recent sociolinguistic research on language and gender. Sociolinguistic studies are divided into two broad types: those which attempt to show differences between the *forms* of grammar and pronunciation that women and men use, and those that plot differences between the interactional *activities* that women and men engage in. It is argued that form-based studies show that women are more linguistically 'conservative' and 'correct' than men; activity-based studies demonstrate that men dominate women in social interaction.

The final section of the chapter proposes that school classrooms are important forums for the learning of gender-differential patterns of linguistic and interactional behaviour, and suggests means of redressing the imbalances through the design of teacher-education programmes.

Introduction

In this chapter we present and discuss a range of research into language and gender. In the main, we shall confine our attention to work which investigates differences in men's and women's use of language and their social-interactional behaviour (Kramer, 1977).

The chapter is organized around two central themes: first, women's and men's use of prestige and low-status linguistic forms and the role of each sex in bringing about language innovations, and second, the alleged tentativeness of women in social interactions and men's dominance in mixed-sex conversations. Although we refer to studies relating to these issues collectively as 'sociolinguistic' research, this is merely a convenient cover term, for they do not share a unitary set of research assumptions and methods. As we shall be passing critical comment upon the assumptions made in some studies, it is helpful to begin with a brief statement explaining two methodologically distinct strains of sociolinguistic work.

Form-based and activity-based approaches

Undoubtedly, there are many dimensions upon which studies of socially-situated language could be arrayed and contrasted. For the purposes of this chapter, however, we shall simply distinguish between form-based and activity-based approaches.

We use the term 'form-based' to denote studies which have emerged from, or are aligned with, a linguistic (as opposed to sociological) tradition of analysis. Studies of this kind take linguistic forms — grammatical constructions, words or pronunciation features — as their basic units of analysis. Samples of language are scanned for instances of particular linguistic forms, and attempts are then made to establish statistical correlations between their incidence and facets of speaker identity. By working in this way, studies have been able to show that language varies not only in accordance with the particulars of the 'local' interactive situation (the setting and purpose of the communication), but also with more 'enduring' speaker characteristics. Social class, education, occupation and, as one might expect, gender have all been established as important predictors of the form one's speech will actually take (Labov, 1972; Trudgill, 1974; Hudson, 1980).

As we shall suggest, form-based studies have yielded much useful information about women's and men's differential use of high- and low-status forms of language, and about gender as a factor in linguistic change. However, we shall also argue that there is a danger of extending this approach into areas it is ill-suited to illuminate. In particular, it would seem that it cannot provide one with reliable information about the claimed tentativeness of women in social interaction (Lakoff, 1975), or men's tendency to dominate mixed-sex talk. If understanding of these issues is to advance, the approach required is an activity-based one.

By 'activity-based' we mean an approach to the study of language in use which takes as its basic elements not linguistic forms but interactional activities. Socially-situated utterances not only express referential meanings but also perform activities (Turner, 1974; Austin, 1976). Conventional labels for these activities include 'questioning', 'promising', 'inviting', 'refusing' and so on, and considerable headway has been established within the sociological sub-discipline of conversation analysis in examining how activities from the various classes are managed and coordinated. (For explanatory introductions to this work, see Atkinson and Drew, 1979, Chapter 1; Wootton, 1981a; for overviews see Atkinson and Heritage, in press, Introduction; Heritage, in press.) A small but growing body of work has begun to use insights provided by this tradition as a resource for investigating gender differences in interaction. Through examining who typically does what in mixed-sex talk, for example interrupting, requesting confirmation or reassurance, or giving or withholding supportive feedback, activity-based studies have made a promising beginning at answering questions of whether women are less assertive than men and how men achieve conversational dominance over women.

Before proceeding to these studies, we shall first examine the issues of gender-differential use of prestige and low-status forms, areas to which the former, form-based studies have made a substantial contribution.

Prestige and low-status forms

Most, if not all, languages are internally differentiated in terms of both grammar and sound structure. As social-psychological investigations have firmly established, certain regionally-marked systems of grammar (dialects) and pronunciation (accents) carry less prestige than others, and tend to be judged negatively in comparison with regionally-neutral systems (Giles *et al*, 1975; Giles and Powesland, 1975).

A large body of form-based sociolinguistic work has been directed towards plotting the incidence of prestige and low-status accent and dialect forms across sub-populations of language communities (Trudgill, 1974; Dittmar, 1976; Hudson, 1980). Studies which have examined the occurrence of such features against speaker gender suggest that, in general, men are most likely to use low-status forms. Some examples of findings from these types of study are represented below. (For a further indication of findings in relation to accent alone, consult Farb, 1973; Kramer, 1975; for a review which includes dialect forms see Trudgill, 1974, Chapter 4.)

With regard to dialect, data from Shuy's study of Detroit English show, as one might predict, that the use of non-standard, multiple negation (for example, 'I don't want none') increases as one descends through the social class bands (UMC, LMC, UWC, LWC). However, within each class, one finds many more instances of these forms being produced by men than by women (Trudgill, 1974). Trudgill has disclosed similar trends in relation to accent, both by reference to the Detroit data and to his own work on Norwich English (1974; 1975a). In respect of the Detroit study, it is shown that some speakers use an 'r' consonant (usually termed 'post-vocalic 'r' ') at the ends of words such as 'car' and 'better' and before other consonants in words like 'hurt' and 'park' whilst others do not. In America, the high-status pronunciation is with the 'r' present and the low-status without the 'r' (in fact, the reverse of the situation for British English). Again, speakers belonging to the lower social groupings utilized more 'r'-absent forms than did those from the higher ones, but men across the social classes used more 'r'-absent forms than did women (see also Levine and Crockett, 1966). A similar pattern is thrown by data from Trudgill's Norwich study where, in words like 'walking' and 'speaking', women of all social classes showed a much lesser tendency than men to use the low-status pronunciation with an 'n' consonant in final position (see also Fischer, 1958). This same type of distribution by gender is also reported in more recent work on language and social networks where it is noted that, with regard to the vowel and consonant systems in Belfast speech, men use 'higher levels of the vernacular variants than women' (Milroy, 1980: 157). And yet further instances are provided by Shuy *et al* (1967) and Wolfram (1969).

There are occasional exceptions to the tendency. For example, Labov (1972) notes that the Chicago accent is undergoing changes to its vowel system, and that these are most apparent in a low-status group: 'young working-class speakers'. Of the vowel shifts recorded in the casual speech of people in this category, though, 'it is the women in the group who show the most extreme forms' (1972: 302). A similar finding is reported in Labov, Yaeger and Steiner (1972) with regard to women's use of non-prestigious vowel pronunciations in New York. However, the general picture is that, as Trudgill says, 'Men's and women's speech . . . is not only different: women's speech is also (socially) "better" than men's' (1974: 94).

There is a good deal of evidence that women's greater linguistic 'correctness' is not only a matter of conventionalized habit, but that their speech may, in fact, be targeted towards prestige norms. When inform-ants are faced with speech situations of increased formality (for example, having to read aloud from prepared texts or word lists), women shift their speech more sharply towards received standards than do men (Fischer, 1958; Labov, 1966; Levine and Crockett, 1966; Labov, 1972). Further, when asked to provide self-reports on pronunciation, women tend to state that they speak in a more standard fashion than they actually do, whereas men evince the opposite trend (Trudgill, 1975a).

Women's and men's different aspirations towards received standards result in a gender-differential division of responsibility for advancing linguistic innovations. In general, the situation is such that the new vernacular forms become established, in the first instance, through the speech of males. Women, on the other hand, tend to be prominent in developing new prestige forms (Anshen, 1969). (See Trudgill, 1974: 98-101 for instances of this trend from American Indian languages, Norwegian, British and American English; see Labov, 1972: 301-304 for some counter-instances.)

An understanding of why women should aspire to the use of high-status forms is, as yet, imperfectly developed. Trudgill, for example, has explained the situation in terms of women being 'more status-conscious than men, generally speaking' (1975a: 91). And their status-consciousness is, he suggests, in turn precipitated by macro-economic and social factors: 'Since they are not rated [by society] by their occu-pation or by their occupational success, other signals of status, including speech, are correspondingly more important' (1975a: 91-92). However, it is quite possible that women's greater 'correctness' has as much to do with gender-differential linguistic socialization as with a general status-consciousness. As Clarricoates remarks in an ethnographic study of a British primary school: 'There was . . . a verbal double standard, with teachers censuring girls more harshly than boys for using improper language' (1980: 33). We shall return to this point in our concluding section where we consider the classroom as a forum for the acquisition of gender-differentiated linguistic and interactional practices.

The avoidance of vernacular forms which carry associations of 'rough-ness' is only one from a range of language features which researchers have attributed to women, and which, it is claimed, render their language behaviour 'more polite than that of boys or men' (Lakoff, 1975: 19).

Other features said to operate to this effect are the tendency to avoid strong expletives (Jespersen, 1922: 246-247; Kramer, 1975; Lakoff, 1975: 10) and terms of obscenity (Miller and Swift, 1977: 111-122), together with 'an absence of . . . strong statement' (Lakoff, 1975; 19). This last claim by Lakoff, that women tend to make greater use of various 'weaker' modes of expression, has initiated a number of empirical studies of the form-based type. We shall examine the claim in some more detail below, and attempt some critical appraisal of the work which has attempted to investigate it.

Tentative expression and male assertiveness

Lakoff suggested that women's avoidance of 'strong statements' was observable in their formal features of intonation and grammar. In particular, tag questions (for example, 'isn't it?', 'aren't you?') and rising intonation were thought to be relevant.

Tag questions are claimed to attenuate or downgrade the force with which statements are expressed. Thus, the sentence with the tag attached ('Books can impart knowledge, can't they?') is said to be less definite and less forceful than its non-tagged equivalent ('Books can impart knowledge'). Lakoff proposed that the tag question 'is more apt to be used by women than men' (1975: 16), and that, by using it, they avoid commitment and hence potential 'conflict with the addressee' (1975: 16-17). Whilst being quite clear that this was an 'impression' and that she did not have 'precise statistical evidence' relating to women's greater use of the form (1975: 16), the contention that women were the predominant tag users nevertheless quickly found its way into subsequent sociolinguistic statements on language and gender (Thorne and Henley, 1975). However, in a thoroughgoing empirical study of tag questions in one (albeit limited) authentic social setting (an academic meeting), Dubois and Crouch have reported that 'men did, and women did not, use tag questions' (1975: 294). To the best of our knowledge, there is no evidence for the view that women and men make differential use of tags as a general feature of their language.

A second indicator of female tentativeness outlined by Lakoff was the use of rising intonation. The production of declarative sentences on rising pitch is said functionally to transform them into 'yes/no' questions ('Books can impart knowledge?'). Lakoff's suggestion was that women use this pattern of pitch in their responses to questions about matters upon which they alone can deliberate (A: 'What time will dinner be ready?' B: 'About six o'clock?'). Thus, answers which one might expect to be delivered in a relatively certain or definitive way are made to sound 'as though one were seeking confirmation' (1975: 17).

Although there is some rather anecdotal indication in a study by Brend that women may make distinctive use of a rising 'request confirmation' contour (1975: 85; Key, 1972), a more recent study by Edelsky

(1979) which set out directly to test Lakoff's hypothesis failed to find supportive evidence. Although Edelsky found that in interviews women did show a very slight tendency to produce a sub-type of rising tone (rise-fall-rise), the functional value of this tone may have been not tentativeness but incompleteness: through its use 'the women might have been trying to facilitate the interview or continue the interaction' (1979: 28). As with tags, there is little empirical support for the view that women make greater use of rising, 'questioning' intonation than men.

Finally, a third form which has been linked with women's inclination towards 'weak' expression is the qualifier. Some types of qualifier which can operate as sentence adverbials are said to downgrade the assertiveness of statements in a way similar to tags ('Perhaps books can impart knowledge' may equal 'Books can impart knowledge, can't they?'). Unlike tags and questioning intonation, there does appear to be some evidence for a gender-differential distribution of these forms. In a study by Hartman (1976) it was found that women made greater use of qualifiers whereas men made more use of absolutes. However, we would suggest that the significance of this finding should be approached with caution in view of the points discussed below.

Of the forms examined here it seems that, with the exception of qualifiers, there is scant evidence of gender-differential usage. One can be sure, however, that further attempts will be made (and probably are being made) to establish such usage. It is clear to us that research into this particular area of language and gender would profit from methodological reflection. The question we would pose is this: if a study were done which linked, unequivocally, the vast majority of tag questions to women, could one then conclude with any certainty that women were more tentative than men in expressing their meanings? Contrary to the reasoning in forming form-based studies in this area, we think not. Our grounds for taking this view concern the disjunction which often exists between researchers' abstract, a-contextual specifications of the meanings of linguistic forms, and the meanings these forms may actually express in empirical instances of usage. It has long been recognized within certain traditions of linguistic philosophy and micro-sociology that there is no homological relationship between linguistic forms and meanings (Garfinkel, 1967). A given meaning (such as 'tentativeness') may be expressed through a variety of linguistic forms, and any form is capable of realizing not one but many meanings (Heritage, 1978). The actual meaning that an empirical production of a form is expressing cannot be derived from linguists' statements about what the form 'seems to mean' when considered out of context, but only by examining it against the backcloth of discourse in which it occurs (Schegloff, 1977). An inkling of how this may relate to tag questions is provided in Dubois and Crouch's study. On the basis of previous work and personal communication, they note that, in addition to 'signalling lack of confidence', tags 'can function as a request'; they can express condescension; and they can be used in an 'overbearing' way to 'forestall opposition' (1975: 292). Yet a further deployment is mentioned in Wootton (1981b) who provides transcripts of interactions where they are used to solicit responses in certain types of communication breakdown. We would be surprised if this list exhausted the functions that tags are capable of fulfilling. In the light of it, though, it becomes clear that a statement of tag frequencies may mask what is happening in interactions. Speakers *might* be expressing tentativeness in using them; on the other hand, they might not. One cannot simply set up tags, or other linguistic forms, as objective indices of speaker tentativeness and then plot their incidence against speaker gender. Or, if one does, one is likely to be rewarded with unreliable information.

This becomes even more apparent when one considers that at least some aspects of women's and men's usage may operate simply to display gender identity. It has long been known that in the Koasati language, for example, women and men until quite recently used different words and constructions to refer to the same objects, events and processes (Haas, 1944). It is now emerging that there are similar (perhaps more subtle and less immediately visible) conventions operating within modern European languages. In Local's (in press) work on Urban Tyneside English, for instance, it was discovered that formal patterns of intonation of the type we have been discussing were used mainly by women. Men used high level tones as their neutral, or unmarked, contour on statements, whereas women's neutral contour was a rise. There is no functional significance attaching to this beyond the display of gender-identity, however; women's rising tones do not signify, and are not taken by their interlocutors as signifying, a confirmation-requesting intent. It is quite possible that women's frequent use of, for example, qualifiers, as found by the Hartman study, has little to do with the meanings 'hesitant' or 'tentative' (1976: 87), but serves simply to mark out their speech as 'female speech'. The interpretation is purely speculative, and there is nothing much to recommend it over other possibilities. This, however, is our whole point. Statements of gender-differential distributions of forms and structures in themselves tell one very little about the sorts of issues at stake here; they allow for *no more than* speculation. Whilst a form-based approach may illuminate women's and men's different orientations towards 'correct' grammar and pronunciation, it is not a suitable tool for investigating the present area. If one is to gain reliable knowledge of whether women are more tentative or less forceful interactants than men, then the place to begin is by looking at the interactional activities women and men perform with respect to one another.

There is, in fact, a small, but rapidly increasing, number of activity-based studies in this area. These studies begin from the proposition that 'power and hierarchical relations are not abstract forces operating on people' and that 'power must be a human accomplishment situated in everyday interaction' (Fishman, 1978: 397). If, as feminist researchers have suggested, male-female relationships are hierarchically organized so that men wield the power (Spender, 1980), then one would expect power to be made manifest in asymmetries between the activities women and men perform in everyday social encounters. Drawing upon the descriptions of, for example, turn-taking systems (Sacks, Schegloff and Jefferson, 1974) and devices for securing speaker attention (Schegloff, 1977; Sacks, 1974) provided by conversation analysts, some researchers of gender have begun to investigate this possibility. To conclude this section we shall briefly consider their findings.

In a study of couples interacting in their homes, Fishman notes that the women, unlike the men, frequently prefaced utterances on new topics with 'attention beginnings'. These activities function to secure the interest and attention of the other party and take such forms as 'this is interesting . . .'. In performing them, Fishman suggests the women were showing that they 'cannot assume the remark itself will be seen as worthy of attention' by their male partners (1978: 401; see also Bernard, 1972). Similarly, once they had begun to speak, the women heavily interspersed their remarks with utterances designed to elicit evidence of listening from their partners (for example, 'y'know?'), thereby showing that they were anticipating problems in being able to hold their attention. When male partners were speaking, however, females showed a strong tendency to insert unsolicited 'minimal responses' like 'yeah', 'umm', 'huh', thus giving the men constant supportive feedback on what they were saying (see also Hirschmann, 1974). In view of these observations, Fishman concludes 'there is a division of labor in conversation' whereby 'the people who do the routine maintenance work' are the women (1978: 404-405).

In contrast to this, men's conversational work is seen as non-supportive. Although they used the same minimal response forms as women, they showed less inclination to insert them within the flow of women's talk. The forms 'yeah' and 'umm' tended to be produced only after the women had completed a lengthy remark, and fulfilled a different type of activity. They were used in a way that displayed 'lack of interest' and served as attempts to 'discourage interaction' (Fishman, 1978: 402). (A purely form-based study undoubtedly would have missed this difference.) This finding was further elaborated in a similar study by Zimmerman and West of talk between acquaintances. Here it was found that not only were men's minimal responses to the women 'retarded beyond the end of the utterance' but sometimes also delayed 'by pauses of up to 10 seconds in length' (1975: 122). The latter study also showed that in single-sex interactional dyads (both female-female and male-male), interruptions 'seem to be fairly equally divided between the first and second speaker' (1975: 115). However, in mixed-sex dyads, of 48 interruptions, 46 were produced by males and only 2 by females. In interpreting the findings, the authors conclude: 'we view the production of both retarded minimal responses and interruptions by male speakers interacting with females as an assertion of the right to control the topic of the conversation reminiscent of adult-child conversations where . . . the child has restricted rights to speak and to be listened to' (1975: 124).

More recent work by Edelsky (1981) on turn-taking and floor-holding in academic meetings bears out this view of men as 'directors' of mixed-sex interactions, but also provides some rather telling findings about the conditions under which interactional inequalities may be levelled. Edelsky distinguishes between two types of conversational floor. The first is 'a singly developed floor' which one speaker holds while others attend. The second type is a more 'collaborative venture where several people seemed to be operating on the same wavelength or engaging in a free-for-all' (Edelsky, 1981: 383). In singly developed floors, 'the men held forth, took longer turns though not more of them . . . dominated the construction of floor by virtue, at least, of the time they took talking' (1981: 415; see also Wood, 1966; Chesler, 1971; Swacker, 1975). In collaborative floors, however, differences in male and female turn length were equalized. Further, in these situations women were found to be 'joking, arguing, directing, and soliciting responses more and men less' (Edelsky, 1981: 415). These findings suggest that when there is a collaborative, or supportive, aspect to the interaction, women feel able and inclined to take an equal part in the proceedings. It was this very element of interactional support that Fishman and Zimmerman and West found being denied to women both by their male acquaintances and their sexual partners.

It is clear that the results of these studies on female-male interaction are of more than purely academic interest, and bear close relevance to the formulation of social and educational policy. We shall take up this point in the concluding section of the chapter.

Conclusion

In substantive terms, two general trends have emerged from the studies of language, interaction and gender discussed here. First, available evidence overwhelmingly suggests that the forms of language women use approximate more closely than those of men to prestige norms, and second, that, in social interactions, the part played by women tends to be supportive while that of men is dominant. In discussing the studies which have produced these findings, we have devoted space to methodological criticism. An awareness of methodological issues is, we believe, extremely important in this area. Given that in many nations gender divisions in society are becoming a subject of political debate, and that the findings of academic researchers may be used to influence social policy, it is necessary that those findings arise from sound methodological footings. Indeed, it is at least partly this type of concern that has dictated the range of topics addressed here. Sociolinguistic study has the potential to illuminate areas of language and gender other than sex-differential usage and interactional behaviour. One such area concerns differences in language (oral and written) used to describe women and men. As yet, however, this field is relatively underdeveloped, with available studies relying quite heavily upon a-contextual methods of linguistic analysis

(Schulz, 1975; Spender, 1980: 14-19) or 'journalistic' commentary (Miller and Swift, 1977: 55-70). Another area of relevance is the disparity between the language used to address women and that used to men. Again, the little available work directly on this topic tends to be form-based (Brouwer *et al*, 1979), and thereby suffers from the problems of interpretation outlined earlier (but see Brooks Gardner, 1980). Accepting for the present, then, the limitations of our focus, what social directions does the work on usage and interaction suggest to us?

In our thinking, the research bears obvious relevance to teachers' practices in the school classroom. We suggested earlier that differences in adult women's and men's use of 'correct' forms may be partly attributable to teachers' enforcing different linguistic standards for girls and boys. As Trudgill (1975b) has pointed out, there are very good reasons for teachers not intervening in any child's use of regional speech, but if we have a situation where some pupils are corrected whilst others are not then this clearly is in need of remediation.

With regard to male dominance in mixed-sex interaction, we have ourselves found evidence of this in British primary school classes of children as young as 10 and 11 years (French and French, 1983). In one lesson, which comprised 66 pupil turns at interaction, 50 of these were produced by boys who numbered less than half the class (see also Brophy and Good, 1970: 373; Galton *et al*, 1980: 66; Stanworth, 1981; Spender, 1982). What is more, a good many of these turns were not 'spontaneously' allocated to boy pupils by the teacher, but achieved through interactional techniques designed to gain the teacher's attention. Whilst the point at which these techniques is acquired is, as yet, unknown, it nevertheless seems clear that a first step towards evening out the imbalance consists in making teachers (in addition to others) aware of them. As we conclude in the original study, 'much would be gained from developing, in the context of teacher education programmes, an interaction-based approach to language and gender which sought to increase teachers' knowledge and awareness of what may be involved' (French and French, 1983: 12).

References

Anshen, F (1969) Speech variation among Negroes in a small Southern community Unpublished dissertation New York University: New York

Atkinson, J M and Drew, P (1979) *Order in Court: The Organization of Verbal Interaction in Judicial Settings* Macmillan: London

Atkinson, J M and Heritage, J C (in press) Conversation analysis *in* Atkinson and Heritage (in press)

Atkinson, J M and Heritage, J C *eds* (in press) *Structures of Social Action* Cambridge University Press: Cambridge

Austin, J L (1976) How to do things with words *in* Urmson and Sbisà

Bernard, J (1972) *The Sex Game* Atheneum: New York

Brend, R M (1975) Male-female intonation patterns in American English *in* Thorne and Henley

Brooks Gardner, C (1980) Street remarks, address rights, and the urban female *in* Zimmerman and West

Brophy, J E and Good, T L (1970) Teachers' communications of differential expectations for children's classroom performance: some behavioural data *Journal of Educational Psychology* **61** 5: 365-74

Brouwer, D, Gerritsen, M and De Haan, D (1979) Speech differences between women and men: on the wrong track? *Language in Society* **8**: 33-50

Chesler, P (1971) Marriage and psychotherapy *in* Radical Therapist Collective

Clarricoates, K (1980) The importance of being Ernest . . . Emma . . . Tom . . . Jane . . . The perception and categorisation of gender conformity and gender deviation in primary schools *in* Deem

Deem, R *ed* (1980) *Schooling for Women's Work* Routledge and Kegan Paul: London

Dittmar, N (1976) *Socio-linguistics: A Critical Survey of Theory and Application* Arnold: London

Dressler, W U *ed* (1977) *Current Trends in Textlinguistics* de Gruyter: Berlin

Dubois, B L and Crouch, I (1975) The question of tag questions in women's speech: they don't really use more of them, do they? *Language in Society* **4**: 289-94

Dubois, B L and Crouch, I *eds* (1976) *The Sociology of the Languages of American Women* PISE Papers IV Trinity University: San Antonio, Texas

Edelsky, C (1979) Question intonation and sex roles *Language in Society* **8**: 15-32

Edelsky, C (1981) Who's got the floor? *Language in Society* **10**: 383-421

Farb, P (1973) *Word Play: What Happens when People Talk* Knopf: New York

Fischer, J L (1958) Social influences on the choice of a linguistic variant *Word* **14**: 47-56

Fishman, P (1978) Interaction: the work women do *Social Problems* **25** 4: 397-406

French, J and French, P (1983) Gender imbalances in the primary classroom: an interactional account Unpublished paper New College: Durham

French, P and MacLure, M *eds* (1981) *Adult-Child Conversation* Croom Helm: London

Galton, M, Simon, B and Croll, P (1980) *Inside the Primary Classroom* Routledge and Kegan Paul: London

Garfinkel, H (1967) *Studies in Ethnomethodology* Prentice Hall: Englewood Cliffs, New Jersey

Giles, H, Bouris, R Y and Davies, A (1975) Prestige speech styles: the imposed norm and inherent value hypotheses *in* McCormack and Wurm (1975)

Giles, H and Powesland, P (1975) *Speech Style and Social Evaluation* Academic Press: London

Haas, M R (1944) Men's and women's speech in Koasati *Language* **20**: 142-49

Hartman, M (1976) A descriptive study of the language of men and women born in Maine around 1900 as it reflects the Lakoff hypothesis *in* Dubois and Crouch

Heritage, J C (1978) Aspects of the flexibilities of natural language use *Sociology* **12**: 79-103

Heritage, J C (in press) Recent developments in conversation analysis *Sociolinguistics Newsletter* special issue edited by Thomas Luckmann (in press)

Hirschman, L (1974) Analysis of supportive and assertive behaviour in conversations Paper delivered to meeting of Linguistic Society of America, July

Hudson, R A (1980) *Socio-Linguistics* Cambridge University Press: Cambridge

Jespersen, O (1922) *Language: its Nature, Development and Origin* Allen and Unwin: London

Johns-Lewis, C *ed* (in press) *Intonation and Discourse* Croom Helm: London

Key, M R (1972) Linguistic behaviour of male and female *Linguistics* **88**: 15-31

Kramer, C (1975) Women's speech: separate but unequal *in* Thorne and Henley

Kramer, C (1977) Perceptions of female and male speech *Language and Speech* **20**: 2: 151-161

Labov, W (1966) *The Social Stratification of Speech in New York City* Centre for Applied Linguistics: Washington, DC

Labov, W (1972) *Sociolinguistic Patterns* University of Pennsylvania Press: Philadelphia

Labov, W, Yaeger, M and Steiner, R (1972) *A Quantitative Study of Sound Change in Progress* Final report on National Science Foundation contract NSF-GS-3287: Philadelphia

Lakoff, R (1975) *Language and Woman's Place* Harper and Row: New York

Levine, L and Crockett, H J Jnr (1966) Speech variation in a Piedmont community: postvocalic r *in* Lieberson

Lieberson, S *ed* (1966) *Explorations in Sociolinguistics* special issue of *Sociological Inquiry* **36** 2

Local, J K (in press) Patterns and problems in a study of Tyneside intonation *in* Johns-Lewis

McCormack, W C and Wurm, S *eds* (1975) *Language in Anthropology IV: Language in Many Ways* Mouton: The Hague

Miller, C and Swift, K (1977) *Words and Women* Gollancz: London

Milroy, L (1980) *Language and Social Networks* Blackwell: Oxford

Radical Therapist Collective *eds* (1971) *The Radical Therapist* Ballantyne: New York

Sacks, H (1974) On the analysability of stories by children *in* Turner

Sacks, H, Schegloff, E A and Jefferson, G (1974) A simplest systematics for the organisation of turn-taking for conversation *Language* **50**: 696-735

Schegloff, E A (1968) Sequencing in conversational openings *American Anthropologist* **70**: 1075-95

Schegloff, E A (1977) On some questions and ambiguities in conversation *in* Dressler

Schulz, M (1975) The semantic derogation of women *in* Thorne and Henley

Shuy, R, Wolfram, W and Riley, W K (1967) *A Study of Social Dialects in Detroit* Final report on Project 6-1347 Office of Education: Washington, DC

Spender, D (1980) *Man Made Language* Routledge and Kegan Paul: London

Spender, D (1982) *Invisible Women: The Schooling Scandal* Writers' and Readers' Co-operative Group with Chameleon Editorial Group: London

Stanworth, M (1981) *Gender and Schooling: A Study of Sexual Divisions in the Classroom* Women's Research and Resources Centre: London

Swacker, M (1975) The sex of the speaker as a sociolinguistic variable *in* Thorne and Henley

Thorne, B and Henley, N (1975) Difference and dominance: an overview of language, gender, and society *in* Thorne and Henley

Thorne, B and Henley, N *eds* (1975) *Language and Sex: Difference and Dominance* Newbury House: Rowley, Mass

Trudgill, P (1974) *Sociolinguistics: An Introduction* Penguin: Harmondsworth

Trudgill, P (1975a) Sex, covert prestige, and linguistic change in the urban British English of Norwich *in* Thorne and Henley

Trudgill, P (1975b) *Accent, Dialect and the School* Arnold: London

Turner, R (1974) Words, utterances and activities *in* Turner

Turner, R *ed* (1974) *Ethnomethodology* Penguin: Harmondsworth

Urmson, J O and Sbisà, M *eds* (1976) *How to do Things with Words* Second Edition Oxford University Press: Oxford

Wolfram, W (1969) Linguistic correlates of social stratification in the speech of Detroit Negroes Unpublished thesis: Hartford Seminary Foundation

Wood, M (1966) The influence of sex and knowledge of communication effectiveness on speech *Word* **22**: 112-37

Wootton, A (1981a) Conversation analysis *in* French and MacLure

Wootton, A (1981b) Children's use of address terms *in* French and MacLure

Zimmerman, D H and West, C (1975) Sex roles, interruptions and silences *in* Thorne and Henley

Zimmerman, D H and West, C *eds* (1980) *Language and Social Interaction* special issue of *Sociological Inquiry* **50**: 3-4

5. Sociology, gender and education

Sandra Acker

Summary: This chapter examines links between education, gender and sociology. Sociologists of education, at least in Britain, have until recently paid little attention to issues of inequality between the sexes. A rapidly developing body of theoretical literature on gender now exists. The chapter outlines major sociological ways of comprehending the structurally subordinate social position of women, through two categories of 'fundamental approaches' (further broken into functionalist, marxist-feminist and radical-feminist forms) and 'implementary approaches'. Fundamental approaches seek to explain why subordination exists, whilst implementary ones focus on processes and practices which perpetuate it. Characteristic applications to educational questions for each approach are discussed and evaluated. The conclusion raises questions of how we choose among alternative approaches and whether a merger of mainstream sociology of education with feminist work on women and education is either possible or desirable.

Introduction

It is the purpose of this chapter to explore possible links between education, gender and sociology. The first section establishes the existence of issues of gender and education that are compatible with the traditional concerns of British sociology of education. The next section reviews approaches available in the 'sociology of gender' to which sociologists of education might turn. The conclusion identifies some of the problems and possibilities raised by an attempt to take gender seriously within the sociology of education.

Questions of education and gender

There are numerous questions sociologists might ask about the education of women and girls. In a world context, the disadvantage to girls, compared with boys, is often pronounced (Deblé, 1980). Yet it is difficult to ascertain why access and provision vary as they do between the sexes and among and within countries. Tradition, religion, economic prosperity, investment in educational expansion and government policy have been among the reasons suggested, but none consistently explains variations across the world (Smock, 1981).

Whereas in some countries different experiences for girls and boys are guaranteed by the provision of single-sex schooling, the great majority of British schools, especially in the state sector, is now mixed-sex. Nevertheless a pattern of different typical outcomes and experiences for the sexes is easy to observe, if not to explain. For example, more boys than girls (but less than 10 per cent of either sex) go on from school to degree courses in higher education. Boys have a greater chance of receiving day-release from employment for part-time study. They are more likely than girls to follow courses in physics, chemistry, engineering and other technological subjects. Girls more often study commercial and domestic subjects and languages. Girls are the majority of those training to teach. About 77 per cent of primary school teachers but only 13 per cent of university teachers are female.

Space does not permit a further and finer exploration of sex differentiation in such experiences and outcomes of education nor a systematic review of available empirical studies. (For reviews, see Acker, 1982; Byrne, 1978; Deem, 1978; MacDonald, 1981a; Sutherland, 1981.) It should, however, be clear that, in the British context alone, there is no shortage of questions we might ask. For example, what factors influence girls' chances of continuing with education to higher levels and studying certain subjects? How does sex interact with class, ethnicity and other such attributes to produce differential distributions of various groups in particular educational institutions, courses and levels? How do patterns of teacher-pupil interaction, the impact of youth culture participation, response to the curriculum, and the process of subject choice vary (if at all) between the sexes? What about the educational personnel and their sex-typed specialties? How do these divisions arise? What impact do they have on children who observe them and adults who experience them? Then there are the thornier questions: does schooling prop up the social and sexual division of labour in society? If so, why and how?

Until recently, British sociology of education has paid little attention to such questions (Acker, 1981). Although a few sociologists noted the neglect of sex as a variable in the 1960s and early 1970s (Jackson and Marsden, 1962: 227-28; King, 1971), questions of social class influence on education have continued to have a prominence in the field never approached by gender or ethnicity. Starting in the mid-1970s, and gaining momentum in the 1980s, a large number of texts, readers, articles, pamphlets and reports became available on 'women and education'. In general, scholarship in this area has flourished outside the major outlets for 'mainstream' sociology of education. Articles on women are more readily found in feminist journals than educational ones; discussions of gender and education in books on gender rather than books on education. There are certainly some signs of a rapprochement between sociology of education and feminist work on education (Banks, 1982; Walker and Barton, 1983), but it is difficult to predict whether this development will herald a significant trend.

Sociological theories of gender

Sociologists of education wishing to acquaint themselves with the theoretical literature on gender will find a rapidly expanding field. Behind much of this work is the explicit or implicit question of why women in most, if not all, cultures are structurally subordinate to men. It is beyond my brief to explicate and synthesize all the various answers offered to such a question, but I shall outline major approaches and their educational applications.

A starting point is a two-fold distinction between *fundamental* and *implementary* approaches (Acker, 1983). Those in the fundamental category seek basic, universal explanations: they ask what features of human nature or social organization require or demand that women be subordinate. Fundamental approaches split into two major sub-groups, emphasizing 'human nature' and 'social structure' respectively. Implementary approaches do not address questions about the underlying reasons for the domination/subordination patterns; instead, they ask how individuals in a given culture go about learning and perpetuating such arrangements.

In the remainder of this section I examine more closely certain fundamental and implementary approaches and their implications for the study of gender and education. Although fundamental theories that emphasize 'human nature' as carrying responsibility for women's subordinate position are often found in educational discussions, they are usually biological and psychological rather than sociological and therefore will not be reviewed here (but see Sayers, Chapter 3 in this volume).

Fundamental approaches

Fundamental theorists of the 'social structure' group argue that when the sexes occupy characteristically different roles within societies, they do so as a consequence of social interpretations of biological differences, not because of the biological differences themselves. Some structuralist anthropologists come close to biological reductionism when they argue that in every culture humans operate with an unconscious nature-culture contrast, sometimes regarded as analogous to female-male polarity (see MacCormack, 1980; Brown and Jordanova, 1981 for reviews). Most social scientists stress instead the diversity of expectations for masculine and feminine behaviour and personality found around the world.

FUNCTIONALIST APPROACHES If not rooted in the human psyche, is the sexual division of labour rooted in some 'needs' of society itself? Functionalist sociologists argue that societies must organize to ensure that resources are produced and distributed, that people have at least a minimal allegiance to their rulers, that populations reproduce themselves biologically. Some functionalists have argued further that the typical split between the responsibilities of men and women within the American nuclear family strengthens the family unit — by shielding the couple from damaging intra-familial competition, clarifying what is expected of each individual, and (most controversially) efficiently matching the capacities of each sex with the tasks required. In turn, a strong family socializes its children more adequately and contributes to social solidarity. (See Zelditch, 1955.)

In functionalist approaches to education, schooling is believed to be an important means by which basic allegiances to society are inculcated and a means of ensuring that advanced training goes to those most suited to it according to their talents. Expanding the education system has generally been regarded as one way to improve the identification and utilization of talent. In the 'human capital' approach often associated with functionalism, investments in a person's own education are thought to bring both personal and social benefit.

Education may be seen to contribute to a clear-cut division of labour between husbands and wives through curricular specialization of the sexes in school (eg domestic science for girls) and perhaps by providing greater opportunities for boys, as potential breadwinners, to acquire advanced vocational skills. However, the functionalist view has never been *opposed* to education for girls. Parsons (1942/1954; 1961), a major functionalist theorist, recognized tensions between the value placed on individual achievement in America and the assumption that all schoolgirls are destined for domesticity. He also argued that a sound education for future mothers would result in better care and education of their children and better companionship for their husbands (Parsons, 1961). 'Womanpower' versions of human capital theory have usually encouraged education for women. The argument is that a society can ill afford to neglect the education of its population if it is to 'keep pace' with its competitors. It must invest in its brilliant women as well as its brilliant men. Such arguments have frequently been adapted for feminist use (Acker, forthcoming) but the arguments are double-edged. They are elitist — what of less talented women? — and can easily be turned about to rationalize less investment in female education in times of labour over-supply.

Functionalist and human capital approaches have lost much of their appeal in recent years. Expanding schooling does not necessarily increase opportunities for women (Smock, 1981: 260) nor does it necessarily reduce occupational sex segregation (Ram, 1980: S75-75). Feminists have frequently taken exception to the restrictions on women's choice of life style implicit in functionalist writings on the family.

MARXIST-FEMINIST APPROACHES In the 1970s and 1980s, theories of gender derived more impetus from marxist and/or feminist analyses of society than functionalist ones.

In the pages that follow, I have followed writers like Banks (1981) and Elshtain (1981) in portraying 'marxist feminism' and 'radical feminism' as distinctly different viewpoints. It is important to remember that such categories are 'ideal' types — mental constructions to aid us in systematic analysis rather than fixed labels — and that a compressed discussion runs the risk of caricature. It should be understood that each term includes a variety of perspectives and that the dividing line might be drawn differently. For example, MacKinnon (1982) contrasts 'marxists' with 'feminists', the latter equivalent to those I have called radical feminists. She uses the term 'socialist feminist' for those who have tried to create a synthesis of marxism and feminism (unsuccessfully, in her view). Other writers use 'socialist feminism' as a synonym for 'marxist feminism' (Banks, 1981: 238). I have not done this because I believe there are a significant number of individuals, at least in Britain, who identify themselves in party political terms as 'socialists' but in sexual political terms as 'radical feminists'. This suggests another difficulty, the blurring between theoretical standpoints and political positions. Those who I term marxist feminists are not necessarily politically committed to orthodox marxism. I use the label to imply that their theoretical views on gender are derived in some way from Marx's work and interpretations of Marx's work. Finally, I refer mainly to British and secondarily to North American varieties of marxist feminists; other countries may identify a quite different group as marxists.

Like the functionalists, marxist theoreticians have typically regarded the family as a unit, linked to the labour market by the husband's relationship to production. Many writers now see this model, with its 'invisible women', as deeply flawed (Garnsey, 1978). Some have turned to Engels' 1884 work which located the origins of female subordination in the development of the system of private property, wherein it was essential for men to be certain that the inheritors of their wealth were their own offspring, and thus monogamy and the fidelity of women were required (Elshtain, 1981). Participation in socialized production would bring about the emancipation of women. Engels' analysis is the starting point of a heated debate among marxists over the best way of conceptualizing 'domestic labour' (Kaluzynska, 1980; Malos, 1980; West, 1982).

Many writers have speculated on ways in which women's subordinate position in general and their domestic role in particular might benefit capitalism (Mitchell, 1971; Kuhn and Wolpe, 1978; Rowbotham, 1973; Sharpe, 1976). Housewives and mothers are sometimes seen as a 'reserve army of labour' available in times of labour shortage, dispensable at other times. Within the family, the women reproduce the labour force by giving birth to and rearing children, together with socializing them into orientations to authority and work appropriate for future workers (Chodorow, 1979). Women act as chief consumers of capitalism's products. By providing both a haven for the male worker wherein he can be fed, clothed and sent off to work each day, and a source of motivation for him (the need to provide sustenance for his family), they increase his incentive to continue his participation in an exploitative system.

This model seems somewhat oversimplified (Breugel, 1979). It does not adequately account for the complex way in which women participate in the labour market, nor why it is women who do housework, nor why women are exploited by men within the family unit (Hartmann, 1979). Another direction taken by some sociologists and economists (both marxist and non-marxist) is the attempt to describe and analyse ways in which the labour market is 'segmented' or 'split' and why women are so frequently found in what is sometimes called the secondary labour market (Barron and Norris, 1976; Bonacich, 1979). It is secondary because training opportunities and career ladders are missing, and employee turnover is high, while pay, autonomy and worker solidarity are all low. This system is thought to work to the advantage of employers in certain industries. Whether it also supports men by ensuring women remain economically dependent on husbands and thus continue to provide for their domestic needs is another question (Hartmann, 1979). It would seem to be women's attachment (by choice or otherwise) to the home and their consequent need for part-time or temporary employment that puts them in a poor bargaining position in the labour market (Garnsey, 1978; Hartmann, 1979).

Does education contribute to the maintenance of this sexual division of labour and the relegation of women to poorly paid jobs and domestic pursuits? Neo-marxist sociologists of education have, in recent years, paid considerable attention to the role of schooling in the reproduction of class relations under Western capitalism (Apple, 1982; Bourdieu, 1977; Bowles and Gintis, 1976). In recent years, feminist theorists have tried to extend these approaches to illuminate the role of school in the reproduction of gender relations (Arnot, 1981; Barrett, 1980; Branson and Miller, 1979; David, 1980; Kelly and Nihlen, 1982; MacDonald, 1980, 1981a, 1981b; Wolpe, 1978). How can we determine whether schools operate so as to reinforce and perpetuate gender relations that subordinate women? We can demonstrate unequal outcomes and differential experiences that seem consistent with the sexual divisions in the labour market and the expectation that women will have prime responsibility within the family. For example, girls in Britain are less likely than boys to go into advanced levels of education and less likely to study science (except biology) and technology. Byrne (1978) shows that many training programmes in the further education sector that lead to skilled manual jobs in technological areas require examination qualifications that are usually acquired in secondary school in subjects that girls are unlikely to have studied. Vocational courses in colleges and government training schemes tend to be highly sex-segregated, though not by any legal requirements (Blunden, this volume, Chapter 12; David, 1980; MacDonald, 1981a: 53). School subjects popular with girls, such as cookery and needlework, have relatively few applications outside the domestic context (unlike 'boys' crafts').

There are other ways in which school experience may pave the way for a sexual division of labour in adulthood. Schools are characterized by what MacDonald (1980) calles 'gender codes': they are organized around the assumption that the sexes have different needs and interests. Sex appears to provide a pervasive basis for differentiation throughout British school life. Children become 'boys' and 'girls' for registration, seating, queuing; they are addressed as such by teachers and set to compete against each other; they are timetabled so that it is difficult for children to choose non-stereotypical subject options even if they wish to do so (Acker, 1981). Within British schools, men dominate authority positions (as well as scientific and technological ones). Only in a single sex girls' school, or in a school catering for children under eight, are children very likely to find women at the helm. It may be that such arrangements signal to children the expected shape of adult life.

In less obvious ways, schools through their typical organization control mothers and limit their participation in the world of work (see David, this volume, Chapter 15). Very few jobs are compatible with school hours and holidays. School teaching is one that has been more compatible than most, and many girls have trained for teaching for no other reason. It is possible that the disproportionate recruitment of women into school teaching has played a part in perpetuating the sexual division of labour, for example by reducing competition for other occupations, by institutionalizing a pattern whereby women adjust their labour force participation to school hours and holidays, and by providing an unspoken message for the younger generation about appropriate feminine pursuits (David, 1980; Deem, 1978).

The literature on women and education summarized above can be used to support arguments about the reinforcement, through schooling, of the sexual division of labour in the economy and the family. However, such use is not without difficulties. One is that this literature can be used equally well to support radical-feminist approaches (which I outline below). Findings tend to illustrate, or be consistent with, a reproduction thesis, rather than provide proof that the system works for this rather than for some other purpose. Secondly, it is not at all clear to what extent the education system is necessarily as it is in order to serve the requirements of capitalism, nor what sort of reform in education or revolution in the economy would alter women's participation in either. Non-capitalist societies also have a sexual division of labour, although it may look different. Efforts to reform education and increase women's participation have been strenuous and sometimes successful in countries with very different political policies and ideologies (for example, the USSR; Cuba; Sweden). Yet educational changes do not inevitably lead to changed patterns of economic participation; economic and educational reforms do not necessarily alter ideologies about domestic life and the subordination of women (MacDonald, 1981a: 88-94; McAuley, this volume, Chapter 16; Molyneux, this volume, Chapter 21).

RADICAL-FEMINIST APPROACHES In the radical-feminist approach patriarchy takes the role capitalism takes for the marxist feminists. History reveals not only the class struggle but the striving of men for power and domination over women, especially over their sexuality and reproductive capacities. There are different meanings attached to the word patriarchy but it can be used to describe a system whereby men are dominant and females subordinate. In the radical-feminist view, patriarchy cannot be explained by the demands of capitalism or any other economic system; it is a more ancient form of oppression with its own logic and its own beneficiaries and victims.

Radical feminists stress the importance of women's personal experience and the necessity of deliberately sharing such experience through consciousness-raising sessions in order to arrive at a clear understanding of why and how women are oppressed (MacKinnon, 1982). They write about experiences unique to women such as lesbianism, childbirth and motherhood and about forms of violence against women such as rape, wife-battering and sexual exploitation.

Radical feminists do not believe that only the interests of capitalism ensure a sexual division of labour, since women are subordinate under all kinds of economic systems. Even though women vary in their links with the class system, either when these are determined by assigning a woman to share the class position of her husband or father, or when determined by the nature of the woman's own position in the labour market, women share certain sorts of oppression simply *because they are women.*

Whilst marxist feminists argue that class divisions make it impossible to speak as if women are a homogeneous group, radical feminists point out that women of all classes share a fear of being raped, and that many apparently 'privileged' women would face penury if their relationships with men were to collapse.

Those arguing from a radical-feminist perspective have made use of much of the same literature as the marxist feminists to explore ways in which schools and colleges shape female identity and encourage subordinate roles for women. However, two additional elements are emphasized in the radical-feminist analysis: first, lowered self-esteem and acceptance of inferiority as derived from women's school experiences; and second, men's control over and definition of 'knowledge' itself.

Studies in Britain and elsewhere find that in mixed sex classrooms, boys get a greater share of teacher attention than girls (Brophy and Good, 1974; Clarricoates, 1978; Evans, 1979; Lobban, 1978; Spender, 1982). Researchers have also reported that classroom projects are designed with boys' interests in mind (Clarricoates, 1978) and that teachers habitually put down girls' academic achievements as due to hard work rather than talent (Clarricoates, 1980; Davies, 1979) or fail to notice them at all (Buswell, 1981; Fuller, 1980; Stanworth, 1981). Teachers have been said to cast slurs on girls' attractiveness and sexuality in order to discipline them (Davies, 1979; Llewellyn, 1980). Several researchers find male students holding negative views about women, including their female classmates (Shaw, 1980; Stanworth, 1981).

It may be that women believe and internalize these messages about their own inferiority. However, it is not clear how deep that internalization is, or whether educational experiences are necessary to create it, or whether education can be used to reverse it. Additionally, as many of the studies are small-scale and anecdotal, we cannot be confident about generalizing from them. It would be important to discover under exactly what circumstances these patterns do or do not obtain.

Another educational area which the radically inclined feminists have particularly stressed is the curriculum, or more broadly the creation and transmission of knowledge in educational institutions and through educational materials. Many disciplines have had their sexist assumptions exposed (Spender, 1981), and there has been an enormous growth, worldwide but especially in the United States, in Women's Studies programmes and courses (Bowles and Duelli Klein, 1983; Duelli Klein, in press).

Some feminists do 'remedial work' in their disciplines, adding studies of women and filling gaps — whilst others insist that the disciplines are so distorted that 'we cannot trust what we know' (Spender, 1982: 2-3). Women's studies are also characterized by attempts to develop an alternative pedagogy, derived from the women's movement and based on the raising of consciousness through sharing of personal experience by equals. This is intended to contrast with the imparting of knowledge by experts through lectures, characteristic of much of higher education.

Implementary approaches

The fundamental approaches reviewed above were linked to marxist or radical feminism. Implementary approaches tend to have more resonance with 'liberal' or 'women's rights' versions of feminism. A key argument is that women are prevented from full realization of their talents by intended or unintended consequences of social conventions and practices. Career 'success' eludes them (relative to equally talented men) because typical female socialization results in attributes unsuitable or inappropriate for it; family role responsibilities, or their anticipation, militate against it; labour market operations and organizational policies which intentionally or otherwise discriminate against women prevent it.

The major concepts in each category are, respectively, 'socialization', 'role' and 'discrimination'. Writers from within this paradigm tend to be impatient with the more abstruse theories of marxist and radical feminists, and with the suggestion that little can alleviate disadvantage for women short of the demise of capitalism and/or patriarchy. It does not matter so much why women are subordinate as what we do about it. Opportunities must be increased, discrimination fought, stereotyping abandoned.

I shall concentrate here on the literature on sex-role socialization, as it is frequently education-related (see also Sayers, this volume, Chapter 3, and Kelly, 1981). Socialization theories are concerned with the construction of gender, that is, how we learn to behave according to a given culture's ideas of masculinity and femininity. Theorists point out that even before birth, the child's sex is a matter for speculation, and 'the gender label attached to the child at birth brings with it a whole range of social apparatus: names, clothes, toys, beliefs, behaviours and values' (Delamont, 1980a: 15). There is a widespread assumption that parents and schools (with the aid of the media) socialize girls towards traditionally feminine personality characteristics such as compliance, nurturance and dependency, traits which lead to restricted vocational choices and prevent significant public career success in adult life. However, there are disputes about exactly how the process works and how reversible it is.

Positions taken on the exact role played by the school are varied and sometimes contradictory. One argument is that schools, especially primary schools, favour girls. Schools have been accused of being feminine environments, staffed by women who respond favourably to feminine behaviour in their charges. Girls flourish; boys, at least the 'masculine' ones, rebel and eventually abandon academic pursuits entirely (Sexton, 1969).

Lee (1973) agrees that the school ethos favours girls, especially in the early years, for they have already been socialized into habits compatible with the needs of teachers for order and conformity. In the long run, however, he believes girls lose by this system; when the time comes for achievement via autonomy and independence they are unable to rise to the occasion. Although some of the American studies of university students do suggest that achievement and affiliation are perceived as incompatible for women (Hoffman, 1972; Komarovsky, 1946), no one has shown that early educational experiences are responsible for the conflict.

Feminist writers who have tackled the question of school socialization in the late 1970s and early 1980s tend to argue that, far from favouring females, schools overtly or covertly discriminate against them, often from the earliest years. The school's continuous reinforcement of boundaries between what is appropriately masculine and what is appropriately feminine contributes to the shaping of sex-differentiated self-concepts and eventually sex-differentiated futures. The school works on the side of tradition; it is more traditional than the outside world (Delamont, 1983). Spender's (1982) research suggests that schools not only treat the sexes differently, but give systematic preferential treatment to boys.

Some puzzles emerge from this brief review. Is the difference between the findings of Sexton (1969) and of Spender (1982) more than ideological? If teachers prefer boys, why do they give girls (as a group) higher marks? How do we explain the results of studies (also conducted by feminists) where girls do not appear to be receiving disadvantageous teacher treatment (Fuller, 1978; Walden and Walkerdine, 1982)? *Why* do teachers give undue attention to boys when they do (French, 1981)? Are they responding to boys' apparently more urgent demands for attention, or prejudices of their own, or pressures from capitalism and patriarchy that somehow filter into everyday life?

The discrepancies between different studies cannot be resolved here without going into detail, nor have I discussed all aspects of school socialization (see also Delamont, 1980b; Lobban, 1978; Spender and Sarah, 1980). And as Arnot argues (1981: 102-103), we need to attend to the source of the 'sex-role ideology' which appears as both cause and effect in so many of these accounts of sex-differentiated educational experiences. To do so would require us to move outside what she calls the cultural perspective (close to the implementary approach of the present chapter) and back to the fundamental approaches earlier discussed. However, the implementary studies have the advantage of calling to our attention some of the gaps left by the fundamental approaches, especially the explanation of how the survival of capitalism or patriarchy or society itself is accomplished by everyday events. They are certainly more optimistic than fundamental approaches, as they assume that educational solutions can be found for what are largely educational problems. If in the past we have socialized girls away from science, then by consciously changing our methods, we can socialize them towards it instead.

Conclusion

This chapter has reviewed some of the major sociological approaches to gender and how they apply to educational questions. Certain problems that arise within each approach have been noted. A question remaining is whether a synthesis is possible between approaches. The fundamental approaches, insofar as they imply that the factors shaping our lives are beyond personal control, appear pessimistic and fatalistic; the reform-oriented implementary ones give us a greater sense of potency but remain incomplete on their own. If we wish to understand both why and how women's subordination occurs, we need to explore possibilities for integration between approaches.

Until we arrive at integration, we need to develop criteria for choosing among approaches. If the approaches are regarded as theories, classical scientific method would have us derive hypotheses from them for testing, the results of which could modify the theory (though not prove it 'correct') (Epstein Jayaratne, 1983). Feminists, like many sociologists, have expressed considerable dissatisfaction with traditional scientific method and positivism as used in social science (Stanley and Wise, 1983). The result is that sometimes global theories become untestable non-negotiable statements of faith. Research results are described in ways compatible with the axioms, but it is not clear what would be sufficient grounds for rejecting the original approach, nor how to choose between approaches (Hargreaves, 1981). We are left not knowing how to reconcile contradictory findings, nor how to evaluate and compare the quality of different studies.

There have been several recent attempts to develop an alternative feminist methodology for social-science-type research (Bowles and Duelli Klein, 1983; Roberts, 1981; Stanley and Wise, 1983). There are also strong arguments *against* the integration of feminist perspectives into traditional disciplines, especially if this means that an autonomous women's studies movement is undermined, and feminism is de-radicalized and distorted in the process (Bowles and Duelli Klein, 1983). Yet I still believe that feminist work can benefit from a sociological understanding — for example, from the debunking qualities and unveiling of ethnocentrism which characterize sociology at its best. Traditional ideas about methods, theories, and standards may need to be revised radically but should not be simply ignored or rejected out of hand.

For their part, sociologists of education seldom actually dismiss the idea of studying gender; rather, they fail to take it seriously. Doubtless some are unconvinced that work based on men-only samples is inadequate; some believe that sex is not as significant a variable as social class; and some regard feminist work as biased by definition. But my guess is that a more significant barrier is that most (male) sociologists of education will have had little acquaintance with work in this area, for they rarely read feminist journals or books on women, however outstanding their quality. Sociologists need to begin taking account of gender in their studies of women and of men (Morgan, 1981). Failure to do so will continue to impoverish an important field of study.

References

Acker, S (1981) No-woman's-land: British sociology of education 1960-1979 *Sociological Review* **29** 1: 77-104

Acker, S (1982) Women and education *in* Hartnett

Acker, S (1983) Women and teaching: a semi-detached sociology of a semi-profession *in* Walker and Barton

Acker, S (in press) Women and higher education: what's the problem? *in* Acker and Warren Piper

Acker, S and Warren Piper, D *eds* (in press) *Is Higher Education Fair to Women?* Society for Research into Higher Education (SRHE): Guildford

Apple, M *ed* (1982) *Cultural and Economic Reproduction in Education* Routledge and Kegan Paul: London

Arnot, M (1981) Culture and political economy: dual perspectives in the sociology of women's education *Educational Analysis* **3** 1: 97-116

Banks, O (1981) *Faces of Feminism* Martin Robertson: Oxford

Banks, O (1982) Sociology of education *in* Cohen *et al*

Barker, D L and Allen, S *eds* (1976) *Dependence and Exploitation in Work and Marriage* Longman: London

Barrett, M (1980) *Women's Oppression Today: Problems in Marxist Feminist Analysis* Verso: London

Barron, R D and Norris, G M (1976) Sexual divisions and the dual labour market *in* Barker and Allen

Barton, L and Meighan, R *eds* (1979) *Schools, Pupils and Deviance* Nafferton: Driffield

Barton, L and Walker, S *eds* (1981) *Schools, Teachers and Teaching* Falmer: Lewes

Bonacich, E (1979) The past, present, and future of split labor market theory *Research in Race and Ethnic Relations: A Research Annual* **1**: 17-64

Bourdieu, P (1977) Cultural reproduction and social reproduction *in* Karabel and Halsey

Bowles, G and Duelli Klein, R (1983) Introduction: theories of women's studies and the autonomy/integration debate *in* Bowles and Duelli Klein

Bowles, G and Duelli Klein, R *eds* (1983) *Theories of Women's Studies* Routledge and Kegan Paul: London

Bowles, S and Gintis, H (1976) *Schooling in Capitalist America* Routledge and Kegan Paul: London

Branson, J and Miller, D B (1979) *Class, Sex and Education in Capitalist Society: Culture, Ideology and the Reproduction of Inequality in Australia* Sorrett: Melbourne

Brophy, J and Good, T (1974) *Teacher-Student Relationships* Holt, Rinehart and Winston: New York

Brown, P and Jordanova, L (1981) Oppressive dichotomies: the nature/culture debate *in* Cambridge Women's Studies Group

Bruegel, I (1979) Women as a reserve army of labour: a note on recent British experience *Feminist Review* 3: 12-23

Buswell, C (1981) Sexism in school routines and classroom practices *Durham and Newcastle Research Review* 9 46: 195-200

Byrne, E (1978) *Women and Education* Tavistock: London

Cambridge Women's Studies Group (1981) *Women in Society* Virago: London

Chetwynd, J and Hartnett, O eds (1978) *The Sex Role System* Routledge and Kegan Paul: London

Chodorow, N (1979) Mothering, male dominance and capitalism *in* Eisenstein

Clarricoates, K (1978) Dinosaurs in the classroom — a re-examination of some aspects of the hidden curriculum in primary schools *Women's Studies International Quarterly* 1 4: 353-64

Clarricoates, K (1980) The importance of being Ernest . . . Emma . . . Tom . . . Jane . . . The perception and categorization of gender conformity and gender deviation in primary schools *in* Deem

Cohen, L *et al* eds (1982) *Educational Research and Development in Britain 1970-1980* NFER/Nelson: Windsor

Dale, R, Esland, G, Fergusson, R and MacDonald, M eds (1981) *Education and the State: Politics, Patriarchy and Practice* Vol 2 Falmer: Lewes

David, M E (1980) *The State, the Family and Education* Routledge and Kegan Paul: London

Davies, L (1979) Deadlier than the male? Girls' conformity and deviance in school *in* Barton and Meighan

Deblé, I (1980) *The School Education of Girls* United Nations Educational Scientific and Cultural Organisation (UNESCO): Paris

Deem, R (1978) *Women and Schooling* Routledge and Kegan Paul: London

Deem, R ed (1980) *Schooling for Women's Work* Routledge and Kegan Paul: London

Delamont, S (1980a) *The Sociology of Women* Allen and Unwin: London

Delamont, S (1980b) *Sex Roles and the School* Methuen: London

Delamont, S (1983) The conservative school? Sex roles at home, at work and at school *in* Walker and Barton

Duelli Klein, R (in press) Women's studies: an intellectual necessity *in* Acker and Warren Piper

Eisenstein, Z ed (1979) *Capitalist Patriarchy and the Case for Socialist Feminism* Monthly Review Press: New York

Elshtain, J B (1981) *Public Man, Private Woman* Martin Robertson: Oxford

Epstein Jayaratne, T (1983) The value of quantitative methodology for feminist research *in* Bowles and Duelli Klein

Evans, T (1979) Creativity, sex-role socialisation and pupil-teacher interaction in early schooling *Sociological Review* 27 1: 139-155

French, J (1981) Classroom interaction: considerations of form and content with particular reference to gender Unpublished MA thesis, University of Manchester: Manchester

Fuller, M (1978) Dimensions of gender in a school Unpublished PhD dissertation University of Bristol: Bristol

Fuller, M (1980) Black girls in a London comprehensive school *in* Deem

Garnsey, E (1978) Women's work and theories of class stratification *Sociology* 12 2: 224-243

Halsey, A H, Floud, J and Anderson, C A eds (1961) *Education, Economy and Society* The Free Press: New York

Hargreaves, D H (1981) Schooling for delinquency *in* Barton and Walker

Hartmann, H (1979) Capitalism, patriarchy and job segregation by sex *in* Eisenstein (1979)

Hartnett, A ed (1982) *The Social Sciences in Educational Studies* Heinemann: London

Hoffman, L (1972) Early childhood experiences and women's achievement motives *Journal of Social Issues* **28**: 129-56

Jackson, B and Marsden, D (1962) *Education and the Working Class* Routledge and Kegan Paul: London

Kaluzynska, E (1980) Wiping the floor with theory: a survey of writings on housework *Feminist Review* **6**: 27-54

Karabel, J and Halsey, A H eds (1977) *Power and Ideology in Education* Oxford University Press: New York

King, R (1971) Unequal access in education — sex and social class *Social and Economic Administration* **5** 3: 167-75

Kelly, A ed (1981) *The Missing Half: Girls and Science Education* University of Manchester Press: Manchester

Kelly, G P and Nihlen, A (1982) Schooling and the reproduction of patriarchy: unequal workloads, unequal rewards *in* Apple

Komarovsky, M (1946) Cultural contradictions and sex roles *American Journal of Sociology* **52**: 184-189

Kuhn, A and Wolpe, A M eds (1978) *Feminism and Materialism* Routledge and Kegan Paul: London

Lee, P C (1973) Male and female teachers in elementary schools: an ecological analysis *Teachers College Record* **75** 1: 79-98

Lobban, G (1978) The influence of the school on sex-role stereotyping *in* Chetwynd and Hartnett

Llewellyn, M (1980) Studying girls at school: the implications of confusion *in* Deem

MacCormack, C (1980) Nature, culture and gender: a critique *in* MacCormack and Strathern *eds*

MacCormack, C and Strathern, M eds (1980) *Nature, Culture and Gender* Cambridge University Press: Cambridge

MacDonald, M (1980) Socio-cultural reproduction and women's education *in* Deem

MacDonald, M (1981a) *Class, Gender and Education* Open University Course E353 Block 4 Units 10-11 The Open University Press: Milton Keynes

MacDonald, M (1981b) Schooling and the reproduction of class and gender relations *in* Dale *et al*

MacKinnon, C A (1982) Feminism, marxism, method, and the state: an agenda for theory *Signs* **7** 3: 515-44

Malos, E ed (1980) *The Politics of Housework* Allison and Busby: London

Mitchell, J (1971) *Woman's Estate* Penguin: Harmondsworth

Morgan, D (1981) Men, masculinity and the process of sociological enquiry *in* Roberts

Parsons, T (1942) Age and sex in the social structure of the United States *in* Parsons

Parsons, T (1954) *Essays in Sociological Theory* The Free Press: Glencoe, Illinois

Parsons, T (1961) The school class as a social system: some of its functions in American society *in* Halsey, Floud and Anderson

Parsons, T and Bales, R F eds (1955) *Family Socialization and Interaction Process* The Free Press: Glencoe, Illinois

Ram, R (1980) Sex differences in the labour market outcomes of education *Comparative Education Review* **24** 2: S53-S77

Roberts, H ed (1981) *Doing Feminist Research* Routledge and Kegan Paul: London

Rowbotham, S (1973) *Woman's Consciousness, Man's World* Penguin: Harmondsworth

Sexton, P (1969) *The Feminized Male: Classrooms, White Collars, and the Decline of Manliness* Vintage: New York

Sharpe, S (1976) *Just Like a Girl* Penguin: Harmondsworth

Shaw, J (1980) Education and the individual: schooling for girls, or mixed schooling — a mixed blessing? *in* Deem

Smock, A C (1981) *Women's Education in Developing Countries* Praeger: New York.

Spender, D (1982) *Invisible Women: The Schooling Scandal* Writers and Readers: London

Spender, D *ed* (1981) *Men's Studies Modified: The Impact of Feminism on the Academic Disciplines* Pergamon: Oxford

Spender, D and Sarah, E *eds* (1980) *Learning to Lose: Sexism and Education* The Women's Press: London

Stanley, L and Wise, S (1983) *Breaking Out: Feminist Consciousness and Feminist Research* Routledge and Kegan Paul: London

Stanworth, M (1981) *Gender and Schooling: A Study of Sexual Divisions in the Classroom* Women's Research and Resources Centre: London

Sutherland, M (1981) *Sex Bias in Education* Blackwell: Oxford

Walden, R and Walkerdine, V (1982) *Girls and Mathematics: The Early Years* Bedford Way Paper No 8 University of London Institute of Education: London

Walker, S and Barton, L *eds* (1983) *Gender, Class and Education* Falmer: Lewes

West, J *ed* (1982) *Work, Women and the Labour Market* Routledge and Kegan Paul: London

Wolpe, A M (1978) Education and the sexual division of labour *in* Kuhn and Wolpe

Zelditch, M (1955) Role differentiation in the nuclear family: a comparative study *in* Parsons and Bales

Acknowledgement

The greater part of this chapter was written in July 1983 while I was a Visiting Scholar in the Women's Studies Department of the University of Washington, Seattle. I am grateful for the space and library access provided. I should also like to thank Geoff Millerson for comments on the chapter.

Part 2:
Case studies of women and education

6. Women's access to education in the Third World: myths and realities

Gail Kelly

Summary: This chapter focuses on factors affecting women's access to education in Third World nations of Asia, Africa, Latin America and the Middle East. While research on the pattern of women's educational participation, as well as the factors affecting it is as yet fragmentary, enough is known to establish that, throughout most of the Third World, females do not attend school at rates equivalent to those of males. Research that seeks to understand the factors affecting women's participation in schooling has focused on social background characteristics of women, cultural and religious milieu and the level of a nation's economic development. Such research has tended to view women's access to schooling as independent of government policy towards women's education and school provision. This chapter argues that, in the Third World as well as elsewhere, the greatest factor influencing women's access to schooling is whether schooling is made available and accessible to women and if so, what type of schooling is offered. These factors are all matters of public policy and therefore amenable to change.

Introduction

Until recently, the determinants of women's access to education have not been a major concern for scholars, schoolmen, or policy makers. While this was the case in the Third World nations of Asia, Africa, and Latin America, it was equally true for North America and Europe. Most international agencies and national governments did not even collect data detailing the number of women, as opposed to men, that entered school or kept themselves in the school system at successive levels of education. Charting women's educational patterns and the factors affecting them are major undertakings that have just begun (Kelly and Kelly, 1982; Deblé, 1980; Bowman and Anderson, 1982; Rogers, 1980). Until our knowledge of women's educational enrollment patterns is more complete, the factors affecting women's access to education in the Third World can only be speculated upon.

The determinants of women's access to education are *not* the same as those for men. Research based on the assumption of similar determinants for both sexes has at best yielded contradictory results; at worst, it has led to conclusions that either 'blame the victim' or attribute female under-enrollment to amorphous factors like 'culture' or 'state of the economy'. It leaves policy makers with no prescriptions for reform. Admittedly, knowledge related to this area is less than it should be; even so, research conducted over the last decade has made it clear that, when all is said and done, the single best predictor of whether girls will attend school is not ethnicity, social class background, religion, demand for educated manpower, or the state of the nation's economic development — though all these may contribute — but rather whether schooling is made available and accessible to women. This is a matter of public policy and choice.

The depressing pattern of women's educational enrollment in the Third World

While statistics on women's participation in education are incomplete, it is easy to discern a pattern in Third World nations. In most of these countries, women do not enter or remain at school at the same rate as men.

Very few Third World nations provide universal primary education. However, most males enter school at rates two to three times those of females. The most recent statistics, compiled by Isabelle Deblé (1980), indicate that in no sub-Saharan African nation, with the exception of Mauritius, do more than 68 per cent of all six- to eight-year-old girls attend schools. In some nations, like Upper Volta, only 6.9 to 9 per cent of all girls in that age group enter school. More commonly, about 30 per cent of the age cohort six- to eight-year-olds enter school. Not all boys attend primary school in these African nations, but male enrollments, as a percentage of their age mates, are double to triple those of females (Deblé, 1980: 32-3; Bowman and Anderson, 1982; Eliou, 1973; Moustaffa-Kedah, 1975/6; O'Shaughnessey, 1978; Youssef, 1976/77; Kotwal, 1975). The gap between male and female enrollments, as a percentage of their age peers, grows exponentially for each year of education. This pattern of inequality in educational participation is replicated in varying degrees of severity in the Middle East, Latin America and Asia. Where primary education approaches universal enrollments, as in parts of Latin America, the disparity between male and female participation rates does not appear among six-, eight- or ten-year-olds, but rather is replicated among children of secondary school age.

The disparity between male and female participation in education has not disappeared with mass expansion of schooling in the Third World, or for that matter in most of North America and Europe. Rather, as school enrollments have doubled and tripled in most countries of Africa, Asia, Latin America, and the Middle East, this expansion has benefited males more than females (Maldonado, 1981; Deblé, 1980; Smock, 1981; Finn, Dulberg and Reis, 1979). More women attend school than ever before, but women's representation in all levels of education has yet to equal males, except in Chile (Schiefelbein and Farrell, 1982). There is some evidence to suggest that Third World governments, once male education enrollments universalize, slacken in their attempt to make provision for women's schooling (Deblé, 1980; Jones, 1982).

While expansion of the school system in most of Asia, Africa, and Latin America has failed to provide equality of educational opportunity for males and females, neither overall educational enrollments nor the disparity between male and female enrollment can necessarily be predicted by a nation's progress toward economic development (Ramirez and Boli-Bennett, 1982; Meyer *et al*, 1977; Meyer and Hannan, 1979). Mauritius enrolls 95.8 per cent of all eight-year-old girls in school, a rate higher than those of several Eastern European nations, including Bulgaria and Yugoslavia (Deblé, 1980). Chile enrolls more women, as a percentage of the age cohort, in higher education than does the United States, Japan, Great Britain, or France (Schiefelbein and Farrell, 1982). In short, women's access to education and the disparity between male and female enrollments at all levels of schooling cannot be predicted by the level or pace of a nation's economic development. Sex inequality in education is not a problem that will go away once a nation has increased its Gross National Product and built an industrial infrastructure (Deblé, 1980; Bowman and Anderson, 1982; Smock, 1981).

If 'development' neither predicts nor explains women's access to education in the Third World, what does? Research has focused on background characteristics of girls and the interplay of economic incentive and reward in girls' access to education and, more recently, on the availability, accessibility and content of schooling.

Background characteristics, economic incentive and women's education

Research on the determinants of access to education in countries in Africa, Asia, Latin America, and the Middle East, conducted for the most part on male populations, has suggested that individual background variables, combined with market forces, impels school enrollments, regardless of sex, in a logical supply-demand model (Foster, 1965; Foster, 1971; Foster, 1977; Ram, 1982). The larger the economic benefits that befall those who are schooled, the greater individual demand for schooling, provided that parents and/or students understand the relation between education and future income generation. Educated parents who themselves work in the market economy by virtue of their schooling tend to share this understanding and are more likely to send their children to school, regardless of their child's gender.

While parental education and income in Third World nations tend to predict a child's educational level, or lack thereof, the relationship as compared to that found in North America and Europe is less strong for males (Foster, 1977; Heyneman, 1976), but more powerful for females (Alexander and Eckland, 1974; Weis, 1980; Bowman and Anderson,

1982; Smith and Cheung, 1982). While not all well-educated parents send their daughters to school, girls who enter school tend, more so than do boys, to come from relatively well-educated and high-income families.

Such findings, generated, in the main, from studies conducted in West Africa, tend to be explained in market terms. Parents, unless wealthy, prefer to educate their sons on the assumption that education 'pays off' in life-time wages more handsomely for males than for females (Ram, 1982; Bowman and Anderson, 1982; Woodhall, 1973; Wickramasinghe and Radcliffe, 1979). In Third World countries, most families have not enough wealth to 'throw away' money on girls' education. The assumption is that girls' education is 'consumption', since they become wives and mothers. Only the very rich can afford such 'frivolity'.

The difficulty with such explanations is that they assume that in many Third World nations women are confined to childbearing and childrearing roles — put another way, to reproduction to the exclusion of production. Once it is recognized that women engage in production, their education can be viewed as investment rather than consumption. In this light, scholars have asked whether and how sex role divisions of labour affect parental decisions to invest in their sons' rather than their daughters' education. Mblinyi (1969) in her study of girls in Tanzania found that it was a greater economic sacrifice for parents to send girls to school than it was to send boys. In female farming areas such as the ones she studied, girls contributed directly to the family's livelihood at an earlier age than did boys. As long as free public education is available, education in this case for a son was not an investment; neither did it represent labour foregone. Findings similar to Mblinyi's have been replicated elsewhere (Naik, 1982; McSweeney and Freedman, 1982; Boserup, 1969).

The sex role division of labour in production which Mblinyi found in Tanzania kept girls from attending school and made investment in female education much more costly than investment in boys. This pattern does not apply to the whole of Africa, much less to the entire Third World. In some places, the very poverty that makes daughters' education too costly an investment for rural Tanzanian families seems to impel parents elsewhere (where the sex role division of labour is different) to favour their daughters' rather than their sons' education. In those parts of the world where girls do not constitute productive labour in the fields, and boys' wages at entry to the labour force and over their lifetimes are higher than those of females, parents view boys' education as too costly an investment and, instead, send their daughters to school and maintain them there longer. This appears to be the case in north-east Brazil and in parts of Mexico. Both these areas are male farming zones and extremely poor regions, relative to the rest of their respective nations. In both, more girls than boys enter school (Goldblatt, 1983; Plank, 1983).

In urban areas wage discrimination favouring men may account for equality in educational enrollments between males and females at all levels of schooling. Schiefelbein and Farrell (1982) found that in Chile parents tended to send their daughters to school for longer than their sons. There, parents perceive that education enables girls to earn a wage equivalent to their brothers who have had less schooling. In Chile, for that reason, more women (as a percentage of their age cohort) attend tertiary institutions than in the United States or Japan.

While there may be no one effect of parental income on girls' access to education across all Third World countries, within many Third World countries ethnicity, as well as parental education, influences which girls will go to school. Most nations in Latin America, Asia, Africa, and the Middle East are plural societies and there is considerable ethnic and regional (often the two coincide) variation in school enrollment regardless of gender (Meyer and Hannan, 1979). In some instances, ethnicity (over and above its association with income and urban/rural residence) seems to affect woman's access to schooling. While girls' rates of school attendance in the few instance studied are lower than boys of the same ethnicity, there are also differences in rates of school attendance among girls according to ethnicity (Anderson and Bowman, 1982; Wang, 1982).

Until there is more research, it is hard to say with certainty how ethnicity affects girls' access to education beyond urban/rural residence or parental income and education. There is some evidence that suggests that differences in female access to education among ethnic groups are a function of government policies that either favour or discriminate against a given ethnic group in education and employment. In Malaysia, for example, the disparity in female enrollments between Chinese and Malays began to lessen after government-initiated programmes favouring Malays in schooling and in government employ took effect.

Often confounded with the effect of ethnicity on women's access to education is religion. Female education, in theory, is depressed among Muslims, given that religion's view of women's place. Some orthodox Muslims practise purdah, which is seclusion of women after either puberty or marriage (Smock, 1982; Boserup, 1969). Whether religion, particularly Islam, depresses women's access to education is not at all clear independent of other factors. In some Islamic nations, women's enrollment ratios are higher than in non-Islamic nations, particularly in higher education (Smock, 1981; Howard-Merriam, 1979; Mustaffa-Kedah, 1975/76; O'Shaughnessey, 1978; Meleis, El-Sanabary and Beeson, 1979). Tunisian and Egyptian female enrollment ratios are higher at the primary and secondary level than in India or Costa Rica (Deblé, 1980). In Malaysia, which is a plural society in which the majority of the population is Muslim, 93.9 per cent of all school-aged girls enter the primary level of education, a rate similar to that of many Eastern European nations (Deblé, 1980). In some Islamic nations, women's enrollments, particularly at the tertiary level, approximate those of males, even, as in Kuwait, in a sex-segregated school system (O'Shaughnessey, 1978; Meleis, El-Sanabary and Beeson, 1979). Sex segregation may, in some instances, actually increase women's access to higher education, simply because there is a demand for women professionals to serve as teachers, doctors, and the like for other women (Boserup, 1969). In short, the impact of religion on women's access to education is not really known. If anything, the studies of the past decade suggest that the assumption that 'immutables' like religion depress women's education, like so many myths about women's nature, has not withstood careful scrutiny.

While there is much that remains to be known about the relation between parental background characteristics and women's access to education, much of the research of the past decade suggests that focus only on class, ethnicity and religion as the determinants of women's access to education has failed to provide a programme for reform that will remove the deep and persistent under-enrollment of girls in schools which is characteristic of most countries of the Third World. Research that dwells solely on the background of girls as an explanation for their lack of schooling runs the risk of assuming that girls' access to education is independent of school provision. All too often girls do not go to school simply because places are not available to them.

School provision and girls' access to education

Therefore, the greatest single indicator of whether or not a girl will attend school may well be whether schooling is made both available and accessible (Deblé, 1980; Hirschman, 1979; Bowman and Anderson, 1982). Research has suggested that when governments provide free education in abundant supply, girls do go to school. Perhaps the clearest example of this is in Tunisia, where the government consciously attempted to provide universal education and to extend equal opportunity to both sexes. Once schools were made available, girls flocked to them, religious beliefs and lack of traditions of female education notwithstanding (Jones, 1982).

The Tunisian case is also instructive because it shows that the type of schooling provided for girls also determines whether or not parents will send their daughters to school and keep them there. In the Tunisian case, demand for girls' education slackened when it became clear, especially in the rural areas, that lesser quality education was being made available. Also in Tunisia, once graduates of general education secondary programmes began to be unemployed, parents insisted that their daughters be given vocational training. In the absence of government response, a trend toward secondary private vocational school enrollment resulted (Jones, 1982).

The demand that schooling for girls be tied directly to remunerative employment is not unique to Tunisia, nor is the finding that girls' enrollment responds to the type and quality of education offered. McSweeney and Freedman's (1982) study of adult learners in Upper Volta suggests that it is not simply enough to provide schools without concern for the content of education and its relation to income generation. In Upper Volta, even when women were freed from tedious household tasks, given leisure time to attend school and given free education, they failed to attend classes unless the education provided for them was directly linked to income generation. The case in Upper Volta suggests that, while there may be little expectation that education might yield women income equal to that of men with comparable educational levels, women do expect education to provide skills for gainful employment.

Thus, research suggests that access to education, school provision, and the relation of the content of education to gainful employment may all be interconnected. Nevertheless, making schools *available* to women needs to be distinguished from making them *accessible* to women. This may well mean that schools may have to respond to the ways girls' lives are structured by work, religion and social norms. Planning provision for female education may not mean the same thing as planning educational provision for males (Naik, 1982). For example, in India government provision of day-time classes that adhere to age-specific guidelines, and to a school calendar that is oblivious to girls' agricultural labour, has done little to extend education to girls. A project undertaken, in conjunction with UNICEF, by the Indian Institute of Education in Pune, Maharastra State, showed that parents were more than happy to send their working daughters to school when schools were structured to accommodate to girls' roles in the family and their work in the fields. In the Pune project, classes were held at night rather than during the day, and in places accessible to the girls. Provision was made to accompany girls from home to class and back again, and villagers were hired to aid in instruction (Naik, 1982). The Pune project suggests that providing a school may not be the total answer to improving women's access to education; rather, attention must also be paid to the relation of the organization, timing, staffing, and nature of instruction to the pace of girls' lives.

The Pune project suggests that how, when and where education is given needs to conform to the pattern of girls' lives. Other research has suggested that women's access to education is affected by whether schools are co-educational or sex segregated (Smock, 1981; Finn, Dulberg and Reis, 1980). Whether co-education or sex segregation stimulates or depresses women's access to education is not known. In some countries where sex segregation is the rule rather than the exception, school provision for females is sometimes constrained, as is the case in Pakistan. As Smock (1981) points out, the Pakistan government, when faced openly with decisions about what type of school to build, tends to build boys' rather than girls' schools. In part, this is because the government associates girls' education with reinforcing traditional values, rather than with efforts towards the nation's modernization. However, in other countries, sex segregation does not always mean that women's educational opportunity is constrained (Meleis, El-Sanabary and Beeson, 1979; O'Shaughnessey, 1978). Certainly more research is necessary before the effect of single-sex and co-education can be disentangled from government policy and a commitment to educate women.

Research that seeks to understand how schools may be made available and accessible to girls in all societies has been rare in the past. It is, however, increasingly of concern to the mainstream of scholarship to understand the causes of female under-education. Isabelle Deblé (1980) succinctly pointed out that one reason women do not receive as much education as men is because governments do not perceive gender inequality as a problem, much less as a problem which they can solve. Research that focuses on how school provision, and the quality, content and organization of education, affects female attendance might well provide an action-oriented agenda for governments on which to base future efforts to eradicate gender-based imbalances in education.

References

Alexander, K and Eckland, Bruce K (1974) Sex differences in the educational attainment process *American Sociological Review* **39**: 668-82

Anderson, C A and Bowman, M J eds (1965) *Education and Economic Development* Cass: London

Altbach, P G, Arnove, R A and Kelly, G P eds (1982) *Comparative Education* Macmillan: New York

Bowman, M J and Anderson, C A (1982) The participation of women in education in the Third World *in* Altbach, Arnove and Kelly

Boserup, E (1969) *Women's Role in Economic Development* St Martin's Press: New York

Deblé, I (1980) *The School Education of Girls* UNESCO: Paris

Eliou, M (1973) The education and advancement of women in Africa: Ivory Coast, Upper Volta, Senegal *International Review of Education* **19**: 30-46

Finn, J D, Dulberg, L and Reis, J (1979) Sex differences in educational attainment: a cross-national perspective *Harvard Educational Review* **49**: 477-503

Foster, P (1965) The vocational school fallacy in development planning *in* Anderson and Bowman

Foster, P (1971) Education, economy, equality *Interchange* **2** 1: 51-61

Foster, P (1977) Education and social differentiation in less developed countries *Comparative Education Review* **21**: 211-29

Goldblatt, P (1983) Progress in schooling in Mexican Municipos Paper presented at the Annual Meeting of the Comparative and International Education Society, Atlanta, Georgia

Heyneman, S P (1976) Influences on academic achievement: a comparison of results from Uganda and more industrialized societies *Sociology of Education* **49**: 200-10

Hirschman, C (1979) Political independence and educational opportunity in peninsular Malaysia *Sociology of Education* **52** 2: 67-83

Howard-Merriam, K (1979) Women, education and the professions in Egypt *Comparative Education Review* **23**: 256-70

Jones, M T (1982) Educating girls in Tunisia: Issues generated by the drive for universal enrollment *in* Kelly and Elliott

Kelly, D H and Kelly, G P (1982) Education of women in developing countries *Educational Documentation and Information* **56** 222 (1st quarter) International Bureau of Education: Geneva

Kelly, G P and Elliott, C M eds (1982) *Women's Education in the Third World: Comparative Perspectives* State University of New York Press: Albany, New York

Kotwal, M (1975) Inequalities in the distribution of education between countries, sexes, generations and individuals *in* OECD

Maldonado, M (1981) Education and the labor force participation of Peruvian women Unpublished PhD dissertation State University of New York at Buffalo

Mblinyi, M (1969) *The Education of Girls in Tanzania* University College: Dar Es Salaam

McSweeney, B G and Freedman, M (1982) Lack of time as an obstacle to women's education: the case of Upper Volta *in* Kelly and Elliott

Meleis, A I, El-Sanabary, N and Beeson, D (1979) Women, modernization and education in Kuwait *Comparative Education Review* 23: 115-24

Meyer, J W and Hannan, M T eds (1979) *National Development and the World System* University of Chicago Press: Chigaco

Meyer, J W *et al* (1977) The world educational revolution, 1950-1970 *Sociology of Education* 50: 242-58

Mustaffa-Kedah, O (1975/76) The education of women in the Arab states *Literacy Discussions* 4 4: 119-39

Naik, C (1982) An action-research project on universal primary education: the plan and the process *in* Kelly and Elliott

OECD (1975) *Education, Inequality and Life Chances* OECD: Paris

O'Shaughnessey, T J (1978) Growth of educational opportunity for Muslim women, 1950 to 1973 *Anthropos* 73 5-6: 887-901

Plank, D (1983) Regional and age differences in Brazilian enrollment robes, 1970 Paper presented at the Annual Meeting of the Comparative and International Education Society, Atlanta, Georgia, March

Ram, R (1982) Sex differences in the labor market outcomes of education *in* Kelly and Elliott

Ramirez, F O and Boli-Bennett, J (1982) Global patterns of educational institutionalization *in* Altbach, Arnove and Kelly

Rogers, B (1980) *The Domestication of Women* Tavistock Publications: London and New York

Schiefelbein, E and Farrell, J P (1982) Women, schooling and work in Chile: evidence from a longitudinal study *in* Kelly and Elliott

Smith, P C and Cheung, P P L (1982) Social origins and sex differential schooling in the Philippines *in* Kelly and Elliott

Smock, A C (1981) *Women's Education in Developing Countries: Opportunities and Outcomes* Praeger: New York

Smock, A C (1982) Sex differences in educational opportunities and labor force participation in six countries *in* Altbach, Arnove and Kelly

Wang, B C (1982) Sex and ethnic differences in educational investment in Malaysia: the effect of reward structures *in* Kelly and Elliott

Weis, L (1980) Women and education in Ghana: some problems in assessing change *International Journal of Women's Studies* 3 5: 431-53

Wickramsinghe, S and Radcliffe, D (1979) Women and education in South Asia *Canadian and International Journal of Education* 8 2: 117-25

Woodhall, M (1973) Investment in women: a reappraisal of the concept of human capital *International Review of Eduation* 19 1: 9-29

Youssef, N H (1976/77) Education and female modernization in the Muslim world *Journal of International Affairs* 30: 191-209

7. Gender differentiation and interaction in Australian primary schools

Terry Evans

Summary: This chapter discusses gender differentiation in the Australian primary school classroom as a reflection of both the occupational structure of primary school teaching and of teachers' perceptions of their careers. A brief synopsis is provided of primary education in contemporary Australia, and of the current concerns about sexism in education. Some details are provided of the policies and practices of the Education Department in the State of Victoria with respect to abolishing sexism in schools and in the employment of staff. In addition, the gender differentiation in some recent employment figures of men and women staff in the teaching and administrative structures in Victoria are discussed. Data are presented and discussed from some of the author's research into differences in the interpretations of personal careers for men and women teachers.

Classroom interaction, curriculum, and teaching materials are discussed in terms of the part they play in the construction of gender. The importance of understanding and focusing upon the taken-for-granted gender assumptions of classroom life is highlighted whilst, simultaneously, the changes which are taking place to the more obvious and superficial features of sexism in schools are acknowledged. Some concluding comments are made about gender differentiation in Australian primary school classrooms and about the need for further research and writing in this area.

Introduction

Gender differentiation in the Australian primary school classroom needs to be seen in relation to the various social, economic and political structures which affect its operation. In particular, the structure and processes of primary schooling are intertwined with those social structures and processes which coalesce to produce social divisions in general, and especially those of gender. Gender differentiation may be seen as the construction and reproduction of masculinity and femininity in social life, and also as the different social relations which result.

It is difficult to separate the structures and processes of gender division from those which produce other social divisions. A recent study by Connell, Ashenden, Kessler and Dowsett (1982) of class, gender and secondary schooling in two metropolitan cities in Australia provided a useful theoretical framework for understanding the construction and reproduction of those two interrelated social divisions in Australian schools. Hence, this chapter briefly sketches the pertinent aspects of Australian social structures, then looks more specifically at the occupational and administrative structures of primary schooling, before discussing primary school teachers' interpretations of their roles and the interaction which takes place in their classrooms. The emphasis is upon Australian literature in the field, to which has been added some hitherto unpublished material from the author's studies of primary school classrooms, aspects of which have been reported elsewhere (see Evans, 1979, 1980, 1982).

Background

Australia is a capitalist society with strong historical, political and cultural ties to Britain (Ehrensaft and Armstrong, 1978). It has more recent and important economic and political relations with the USA, Japan, South East Asia and the South Pacific Region, especially New Zealand and Papua New Guinea. In many respects, Australia's federal system of educational structures and practices most closely resembles those of Britain, although with many developments which reflect Australia's own particular geographical, economic and social circumstances. In particular, the diversity of ethnic backgrounds in Australia outside of the dominant, white Anglo-Celtic mass has led to various accommodations to multicultural education and aboriginal education (Martin, 1978).

Several authors have pointed to the sexist nature of contemporary Australian society dating back over the past two centuries when British men first established their culture and communities on the East coast of Australia (Dixson, 1976; Mercer, 1975; Summers, 1975). The resurgence of the women's movement during the 1970s has initiated many changes in the legal, political and educational fields, not the least of which is the developing equal opportunity legislation. To some extent, the last decade or more has seen important changes to the nature and degree of gender differentiation in Australia; however, those committed to equality would argue that, as in other societies, there is much still to be done. In aspects of the legal, educational, social welfare and business institutions of Australian society women are being seen and encouraged to occupy their rightful places. In some business, government and union organizations, people are being employed actively to promote equality of opportunity; theirs is a difficult task — which meets with resistance — but their presence ensures that the issues of equality are often brought into focus.

At the school level, especially in primary schools where the vast majority of teachers are women, the issues of gender differentiation and equal opportunity would seem to be most pertinent. There has been considerable research in some educational settings about the nature of gender differentiation and, more usually, its consequences in terms of male and female aspirations, achievement and subject choices. However, as happens all too often, the primary school has been omitted by the majority of writers and researchers, although there are signs that some more interest is being taken in this crucial agency of child socialization.

Gender differentiation in the administrative and occupational structures of primary school teaching

The administration of schooling in Australia is principally the responsibility of the individual state governments, although the federal government increasingly exerts considerable influence through the allocation of funds and its various national organizations which have responsibilities concerning schools (for example, the Schools Commission). There are some differences between the states in their administration of primary schooling, but they each follow relatively common procedures. Victoria, which is the second most populous state in Australia with approximately three-and-a-quarter million people (about one-quarter of Australia's population), serves as a useful example of an Australian primary school administration. All the state's schools are administered by the Education Department of Victoria which, until recently, contained separate divisions for the employment and administration of primary, secondary and technical schooling.

Primary schooling is for children of ages between five and 11 years. In terms of staffing structures, the primary schools division contains a considerable imbalance between the sexes despite various efforts to combat it. For example, successive governments and the Education Department have avowed that the elimination of sexism was an important priority; the primary teachers' union has similar policies and practices in these respects; and many reports, programmes and curricular materials have addressed the problem and initiated changes (see, for example, Sampson, 1977; Schools Commission, 1975). Nevertheless, the upper echelons of the administrative structure of the Education Department are entirely occupied by men; the most senior women are employed at the level of Assistant Regional Director.

In the primary schools division (where approximately 80 per cent of employees are women) about 25 per cent of principals are women. Such figures reflect the personal career decisions of men and women, based upon their own gender-related socialization (that is, through the family, schooling, mass media, etc). The consequences of such a degree of gender differentiation in the occupational structure of primary school teaching in Victoria go far beyond the lack of female senior career role models for the pupils or the domination of junior career role models by women. Hence, both boys and girls are encouraged to identify with career paths which may not be those which they would otherwise choose. Usually the consequences *within* the primary school are that pupils experience women teachers in their classrooms who often have deflated views of their own competence, capacity for promotion and their contribution to the decision-making process in their schools. In contrast, the pupils experience men teachers who may have anxious views of their needs for promotion and may have inflated views of their own competence and capacity, as well as a tendency to assert themselves disproportionately in school decision-making structures.

The established patterns of school structures continue to reinforce these gender differentiated perceptions in existing staff, and help to construct them in novitiates. A study by Wentworth (1979) of final year primary teacher trainees in Victoria has shown that the traditional gender differentiation in career aspirations is well established before the commencement of work in schools. The construction of gender differences in the career aspirations of primary teachers is embedded in the socialization experience of their earlier lives, as well as in their contemporary professional and peer socialization.

Primary school teachers' gender differentiated career perceptions and classroom behaviour

In 1980, the author completed a study in two primary schools in Victoria which have been called Pinedale and Walkwood. This study, details of which have been reported elsewhere (Evans, 1982), involved the interviewing of teachers and observation of their classrooms in order to understand that part of the process of gender-role socialization which stems from teachers' perceptions of gender, especially in relation to their own personal biographies and careers. The following is an answer from a male teacher at Pinedale, aged in his late twenties, about the career opportunities for *women* in primary teaching:

> *Pinedale male teacher:* 'I think primary teaching has been a casualty of the career aspirations of men. The social acceptability scale of teaching, particularly primary teaching, was not that high. In order to get into teaching, you've got to be fairly bright, your aspirations have got to be higher than a primary teacher if you're a bloke, and, consequently, you've got a higher proportion of women coming into primary teaching. You see, blokes would be going to look to be an engineer, doctor, dentist, even secondary teaching, before they come down to primary. Primary is a last ditch thing. I have only got to look at myself, I'm a failed dentist, I always wanted to be a dentist, but my marks were not good enough . . . I think a lot of blokes fall into it [primary teaching]. There's a lot of women in the primary service, for sure, that's probably because blokes have looked for something that, perhaps pays more . . . the brighter ones go for something more.'
> *The author:* 'You mean brighter men?'
> *Pinedale male teacher:* 'Yes, the brighter men go for something better and the blokes who aren't so well endowed obviously get something worse.'
> *The author:* 'Where does that leave the women?'
> *Pinedale male teacher:* 'In the middle, yes, and that's why you get so many women in primary teaching.'

This male teacher's perceptions of his female colleagues probably require little elucidation. The initial question was specifically about the career opportunities for women, and yet he only explained women as, in effect, filling the vacuum left because 'blokes' did not aspire to such teaching. Contrast the male teacher's comments with those of a female teacher of similar age from Walkwood School, when she was asked about whether the career opportunities for women had changed in primary school teaching:

> *Walkwood female teacher:* 'Definitely more equality. There are still some fields where women are restricted, and I think there are some males who do not like to think of women taking over senior positions, because they still class them as the child bearer. [They] think women run off and have kids and then the position is vacant, and so why didn't a man have it anyway. I know my father and my younger brother will say that.'
> *The author:* 'What about senior positions (in teaching)?'
> *Walkwood female teacher:* 'Yes, I think so, there are more female principals now than there were before. I don't know whether the primary [school] structure is good for men, though I think it is very hard to be promoted for men. Particularly at the lower levels and with the staffing changes it's going to be more difficult for younger 'fellas' to get to the principal class.'
> *The author:* 'So you say it's easier for you?'
> *Walkwood female teacher:* 'No, I think it's difficult for everybody. But for a man who, maybe, you would consider would want to stay in this career for ever, I mean it's his life support, then it's just as hard for him to be promoted . . .'

For this teacher, her answer is also centred upon men. Not only does she feel sorry for men's lack of opportunities for promotion, which she acknowledges are no different for women, but she also sees men as being sole bread winners. As a consequence, she defines women teachers, and thereby herself, as only having a job as a secondary 'life support', the first presumably being from the man to whom she is attached. One might conclude that this teacher has not, in fact, completely rejected the views of her father and brother on women as childbearers, but has moderated them instead. This points to the power of family relationships in producing gender differentiation.

In fact, the Victorian Education Department has been a fairly progressive employer with respect to recognizing the maternity leave needs of women teachers and is planning to introduce a seven-year parental (unpaid) leave entitlement which, one is given to understand, will make no distinction between the sex of the parent except for a paid leave component for women similar to the current maternity leave provisions. It appears the system will allow either, but not both, parents to take or share leave for up to seven years in a career and will enable some equalization of the career prospects between male and female teachers who are parents. The current unemployment amongst primary teachers makes the new system attractive for reasons other than shared parenthood and equality of teaching career prospects.

To return to the two teachers, it seems they failed to recognize the relative equality of career opportunities in primary teaching and they based their own interpretation more upon what might be called traditional family and societal divisions between the sexes. This raises the question of what is then passed on in their classrooms as appropriate gender roles for their male and female pupils. The deeply entrenched nature of gender differentiation in the consciousness of most men and women teachers (and in most people) makes it difficult for them to see the restrictions and limitations they apply to each other, especially men to women, and to themselves. This also leads to a failure to recognize the gender differentiation they are helping to produce in their classrooms. The patriarchal domination of Australian school structures and systems can be seen to be reflected, partly through the teachers, in primary school classrooms.

Gender differentiation in the pupils' classroom lives

As has been demonstrated, gender differentiation is usually carried across the threshold of the primary school classroom by the teacher. The pupils also bring their own less well constructed versions into the classroom along with contributions from curriculum materials, books and mass media. The interaction between all these elements provides the classroom researcher with an ever-changing array of events to observe and record. One does not have to spend long in an Australian primary school classroom before evidence of gender differentiation emerges.

A study by the author in 1976 of classroom interaction between teachers and their nominated most, and least, creative pupils showed that teachers interacted twice as frequently with the most creative males than females, and about one-fifth more frequently with the least creative males than females (Evans, 1979). The study at Pinedale and Walkwood schools, four years later, substantiated this difference where usually teachers would interact two to three times more frequently with boys than girls. However, gender differentiation emerges not only in different frequencies of interaction; it also markedly affects the nature of those interactions. This throws light on the way in which gender is produced and reproduced, and on its ideological basis.

An example from the Pinedale and Walkwood study may be useful to explain the importance of understanding the nature of classroom interactions in order to study gender in the primary school classroom. The first example comes from a lesson being given by a Walkwood teacher to her grade 4-5 class (ages of nine and ten years) on the topic of houses. The teacher asked a question about architects, and a boy, Mark, immediately raised his hand to answer. The teacher sees him but ignores him and gives others the chance to answer first. The teacher accepts some answers and then says, 'Mark has got some good ideas for us'. Mark then gives his answer, which refers to architects being of the masculine gender, while the teacher nods and occasionally comments approvingly as Mark speaks. This is one example which is typical of a process through which both males and masculinity are seen to be important. In the observed classroom discussions, architects were never referred to as anything but male by both teacher and pupils — as if there were no women architects in Australia!

Perhaps the real significance of these types of interaction relates to the ways in which the teacher was able to, and was seen to, 'ignore' Mark in a manner which implied that the best or good answers should come last in order to allow the pupils with the less suitable answers to respond first. This raises questions about how the teacher *knew* that Mark would have some good ideas about architecture. For example, was this purely a matter of her understanding of Mark's capabilities and interest, or was there an element of gender-related expectation? The above item of class-room interaction is an example of a primary schooling process which serves to establish the importance of the male intellect and to attribute masculinity to certain types of occupation.

Such incidents are not isolated occurrences but are part of a structure of gender-differentiated socialization in primary schools — a structure which is a part of common, everyday teaching and is almost universally accepted. However, there are other more obvious elements of gender differentiation in primary school classroom life which are becoming less accepted, often challenged and gradually eroded.

Developments in gender differentiation

Since the mid-1970s, considerable literature has been published in Australia within the area of gender and education, although material on primary schooling has occupied only a small part of that literature. In terms of the primary school curriculum and curriculum materials there has been both evidence and criticism of the traditional sex-biases and emphases upon masculinity (Bradley and Mortimer, 1973; Healy and Ryan, 1975; Sampson, 1975; Sampson, 1977). These criticisms have been transformed into positive action through the recommendations of govern-ments, committees and employing authorities, teachers' unions, women teachers' groups and individual teachers in schools. Many schools continue to use the sexist readers and materials of the past, if only because the cost of replacement is prohibitive in times of financial stringency in education.

However, increasingly teachers are becoming aware of gender differ-entiation in their classrooms and are beginning to modify their curricula, materials and practices. These instances are still not universal and they only represent a beginning to the elimination of gender differentiation in schools. Many simple and obvious forms of sexist practices that have been eliminated in some schools remain in others. For example, some schools segregate 'lining-up' for boys and girls; others allocate physical tasks to boys and dexterous or domestic tasks to girls. In the primary school, there is little gender differentiation in the subjects taught, although, as has been shown earlier, there is gender differentiation in the way such subjects are taught.

Currently, there is concern at the prevalence of negative attitudes to mathematics among girls compared with boys and debate about the reasons. The main concern stems not so much from girls' performance at mathematics in the primary school, where they are about equal to boys (Moss, 1982), but rather from their subsequent poor performance at secondary school and tertiary education. The decline has been attributed to the masculine nature of mathematics texts and mathematics problems given at school which Leder (1974) has shown affects girls' preference for mathematics. Schofield (1981) has demonstrated that primary school girls' and boys' attitudes towards mathematics affect their achievement, and that traditional gender stereotypes encourage poor attitudes to mathematics on the part of girls.

An area of the primary school curriculum which has proved resistant to the removal of gender differentiation concerns sports. Girls have no place at all in the popular codes of football (rugby league, and Australian rules football), which are ruled by patriarchal administrative bodies, which exhalt physical confrontation and aggressive masculinity, and are reinforced in this by the mass media. Therefore, if the primary school chooses to teach such sports, girls are usually excluded. Many primary schools, for reasons of encouraging less aggressive sports as well as mixed-sex participation, now choose to emphasize other team games or individual sports. At primary schools, physical development, if anything, favours girls rather than boys, so, to the egalitarian teacher, there are few obstacles to prevent an integrated sports curriculum. A developing interest in Australia in fitness and health, together with similar calls for leisure education in schools, should provide a useful opportunity for the construction of non-sexist sports and leisure curricula which reflect a wide range of participant sports and activities.

Conclusion

In recent years there have been many concerted attempts to remove some aspects of sexism from primary schooling in Australia. While there have been variations between the individual states in the movement toward the abolition of sexism, it would seem that New South Wales, South Australia and Victoria have been most active in these respects. Furthermore, this trend has been promoted and supported by the various teachers' unions, by women's groups, and by the Australian Schools Commission. In these respects, it is reasonable to expect a diminishing of the more overt features of gender differentiation in the Australian primary school in the future. However, the extent to which women occupy the subordinate teaching positions, and men occupy the senior administrative positions, suggests that it will be many years before men and women achieve equality in their teaching careers.

These differences in the careers of men and women in primary schooling are not so much to do with barriers to career opportunities in the employing authorities, but rather to do with the different career aspirations of men and women. This suggests that wider societal factors, especially the family and mass-media socialization, together with patriarchal power structures in virtually every aspect of social life, are largely the cause. Classroom interaction can be seen to reflect a gender-differentiated state of affairs — to the extent that much of everyday classroom practice may be seen to comprise 'taken-for-granted' gender differentiation.

The literature on gender differentiation in Australian primary school classrooms is limited, although there is considerably more material on other sectors of education. Researchers are just beginning to provide explanations of the processes associated with primary school classrooms. What is certain from the evidence available is that gender differentiation is deeply entrenched in the consciousness of teachers and pupils and therefore in the interaction between them; thus the various moves to eliminate sexism or sex bias in school curricula, materials and formal procedures, represent largely superficial changes. A wider range of research into gender relations in primary school classrooms will assist the processes involved in the creation of more fundamental changes.

References

Bradley, D and Mortimer, M (1973) Sex role stereotyping in children's picture books *Refractory Girl* 1

Connell, R W, Ashenden, D J, Kessler, S and Dowsett, G W (1982) *Making the Difference: Schools, Families and Social Divisions* George Allen and Unwin: Sydney

Dixson, M (1976) *The Real Matilda: Women and Identity in Australia 1788-1975* Penguin: Ringwood

Ehrensaft, P and Armstrong, W (1978) Dominion capitalism: a first statement *Australian and New Zealand Journal of Sociology* 14 3: 352-63

Evans, T D (1979) Creativity, sex-role socialisation and pupil-teacher interactions in early schooling *Sociological Review* 27 1: 139-55

Evans, T D (1980) Pre-school and primary teachers' interaction with their most and least creative pupils *Research in Education* 24: 31-43

Evans, T D (1982) Being and becoming: teachers' perceptions of sex-roles and actions toward their male and female pupils *British Journal of Sociology of Education* 3 2: 127-43

Evans, T D (1983) Gender, class and education: a teaching bibliography of Australian and New Zealand studies *in* Walker and Barton

Healy, P and Ryan, P (1975) Sex stereotyping in children's books *in* Mercer

Leder, G C (1974) Sex differences in mathematics problem appeal as a function of problem context *Journal of Educational Research* 67 8: 351-53

Martin, J (1978) *The Migrant Presence* Allen and Unwin: Sydney

Mercer, J ed (1975) *The Other Half: Women in Australian Society* Penguin: Ringwood

Moss, J (1982) *Towards Equality: Progress by Girls in Mathematics in Australian Secondary Schools* Australian Council for Educational Research: Melbourne

Sampson, S N (1975) Sex role enculturation in schools *in Education News* 15 4 and 5: 34-39

Sampson, S N (1977) Chairperson Victorian Committee on Equal Opportunity *Report to the Premier of Victoria* Government Printer: Melbourne

Schofield, H (1981) Grade level and the relationship between mathematics attitude and achievement in children *Journal of Educational Research* 75

Schools Commission (1975) *Girls School and Society* Australian Government Publishing Service: Canberra

Summers, A (1975) *Damned Whores and God's Police: The Colonization of Women in Australia* Penguin: Ringwood

Walker, S and Barton, L *eds* (1983) *Gender, Class and Education* Falmer Press: Lewes

Wentworth, R D (1979) A comparison of the career aspirations of men and women trainee teachers *South Pacific Journal of Teacher Education* **7** 3 and 4: 85-91

Acknowledgement

The author is indebted to his colleague, Daryl Nation, for his critical comments on an earlier draft of this chapter.

8. Sponsoring and stereotyping in a working-class English secondary school

Carol Buswell

Summary: This chapter is based on fieldwork conducted over two years in a large comprehensive secondary school (1,500 pupils and 100 teachers) in the north of England. Through the use of individual case studies — one boy and three girls — some subtle, but important, processes of gender interaction are identified. Some boys with marginal examination achievements are 'sponsored' by male teachers, in the sense that they are given extra opportunities and encouragement to reach a higher level of achievement. At the same time, some girls who have singular, and often aggressive, characteristics are 'nurtured' and these characteristics redefined in psycho-emotional terms. In responding to this, the girls learn to manipulate interpersonal relations with men which, in the future, will emphasize the traits which legitimate their subordinate position. Some girls of high ability 'acquiesce' in responding to the school's wishes possibly to their own future detriment and other girls are simply 'invisible'.

The girls cope with contradictory social messages by accommodating and resisting, but this behaviour is a product of the social relations they experience which reflect structural realities. Thus, in spite of the official ideology of 'equality' within schools there are processes of interaction between teachers and pupils that serve to reinforce and reproduce the dependency relations which characterize wider social and interpersonal relations between the sexes.

Introduction

During the last year of compulsory schooling in England and Wales most pupils now take public examinations. 'High achievers' gain between five and ten passes, in different subjects, at 'Ordinary' (O) level. In the past, many of these pupils would have stayed on in the school sixth form for two extra years of schooling to take two or three subjects at 'Advanced' (A) level for entry into higher education (universities) or jobs requiring extended schooling. The growth of 'credentialism' and unemployment has, however, increased the numbers of pupils staying on at school beyond the statutory age and schools now offer a sixth form curriculum that includes vocational and lower-level qualifications as well as the traditional, and newer, A level subjects. By 1981, roughly the same number of boys and girls were staying on in the sixth form of the large comprehensive school under study here. However, the school hierarchy — in common with others (Acker, 1983) — was male-dominated in the sense that the senior staff were predominantly men and insofar as women teachers taught sixth-formers at all, they by and large taught the lower level vocational courses.

Gender stratification structures, with males as the dominant group, are characterized by the dependency of women on men — in the private sphere in terms of the social relations of domestic organization and in the public sphere in terms of the social relations of production. Dependency relations penetrate interpersonal and social relations, but the social construction of gender only has meaning when the concepts of masculinity and femininity are recognized as a pair (MacDonald, 1981) and the female role is a relational one deriving from women's position *vis-à-vis* men (Davies, 1983). It is, therefore, necessary to have regard for the cultural processes of reproduction for men as well as women and for the relationship between the two. The cultures of males and females act to legitimate individual and group locations. It is the cultural reproduction of dependency relationships within a school that will be investigated in this chapter. Four case studies (one boy and three girls) illustrate the subtle processes which, at this higher level of the school, contribute to the cultural reproduction of dependency.

A sponsored boy

There seems to have been a tendency, in predicting O level results, for teachers to overestimate some boys' results, but to be fairly accurate regarding all the girls. The tendency was most marked with regard to a few boys who were expected to pass five or more subjects and, in the event, passed between one and three. These boys could be called marginal achievers but they were not seen by the teachers, or by themselves, in this way.

Peter, one of these boys, intended to stay on at school to take three A levels and become a teacher. He explained that he might well not have considered staying on because he had been in trouble in the fifth year for fighting. But some of the teachers supported him, including two male teachers who were involved in the football teams for which he played — and they advised him to change his ways, his appearance and his friends so that he would be allowed to stay on. Thus, through the informal network of sports teams, Peter had developed relationships with teachers who were supportive of him. Reports from teachers regarding Peter, just before O levels, were glowing: 'extrovert', 'very articulate', 'very mature', 'a great lad' etc. At this time, a teacher, Mr T, described Peter as having a 'very able mind' and also said: 'His parents give him support. His work is good. I think he'll really blossom in the sixth form'.

In the event, Peter only passed three out of six O level subjects but in the sixth form started studying for three A levels and two new O levels.

A few weeks after entering the sixth form he was 'very depressed and bored' as the amount of work expected left no time for anything else — if it were done. Peter, however, decided to continue to spend his time on sport and recreation and as he was doing no work he was 'called in' by his tutor about the matter several times during the first term. His school report at this time said he did insufficient homework and his lack of progress was blamed on this.

Thus, whatever his examination and coursework results, no one ever suggests that Peter is not 'able' or capable of doing the work. By the beginning of the next term, the teacher who had previously described Peter's parents as supportive said that 'he gets no support from home'. Peter said the opposite and stressed that his parents wanted him to work and they were pressing him to do well because his father did not want him 'to put on overalls' (work in a factory). Throughout the next term, the pattern was the same — Peter doing no work and the teachers 'chasing him up'. Half way through the year he failed two of the three internal school exams on the A level subjects and was surprised because one of the subjects he failed was supposed to be his best subject. He failed, he explained, 'because of the way that teachers mark. Everyone did badly except one girl'. He also said he was not worried about being sent for after the exams: 'I didn't really get told off, they just try and point out that I must work if I'm going to pass'. His report at the end of term stressed his lack of effort and waste of talents. The next year followed exactly the same pattern, and in the summer he just passed one of his A levels but failed the other two.

The general expectancy model applied to success and failure maintains that when performance is inconsistent with expectancy it is attributed to one or more temporary factors like luck or effort rather than to a stable factor such as ability. It has been found that males, having more positive expectations than females, will be more likely to explain their success in terms of ability and their failure in terms of an unstable factor (Viaene, 1979). This process is clearly in operation here, where neither Peter nor his teachers ever call his ability into question, even when his performance suggests it might be. This is also consistent with Bisseret's findings with regard to male students who attributed their exam failure to similar temporary factors — boredom, lack of effort etc — and even said that exam success was the sign of not being intelligent! (Bisseret, 1979).

The 'sponsoring' process has been illustrated by considering the career of one boy, but other boys in this category have similar case histories. This is not to say that they were being 'chased up' and similar girls were not; the point is that the A level girls were all doing some work and were anyway less marginal in examination terms. These boys were being given *extra* chances and opportunities — whether or not they decided to take them. This process takes on crucial structural importance if one considers the view that, in bourgeois society, forms of exclusion are based on the right to nominate successors through systems of sponsorship (Parkin, 1974).

Thus, the sponsoring of boys by male teachers is, as far as girls are cconcerned, a form of exclusion in itself.

Some girls in the sixth form were encouraged by teachers and some very able ones even described the encouragement as being pushed, and restricted the amount of work they did in order to have some social life as well. The important difference between encouragement for these girls and the sponsorship of marginal boys was that the girls were encouraged *after*|they had already proved themselves. One of these girls, Mandy, at the end of the fifth year said: 'I didn't like school for five years because they didn't know who I was. Then – all of a sudden – when I was doing O levels – they all wanted to know what I was going to do. I know all the teachers can't know all the pupils, but I was a bit disillusioned that – all of a sudden – they wanted to know me'.

A nurtured girl

One girl, Judy, had something in common with Peter inasmuch as she, too, had flirted with a counter-culture in the fifth form and had left school to work in a shop. At the beginning of the second year in the sixth form, two of the A level sixth-form girls had persuaded her to come back to school and take some O levels. Soon after she returned to school, Judy said: 'Some people don't like me because I'm not all quiet and sweet. But I know that Mr T and them are pleased I'm doing all right. As soon as someone gives us a bit of confidence I'm all right – but it just takes one dirty look from a teacher and it all goes away'. This theme of being sensitive to what (male) teachers think of her runs through Judy's account of events – confidence is something that staff dispense or withhold rather than something developed internally. Soon after she returned to school a teacher was overheard describing her as 'highly strung' and a senior member of staff, Mr S, complained to her tutor about her noisiness and the fact she was setting a bad example to other pupils. She was 'seen' about her behaviour and her report at the end of the first term suggested that she 'lacks confidence' and had a 'fear of failure'.

At the beginning of the next year, Judy shouted at Mr S and the whole of the next day revolved around teachers attempting to persuade her to go to him with the written apology he demanded. A teacher described her as 'neurotic' and when Mr T was trying to persuade her to apologise she said, 'You're trained to break my spirit' and rushed out of the room. She did, eventually, produce the apology for Mr S and he described her as 'spoilt'.

A fairly typical exchange during a lesson between Judy and a male teacher is exemplified by the following:

Judy: Do I have to do this?
Mr C: No. It's your decision.
Judy: Don't be horrible! (pouting)
Mr C: I'm not being horrible, love (Puts his arm round her shoulder in a friendly fashion).

So, by playing the tentative, moody, unconfident female she elicits friendly and supportive responses. It is the aggressive, argumentative loud-mouth the teachers do not like. Judy's work does not figure highly in her story at all: she does hardly any, but is not 'seen' about that. But when asked in the upper sixth if she thought she might have been able to do O levels in the fifth form she replied: 'Nobody ever bothered with me then. I didn't know how to revise until the other day — Anne showed me . . . and if Sue and Lesley hadn't bothered with me I wouldn't be here now'. So there is a sponsorship system for girls; they sometimes sponsor each other.

Mr C said that he went through a 'bad patch' with Judy because she always wanted to be a special case and he had not the time to deal with it — 'But we're over that now. I think chiefly because I handled it in a good-natured way'. This was the teacher in the lesson quoted earlier — so it might be suggested that an improvement in their relationship was also because she had learned to manipulate him by using insecure, rather than aggressive, signals. He described her as 'manic depressive'.

Another male teacher explained: 'She wants attention all the time. She lacks confidence. She's spoilt. She stormed out of the lesson last week'. As a result, she asked if she could leave doing the exam course in that subject and was allowed to go to the lessons and do easier work; she did very badly in the school exams at this time.

This girl, who had shouted at a senior member of staff, told a teacher that he was trained to break her spirit and had stormed out of a lesson, might have been described as aggressive, rude and unpredictable. However, she had, in fact, been variously described as highly strung, lacking in confidence, neurotic, spoilt and manic-depressive — a thumb-nail sketch of a person who could only be female, according to traditional stereo-types. The labelling of her attributes in this way is important because it 'constructs' a person who needs nurturing. The image of an aggressive loud-mouth who does no work and misses lessons would have suggested quite different treatment.

Judy gained a few credentials from her extra two years at school and went to a further education college to train for a traditional female occu-pation. What she learned in school was to manipulate and control men with an acceptable set of traits and behaviour patterns. The school felt it had been successful because someone they had hardly been able to control had 'grown up'. Hunt (1980) maintains that, through socialization, boys learn to control the world and girls to be controlled by it, while Middleton (1974) comments that sexist ideology under capitalism con-firms the notion that women invariably live *through* other people — something which some girls in this school learned. Boys present images as well — but the ones which girls like Judy are learning will only be of benefit in interpersonal relations of an unequal kind. By adopting this behaviour, girls will 'locate' themselves in powerless and traditional positions, always dependent on the group they think they are controlling. This situation is very like that of the working-class boys that Willis (1977) describes. Davies (1979), in studying 'oppositional girls', points out that these girls are closing future avenues to themselves. But the girl described here was not a member of any counter-culture — she was learning to behave in an approved way, to be a 'good pupil', and thereafter a 'good woman'.

An acquiescent girl

Sensitivity to teachers' responses and the perceived needs of the school are exemplified by a high achieving girl who will, ultimately, be affected by following the wishes of others. In the middle of the fifth year, Anne, who was regarded as very clever but diffident, said that her only aim in life was to become an accountant, and that she wished to go to university to qualify towards that end. Anne came from a working-class background and her parents knew very little about education. Having achieved high grade passes in all the O levels she took, Anne returned to school intending to take A level accounts, maths and history. But Mr S persuaded her to take English instead of accounts. She explained this in the following way: 'He said accountancy wasn't accepted as an academic subject, and he thinks if I got good enough grades I could go to Oxford or Cambridge — and he says that it would be better to get a good general education and then, after that, I could do what I want. But if I did that for three years, then I'd have to start all over again doing accounts, because they don't do that at Oxford or Cambridge. If I'd have got lower grades (at O level), and if I hadn't passed French and German, they wouldn't have bothered with me, because you need languages for Oxford or Cambridge and I'm the only one who passed them and stayed on. So they've pinned all their hopes on me — which is a bit hard. It makes me worry — because if I failed before, it wasn't hard for nobody but me. But now Mr S says it'll be good for the school — and I don't want to let the school down; it's not just for me now'.

Anne achieved entry to Oxbridge to study a humanities subject. Whether this will secure a better future for her than accountancy is a matter of conjecture. However, Roger also wanted to go into accountancy or banking and he, too, was an able pupil who passed the O levels he took and returned to school to take A level accounts, maths and history — the subjects Anne had intended to do. At the end of two years he went to university to study finance and accounting.

The school's assumption seemed to be that a 'general' education — especially at a high status university or college — is a good choice for able girls because there is no need to look further ahead than that for women, but that concrete careers are important for boys. This could be the modern educational equivalent of the middle-class Victorian emphasis on music and polite skills for girls, compared with professional and business acumen for boys. The school did not force these particular career choices on the pupils — however, Roger informed the teachers about what he wanted to do and Anne allowed herself to be told by them what they thought she should do.

An invisible girl

Many girls are neither so clever that the school directs them, nor have the personal characteristics that put them into the nurtured category; they could best be labelled 'invisible'. Pat, one such pupil, was described as 'pleasant', 'reliable' and 'neat'. In the fifth year she intended to find a job after her A levels, and at this time she said, 'The subject teachers hardly know you — they take more notice of you if you do well in a subject — if you don't you're just background'. Like Anne, she had parents who knew little about education. Having started two A level subjects in the sixth form, Pat considered asking if she could drop one of them as she was finding it difficult. With regard to this particular subject, she commented: 'Mr T has got his favourites. He doesn't like the girls. He laughs at the boys' jokes and talks towards them all the time. Some of the lessons are just conversations between him and Peter. You can *really* tell he doesn't like us because, you know, he's just not bothered about us at all'.

Shortly after this she began to find the subject easier and decided, mainly because of encouragement from her friend, that she might be able to cope with a third A level. She tentatively suggested the idea to a teacher. One of the reasons she wanted to take another subject was because she felt she had not got enough work to do: 'I'd stay in every night and do work. But I'm having it easy compared with last year. I thought it would be writing notes *every* night. There's not much work to do — like Mr T gave us an essay last week and I thought I'd do it straight away while it was fresh in my mind. Then we went to the lesson and he said "We'll take half the lesson to do a plan of the essay" — and I'd already done it!'

Compare this girl, who wants to do more work, who is not being noticed in lessons and who is regarded simply as 'pleasant' and 'neat', with the boys who are simultaneously being sponsored — although they are doing no work at all. Pat, too, has a hand in her own invisibility — she did not even tell Mr T that she had already completed the essay that he asked them to plan.

Accommodation, resistance and conflict

Anyon (1983) has noted that: 'complete acceptance (as well as complete rejection) of sex-role-appropriate attitudes and behaviours is actually rather rare'. Instead, she suggests, there are processes of 'accommodation and resistance', which involve girls in a series of attempts to cope with contradictory social messages. Girls sometimes use female-appropriate behaviour to resist the demands of work and the teachers — as in the case of Judy. Mandy — who resented the school's sudden interest in her after five years — also resisted attempts for her to achieve the highest academic grades and, in the end, decided not to go into higher education at all but to enter a 'female' semi-profession which was her mother's wish. She maintained that she was not pressured by her mother into this choice, but she obviously found the school's demands easier to resist because she experienced little interest from her teachers until late in her school career. Anne's behaviour, on the other hand, could be construed as accommodation. Pat experienced conflict between her parents' expectations that she would leave school and obtain a job and her own increasing confidence and desire to go into higher education. She left her decision until the last moment and eventually compromised by entering a local college to which she could travel daily whilst still living at home.

Where girls exercised 'choice' it was usually a choice between that which various other people expected of them. This was also the case for some boys. However, significantly, there were some boys who followed their own inclinations entirely, against the wishes of both parents and teachers. Peter was one example.

Conclusion

All the teachers mentioned in this chapter are male and are clearly acting out their own roles in interpersonal relations with the pupils. It has been maintained (Clarricoates, 1980) that different schools transmit a different female sub-culture depending on the school's location and intake. The school described in this paper is in a working-class area, but the attempt has been made to illustrate that it transmits several ideas of 'female'. Most, if not all, the girls fit into the nurtured, acquiescent or invisible categories and none at all into the sponsored one. It is suggested that the school is constructing, placing and responding to girls according to versions of well-known adult female stereotypes — women in need of love and protection, women who are clever but malleable, and women who are invisible. It is important to see the dependency relations of girls with male teachers alongside the relationships of such teachers to boys, and to remember that positive stereotypes (of the dominant group) are an important part of ideology (Perkins, 1979) and that dependence is more than a personality trait because it involves power and subordination.

It is not argued that the girls' responses turn them into 'types' (behaviour is partly the *product* of the social relations within an organisation) but that the girls' responses will serve to locate them in traditional positions *vis-à-vis* men. The girls are learning to shape interpersonal relations, but not to question the structures that determine those relations. Nor could they change these gender structures, even if they did question them: material conditions are powerful, and power is more important in changing structures than attitudes. The material conditions that are particularly relevant here are those concerned with the labour market and the future position of girls in the occupational structure. If there is a dual labour market (Edwards, 1975) with primary and secondary sectors — the latter comprised of non-career jobs — and if, even in mass middle-level occupations, there is a deskilled lower sector developing, where women disproportionately congregate (Braverman, 1974), this makes educational qualifications much less important for women than the fact of their gender.

The data does suggest that what Bourdieu (1976) maintains with regard to the working-class is also true for girls. That is, objective chances are *intuitively* perceived and internalized and shape 'choices' and behaviour. In other words, the girls 'know' at their own level what is true at the structural level — that there are only certain opportunities. They act according to this knowledge, so that their wishes never materialize as long as the real chances of success are slim.

Thus, some girls, like Judy, stay on at school to do some O levels, but do not take the work very seriously. They pay lip-service to the notion that extra qualifications are desirable, but their actions suggest that they do not really believe this. Empirically, they are correct: the labour market is not as highly differentiated for girls as for boys. Similarly, the girls' responses at an interpersonal level show perception of structural realities.

The processes of gender interaction at senior school level also illustrate one of the contradictions of our ideology — that of offering (in theory) short-term equality within educational institutions and, at the same time, 'cooling out' aspirations in preparation for a long-term future of inequality. What is important is the dialectical process of a division of labour which presents girls with certain modes of behaviour, the adoption of which legitimates the structure.

References

Acker, S (1983) Women and teaching: a semi-detached sociology of a semi-profession *in* Walker and Burton

Anyon, J (1983) Intersections of gender and class: accommodation and resistance by working-class and affluent females to contradictory sex-role ideologies *in* Walker and Barton

Barrett, M *et al eds* (1979) *Ideology and Cultural Reproduction* Croom Helm: London

Barton, L and Meighan, R *eds* (1979) *Schools, Pupils and Deviance* Nafferton Books: Driffield

Bisseret, N (1979) *Education, Class Language and Ideology* Routledge and Kegan Paul: London

Bourdieu, P (1976) The school as a conservative force *in* Dale *et al*

Braverman, H (1974) *Labor and Monopoly Capital* Monthly Review Press: New York

Clarricoates, K (1980) The perception and categorisation of gender conformity and gender deviation in primary schools *in* Deem

Dale, R *et al eds* (1976) *Schooling and Capitalism* Routledge and Kegan Paul: London

Dale, R *et al eds* (1981) *Schooling and the National Interest* Falmer Press: Lewes

Davies, L (1979) Deadlier than the male? Girls' conformity and deviance in school *in* Barton and Meighan

Davies, L (1983) Gender, resistance and power *in* Walker and Barton
Deem, R ed (1980) *Schooling for Women's Work* Routledge and Kegan Paul: London
Edwards, R (1975) *Labor Market Segmentation* Lexington: Mass
Hartnett, O *et al* eds (1979) *Sex Role Stereotyping* Tavistock: London
Hunt, P (1980) *Gender and Class Consciousness* Macmillan: London
MacDonald, M (1981) Schooling and the reproduction of class and gender relations *in* Dale *et al*
Middleton, C (1974) Sexual inequality and stratification theory *in* Parkin
Parkin, F ed (1974) *The Social Analysis of Class Structure* Tavistock: London
Perkins, T (1979) Rethinking stereotypes *in* Barrett
Viaene, N (1979) Sex differences in explanations of success and failure *in* Hartnett *et al*
Walker, S and Barton, L eds (1983) *Gender, Class and Education* Falmer Press: Lewes
Willis, P (1977) *Learning to Labour* Saxon House: Farnborough

9. Educational opportunities for girls in Malaysian secondary schools

Fatimah Hamid Don

Summary: Educational opportunities for girls in Malaysia have increased tremendously since the country achieved its independence in 1957. The quantitative expansion of the national education system provided opportunities to a greater number of pupils; enrolment figures over the decades showed that girls were not left behind in availing themselves of this new opportunity. Imbalances in the male-female enrolment at the primary levels which existed in the early 1950s were almost completely eliminated by the 1970s with the implementation of the policy of free, universal primary education and the practice of automatic promotions and policies aimed at minimizing the dropout rates.

At the secondary level, although access is non-discriminatory to girls, the remnants of traditional attitudes among parents and among the girls themselves have resulted in a slightly lower (5 per cent) proportion of girls being enrolled in secondary schools as compared with boys. The access of girls to the vocational secondary schools is limited by the lack of appropriate facilities and diversity in the vocational courses offered. In both the Government and private vocational schools, girls tended to gravitate towards traditionally recognized female vocational courses. Research studies indicate that the vocational preferences of girls are gradually widening with greater opportunities.

The academic schools provide no curricular differentiation for boys and girls. With the exception of home science courses and certain sports and co-curricular activities, the rest of the curriculum is standard and uniform.

Religious schools show higher enrolment of girls than of boys. This may be interpreted as reflecting certain preferences in the role of women and of societal values of some groups.

Opportunities in university education are generally available to those who aspire to and have acquired the necessary qualifications for university entrance. Limitations are posed by the capacity of existing institutions and the financial standing of the candidates. Participation rates of girls in tertiary education are about one-third of the total enrolment. A preponderance of girls is found in the arts and humanities, education, law, medicine and dentistry. There is evidence that some universities impose a limit on the number of women to be admitted. With the expansion of vocational schools and polytechnics with a wider range of course offerings, it is envisaged that women will gradually break away from the traditionally 'female' studies.

The Malaysian context

Malaysia is a federation of 13 states, comprising 11 states in Peninsula

Malaysia and two states in the northern part of the island of Borneo or Kalimantan. A Federal Territory makes up the fourteenth entity within the federation. The country has a population of approximately 14.3 million (1980 estimate) with an annual growth rate of 2.6 per cent. The population is cosmopolitan, with the indigenous communities (Malays and other Bumiputras[1]) comprising 54 per cent of the population, the Chinese 34 per cent, the Indians (including Sri Lankans, Bangladeshis and Pakistanis) 9 per cent, and the remaining 2 per cent comprising the Europeans and Eurasians, Indonesians, Philippinos and other Asian communities. The female/male ratio is approximately 98.3 females for every 100 males on average (1979 estimates).

The independent state of Malaysia (originally known as the Federation of Malaya) came into existence in 1957; prior to this the geographical area constituted the British Straits Settlements, the Malay Sultanates and the Colonies. Politically, Malaysia is a democracy with a parliamentary system of government. The Constitution provides for a Head of State (the Yang Di Pertuan Agong), the Senate (Dewan Negara) and the House of Representatives (Dewan Rakyat). The members of the House of Representatives are elected once every five years. The present government is a coalition of the main ethnic political parties collectively known as the National Front. The Yang Di Pertuan Agong is elected once every five years from among the nine Malay Sultans who, together with the four Governors of the former colonies and the Straits Settlements, form the Council of Rulers.

The official language is Bahasa Malaysia,[2] with English and Chinese as the next most widely used languages in education and commerce. Islam is the official religion, but other religions are widely practised. Christians make up 7 per cent of the population, Hindus 7 per cent and Buddhists 17 per cent. There are other religious sects as well as those who practise animism.

The indigenous population is by and large concentrated in the rural areas and comprises mainly agricultural workers and fisherfolks. The Chinese and Indians, descendants of earlier immigrants, live in urban areas and are engaged in commerce and industry and in the tin mines and rubber estates. The government's development policy is seeking to restructure the Malaysian society to eliminate the identification of ethnic groups with economic function and to eradicate economic imbalances characterizing the Malaysian economy.

About 33.9 per cent of the population of Peninsula Malaysia is located in the urban areas and about 66.1 per cent in the rural areas. By 1990 the urban population is expected to increase to about 42 per cent of the total population.

The age structure of the population indicates extreme youthfulness, with 42 per cent in the 0-14 age group. Married women between the ages of 15 and 49 are estimated to be 14 per cent of the population. The marriage system varies from the Westernized approach of choosing one's own mate to a basically traditional and conservative approach where the parents arrange for a suitable partner. The traditional pattern of marriage is still prevalent in the rural areas. Malay marriages are conducted in accordance with Islamic laws, while traditional Chinese and Indian marriages are registered under civil law.

The major features of the education system

The formal education system has a pyramidal structure with 95 per cent of the age cohort in the primary school, 82.8 per cent in the lower secondary schools, 38.8 per cent at upper secondary level, 9.1 per cent at post-secondary and 1.65 at university level. The school system has a 6-3-2-2 structure: six years of primary education, three years of lower secondary (comprehensive) education, two years of upper secondary education and two to three years of post-secondary education. Vocational and technical education at the upper secondary level constitutes only 4.6 per cent of the total enrolment at this level.

The main language of instruction at all levels is Bahasa Malaysia. Only in the vernacular primary schools are Chinese and Tamil used as languages of instruction. English is taught as a compulsory second language from the first year of schooling in all national schools, while Chinese, Tamil, Arabic and other foreign languages are taught as third language options in a number of schools.

A common content curriculum, centrally planned and developed by the Ministry of Education, is used throughout all national and national-type schools.[3] The school syllabuses lead to common public examinations at the end of the lower secondary level, the upper secondary level and the post-secondary level.

Access to education

The formal education system gives every child, regardless of sex, the right to nine years of basic education up to the age of 15-plus. Pupils enter the primary school at the age of six-plus and primary education is provided free to all. Automatic promotion ensures that everyone, in theory, completes nine years of schooling. In practice, a sizeable proportion of dropouts has been reported. To reduce the incidence of dropouts, which was reported to be as high as 40 per cent among girls in the rural areas (Ministry of Education, 1973), a number of facilities and provisions have been made. These include residential schools for rural children, the award of scholarships to needy pupils at the secondary level, a textbook loan scheme introduced in 1975 to provide basic learning facility to pupils from the low income group, and supplementary feeding programmes in schools to improve the health of rural children and their performance in schools. Compulsory schooling has not yet been enforced, but has repeatedly been recommended by concerned groups.[4]

The decade 1970 to 1980 saw a tremendous expansion of educational facilities. During this period primary school enrolment increased by 19.5 per cent, lower secondary enrolment by 87.7 per cent and upper secondary enrolment by 143.2 per cent.[5] Vocational and technical education increased by 272.2 per cent (Government of Malaysia, 1981-85: 345-6). The participation rates of girls increased phenomenally: statistics show a difference of only 3 to 4 per cent between males and females of the relevant age-groups enrolled at the appropriate school levels.

Post-Independence development of the educational system provides every child, regardless of race or sex, with the right to nine years of basic education as defined by the schools system. To ensure that this right is used by parents, education is provided free in the first six years — after which a nominal fee is charged for the lower secondary levels. Promotion through the grades is automatic, so that no child is retained at any grade level except by parental consent and at the teachers' discretion, and no child can be dismissed from school either because of failure or frequent absence.

The lower secondary level has been designed to cater for a variety of abilities and aptitudes. The level is characterized by what is known as the 'comprehensive' system whereby, along with 'core courses' aimed at providing a basic education, children may take elective courses of a pre-vocational nature.[6] In this way, whether the child is good with his head or with his hands, he has the opportunity to complete the nine years of universal education which the system provides.

Enrolment ratios of girls and boys

The percentage of the relevant age-groups enrolled at the various levels of the educational structure for 1979 is given as follows:

Levels	Age-Groups	Enrolment (%)
Primary education	6-11+	95.6%
Lower secondary education	12-14+	82.8%
Upper secondary education	15-16+	38.8%
Post-secondary education	17-18+	9.1%
University level education	19-24+	1.6%

(Source: *Educational Statistics of Malaysia 1976-1979*, Ministry of Education, 1980)

Table 1. *Enrolment rates by age-groups at various educational levels, 1979*

The participation rate of girls compared with that of boys at each educational level is given in Table 2.

Level of education	Enrolment		
	Males %	*Females %*	*Total*
Primary education			
Standard 1	51.24	48.76	286 348
Standard 2	51.26	48.74	284 807
Standard 3	51.24	48.75	273 162
Standard 4	51.08	48.92	266 882
Standard 5	51.36	48.64	273 881
Standard 6	51.53	48.47	263 437
Lower secondary education			
Remove class assisted schools	52.50	47.50	71 497
Form I	52.25	47.75	219 518
Form II	52.29	47.71	198 268
Form III	52.17	47.83	192 710
Upper secondary			
Form IV	52.49	47.51	102 088
Form V	51.59	48.41	100 354
Post-secondary education			
Form VI (Assisted schools)	51.03	48.97	22 702
Form VI (TAR college)	59.66	40.34	3 713
Teacher training institutions	54.53	45.47	10 965
Colleges and polytechnics	67.77	37.23	12 501
University level education			
University of Malaya	59.43	40.57	8 480
Science University of Malaysia	65.59	34.41	2 752
National University of Malaysia	64.76	35.24	4 968
Agricultural University	73.96	26.04	3 221
University of Technology	77.27	22.73	3 607

(Source: *Educational Statistics of Malaysia 1976-1979.* Ministry of Education, EPRD The Government Press, 1980).

Table 2. *Enrolment by grade level of education, 1979*

There have been phenomenal increases in school enrolments over the decades after Independence. The increased participation of girls pointed to the changing attitudes of parents of all communities with regard to the school education of girls. This change in attitudes was brought about by the fact that more educational facilities are being provided and that fewer parents now have to make the choice of whether to educate sons or daughters when there are limited financial resources and facilities for educating their children.

This change in attitudes has been well documented in statistics and by the study made by Singh (1967). She pointed out that in the early post-war years (1946-47), when Asian traditions emphasized the importance of boys as potential breadwinners, the enrolment ratio in schools was 306 girls for every 1,000 boys (at a time when the population sex ratio was 891 : 1,000). The Malay community had the lowest ratio, 123 girls enrolled per 1,000 boys, while the Chinese and Indians showed a slightly better ratio. Wastage was high and the award of free places favoured boys over girls. Subsequent development saw a remarkable change in the pattern of statistics. In 1966, the ratio of girls was 874 per 1,000 boys in the primary schools and 608 girls per 1,000 boys in the secondary schools in 1966. Now, among the Malay community, the ratio of girls to boys in Malay schools is 900 : 1,000, and similar increases are apparent in the ratio of girls to boys in the Chinese and Indian communities.

Equality is still far from being attained. The dropout rates from Standard 6 and the first year of secondary schooling were found to be higher among girls than among boys. A paper on educational wastage submitted to UNESCO in 1966 reported that 37 per cent of girls as against 30 per cent of boys dropped out in 1965 and 35 per cent of girls as against 27 per cent of boys failed to continue schooling in 1966 (UNESCO, 1966).

Among the reasons given in the report for the high dropout rates among the girls were parental attitudes, especially 'where the parents themselves are illiterates and/or conservative'. This discrepancy, however, was 'not as serious as it used to be'. The latest statistics on dropout rates showed that there is now a great reduction in dropout rates for both boys and girls, due to governmental policy which included the provision of residential schools, a textbook loan scheme, and support for low income families (free uniforms, shoes, meals, etc).

The gap between participation rates of girls and boys has narrowed considerably. There is now, on average, a difference of 2 per cent between the enrolment of boys and girls at every level of schooling as can be seen in Table 2 (see page 114). The gap gradually widens at the post-secondary and tertiary levels, where the difference may be as high as 10 per cent. At the university level, the proportion of girls to boys is about half, especially in the newer universities — namely, the Agricultural, Science and Technology universities. This is due to the recruitment policies of these institutions, which restrict the participation of girls in certain courses and impose a ceiling for girls in other areas of study.[7]

Another interesting feature is the participation of girls in religious (Islamic) schools. The enrolment in religious schools, administered by the Ministry of Education in 1979 in the various States, showed a larger percentage of girls than boys in almost every case, as may be seen in Table 3 (see p 116).

The data seem to suggest that there are many Muslim parents today who value a religious education for their daughters over a secular one. Some of the reasons commonly given were the following: girls would one day become mothers and would have to shoulder the responsibility of providing their children with a religious upbringing; a religious home is a more harmonious one; with religious education, girls are less likely to be wayward; they make 'better' wives in the sense that they are well-versed

Selected states	Enrolment		
	Males	*Females*	*Total*
Perlis	181	232	413
P Pinang	221	300	521
Selangor	144	155	299
N Sembilan	120	192	312
Melaka	251	395	646
Johor	85	123	208
Trengganu	284	348	632
Kelantan	140	356	496

(Source: Educational Statistics of Malaysia (1976-1979), Ministry of Education, 1979)

Table 3. *Enrolment of boys and girls in religious schools, 1979*

in the duties and responsibilities towards their husbands and their off-spring as required by Islam. Another reason is the reluctance of some parents to allow their daughters to enrol in co-educational schools where activities are participated in jointly by girls and boys. Such 'free' mixing is thought to be socially and morally unhealthy for the girls.

Age-group (in years)	Number (000)	Educational attainment							
		No schooling		*Primary*		*Lower secondary*		*Upper secondary*	
		M%	F%	M%	F%	M%	F%	M%	F%
5 - 9	1,781.1	38	39	62	61	:	:	:	:
10 - 14	1,630.5	4	5	57	58	39	37	:	:
15 - 19	1,484.6	5	8	19	24	40	36	36	32
20 - 29	2,298.2	8	15	35	42	26	19	31	24
30 - 39	1,534.9	13	32	52	49	16	9	19	10
40 - 49	1,090.6	25	58	57	35	8	4	10	3
50 - 59	731.0	37	75	54	21	4	2	5	1
60 and over	741.9	56	90	38	9	3	1	3	1
5 and over	11,292.8	19	32	46	42	20	16	15	11

(Source: Preliminary 1980 Census Returns, Department of Statistics, Malaysia, 1983)

Table 4. *Percentage distribution of the population by highest educational attainment, age-group and sex, 1980*

The progress of women in utilizing the educational opportunities offered by the national education system over the years may be seen in Table 4. The participation rates of boys and girls in the younger age-groups, namely five to nine and 10 to 14, are more or less equal. However, among the older age-groups, the gap between males and females widens considerably. For instance, it is evident that there is a higher illiteracy rate among women than among men in the age-groups above 20. Women with primary education only outnumber men in the 15 to 29 age-groups, indicating that not as many women as men proceeded to secondary education, and in the older age-groups there are even fewer women with primary education as compared with men.

At the secondary educational level, only 19 per cent of the women in the 20 to 29 age-group attained a lower secondary education as compared with 26 per cent of the males; 31 per cent of males attained the upper secondary level as opposed to 24 per cent of females. The percentages are progressively smaller for the women of the older age-groups. It could be seen that only 19 per cent of women in the 30 to 39 age-group, and 7 per cent of the 40 to 49 age-group, had secondary education (lower or upper).

With the present trend of participation among the younger age-groups it would be expected that, in a decade or two, the discrepancy between the educational levels attained by men and women will gradually diminish as women participate on equal terms with the men under conditions of equal opportunity within the educational system.

Some limitations to girls' opportunities

Despite the attitudinal change towards formal education for girls, and the expansion of educational facilities, there are still a number of factors that may hinder the full participation of girls in formal education. Low family income may force the girls to leave school earlier in order to work and supplement the family income or to assist the mother in household work, if she is gainfully employed elsewhere. There are also some conservative parents who would prefer single-sex schools for their daughters, once they have attained the age of puberty. Most schools, however, are co-educational. Having to attend a co-educational school may deter some girls from continuing their secondary education. Many would prefer to enrol in religious schools where males and females are generally segregated.

The Table on page 118 shows the number of boys' schools, girls' schools and co-educational schools in the states of Peninsula Malaysia in 1981. The number of co-educational schools clearly outnumbers the single-sex schools, many of which are, in fact, predominantly boys' schools with co-educational sixth-form classes.

Other persistent deterrents include low parental educational level, distance from home to school, traditional perceptions of parents, early marriage, relative poverty levels, and the preferences of girls themselves regarding their roles. Many girls in the rural areas, for instance, do not continue their upper secondary formal education but prefer to gain employment as factory workers in multinational corporations. There is still a widespread belief that education for a girl should be a stop gap measure until she is suitably married off or reaches a point when she decides to become a homemaker. As many a prospective mate today would prefer a girl with some education (but not too high), parents see to it that the opportunities provided by the system are utilized accordingly.

The curriculum for general education makes no provision for sex differences; such provision might be construed by some as discriminatory. However, in many girls' schools domestic science, cookery and handicraft are subjects taught at the lower secondary level. In the comprehensive school system the prevocational options for girls include commerce, secretarial courses, book-keeping, home science and agricultural science. Those for boys include mechanical and woodwork, construction and electrical engineering.

To some extent there are parents who feel that the basic school curriculum is unsuitable for girls in their potential role as homemakers. These parents may choose to terminate their daughters' schooling after the primary or lower secondary level and seek alternatives in non-formal education or in religious institutions.

State	All-boys schools	All-girls schools	Co-Ed schools	Total
Johor	4	12	96	112
Kedah	2	8	66	76
Kelantan	2	4	65	71
Melaka	3	8	33	44
Negeri Sembilan	3	4	43	50
Pahang	1	3	68	72
Perak	6	14	102	122
Perlis	—	1	14	15
P Pinang	7	15	36	58
Selangor	3	8	73	84
Trengganu	—	—	33	33
West Persekutuan	10	15	26	51

(Source: *List of Assisted Schools, 1981.* Prepared by the Educational Planning and Research Division, Ministry of Education)

Table 5. *Boys', girls' and co-educational schools in Peninsula Malaysia*

Opportunities in vocational education

Statistics pertaining to the participation of girls in vocational secondary schools are incomplete. There are presently 25 vocational secondary schools (Sekolah Menengah Vokesyenal) in Peninsula Malaysia of which four are all-girls schools. These schools are characterized by their curricular offerings, namely home science or home economics.

The following tables shows the participation rates of boys and girls in secondary vocational schools for the years 1968 and 1975.

Type of school	Enrolment 1968			Enrolment 1975		
	M%	F%	Total	M%	F%	Total
Assisted vocational schools	87	13	999	73	27	7,807
Private vocational schools	40	60	7,601	28	72	9,657

Source: *Educational Statistics of Malaysia* (1974-75) Ministry of Education (1975)

Table 6. *Secondary vocational schools and enrolment by sex, 1968 and 1975*

It is clearly seen that opportunities were limited for girls in the government-assisted schools in the last two decades. A higher proportion of girls than boys were enrolled in private schools — as much as 72 per cent of the enrolment of these institutions were girls. The reverse is the case with the government-assisted vocational schools, where girls constituted only 27 per cent in 1975.

The enrolment according to the various training courses in the commercial or private schools is given in the table below:

Courses	Boys %	Girls %	Total numbers
Shorthand	2.1	97.9	1.356
Trengkas (Malay language)	8.0	92.0	573
Typing	13.9	86.1	4,048
Book-keeping	47.6	52.4	2,843
Private secretaryship	—	100	593
Accounts	57.8	42.2	1,197
Accountancy (ACA)	59.6	40.4	459
Telephone operator	6.4	93.6	31
English	48.5	51.5	237
Bahasa Malaysia	60.6	39.4	203

(Data obtained from the Selangor State Education Department, 1977)

Table 7. *Enrolment in various courses by sex in private schools*

The above data seemed to support the view expressed by Gerhold (1971) that the utilization of educational facilities by women tended to be complementary to that by men, that is to say, that female participation decreased when the male utilization of economically advantageous education was higher. Women generally tended to be high users of the less economically advantageous educational opportunities.

Vocational training opportunities are also provided by Majlis Amanah Rakyat (MARA — a trustee organization for increasing the participation of indigenous peoples in development). Courses ranging from 18 months to two years are aimed at developing vocational skills for self-employment or work in the public and private sectors. The trainees are provided with accommodation, food, and allowances. There is an intake of 1,200 to 1,300 trainees annually.

While no discrimination is intended, a breakdown of the selected candidates for 1978 and 1979 shows a low percentage of girls (15.3 per cent). This reflects clearly the male bias in selection, in the range of courses offered, in the facilities (eg accommodation) provided. There is also an over-subscription of females in courses perceived as suitable for girls, ie sewing, hairdressing, secretarial and handicrafts.

An interesting study conducted by Goon (1975) on the vocational preferences of Form Five girls revealed that over 90 per cent of those surveyed wished to pursue higher education or some special training for employment. The leading preference was accountancy. The girls did not seem to hold extreme views on home-making and career roles but were prepared to assume dual roles if required. The parents as a whole regarded the career role of girls as equal in importance to that of boys.

Goon (1975) observed: 'Recalling that the majority of the mothers are full-time housewives . . . it illustrates the attitude changes that have occurred within the country in recent decades . . . Women who are largely housewives believed that the full-time paid employment of females is important, more important than their husbands believed it to be.'

In an analysis of the views of the various ethnic groups, it was found that the Malay girls have the highest mean level of educational aspirations, followed closely by the Chinese and Indians. This led Goon to conclude that the Malays, 'with a cultural background that traditionally manifested greater respect and freedom for the individuality of women' have provided an extremely favourable climate for the acceptance of the expanding roles of the educated female (see also Swift, 1963).

The study by Goon also found that 92 per cent of her subjects aspire to some form of vocational or specialized training after their upper secondary education. Fifty-seven per cent planned to undertake professional or college level education and 14.3 per cent aspired to seek university level education. In terms of professional preferences, the top four professions are accountancy, nursing, teaching and medicine. While the study discovered that there was a 'slight broadening of the range of preferences and trends of an increase in non-traditional female vocations' the reality showed that educated girls still orientate largely towards professional and clerical jobs.

Conclusion

The broad national educational policy in Malaysia is aimed at providing every individual with the right to an education that would contribute to and accelerate national development and growth economically, culturally, socially, and politically. The eradication of poverty, the elimination of economic imbalances between the communities and ethnic groups, and the fostering of national unity have become the main foci of all development policies, including that of education. Under the umbrella of national development plans, women have been accorded special recognition as having an important role to play. Women have therefore enjoyed access to as many educational and training opportunities as there are facilities, not just in proportion to the sex-ratio of the population but even more generously in order to supplement the shortage of available male resources in many instances.

However, in the implementation of specific policies, not all decision-makers are sympathetic or emancipated with regard to the status of women. Certain plans failed to take into account the full participation of women, for example, in the planning of vocational institutes and polytechnics. Some individuals who were in charge of implementing specific programmes made the assumption that women were to be excluded or needed only to be represented by a token few. The National Council of Women's Organizations had on many occasions stressed the need to have women in charge of decision-making bodies and implementing bodies.

There has been no in-depth study of the extent to which sexism prevails in the school curriculum. The portrayal of stereotypes in textbooks or by the teachers themselves is frequent and there has been little pressure to forbid or eliminate them. However, the language of instruction, Bahasa Malaysia, is non-discriminatory in the sense that pronouns are common for both the sexes and so the process of translating from English to Bahasa serves to eliminate some of the sex identification, except by the most facetious of translators. And then again what may be regarded as sexism in Western societies may not be deemed so in the Asian or in the Islamic context. A consensus on the concept of equality between men's and women's role is still being sought. The establishment of the National Council for the Integration of Women in Development (NACIWID) within the Implementation Co-ordination Unit of the Prime Minister's Department in 1975 is seen as a positive step in advancing the status of women and combating practices which discriminate against them.

Notes

1 Literally means 'sons of the soil'. This is the official term used collectively for all the indigenous peoples of the Malay Peninsula and the Territories of Sabah and Sarawak. The descendants of the immigrant settlers, namely the Chinese, Indians and Eurasians, are excluded except in cases of inter-marriages with male Bumiputras.

2   Also known as the Malay language, Bahasa Malaysia has considerable sim-
    ilarities with Bahasa Indonesia having evolved from the same parent language,
    Bahasa Melayu Riau. An intergovernmental Committee comprising language
    and education experts from Malaysia and Indonesia, meets regularly to seek
    greater uniformity between the two languages.
3   These refer to Government-aided primary schools where the medium of
    instruction is not in the national language. Transition from the Chinese
    medium and Tamil medium National-Type Primary schools into the National
    Secondary schools is provided through a system of Remove Classes of one-
    year duration where intensive instruction in the Bahasa Malaysia is given.
4   The National Council of Women's Organizations (NCWO) has made this
    recommendation on several occasions. A Mid-Decade Seminar of the Inter-
    national Decade for Women organized by the NCWO reiterated this
    recommendation, among several others.
5   The raising of the school-leaving age from 11-plus to 15-plus which started in
    1965 began to take full effect by this time as more schools and classrooms
    were added.
6   The development of the Comprehensive Education System has not been up to
    expectation. The elective courses remained limited to such subjects as home
    science, secretarial courses and commerce for the girls and metalcraft, wood-
    work, electrical repairs and maintenance and agricultural science for the
    boys. The preference for academic subjects by parents and educational
    authorities alike has led to the neglect of further developments of the com-
    prehensive system. Vocational subjects became the concern of the Vocational
    Secondary Schools.
7   This was communicated to the writer by the institutions concerned in in-
    formal discussions. The International Islamic University which opened in July
    1983 in Kuala Lumpur with a pioneer batch of 132 students has women as
    about one-third of its enrolment.

References

Gerhold, Caroline Rose (1971) Factors relating to educational opportunity for
    women residents in the Malay Peninsula PhD Thesis Cornell University
    Unpublished
Goon, Ai Chin Cecelia (1975) Patterns of vocational preferences of Form Five girls
    in selected English medium schools in Selangor MEd Dissertation University of
    Malaya: Kuala Lumpur Unpublished
Government of Malaysia (1981) *The Fourth Malaysia Plan 1981-1985* Government
    Printers: Kuala Lumpur
Ministry of Education (1973) *The Dropout Study* Government Printers: Kuala
    Lumpur
Ministry of Education (1980) *Education in Malaysia* Government Printers: Kuala
    Lumpur
Ministry of Education (1982) *Educational Statistics of Malaysia: 1976-1979* Govern-
    ment Printers: Kuala Lumpur
Malaysia (1980) *Population and Households Census* Department of Statistics: Kuala
    Lumpur
Malaysia (1983) *Preliminary 1980 Census Returns* Department of Statistics: Kuala
    Lumpur
Singh Sarjit , Jasbir (1967) Equality of educational opportunity in Peninsula Malaysia
    BEd Academic Exercise University of Malaya: Kuala Lumpur Unpublished
Swift, Michael (1963) Men and women in Malay society *in Women in New Asia:
    The Changing Roles of Men and Women in South and Southeast Asia* Ed Ward,
    Barbara UNESCO: Paris
United Nations Educational Scientific and Cultural Organization (1966) *Technical
    Seminar on Educational Wastage and School Dropout* Report of Malaysia: Bangkok

10. Sex roles and secondary education in Jamaica

Marlene Hamilton and Elsa Leo-Rhynie

Summary: A brief outline of the structure of Jamaica's educational system sets the stage for a discussion of sex role differences at the secondary level of schooling. These are identified mainly through a review of local research carried out within the last decade. Differential access to secondary schooling, the part played by the school in the socialization process, and the outcomes of this socialization in terms of cognitive abilities, personality characteristics and academic attainment, are examined and discussed to reveal the implications for sex role development. Despite certain similarities between the sexes, especially in important areas such as motivation and achievement, the differences identified suggest that the active, independent male and passive, dependent female stereotypes still persist. The chapter appeals for educational targets for the development and ultimate utilization of human potential (of *both* sexes) to be stated explicitly and for these to be employed by educators in preparing all students to make a full contribution in every sphere of national life.

The contextual setting

An overview

The educational system in Jamaica has evolved from efforts to serve the needs of the island's diverse population. It consists of a number of tiers (see Figure 1), with progression from one level to the next being contingent on students' facing and clearing various selection hurdles. There are several different types of institution found at each stage — some privately funded, most owned or aided by government — and they inevitably represent a hierarchy which reflects the economic and cultural disparities existing within the Jamaican society. It is perhaps at the secondary level that this is most pronounced, for the goal of *all* Grade 6 students, their parents and teachers, is to gain one of the coveted places in a limited number of traditional high schools. Some idea of student enrolment in secondary-level institutions for 1979-80 is given in Table 1.

The Common Entrance Examination (11+) is designed to identify those who merit selection for the places available in traditional high schools and is based on an 'equal opportunity for all' policy. The examination is a formidable hurdle, since only between 20 per cent and 25 per cent of the candidates are awarded places. Results for the 1980 and 1981 examinations

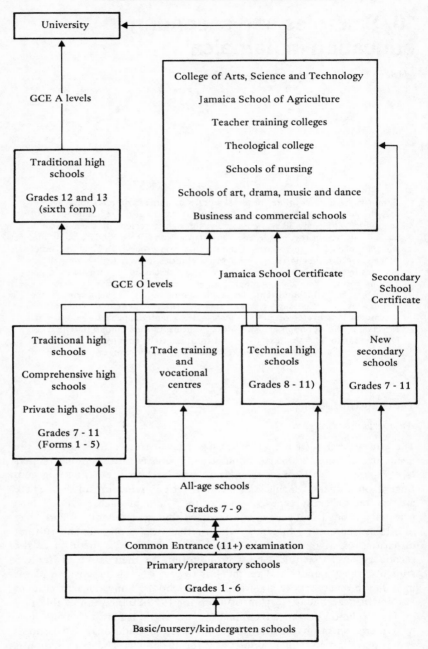

Figure 1. *The system of education in Jamaica*

Type of school	Number of institutions	Number of students		
		Male	Female	Total
Traditional high	46	21,376	30,104	51,480
Comprehensive high	5	3,271	3,824	7,095
Technical high	7	3,304	3,291	6,595
New secondary	78	50,862	49,333	100,195
Vocational/technical	2	152	250	402
All-age	455	36,543	37,205	73,748

Source: *Economic and Social Survey*, Jamaica (1980)
National Planning Agency, Kingston, Jamaica

Table 1. *Student enrolment in the secondary institutions of Jamaica (1979-1980)*

are shown in Table 2, where it is seen that, in both years, entries and awards for girls exceeded those for boys, although it is evident that a larger percentage of the male entry was afforded high school places (27 per cent and 31 per cent boys, as against 21 per cent and 24 per cent girls) in these two years.

Year	Entries			Awards		
	Total	Males	Females	Total	Males	Females
1980	38,106	13,796	24,310	8,766	3,735	5,031
1981	39,786	14,720	25,066	10,608	4,580	6,028

Source: *Statistics, Secondary High Schools* (1980, 1981)
Ministry of Education, Jamaica

Table 2. *Sex comparisons of performance in the Common Entrance examination (1980 and 1981)*

The charge that many low-performing boys are given places at the expense of higher-performing girls has been denied by the Ministry of Education (*Daily Gleaner*, 16 March 1982), but no data have been produced to support this denial. Thus, there continues to be a strong feeling among local educators that there is a sex bias in the allotment of these places. One such educator has gone so far as to point out that: 'In the case of co-educational schools with an equal allocation of boys and girls, there is some discrimination against the girls who generally perform better. It is argued, however, that the boys are later developers and hence the allocations tend to be equally dispersed between boys and girls' (Sangster, 1982). The ideological concept of equal opportunity seems, therefore, to override the available evidence.

In the light of the overriding importance of the 11+ examination outcomes, there has been, over the years, a number of locally-based researches designed to look at a range of relevant aspects. One topic which has been fairly widely explored is that of sex differences among students who are in their final year of primary education and thus about to embark upon secondary schooling. Although some significant differences have been noted, by and large the sexes appear to be fairly similar in respect of those variables which have been considered. Isaacs (1975) found, for example, that boys and girls did not differ significantly in their performance on Piaget-style tasks of conservation of length, area, quantity or displaced volume. However, boys were superior to girls at conserving internal volume (p < .01) and water levels (p < .001), while girls, surprisingly, performed better on conservation of weight (p < .05). Isaacs has explained this last-mentioned finding thus: 'The girls go to buy things which are weighed out on scales a great deal more often than do the boys' (1975: 15).

Roach (1978) reported no significant difference between the sexes on Witkin's test of field independence, but the girls in his Grade 6 sample out-performed the boys on a test of mathematics. The importance of the home environment in relation to the favourable performance of girls was also evidenced from Roach's results: for this sex only, significant correlations emerged between father-presence in the home and field independence, as well as between parents' occupational level and field independence.

Even more recently, Jarrett (1983) found that boys and girls held comparable views of themselves, and were similarly motivated to achieve academically. However, girls revealed themselves to be significantly more anxious about school than boys, despite the fact that teachers demonstrated no sex bias in the expectations they had of students, nor did the students of different sexes perceive any differences in their teachers' expectations of them.

The secondary school as an agent of socialization

A number of features of both the home and school have implications for the sex role development of students of all ages, especially for the adolescent. Wong (1983) has explored the effects of father-absence on certain personality characteristics of a sample of high school boys. Although there was no significant difference between father-absent and father-present boys on measures of responsibility, self-control and aggression, those whose fathers were present in the home had more favourable opinions of women, and also had a greater tendency to view male/female relationships as a partnership than had boys from father-absent homes. The subjects who felt themselves to be female-dominated at home also expressed a strong sense of female domination at school.

The presence of male teachers in schools has, in the past, served the purpose of exposing boys to responsible male models, a feature of particular importance to those from working-class families for whom a male model in the home is a fairly uncommon feature. Unfortunately, the 'feminization' of education in Jamaica, brought about by an exodus of male teachers seeking better paid jobs, has reduced such exposure. Furthermore, as the number of men in the profession decreases, the stereotype of the teacher as female is reinforced, and this inevitably deters boys from selecting teaching as a profession.

Nowadays, the strong female presence is to be found in single-sex, as well as co-educational institutions, although 25 years ago a female teacher in a boys' school was almost unheard of. Today, the majority of secondary schools in the island are co-educational, even though the traditional high schools still boast a number of single-sex institutions among their ranks. These tend to be regarded as 'high prestige' schools, and although there has been a broadening of their curricular offerings to include business education, home economics, woodwork, metalwork and the like, their main thrust is strongly academic.

Sex differences are markedly reflected in students' choice of subjects. Boys still tend to select science subjects, and girls the arts; as a concession to the schools' rule that each student studies at least one science subject, girls also generally do biology. This feature has been aptly demonstrated by Glasgow (1978), who noted that of the 502 randomly selected Grade 11 students preparing two or more science subjects for the Cambridge examinations, 331 were boys, and 171 girls. Biology was the preferred science subject of 64.9 per cent of girls and 25.1 per cent of boys ($p < .001$), while physics was listed as the favourite subject of 40.8 per cent of boys, but only 4.1 per cent of girls ($p < .001$). Even those girls planning science-based careers were interested in the ones with a biological emphasis (for example, nursing), whereas boys were more likely to select careers such as engineering, linked to the physical sciences. Hamilton (1976) recorded similar results for a sample of Grade 11 students, and in subsequent work staged at Grade 13, Hamilton (1981) provided further proof of academic bias (arts/sciences) related to sex. Leo-Rhynie's (1978) investigation, while containing corroborative evidence, showed, however, that the girls/arts link was more marked than that of the boys/sciences at this level.

Male/female differences in the vocational subjects studied by those students attending technical high schools are readily evident, there being a strong inclination of girls toward secretarial and home economics courses, and of boys towards industrial offerings, as well as to the accounts side of business education. The same trend holds for the new secondary schools, where work experience programmes allow students a three-week exposure to the practical skills needed in real job situations. Table 3 reveals the registration of final year students in this programme by sex and vocational area for 1979-80 and 1980-81.

There are, admittedly, no overt measures taken to channel students into sex-appropriate curriculum areas, yet local research has shown that there are a number of covert influences at work — part of the 'hidden curriculum'. A UNESCO document on curricular and educational and

Course	1979-80			1980-81		
	Male	Female	Total	Male	Female	Total
Agriculture	532	252	784	508	279	787
Art	16	31	47	51	66	117
Craft	313	439	752	389	271	660
Business education	254	1,655	1,774	375	1,259	1,634
Home economics	178	5,655	5,833	306	5,706	6,012
Beauty culture	—	108	108	172	173	
Child care	2	1,838	1,840	—	1,926	1,926
Clothing and textile	8	1,640	1,648	5	1,664	1,669
Food and nutrition	168	2,068	2,237	300	1,944	2,244
Industrial/technical	6,484	134	6,618	6,121	136	6,257
Auto mechanics	792	42	834	855	51	906
Carpentry and cabinet making	1,773	3	1,776	1,692	2	1,694
Drafting	86	19	105	138	18	156
Electrical installation	1,904	62	1,966	1,604	53	1,657
Farm mechanics	24	—	24	17	—	17
Machine shop and welding	1,517	5	1,522	1,433	12	1,445
Plumbing and pipe fitting	388	3	391	382	—	382
Total	7,777	8,031	15,808	7,747	7,841	15,588

Source: Ministry of Education Statistics Section, Kingston, Jamaica

Table 3. *Grade 11 Students in Work Experience Programme by Course and Sex, 1979-80 and 1980-81*

training standards for boys and girls in secondary schools reports answers to questions probing sex differences in the selection of subject areas by each sex: 'There is a tendency for boys (or girls) to choose more masculine (or feminine) subjects as this is the traditional approach' (UNESCO, 1978: 13). This 'traditional approach' was said to reflect 'social expectations at work'. Other investigations have highlighted the effect of factors such as attitudes transmitted by parents, teachers and other students, the portrayal of sex stereotyping in textbooks, and even subtle variations in provisions found in certain schools, which, in various ways, affect subject choice. To give an example, Hamilton and Leo-Rhynie (1979-80) have pointed out that: 'The suggestion that any girl with ability could be hindered from doing physics at A level would be denied, yet two of the seven girls' schools in the capital city do not offer this subject' (1979-80: 53).

The implication to be drawn from such situations is that, even though sex role stereotyping may be initiated in the home, the process is reinforced throughout the entire period of schooling in many different, often insidious ways, especially in the traditional high schools. Sex role differences among students emerge as an attitude or orientation which is revealed by the use to which their education is put.

The results of socialization

One cannot overlook the possibility of biological determinism in relation to both the cognitive and personality domains; yet there is an ever-increasing body of evidence which points to the consequences of one's environment affecting the individual positively or negatively. 'Human behaviour is the product of a biological organism developing in a social context' (Griffiths and Saraga, 1979). This context affects the conscious and unconscious minds of males and females differently, and thus fashions their development and behaviour in different ways.

Cognitive concerns

Local research has tended to support well-established international findings on male/female variations in certain cognitive functions. Perhaps the most extensive investigations pertain to spatial and abstract reasoning abilities manifested at Grades 11 and 13 (the two terminal points of Jamaica's secondary school structure), as these are relevant to students' academic orientation toward the arts or sciences. Cognitive style, verbal reasoning and creativity have also been examined at these levels, although some researchers have concentrated on their measurement in lower grades.

In respect of spatial ability, Mitchelmore (1974) administered the I-D Boxes and Three Dimensional Drawing tests to Grade 9 students attending high and new secondary schools, and established boys' significant superiority to girls on both tests. This tendency might explain (at least in part) why Hamilton (1976), investigating science orientation in a randomly selected sample of 576 Grade 11 high school students, found that most of those classified as 'science-oriented' were boys, and that males in general scored markedly higher than females on the DAT Space Relations test ($p < .001$). The same trend was established for abstract reasoning ($p < .01$). A significant relationship between achievement in the sciences and these two measures existed for both sexes, while, from multiple regression analyses, abstract reasoning (for boys) and space relations (for girls) were among the best predictors of science achievement obtained. That there was such a markedly lower proportion of science oriented girls in the sample caused Hamilton (1976) to conclude: 'For girls, the picture seems less encouraging due to societal mores tending to discourage females entering scientific fields. Indications are that certain cognitive inputs are essential in fostering science orientation among girls, for example, their skill at perceiving spatial relations . . . hence it is essential for these features to be nurtured, encouraged and emphasized' 1976: 344.

In Leo-Rhynie's (1978) research the male/female differences in spatial ability and abstract reasoning identified by Hamilton were shown to persist at a higher educational level (Grade 13). Her findings were extended to encompass cognitive style, and, on Witkin's test of field independence, boys scored significantly higher than girls ($p < .001$). When the sample of 203 students was partitioned according to subject emphasis (arts/sciences), Leo-Rhynie established that the science-emphasis group (comprised mainly of boys) gained significantly higher scores than their arts-emphasis counterparts (the large majority of whom were girls) on all three cognitive measures. She also found that abstract reasoning proved to be a contributor to success in the Cambridge A level examinations for the science-emphasis group, while field dependence operated similarly for arts-emphasis subjects. In the light of these outcomes, Leo-Rhynie pointed out that: 'Recognition of the importance of the analytic thinking skills in effective functioning at this level renders imperative the fostering of their development (in girls as well as boys), as they are not merely necessary for examination success but are also essential for coping with life in a dynamic society. (Unfortunately) the development in girls of the intellectual skills traditionally associated with masculine interests has been regarded as a defiance of the "appropriate" feminine role' (1978: 289-90).

There has not been a great deal of local reseach reported on verbal abilities, perhaps because of the unavailability of suitable instruments. However, Parchment (1982), in exploring factors related to achievement in modern languages, did administer the DAT Verbal Reasoning test to a sample of 162 Grade 11 students. A marked relationship between this variable and achievement in Spanish was established for girls, whilst for boys, an inverse, non-significant correlation was reported. Parchment further showed that verbal reasoning correlated significantly with girls' aptitude for learning a foreign language; but, in the case of boys, the two significant relations emerging in this area (verbal reasoning with motivation and academic self-concept) were both inverse. Her explanation of these outcomes was that: 'In Jamaican schools, Spanish is generally thought of as a "feminine" subject, and as such, one finds more girls than boys taking the subject, possibly because they feel this is expected of them' (1982: 85). Parchment therefore drew attention to the necessity of cultivating in boys a positive attitude to Spanish, and of developing their motivation to study this subject at the same time, partly by removing the sex bias attached to it. She also emphasized the importance of teaching some amount of English grammar along with Spanish, for, in her opinion, a knowledge of linguistic constructs and analogies could meaningfully be applied to the study of modern languages.

The final cognitive factor considered — creativity — is one whose exploration within a formal research setting is quite new to Jamaica. Of particular relevance is Edwards' (1982) work on the relationship between creativity (both fluency and originality dimensions) and subject orientation at Grade 11 of high school. As in earlier investigations, Edwards ascertained that some 70 per cent of the girls in her sample of 275 students were oriented toward the arts, while 55 per cent of the boys (albeit a lower proportion) could be classified as science-oriented. She went on to demonstrate that girls displaying an arts bias performed relatively better on a battery of creativity tests than the other students (especially science-oriented males), this being particularly marked for the originality dimension of the Circles test, and on verbal measures such as the Remote Associates test of creativity.

Further evidence of what Edwards considered to be a predisposition toward the arts or sciences appeared through a field independence/sciences orientation relationship on the one hand, as against a field dependence/ arts orientation link associated with the verbal side of creativity, on the other. Based on these outcomes (and especially on the absence of significant correlates of creativity for science-oriented students), Edwards opined that: '. . . early subject specialization in Jamaican high schools imposes several restrictions to the development of creative talent, originality and inventiveness' (1982: 126). This was especially the case in science-based fields of study. This, she felt, strongly reflects the fact that from an early stage (even Grade 7 in instances), boys are: 'channelled into the sciences (where they inevitably become more convergent in their mental functioning), and girls are encouraged to pursue the arts' (1982: 127).

Hamilton (1982a) narrowed Edwards' concerns to focus specifically on qualitative differences in creativity. Having discerned the absence of significant differences in fluency, flexibility and originality between a sample of 247 Grade 11 girls and boys in the Circles test, she proceeded to examine the content of the drawings. The unequivocal outcome was that boys made a significantly greater contribution than girls to two of eight categories of drawings defined: 'scientific/technical/mechanical' and 'sports/games'. Girls, on the other hand, scored higher on the remaining categories, but only in the case of 'life' (representations of animate beings or their parts) was this markedly greater than for boys.

Hamilton argued that the different modes of socialization accorded to girls and boys were being demonstrated in a corresponding development of interests along culturally prescribed lines. In her opinion, qualitative variations in the pattern of creative performance displayed by each sex reflected the pervasive effects of sex role stereotyping on these students. Such a situation was felt to be untenable, for: 'Where school and society attempt to prescribe stereotyped behaviours which are "acceptable" for each sex, and where sex roles are internalized to the extent that they even appear in innocuous situations such as the Circles Test, there is cause for concern' (1982a: 131).

The personality domain

A recent concern of educators has been the number of Jamaican youth involved in acts of vandalism, violence, and general anti-social behaviour. This has prompted investigation into the degree of alienation experienced by young people in general, and the different sexes in particular. Two separate studies on alienation at the secondary school level were conducted. Although no significant sex differences emerged, one researcher, Degazon-Johnson (1983) was able to identify differences in the methods employed by each sex in demonstrating this behaviour; for example, the high incidence of teenage mothers indicated one way in which girls manifested their alienation from society. Gordon (1983), in her study of the incidence of problems experienced by Jamaican adolescents, corroborates the existence of the motherhood problem but she attributes it to a lack of security and search for independence being manifested by these girls.

Several other local investigators have examined whether aspects of personality bear an apparent relation to sex. At Grade 11, Hamilton (1976) noted significant differences in favour of males on measures of convergency, authoritarianism and social introversion, while Cameron (1982) found that females were more extraverted and neurotic, and, at the same time, more anxious about school (although not significantly so) than males. He also reported a significant correlation between school anxiety and neuroticism for girls (p < .01), but found no such relation for boys.

It would seem that the differential effects of socialization on the personality, which can be observed by the time students have completed Grade 11, are even more strongly apparent among those young people who are motivated to enter Grades 12 and 13 to do further studies. Morris (1978) demonstrated that at Grade 13, girls were significantly more extraverted (p < .01) and neurotic (p < .01) than boys (these results providing earlier evidence of Cameron's Grade 11 trend); while Stokes (1983) found females displaying stronger attitudes to religion, more favourable opinions of church, and a stronger belief in God, the Bible and life after death, than did males investigated. Stokes' findings agree with certain aspects of Bell's (1981) on character development. Bell ascertained that, although males scored significantly higher on her measure of character than females (p < .05), the shaping of girls' character was much more strongly affected by environmental inputs such as the influence of religion. The impact of religious influences has also surfaced in Richardson's (1980) identity study and Sinanan's (1983) investigation of control orientation.

Motivation has received quite a bit of attention at the local level, and research findings have generally pointed to boys' superiority in this area. There are, however, so many intervening variables to be considered when studying motivation that one must exercise caution when attempting to draw inferences from such findings. Figueroa (1976), in researching achievement value-orientation among a sample of Grade 8 boys, discovered a strong socio-economic status (SES) input at work, for it was those of the higher social stratum who were, in fact, high on his criterion measure. Ragbir (1975) similarly established a high SES/high motivation link which persisted when he broke down his motivation variable into its different components (for example, academic initiative, need for achievement and academic self-concept).

However, Jackson's (1979) study of need achievement among a sample of girls attending different types of secondary schools gave the opposite results; for those of the upper and upper-middle strata gained the lowest need achievement (N-Ach) scores. A possible explanation offered was that: 'The high school (typically middle and upper class) girls, see that their future lies in the security of marriage at an early date . . . (so that) marriage, motherhood and the homemaker role is more important than a career . . . On the other hand, the working class student attending the 'low status' school realizes that she has to make her own way in this society' (1979: 206-7).

At Grade 13, global measures of motivation do not effectively discriminate between the sexes. However, it has been established that on certain specific dimensions such as vocational aspirations, male students are seemingly much more likely to register higher scores (Leo-Rhynie, 1978). Vocational aspirations have also been shown to affect students' attitudes to specific subject areas — for example, Campbell (1980) reported that Grade 10 girls were more favourably disposed towards business studies than boys, and likewise, held stronger vocational aspirations in respect of this area of the curriculum. Hamilton (1982b) similarly discovered that both male and female Grade 13 students who planned to pursue the sciences at university held more favourable attitudes to science than did their peers specializing in other fields. Of particular interest was the finding that science-oriented Grade 13 girls held more favourable attitudes to science than their male counterparts! In light of this result, she concluded that attitudes appear to play a more vital role where girls are concerned (at least for the sciences), and has thus strongly supported the earlier stand of Hamilton and Leo-Rhynie (1979-1980) that: 'It is not sufficient to make equal educational provisions for students of different sexes: a change is needed in the attitudes and prejudices which have persisted through many generations, and which many people hold without being fully aware of . . . Girls must be encouraged at home and school to develop a sense of responsibility and independence, to think analytically, and to question issues rather than to accept passively: in this way they can develop the interest, competence, and confidence to be successful in careers which have traditionally been closed to them' (1979-1980: 55).

Academic performance

The tangible product of the educational process is performance in terminal examinations. Despite criticisms of this criterion, it is the yardstick employed by society to assess the use to which students have put their school years, their aptitude for certain occupations, and their ability to benefit from further education. In Jamaica, tertiary education has always been made available to both sexes, so the incentive for those who are academically highly motivated and who display the ability is offered without sex bias by society. That male and female students perform well enough to take advantage of this opportunity is attested to by local researchers, who report no significant difference between boys and girls on a Cambridge A level examination (Leo-Rhynie, 1978; Morris, 1978). However, at O levels (Grade 11), Seaton (1980) found that her sample of girls had been successful in a larger number of subjects than boys (p < .001). Although this result suggests that girls have a wider educational base, it also points to the early specialization of boys, for whom this may be indicative of a definite sense of vocational purpose. As mentioned previously, Leo-Rhynie (1978) recorded a significant difference in the vocational aspirations of boys and girls preparing to sit the A level examination — boys had higher aspirations and were more certain of their career goals than girls (p < .01).

Subtle sex differences in attainment come to light when the data are observed from different perspectives. Hamilton (1976) reported that boys were more successful than girls in O level science subjects, while Williams' (1981) results showed that girls attending co-educational schools not only entered for fewer subjects at O level than girls at single-sex institutions (p < .01), but also were less successful than their counterparts in these schools (p < .01). The girls in this investigation did not differ significantly in terms of life-style, early educational experience or academic motivation.

Williams' findings are supportive of the work of McMillan (1982) who carried out a random selection, from those schools catering for girls of similar social status, of three single-sex girls' and three co-educational institutions. In 1978, 13.1 per cent of the co-educational girls, as compared with 22.5 per cent of those from single-sex schools, achieved five or more passes at O level. In 1979, the corresponding figures were 6.7 per cent and 24.2 per cent. McMillan considered that such markedly different results reflected assumptions made by girls in the co-educational setting that boys ought to be the achievers, and that scholastic attainment is not as important for girls. This trend suggests that the move towards co-education in Jamaican schools may well have adverse effects on the achievement of girls.

The same can be said of boys. Parchment's (1982) finding that boys in single-sex high schools demonstrated higher levels of achievement in Spanish than those in co-educational institutions, led her to recommend that, wherever possible, the sexes be taught Spanish separately in co-educational schools. In Parchment's opinion, where boys are taught this subject apart from girls, they are probably not faced with the assumption that they are doing a 'feminine' subject.

The strong support from school sources, needed to bolster the efforts of girls in their academic pursuits, is reflected in the correlates of achievement at O and A levels. Hamilton (1976) found that the school played a vital role in O level science achievement of girls through their early educational experiences, the provision of proper facilities, and the science teachers assigned. For boys, however, these factors were relatively unimportant — their success being more strongly characterized by the strong internal motivation of vocational aspirations spurred on by parental interest. Parental control, which was the variable examined by Seaton (1980), was found to be negatively related to A level performance in the sciences. Interestingly, girls were subjected to significantly greater control than boys (p < .02). This led the researcher to conclude that over-restrictiveness on the part of parents, particularly with their daughters, may militate against students performing successfully in the science examinations.

Leo-Rhynie (1978) reported a noteworthy sex difference related to social status, establishing that whereas SES variables were predictive of success for Grade 13 boys, the relationship was an inverse one for girls. Girls from the upper social echelons seemed to display a certain sense of security in terms of social status, whereas those from working class families who could only gain such status through certification, appeared to value, and to work harder to achieve, academic success. The upper SES boys in Leo-Rhynie's sample were not as complacent as their female counterparts of similar social status, probably because they had been encouraged to retain such status through educational attainment.

The reactions of Grade 13 boys and girls to their course of study are also revealing. Leo-Rhynie (1983) recorded that boys were significantly more confident of success than girls (p < .01), even though they admitted that they experienced greater difficulty in making the transition from O to A level work (p < .01). This seeming contradiction was explained in terms of a defence mechanism operating in boys to bolster their self-esteem which, because of societal expectations for males, cannot envisage failure, even in the face of difficulty. Girls may not find failure as damaging to their self-esteem, so that, for them, this transition may be accomplished with less difficulty, and they can apparently face the possibility of failure with greater honesty. Alternatively, it could be that the boys, having recognized, and faced up to, the difficulties involved in A level work, have realistically set about overcoming these, to the extent that they can express confidence in the outcome of their programme of study.

Implications and conclusions

The similarities and differences between the sexes revealed by these studies are thought-provoking in terms of the evidence they provide regarding the sex role positions occupied by Jamaican students at the secondary level. The cognitive abilities and personality traits which characterize male students, hint at self-sufficiency and independence in relation to their educational experience. This disposition contrasts with the strong need amongst girls for support and encouragement in their endeavours.

Contrasting images persist of an active, responsible, analytically-thinking, confident male, preparing himself for work in an age of science and technology, versus that of a girl who may be strongly motivated academically, but is also anxious and uncertain, and needs the support of home and school to achieve the educational goals which she sets herself. She is thus more likely to select a 'safe' course of study than a challenging, traditionally male-dominated one.

The contrast is even more disturbing because of the similarities in ability and achievement levels demonstrated by boys and girls. This points to the fact that, although the potential of both sexes is being channelled along common paths, there exist factors within the society which perpetuate sex role stereotyping, and thereby emphasize differences which are in fact far greater within, than between, the sexes. This has been a recurrent theme in this chapter, for the roles which adolescent boys and girls adopt, the attitudes they hold, and the goals for which they strive have repeatedly been shown to mirror societal influences in one way or another. Educators have a responsibility to recognize where such influences are counter-productive, and to devise means whereby they can be eliminated.

If educational planners are committed to a system which will develop and utilize the full potential of its human resources — both male and female — so as to advance the nation's progress, they must be sensitized to gender differences. Awareness of the problem, and identification of those factors which contribute to its perpetuation, can then lead to the development of strategies to be employed in schools so as to rid adolescent girls of the feminine image of passivity, and of the anxiety which accompanies their striving to escape this stereotype.

In order to reduce disparities in gender roles, terms such as 'equality of opportunity', which are descriptive of educational goals, must be replaced with explicit statements intended to draw attention to societal expectations. For example, targets can be set for the school achievements of boys and girls, and their preparation for the world of work. As it now stands, males are given the advantage in respect of demonstrating an ability to cope with the demands of living in a period of rapid technological change. The existence of this situation makes it imperative for the focus to be on girls, so as to develop in them the confidence and self-assurance which will enable them to assume roles through which they can achieve their potential in all spheres of development, and thus make a more far-reaching contribution to national life.

References

Bell, M (1981) *The Effect of Environmental Factors on Character Development: an Investigation Mounted on a Sample of Older Jamaican Adolescents* unpublished MA thesis, University of the West Indies

Cameron, A (1982) *School Anxiety and Academic Achievement in a Sample of Jamaican Students* unpublished MA thesis, University of the West Indies

Campbell, M (1980) *The Development of an Instrument for Measuring Attitudes of Jamaican 10th Graders to Business Education* unpublished MEd thesis, University of the West Indies

Degazon-Johnson, R (1983) *An Investigation into Home and School Correlates of Alienation among a Sample of Jamaican Youth* unpublished MA thesis, University of the West Indies

Edwards, C (1982) *The Relationship between Creativity and Subject Orientation, among a Sample of Jamaican Adolescents* unpublished MA thesis, University of the West Indies.

Figueroa, P (1976) Values and academic achievement among high school boys in Kingston, Jamaica in Figueroa and Persaud

Figueroa, P and Persaud, G eds (1976) Sociology of Education — A Caribbean Reader Oxford University Press: London

Glasgow, J (1978) Science in the Jamaican Community: a Survey of some Aspects of the Provision for Training in Science unpublished MA thesis, University of the West Indies

Gordon, C (1983) Interpersonal Relations as a Source of Problems Experienced by Jamaican Adolescents unpublished MA thesis, University of the West Indies

Griffiths, D and Saraga, E (1979) Sex differences and cognitive abilities: a sterile field of enquiry? in Hartnett, Boden and Fuller (1979)

Hamilton, M (1976) A Study of Certain Personality, Educational and Environmental Variables Associated with Science Orientation in a Selected Group of 5th Form Students, in Secondary Schools of Jamaica unpublished PhD thesis, University of the West Indies

Hamilton, M A (1981) The prediction of academic success — an interim report Caribbean Journal of Education 8 1: 43-58

Hamilton, M A (1982a) Sex differences in the qualitative performance of Jamaican adolescents in the circles test of creativity Caribbean Journal of Education 9 2: 124-34

Hamilton, M A (1982b) Jamaican students' attitude to science as it relates to achievement in external examinations Science Education 66 2: 155-69

Hamilton, M A and Leo-Rhynie, E A (1979-80) Sex-role stereotyping and education: the Jamaican perspective Interchange 10 2: 46-56

Hartnett, O, Boden, G and Fuller, M eds (1979) Sex-role Stereotyping Tavistock: London

Isaacs, P (1975) Conservation of a Selection of Scientific and Mathematical Concepts among some Grade 6 Children in Jamaica unpublished MA thesis, University of the West Indies

Jackson, J (1979) An Exploratory Study of Achievement Need among Girls Attending Secondary Schools in Jamaica unpublished MA thesis, University of the West Indies

Jarrett, J (1983) Expectancy Effects and their Relationship to the Academic Performance of Grade 6 Students unpublished MA thesis, University of the West Indies

Leo-Rhynie, E (1978) An Investigation into the Relationship of Certain Cognitive Environmental, Experiential and Motivational Variables to the Academic Achievement of Selected Jamaican 6th Form Students unpublished PhD thesis, University of the West Indies

Leo-Rhynie, E A (1982) Educational research of some graduate students of UWI — a commentary Caribbean Journal of Education 9 2: 135-51

Leo-Rhynie, E A (1983) Approaches to A level work and study used by a sample of Jamaican sixth formers Caribbean Journal of Education 10 2

McMillan, V (1982) Academic Motivation of Adolescent Jamaican Girls in Selected Single-Sex and Co-Educational Schools unpublished MEd thesis, University of the West Indies

Mitchelmore, M (1974) The Perceptual Development of Jamaican Students, with Special Reference to Visualization and Drawing of 3-Dimensional Geometrical Figures and the Effects of Spatial Training unpublished doctoral dissertation, The Ohio State University

Morris, M (1978) The Effects of Certain Personality and Related Variables on Academic Achievement unpublished MA thesis, University of the West Indies

Parchment, V (1982) The Effect of Selected Cognitive, Motivational and Attitudinal Variables on Students' Achievement in the CXC/GCE Spanish Examinations unpublished MA thesis, University of the West Indies

Ragbir, L (1975) Measured Intelligence, Social Class, Academic Achievement and Academic Achievement Motivation in Selected Jamaican High School Students unpublished MA thesis, University of the West Indies

Richardson, M (1980) *Identity in the Jamaican Context: its Measurement and Relationship to Certain Biographical, Environmental, Personality and Attitudinal Variables* unpublished PhD thesis, University of the West Indies

Roach, D (1978) *The Effect of Cognitive Style and Other Related Variables on the Achievement in Mathematics of some Jamaican Elementary School Children* unpublished PhD thesis, University of the West Indies

Sangster, A W (1982) Looking at the common entrance exams *The Sunday Gleaner*, 10 October

Seaton, H (1980) *The Relarionship of Selected Motivational Variables to the 'A' Level Science Achievement of Jamaican Students* unpublished MA thesis, University of the West Indies

Sinanan, J (1983) *The Measurement of Locus of Control and an Investigation of Factors Related to Locus of Control among a Sample of Young Jamaican Adults* unpublished PhD thesis, University of the West Indies

Stokes, B (1983) *Correlates of Alienation among Selected Jamaican Adolescents* PhD thesis in preparation, University of the West Indies

UNESCO (1978) *A Study on Curricula and Standards of Education and Training for Boys and Girls in Secondary Schools and Teacher Colleges in Jamaica.* document ED-78/WS/112 Research conducted by Jennings-Wray, Z, Persaud, G and Turner, T, of the Caribbean Society of Educational Administrators (CARSEA) for the Jamaican National Commission for UNESCO, November

Williams, C (1981) *The Relationship between Achievement Motivation, Academic Performance and Certain Selected Variables in a Sample of 5th Form Jamaican Students* unpublished BEd study, University of the West Indies

Wong, J (1983) *The Effect of Father-Absence on Certain Personality and Related Variables among Selected Jamaican Adolescent Boys* MA thesis in preparation, University of the West Indies

11. Pursuing the Baccalaureate degree in the United States: the case of African American women

Beverly Lindsay

Summary: This chapter discusses conditions affecting African American women pursuing the undergraduate baccalaureate degree. In accomplishing this examination, the chapter focuses on four major areas: (i) providing descriptive statistical indices of the access, distribution, and retention or completion rates of African American women: (ii) explaining college enrolment and retention in the light of individual characteristics and structural conditions; (iii) discussing historical and contemporary legal requirements and executive orders which have an impact on colleges; and (iv) portraying future research needs and policy considerations. Many of the conditions affecting African American women students are similar to those of African American men, of other minorities, and of other women. Thus data and examples for these groups are also used to examine the condition and status of African American women students. This chapter provides some recommendations regarding college characteristics which may be altered to enhance African American women's chances of graduation. Finally, the chapter concludes by discussing future research areas − financial aid, post-baccalaureate opportunities, and subtle discrimination − in relation to legal and economic policies.

Introduction

'Who should go to college then? Not everyone. Only those who are qualified. And by 'qualified' one should mean those able to benefit from the training in the institution selected . . .' (Bailey, 1978: 85).

This quote contains a *double entendre* if we examine it in relation to African American women in the United States. Perhaps African American women are qualified for and benefit tremendously from post-secondary training? Perhaps African American women are frequently included in the category of 'not everyone'? Or perhaps both positions are evident, since more African American women than ever are attending college? However, their graduation rates are consistently lower than those for white men and women. Why are such discrepancies apparent? Does pre-college education play a role? Does the socialization process continue to influence college

This article was written by the author in a private capacity. The views expressed are those of the author and do not reflect the policies of the National Institute of Education or other bodies cited.

women? Does the college environment and structure inhibit women's graduation? Does the enactment of financial and legal policies curtail graduation rates?

The primary purpose of this chapter is to provide a critical overview of the position of African American women in baccalaureate degree programmes and the conditions affecting them. The American baccalaureate (or bachelor's) degree is normally pursued after completing 12 years of primary and secondary education or the equivalent, and it takes approximately four years to complete. The focus is primarily on baccalaureate undergraduate degree programmes since the attainment of this degree is a prerequisite for entering a professional career, reaping personal benefits, and making economic and social contributions to society. In addition, relatively more comprehensive data are available for undergraduate institutional studies.

To accomplish the primary purpose, this chapter focuses on four basic concerns:

1. providing descriptive statistical indices of the access, distribution, and retention or completion rates of African American women;
2. explaining college enrolment and retention in the light of individual characteristics and structural conditions;
3. discussing historical and contemporary legal requirements and executive orders which have an impact on colleges;
4. portraying future research needs and policy considerations.

The term 'African American' applies to Americans of African descent, formerly known as 'Negroes' or 'coloureds'. Many of the conditions affecting African American women students are similar to those of African American men, of other minorities, and of women in general. Thus data and examples for these groups may also be used to examine the conditions and status of African American women students.

Indices of access, distribution, and retention

Access to baccalaureate programmes may be initially viewed by examining secondary school graduation rates. These graduates provide the available pool of potential students. In 1970, approximately 60 per cent of African Americans graduated from secondary school, and this increased to approximately 70 per cent by 1980. In contrast, approximately 81 per cent and 83 per cent of white youth graduated in 1970 and 1980 respectively. Thus, the lower secondary school graduation rates initially contribute to the smaller percentage of African Americans enrolled in baccalaureate programmes. Based upon a nationally representative sample of colleges and universities, about 6.2 per cent of the first-year students were African Americans in 1970, 8.4 per cent in 1977, and 8.8 per cent in 1980 (Astin, 1982a: 26). African Americans would need to increase their representation by about 40 per cent to equal that of the general population.

After initial entrance, indices of distribution can be viewed in terms of the types of college attended — two- or four-year — and the major subject studied. In 1975, about 50 per cent of all African American students were in two-year institutions; about 37 per cent of full-time African American students were enrolled in these institutions (Olivas, 1979: 25, 27). In 1980, about 42 per cent of African Americans were enrolled in two-year colleges and about 34 per cent of these were full-time students seeking a degree (Hill, 1983: 8). Yet, in the 1975-76 academic year, only 8.4 per cent of the associate degrees (two-year college degrees which can be used toward the baccalaureate) were awarded to African Americans. In the 1980-81 academic year, this figure had increased slightly to 9.2 per cent. (Students may transfer to four-year institutions without an associate degree; but many two-year colleges design their academic associate degrees in the light of four-year college requirements). In the two academic periods, the highest percentage of degrees were awarded in public service technologies, data processing technologies, and business and commerce technologies (Hill, 1983: 31).

In the 1975-76 and 1980-81 academic years, African Americans earned about 6.3 per cent and 6.5 per cent respectively of all baccalaureate degrees. Of baccalaureate degrees awarded, 3.6 per cent in 1975-76 and 3.9 per cent in 1980-81 went to African American women. White men received 47.8 per cent of the degrees in 1975-76 and 43.4 per cent of the degrees in 1980-81. The corresponding percentages for white women were 39.2 per cent and 42.3 per cent (Trent, 1983: 19; Hill, 1983: 15). (These figures do not include those for other American minority groups; hence the percentages do not equal 100.) In 1975-76, African American women most often earned degrees in education (about 32 per cent), the social sciences (about 16 per cent) and business (about 11 per cent). By 1980-81, about 19 per cent of the degrees awarded to African American women were in education, about 12 per cent in the social sciences, and about 19 per cent in business.

For white men in 1975-76, 23 per cent of the degrees were in business, 15 per cent in the social sciences, and 11 per cent in mathematics. In 1980-81, the figures were: almost 28 per cent in business, 13 per cent in engineering, and 12 per cent in the social sciences. Comparable figures for African American men were 23 per cent and 27 per cent in business, 22 per cent and 15 per cent in the social sciences, and about 15 per cent and 10 per cent in education. For white women during this period, about 27 per cent and 18 per cent of the degrees were in education, 11 per cent and 9 per cent in the social sciences, and 10 per cent and 12 per cent in the health professions (Trent, 1983: 21).

The retention or graduation rates of African American women are lower than those of white students. Only about 24 per cent of the African American women and men complete a baccalaureate degree approximately four years or so later, compared to 34 per cent of whites (Astin, 1982b: 14, 15). These discrepancies are caused by attrition at key points: secondary schools; two-year colleges (less than 25 per cent of all students enter four-year colleges after completing two-year college courses); and attrition at the end of the first or second year of four-year institutions (Astin, 1982b: 16). What are the factors which contribute to college retention through to the baccalaureate degree?

College enrolment and retention

College retention may be viewed in the light of three categories of students: persisters, stopouts, and dropouts. Persisters complete their baccalaureate degree within a period of four years or so (or slightly longer depending upon the nature of the programme). Stopouts have not completed the baccalaureate degree within the normally prescribed period: but they are still pursuing the degree on a full- or part-time basis. Dropouts have not completed the baccalaureate degree are not enrolled in a concentrated programme, nor have they been enrolled during the preceding academic year (Astin, 1975: 9, 10; Churchill and Iwai, 1981: 353). When discussing dropouts, we should be aware that some students did not intend to complete the baccalaureate degree. Some researchers state, however, that more than two-thirds of the entering students want to earn at least a baccalaureate degree (Alba and Lavin, 1981: 235). Although this general figure is presented, it is often difficult to ascertain clearly whether students entered college with the idea of dropping out, or whether this view was developed later. Nevertheless, the basic fact remains that many do not finish.

The lack of adequate academic preparation in secondary schools is one reason why students fail to persist. Various writers state that the quality of academic instruction in many urban schools attended by African American girls is not comparable to that in many white suburban schools. Low enrolment in academic or college preparatory curriculum tracks, inadequate academic counselling, and infrequent participation in extra-curricular academic activities can hinder African American girls' readiness for college work (Bailey, 1978: 20; Astin, 1975: 45; and Lewis et al, in press). Students who graduate with low academic averages and limited participation in school activities simply do not perform as well, or persist as readily in college, as their peers who have higher averages and more active involvement in secondary school.

A body of literature focuses on psychological and socialization processes as they affect women students in general and African American women students in particular. In a succinct summary of the literature, Thomas and Hargett (1981: 68, 69) analyse several salient issues associated with the socialization process and its relation to individual psychological features. First, there is an absence of professional African American women as role models. Some researchers contend that the absence of professional role models contributes to negative socialization so that students do not envisage themselves in a variety of roles. Second, despite the absence of adequate role models, African American women frequently have higher academic performance and educational attainment in secondary schools than African American men. However, these positive features begin to disappear in college. Third, the apparent disappearance of positive features may be due to the 'fear of success' (Horner, 1972: 157-75). Horner argues that women consciously select less competitive majors, and lower their educational aspirations and attainment as a means of reducing psychological barriers that confront successful professional women. Moreover, the socialization process which contributes to the 'fear of success' can also contribute to women's concerns with affective relationships which may interfere with academic pursuits. Thomas and Hargett (1981) and other researchers point out that Horner's model may be a partial explanation with limited applicability; other major individual and structural explanations should be considered.

Other literature suggests that attrition or dropout rates may be high for African American women because they experience more psychological stress on white campuses than do white students and African American men students. Fleming (1981: 307-18) conducted a study of African Americans attending white and African American colleges. African American women were much more unhappy, and experienced more psychological stress, on white campuses than other groups. This was not evident with women at African American colleges. African American colleges were primarily established in the mid-1800s and thereafter to provide education for people of African origin, known then as Negroes or coloureds. In most instances African Americans were legally required to attend segregated institutions. Today, well over 75 per cent of African American sudents attend predominantly white colleges. Attending a white college can necessitate a tremendous adjustment if the student did not previously attend a white secondary school.

Yet, interestingly enough, several researchers have concluded that college persistence rates for African American women are higher than those of white women with similar backgrounds. African American persistence rates, in general, are higher than those for whites with similar abilities (Cross and Astin, 1981: 89; Astin, 1978: 129, 218). Such differences in persistence rates are not readily discernible because academic and socio-economic backgrounds are seldom comparable between African Americans and whites.

Individual experiences and characteristics are one important way of examining causes of attrition or dropout. Equally, if not more important, are structural explanations which take into account components of colleges and external social institutions. To paraphrase one writer, it is necessary to focus on college characteristics, and what they mean to the collegiate experience of different students (Astin, 1978: 30). Two-year colleges are a major illustration.

The characteristics and structures of two-year colleges are ostensibly designed to provide access and graduation opportunities; often they have curtailed educational opportunities. Various researchers have depicted the high attrition rates, the limited academic opportunities, and the failure or inability of students to transfer to four-year baccalaureate programmes (Arce, 1978: 167; Olivas, 1979: 133-40; and Astin, 1978: 250-51). Two-year colleges normally have open admissions, that is, students who graduate from secondary schools can enter regardless of their prior academic backgrounds. These colleges, however, frequently do not provide adequate academic support programmes, counselling, and campus activities to buttress the relatively weak students' backgrounds. Various writers have, in fact, argued that two-year colleges are fulfilling their implicit function: the weakest students are offered the most limited educational opportunities in the lowest tier of the formal post-secondary education structure, and a 'weeding-out' or 'cooling-out' process occurs as students are systematically eliminated (Clark, 1960: 165; Olivas, 1979: 1, 3; and Astin, 1978: 251), although more transfer from sites with stronger academic programmes (Alba and Lavin, 1981: 243-36). This is not a readily apparent function. The illusion of opportunity is important, rather than authentic educational opportunities. Over 50 per cent of African American students are at two-year colleges; over half of these are women.

As mentioned previously, African American students — and women in particular — encounter various psychological stresses at four-year, predominantly white, colleges. African American students who express positive views of campus race relations, who interact regularly with faculty, who are satisfied with their housing, and who participate in campus activities, generally earn higher academic evaluations and are more likely to graduate within the normally prescibed period or shortly thereafter (Allen, 1981: 136; Astin, 1978: 186-87). The racial climate of colleges, faculty relations with students, and the scope and breadth of campus activities are integral components of the college structure. Such components can be altered to enhance the academic achievement and graduation rates of African American students.

Several recurrent themes emerge regarding means of altering components of the college structure to provide viable support services.

Orientation sessions should be conducted, wherein all students are provided assurances of belonging, the opportunity to learn what their baccalaureate programmes require, and detailed information on academic and personal resources for assistance.

Counselling should be available by professional counsellors who understand the nature of academic course requirements and are sensitive to the cultural and psychological needs of African American students.

White faculty and administrators should learn to interact regularly with African American students and counsel them regarding academic expectations. Administrators should be actively involved in efforts to recruit African American women and men to faculty, administration, and professional staff.

African American faculty and administrators should perform in a similar way to their white colleagues; but they should also be fully aware that they are role models.

Housing accommodation should be available on campus, wherein students can exercise choices about their room mates and about types of housing or dormitory activities.

Extracurricular activities should encompass academic and cultural features. Participation in honours societies and clubs associated with academic fields should be encouraged. African American cultural centers and programmes can enhance a sense of belonging for African American students and provide white students and professionals with the opportunity to learn about different cultures (Smith, 1981: 299-306; Cross and Astin, 1981: 88-9; Astin, 1982b: 28-9).

During the late 1960s and early 1970s, many four-year colleges established African American, Ethnic, or Third World study programmes to ensure that the social, political, and economic perspectives and needs of minority Americans were represented. Simultaneously, minority cultural centers and remedial or developmental education programmes were established. Such programmes, as mentioned in the previous paragraph, may enhance academic achievement and graduation rates. But they should be integrally linked to the overall campus structure and not be peripheral components as they often are. For example, the funding for an African American Studies Center or Afro-American Cultural Center should be a budget line item as are other student centers. Equally important is the integration of African American students, especially women, into the complete academic life of the college. Many African American students, for instance, have entered colleges through special recruitment programmes, wherein such recruits are designated as 'non-traditional, disadvantaged, or developmental students'. Such terms frequently carry negative connotations within the campus community (and elsewhere). Special recruitment efforts and related support programmes may be established; but this can be accomplished in a creative manner whereby the negative stigma is lessened, if not eradicated.

An example of this creative approach may be witnessed at Oakes College, a residential liberal arts college within the University of California, Santa Cruz. Mainly African American students, other ethnic and racial minorities, and women — usually with academic deficiencies — attend this college. Of the 600 students enrolled at Oakes, over half are minorities. The students are called 'New Students'. The provost states that: 'The concept New Student was developed to designate those students who have traditionally been denied access to higher education . . . We prefer the designation New Student [because] . . . the concept recognizes the strengths and unique qualities of the student without minimizing their academic deficiencies' (Blake, 1982: 9).

The college curriculum for the New Students emphasizes science and takes account of the experience of ethnic minorities. The students often arrive from communities lacking medical, scientific, and technological expertise. About half of the minority students major in the natural or physical sciences. This college appears to be successful in retaining and graduating students with these majors; over half graduate within five or more years, which is not unusual for science majors. In 1980 and 1981, about 40 per cent of the minority students who graduated with science degrees were accepted by top medical schools such as Harvard

University and the University of California, San Francisco. About half
of these were women (Blake, 1982: 11). Creative approaches to teaching,
counselling, and learning; a residential college where most students live
on campus; and Oakes' establishment as a college comparable to others
at this site account for these apparent successes. In essence, the structure
within the college and the University are conducive to New Students'
access and graduation.

Looking beyond the institutions, it is necessary to examine structural
conditions within the larger society — particularly economic conditions
and financial aid programmes for college students. During the early 1980s,
about 70 per cent of white college students were from families with
incomes of at least $25,000. The median white family income in the US
was about $25,000. In 1980 and 1981, almost 70 per cent of all first-year
college students were relying on some form of parental aid. About half of
these students were receiving at least $1,000 from this source (Astin,
1982a: 28). In contrast, the median family income for African American
families was $12,600 in 1980 (Cross, 1983: 7). In the fall of 1981, over
70 per cent of African American men and over 85 per cent of women
from this group at historically African American colleges were from
families with incomes of less than $25,000. At predominantly white
colleges, at least 70 per cent of African American students were from
this background (Astin, 1981: 16, 32). Yet, in 1981, average college
expenses totalled over $4,400 at public colleges and $8,569 at private
colleges (Ottinger, 1982: 3). Thus it is not surprising that various studies
indicate that students from higher family incomes tend to persist and
graduate from college more often than those with lower family incomes.

Financial aid programmes — federal, state, and individual college —
were designed, particularly during the 1960s and early 1970s, to provide
opportunities for needy students. In general, enrolment of low income
students increased, especially in the early 1970s. From that time to 1976,
African American student enrolment also increased. Part of this increase
is traceable to federal financial aid packages (Davis and Johns, 1982: 5-10;
Hill, 1983: 7) which may be a combination of scholarships, grants, loans,
and work-study programmes. (Scholarships are usually monies awarded
for academic achievement and do not have to be repaid; grants are similar
but they are usually based on need; loans are awarded on the basis of need
and must be repaid with interest to the lending institution; and work-
study programmes require students to work part-time each week to earn
money for tuition, fees, or other college-related expenses.) Researchers
have indicated that the availability and type of financial aid packages to
African American students are related to their college persistence. For
example, nearly 55 per cent of African American students receive
scholarships during their first year. Students who receive scholarships
tend to persist more often than those who primarily receive loans. In
predominantly African American colleges, loans have no clear relationship
to persistence; but they appear to be an asset for African American
students at predominantly white colleges. An 8 per cent reduction in

attrition rates is associated with students who secure loans compared with those who do not. Students who earn part of their financial aid through federal work-study programmes tend to participate more in campus activities. This appears more prevalent among African American women and men and white women than among white men (Astin, 1975: 56-70; Cross and Astin, 1981: 78-79). Perhaps this is related to the fact that white men have various ways of participating in campus activities. As discussed previously, participation enhances persistence.

The quality of academic programmes, the economic status of institutions, and the continued availability of individual student aid packages are threatened by limitations in the amount of funding for federal financial programmes. This is evident by the average Pell grant of just over $900 in the 1982-83 academic year for needy students (Ottinger, 1982: 4). For the 1983-84 academic year the average award will be approximately the same. Given inflation, the award is actually less.

One national body, the Commission on the Higher Education of Minorities, recommends that, whenever possible, needy minority American students be given grants and that work-study programmes be packaged so that students work less than half-time at on-campus jobs. Grants and work-study programmes contribute to persistence (Astin, 1982b: 30-31). Since it is unlikely that federal grants and work-study programmes will be increased, it is doubtful whether these components of financial aid can continue to be paths for enhancing the access and persistence of African American women.

Legal decisions and executive orders

Prior to 1954, segregation of racial groups was legal in the United States. In 1954, the Supreme Court of the United States in *Brown v Board of Education* declared that official or *de jure* segregation in public schools was unconstitutional. The decision extended to all tiers of the formal *public* education system. Although an official decision was reached, contemporary practices and institutional structures often served as a means of excluding African Americans. In the late 1950s and early 1960s, the federal military was used to enforce desegregation in post-secondary institutions, as, for instance, at the Universities of Mississippi, Alabama, and Georgia. By the mid-1960s, this was no longer necessary. But few racial minority students and professionals were present on predominantly white college campuses and in other major business, social and public agencies. The United States Congress passed the Civil Rights Act of 1964 as an attempt to prohibit discrimination due to race, colour, religion, sex, or national origin in employment policies and practices. Related to this Act was the Executive Order 11246 issued in 1965 by President Lyndon Johnson. This Order prohibited federal contractors from discriminating on the basis of race, colour, religion, and national origin. The Order was amended in 1968 by Executive Order 11375 to include discrimination based on sex (Raffel, 1979: 110-11; Moore and Wagstaff, 1974: 73-4; and Bailey, 1978: 75).

As a result of these Executive Orders, affirmative action plans were introduced as a policy and strategy to promote fair treatment for those groups 'who would in the ordinary course of events be victimized by discrimination' (Swinton, 1978: 111). When affirmative action plans were introduced on college campuses, they included not only employment policies and practices for staff, but recruitment and admissions policies for minority women students. With reference to affirmative action plans for students, alternative admission standards were initiated so that scores on standardized tests and related assessments were not the sole criteria. Affirmative action plans included such measures as: goals for recruiting an approximate number or percentage of minority students; timetables for approximate target dates for recruitment and related activities; and, in the earlier years, quotas which specified the number of particular types of students to be admitted. Although many of these plans were introduced for post-baccalaureate students, baccalaureate degree institutions and programmes adopted similar practices.

In 1978, the Supreme Court declared in the *University of California v Bakke* that race could be used as a criterion for a constitutionally accepted admissions programme. But special admissions based on 'naked racial quotas' are not valid when:

1. there are no specific findings of racial discrimination;
2. minorities receiving the benefits have not been victimized by specific discriminatory actions;
3. identifiable whites — who did not contribute [to] or directly benefit from discriminatory policies — are not seriously harmed by the preferential policy (Bell, 1980: 452).

What are the immediate implications for African American women? The race (and sex) of African American women students can still be used legally as criteria for admission to baccalaureate programmes.

Despite the Supreme Court decision, many critics of affirmative action contend that white males are being discriminated against and that negative stigmas are attached to African American women and men whether or not admitted through affirmative action. The United States Commission on Civil Rights states that affirmative action plans are not designed to establish the superiority of minorities and women over white males. Rather, they are a means to establish equal opportunity for all students. Moreover, affirmative action does not advocate the lowering of standards; it does require the examination of traditional standards (United States Commission on Civil Rights, 1981: 37-9), many of which may not be clearly related to academic or successful career performance. Perhaps the illustration from Oakes College can again shed some light on the issue of 'proper' admission criteria.

One noted African American political scientist contends that it is quite important to link affirmative action for African Americans with compelling state interests (Hamilton, 1978: 71). Health care for poor people, quality teachers for urban schools, and computer and business experts to service the minority community are all major state interests. These needs must be met by the state. Therefore it is in the state's compelling interest to see that competent professionals meet the needs of the constituents for health care, education, and business. Historical and contemporary data clearly show that African American professionals normally serve similar racial constituencies. These professionals — both women and men — must be initially educated and trained. Affirmative action is a major avenue for achieving this goal.

Future research and policy considerations

The preceding discussion has highlighted the descriptive indices of African American women's access to baccalaureate programmes; their distribution within types of colleges and academic majors; their persistence and/or graduation rates; their individual social and psychological features; and the structural conditions within the college and larger society which affect the pursuit of the baccalaureate degree. Some progress has been made; but much remains to be done before parity with white males will be achieved. Several basic research issues and policy considerations must be seriously entertained when examining parity for African American women.

The reader may wish to note the following publications on undergraduate and graduate education opportunities, career goals, and social conditions affecting African American women (see: Lindsay, 1980; Sims-Wood, 1980; Thomas, 1981a; and *Journal of Social and Behavioural Sciences* 1981: 68-201. There is some literature on post-baccalaureate opportunities for women. Follow-up research data on their post-college experiences in graduate or professional school, careers or vocations, and domestic or personal life, should be viewed in conjunction with their undergraduate experience. For example, about 19 per cent of African American women graduates in 1980 earned degrees in business compared with about 11 per cent five years earlier. What indicators may be available within a few years to portray what types of real benefit have accrued to these business graduates? Or has the content of or concentration within the undergraduate business curriculum prepared them to assume a variety of business careers? Are they actually employed in business or the corporate world? Such data would be useful to education policy makers and faculty as they continue recruiting and educating future undergraduate African American women.

Particular research should focus on an in-depth examination of the structure of financial aid packages by federal and state bodies and their impact on African American women students' access, distribution, and graduation. As cited earlier, there are various views regarding 'the most appropriate' financial aid packages which can enhance persistence. Cross (1983: 11-13) acknowledges the various views, but notes that the sheer availability of adequate financial aid through federal programmes is a larger issue. Thus, additional research which examines the linkages among the availability of federal aid, the criteria for awards, and access and persistence rates, must be continually focused on African American women and men in various types of colleges and universities.

From 1970 to 1978, the percentage of African American full-time students who earned degrees steadily increased. Yet from 1979 to the present, no increase or decrease has been evident; progress has ceased. Are new or subtle forms of discrimination present? Is there less attention and concern with affirmative action programmes in the light of the Supreme Court decision on Bakke? Or has the national (and international) economic downturn, evident since the late 1970s, simply provided a convenient rationale for excluding African Americans' quest for education? Responses to such policy-relevant research questions will help us gain a better understanding of viable alternatives to enhance African American women's access and success in pursuing the baccalaureate degree.

An understanding of alternative perspectives ultimately provides different criteria for examining the quality of applicants and students. We return to our first quote. 'Who should go to college then? Only those who are qualified'. A statement by the president of Georgetown University in Washington, DC provides the best response. 'If . . . the notion of "quality" is tied to the automatic exclusion of any percentage of the population, any racial . . . or ethnic group, it simply is not acceptable in America. If . . . "quality" indicates a goal to be aimed at . . . or an achievement to be defended, then it clearly is compatible with a great measure of equality' (Healey, 1976: 8). Equality of access and success is the goal to be achieved for *all* quality students.

References

Alba, R D and Lavin, D E (1981) Community colleges and tracking in higher education *Sociology of Education* 54 4: 223-37

Allen, W R (1981) Correlates of Black student adjustment, achievement, and aspirations at a predominantly white southern university *in* Thomas

Arce, C H (1978) Minorities in higher education: recent advances and current problems *in* Smith

Astin, A (1982a) *The American Freshman, 1966-1981: Some Implications for Educational Policy and Practice* National Commission on Excellence in Education, Department of Education: Washington, DC

Astin, A (1982b) *Final Report of the Commission on the Higher Education of Minorities* Higher Education Research Institute Inc: Los Angeles, California

Astin, A (1978) *Four Critical Years* Jossey-Bass: San Francisco, California

Astin, A (1975) *Preventing Students From Dropping Out* Jossey-Bass: San Francisco, California

Astin, A *et al* (1981) *The American Freshman: National Norms For Fall 1981* Higher Education Research Institute and American Council on Education: Los Angeles, California

Bailey, R L (1978) *Minority Admissions* D C Heath and Company: Lexington, Massachusetts

Bell, D A (1980) *Race, Racism and American Law* Little, Brown and Company: Boston, Massachusetts

Blake, J H (1982) *Demographic Change and Curriculum. 'New' Students in Higher Education* National Commission on Excellence in Education, Department of Education: Washington, DC

Churchill, W D and Iwai, S (1981) College attrition, students' use of campus facilities, and a consideration of self-reported personal problems *Research in Higher Education* **14** 4: 355-62

Clark, B R (1960) *The Open Door College: A Case Study* McGraw-Hill: New York, New York

Cross, D (1983) The issue of equity: current realities and the task ahead Paper presented at the American Educational Research Association (AERA) annual conference in Montreal, Canada. AERA office: Washington, DC

Cross, P H and Astin, H S (1981) Factors affecting Black students' persistence in college *in* Thomas

Davis, J S and Johns, K (1982) Law and family income: a continuing barrier to college enrollment *The Journal of Student Financial Aid* **12** 1: 5-10

Fleming, J (1981) Stress and satisfaction in college years of Black students *Journal of Negro Education* **50** 3: 307-18

Hamilton, C V (1978) Public responsibility or equality and justice *in* Smith

Healey, T (1976) Can quality coexist with equality in a just community? *The College Board* **102**: 8-11

Hill, S T (1983) *Participation of Black Students in Higher Education: A Statistical Profile from 1970-71 to 1980-81* National Center for Education Statistics, Department of Education: Washington, DC

Horner, M (1972) Toward an understanding of achievement related conflicts in women *Journal of Social Issues* **28** 2: 157-75

Journal of Social and Behavioral Sciences (1981) **27** 3: 68-201 Special issue on Education, Socialization and Traditional Versus Non-Traditional Career Paths of Black Females: Theoretical and Empirical Evidence

Kline, S ed (in press) *Achieving Sex Equity Through Education* The Johns Hopkins University Press: Baltimore, Maryland

Lewis, S et al (in press) Achieving sex equity for minority women *in* Kline

Lindsay, B ed (1980) *Comparative Perspectives of Third World Women: The Impact of Race, Sex, and Class* Praeger: New York

Moore, W and Wagstaff, L H (1974) *Black Educators in White Colleges* Jossey-Bass: San Francisco, California

Olivas, M (1979) *The Dilemma of Access: Minorities in Two Year Colleges* Howard University Press: Washington, DC

Ottinger, C (1982) *Student Loan Options: What is Happening?* American Council on Education Policy Brief: Washington, DC

Raffel, N R (1979) Federal laws and regulations prohibiting sex discrimination *in* Snyder

Sims-Wood, J (1980) *The Progress of Afro-American Women: A Selected Bibliography and Resources Guide* Greenwood Press: Westport, Connecticut

Smith, C (1978) *Advancing Equality of Opportunity: A Matter of Justice* Howard University Press: Washington, DC

Smith, D H (1981) Social and academic environment of Black students on white campuses *Journal of Negro Education* **50** 3: 299-306

Snyder, E ed (1979) *The Study of Women: Enlarging Perspectives of Social Reality* Harper and Row: New York

Swinton, D (1978) Affirmative action in a declining economy *in* Smith

Thomas, G E ed (1981a) *Black Students in Higher Education: Conditions and Experiences in the 1970s* Greenwood Press: Westport, Connecticut

Thomas, G E (1981b) College characteristics and Black students' four-year college graduation *Journal of Negro Education* **50** 3: 328-45

Thomas, G E and Hargett, S L (1981) Socialization effects and Black college women: Educational and occupational orientations *Journal of Social and Behavioral Sciences* **27** 3: 65-72

Trent, W T (1983) *Race and Sex Difference in Degree Attainment and Major Field Distributions from 1975-76 to 1980-81* The Johns Hopkins University Center for Social Organization of Schools Report Number 339: Baltimore, Maryland

United States Commission on Civil Rights (1981) *Affirmative Action in the 1980s: Dismantling the Process of Discrimination* United States Commission on Civil Rights Clearing House Publication 70: Washington, DC

12. Vocational education for women's work in England and Wales

Gillian Blunden

Summary: This chapter considers some aspects of women's vocational education in England. Using historical material gathered in the course of my doctoral research and data collected from my current students, underlying trends and assumptions in provision of further education for female students are analysed. These may be seen as institutionalizing sex discrimination within the further education sector. Little in the provision directed towards the growing numbers of unemployed young women and men appears to contradict this underlying assumption.

Certain aspects of women's vocational education in the 1980s are considered first. Then historical developments are examined and finally I begin to explore the future direction of vocational education for women's work.

Introduction

Women's vocational education has a long, if unacknowledged, history in England and Wales. It is now generally provided in one of two ways after a secondary school education. It may comprise part of the local education authority's further education provision. Increasingly it is being supplied through the various schemes (run by the Manpower Services Commission) that attempt to cope with the growth in youth unemployment. Except in specific areas such as medicine or veterinary science, 'higher education' at first degree level in Britain is not generally concerned with directly vocational courses. This chapter analyses the position of women and girls as students in non-advanced further education. Throughout this chapter the term 'further education' refers to that sector of the public education system in England and Wales that is maintained by the local education authority but not conducted under school regulations. 'Non-advanced further education' refers to courses up to and including GCE A level (matriculation), or its equivalent, and 'advanced further education' to full- or part-time higher diploma, degree or degree level courses outside the universities and colleges of education.

Women and girls have always been able to study and educate themselves after leaving school. They have never been formally and wholly excluded from further education as they once were from the universities. Yet, a hundred years ago, they did not enrol on every course, nor do they now. In the 1890s women were confined to the domestic, art and languages courses. Men's options were not as limited but they were prevented from attending classes in domestic subjects. In the 1980s both sexes enrol on a wider variety of courses but it is still unusual to find a girl studying motor mechanics or a boy, childcare.

In this chapter I shall outline current trends in the provision for female students before outlining the historical development of such trends. I shall conclude by raising questions about possible future directions for women's vocational education. These must be examined in the light of the growing numbers of unemployed school leavers and the policies of successive governments that have been directed towards this problem.

Current trends in non-advanced further education

In England and Wales, some three and three-quarter million people take further education courses each year: 60 per cent of these students are women. The non-advanced further education sector in the 1980s accounts for about 35 per cent of all 16 to 19 year olds. Ten per cent of the age group is enrolled on full-time courses at college; twenty-five per cent is in education or training associated with employment or on government schemes connected with youth unemployment. A further 20 per cent of the age group is still at school. The remaining 45 per cent receives no further day-time education. This age group is deemed to have not yet entered the higher education sector. The present Conservative British Government is restructuring the provision for unemployed school leavers.

The Youth Opportunities Programme (YOP) has now ceased and is being replaced by the Youth Training Scheme (YTS). A pilot YTS was held in the four Bristol technical colleges during 1982/3. Each college provided 100 places for voluntary trainees. The courses included college-based learning and work experience. None led to any recognized qualifications. For those in attendance their supplementary benefit allowance was raised from £16-£17 per week to a £25 per week training allowance. Most of the trainees were young women taking courses such as the Retailing and Distributive Trades course. Initial research showed that their main reason for enrolment was: 'It's something to do, isn't it?' Young women tend to have fewer 'street-corner' activities than do young men to occupy their time. As their friends returned to school or college in the autumn of 1982, so the young women drifted into the pilot YTS courses.

Provision for the 16 to 19 year old age group is characterized by inequality. The well-provided-for client groups are the prospective higher education entrants and the politically visible young unemployed. The inequalities are manifest: those entering employment without any structured training receive the least amount of further education (see Table 1 on p 155). Despite this, it has been youth unemployment and not egalitarian reform that has kept the provision for the 16 to 19 year

Main types of provision	Client groups	Client groups as percentage of age group (1981)	Percentage of client group provided for (1981)
Unified vocational preparation (pilot schemes)	Those entering employment without any structured training	11-16	1.6 - 2.5
Young operatives courses	Those entering employment with opportunity for structured training	27	56
Youth Opportunities Programme	Unemployed	11-16	63 - 95*
Full-time A level courses (school or college)	Prospective higher education entrants	21	84
Vocational qualifications	Full-time students seeking vocational qualifications	11	70
General educational qualifications (school or college)	Full-time general education students	11	67.5
Literacy and numeracy	Those requiring remedial education	3	10
Totals	1,850,000	100	

Note
* In the first part of 1981, only 36 per cent of YOPs entered a job or education or training

Source: Adapted from *Education for 16 - 19 Year Olds*, Department of Education and Science, January 1981.

Table 1: Provision for 16 to 19 year olds in a single year in England and Wales

olds on the political agenda since the Conservatives took office in 1979 (Blackstone and Lodge, 1982).

Female students are clustered in the low-level courses in the further education sector. They are outnumbered by 4 : 1 on advanced courses, despite the fact that they make up the majority of all further education students (Department of Education and Science, 1978: 5). One explanation for this is that girls and boys have often followed somewhat different curricula in their secondary schools. The secondary education that many girls receive, in spite of the existence of the Sex Discrimination Act 1975, does not equip them even to apply for many further education courses. Ninety per cent of all courses above craft level require an applicant to possess a minimum of four or five GCE O level passes. For two-thirds of further education courses a candidate must offer subjects chosen from a limited range of core subjects that include mathematics, English, physics, chemistry and a technical craft. Boys have more passes in all of these subjects except English. Subjects that the girls hold, such as housecraft, are often specifically precluded from fulfilling entry requirements (Byrne, 1978).

In addition to the teenagers, there are two million adults involved in non-advanced further education, mostly on a part-time basis. The majority of these are women. Of the students enrolled on my adult courses during 1982-3, between half and three-quarters were taking the subject with a view to enhancing their present or future work prospects.

Some of these women students were employed, yet wanted a change of direction:

'Have been trying to find a job in Social Administration/advice/ information work since graduation — no success. Hoped this (GCE A level) course might be useful — and also interesting for my own sake — particularly to relieve the boredom of my job.'

'Having been a secretary for seven years I would like to move on to a more responsible post within local government and hope that this (GCE A level) course will give me some insights into the various aspects.'

'I work with old people in an old people's home (as a domestic) and I find it such rewarding work that I have decided that this should be my career, working with people.'

Some students had full-time family commitments but were concerned to further their future employment prospects:

'I chose to do this (GCE O level) course after having had some interesting discussions with a student who attended last year. Also to further my education for the future. Also to help me sort out my views on these issues.'

'I thought it would be an interesting subject and get my mind thinking of other items than family and housework. Also with the other subjects that I hope to take over the next few years it would be helpful when I apply for a job in the future to get some O levels as this seems to be required for any interesting jobs.'

Of the 50 per cent of my students who did not enrol for any directly vocational reasons, the following statements are typical:

'I became involved and interested in this subject during the time that one of my daughters was taking it at O and A level.'

'The reason that I wanted to take this subject is because my cousin said that it is very interesting. It was the only course on the night I could make which offered an examination.'

'I want to study this subject to get away from nappies.'

A somewhat unusual motivation was expounded by a retired primary schoolmistress:

'I need the vocabulary of this subject so that I can understand writings on feminism and modern politics.'

(All quotations are taken from the author's original research on student enrolment in September/October 1982).

Vocational education for women's work

For women, much more than for men, family considerations, either actual or potential, figure largely in their choices of vocational education and employment. Any analysis that seeks to understand their position as students within the non-advanced further education sector cannot ignore the dual nature of 'women's work' in modern industrial society. In this chapter, the term 'women's work' includes both paid and unpaid activity. The original material referred to in this section is to be found in my doctoral thesis (Blunden, 1982). Three historical case studies were conducted in order to examine the relationship between the local labour market and women's non-advanced further education. These were of Cinderford and Stroud in Gloucestershire and Swindon in Wiltshire, England.

Unpaid domestic labour, generally performed by women, is as necessary to the maintenance of modern industrial society as paid labour. This is because housework and child-care, on a daily and generational basis, physically and emotionally reproduce the labour power that is employed to produce profits directly for the industrialist (Malos, 1980). Work caring for husbands and children or for fathers and brothers is of wide significance in the economy: its effects are not limited to each individual household. Vocational education for women in England and Wales has reinforced this dual definition of what constitutes women's work, whereas the provision made for men has been limited to those forms of knowledge that are relevant to men's paid employment only.

Since the mid-nineteenth century, there has been a strong relationship between the local labour market and further education provision. Courses were generally initiated where they were perceived to be in the local economic interest. In the 1890s, many firms were swift to take advantage of local government funds being made available for training of their labour force. With the sharpening of international industrial competition, a more skilled worker was required than had previously been the case, if Britain were to retain its favourable economic position. Since vocational

education was developed and supplied with the assistance of government monies, individual firms were no longer responsible for the whole
costs of training their workforce. Nevertheless, they did not lose much
of their control over the type of education that their employees received
since, in the early days, they were heavily represented on the relevant
local government committees.

Within this framework, the resources that were made available to
supporting vocational education were directed towards providing those
kinds of courses that would equip the local economy with the skilled
workforce it needed. For example, in Swindon the Great Western Railway
Company had developed its Locomotive and Carriage Works. These
employed 80 per cent of the economically active men in the town by
1908. The local authority provided an extensive scheme of engineering
courses that the company encouraged its employees to attend. In 1903-4,
part-time day courses in mechanical engineering were introduced, whereby
selected apprentices were released from work to attend, their wages being
paid by the company as if they were at work. A similar scheme for clerical
workers was inaugurated in the 1920s.

In Gloucestershire, after 1890 vocational education was developed
related to the dominant industries of the county: agricultural instruction
throughout the county; mining instruction in the Forest of Dean, relevant
to the thriving mining industry of the area; and textile education based on
Stroud, in an attempt to resurrect the dying textile industry. Nor were
the claims of women and girls to a share in this type of provision entirely
ignored. Where they were employed in a skilled capacity and required in
certain kinds of paid employment in the locality, then courses were
provided for their further education. This was especially true in Stroud,
where the local middle classes sought to establish a School of Domestic
Economy in an attempt to provide themselves with a pool of suitably
trained women domestic workers.

For women, however, the relationship between their vocational education and the needs of the local economy was not as straightforward as
it was for men. Even when they were not engaged in paid occupations,
they were not wholly excluded from the further education sector. Certain
courses, namely those associated with domestic skills and 'womanly'
accomplishments, were always provided for them, albeit in a somewhat
haphazard fashion.

Women's position, both within and outside the paid labour force,
affected their further education opportunities in four main ways. They
are illustrated below by reference to policies pursued in Gloucestershire
and Swindon in the early part of this century.

Firstly, when women worked in those occupations where further
education was deemed necessary to ensure that the workforce was
equipped with the skills appropriate to the work task, then further education opportunities were provided for them. Where the interests of both
women themselves and those of their employers coincided, then women's
further education opportunities were broadened. This was especially

true of the expansion of women's commercial education in the 1920s.

Most such courses also included domestic education in their curricula, hardly a vital requirement in most secretarial posts. Yet the male-dominated education committees of the time argued that, even where girls were being trained to take up non-domestic vocations, their training as the nation's wives and mothers should not be neglected. The curriculum was broadened not in order to equip girls to secure better jobs and good prospects of promotion in their chosen occupations, but rather to perpetuate the notion that women's first responsibilities were to their homes and families. In Swindon, girl employees' domestic education took two forms. Initially, special domestic science evening classes were provided for the girls employed in a clothing factory before the first world war. Later on, when young women were released from work during the day to attend classes, as they were by a Swindon tobacco firm immediately after the war, it was to improve their domestic, not their technical skills. Such courses as these were both directly and indirectly beneficial to the local economy. Women were being trained to perform well in paid employment, when this was economically desirable, and to improve their capacities for reproducing men as the current and children as the future workforce.

The second way that women's opportunities were affected by the kinds of work that they did was a restrictive one. If women did not work in those sectors of the local economy where further skills were required, then they missed out on the educational provision that existed for male workers in these other sectors. With the growth of day-release courses in engineering and similar subjects, these limitations were especially marked.

In this way, the policies of the local education authority contributed to the institutionalization of sex-discrimination. The Gloucestershire County Council considered that the visible economic needs of the area were very important and diverted further education spending in order to satisfy them. In doing so, the council was adopting a policy of allocation and provision that indirectly resulted in the exclusion of women from any great share in it. Where men were employed in the dominant sector of the local economy, it was they who reaped the very real benefits of further education: from widened horizons; educated companionship; increased promotion prospects; scholarships; organized trips and enhanced status in the local community.

The local authority did not deliberately set out to discriminate against women and deny them these advantages; indirect discrimination against women was, however, a consequence of this policy. The consequences of discrimination are no less real to the women who suffer them by virtue of their not being intentional. Indeed, if discriminatory practices are hidden, they present great problems for those concerned with their eradication. When these practices can be explained away as the unintended consequences of a particular policy, they can be seen as inevitable and consequently nothing need or should be done to combat them.

This is also true in considering the third type of relationship that existed between women's work and their further education opportunities.

Even where women were employed in an industry for which the local education authority made vocational provision, if they were not employed in a skilled capacity or at a supervisory level then their actual or potential claim to further education was not considered. Although women made up a large proportion of the workforce in the textile and clothing industries in Stroud, they did not reap the benefits of the local authority's investment in textile education in the area. The classes were intended for managers and foremen, and this policy had repercussions for women's opportunities. Women did not hold positions of formal responsibility in the textile mills, despite being a high proportion of the workforce, and they were therefore excluded from these courses. They were not excluded directly because of their sex, but because of the indirect effects of the sexual division of labour in the local economy. This was not merely a straightforward example of the local economy determining educational provision. The very exclusion of women from these courses for managers and foremen served to perpetuate the notion that women's position in the factory was a less responsible, and consequently less well-paid one, than men's.

Finally, it was generally the case that if women wanted instruction that was not beneficial to the local economy, then that demand remained unsatisfied. There was a considerable demand for art education in Stroud, articulated by middle class women. However, the relationship between art education and local industry in Stroud was virtually non-existent. Further education of this nature in Stroud did not form one of the local education authority's priorities and when resources were scarce, Art education undoubtedly suffered. This has severe consequences for further education prospects for women in so far as it was acknowledged that many of the potential art students were female. A shortage of resources devoted to art education resulted in restrictions in women's further education opportunities.

Women's vocational education in England and Wales developed in order to prepare them for their perceived adult roles. These were first and foremost as wives and mothers, and such training as they did receive was directed to this end. Their unpaid, private, domestic labour was important both to the economy, since it ensured the daily and generational reproduction of labour power, and to men, since they benefit from women's domestic services. However, when labour was scarce, and the local economy required women to work in a skilled, paid capacity, the further education system facilitated women's entry into paid employment. The patriarchal power structure required that, when this occurred, men should not lose the benefits of women's services, so women were trained in so limited a manner that their long-term participation in the paid labour force was unlikely. When they were excluded from training, their exclusion helped perpetuate a belief in the inferiority of their skills. Married women were expected to participate in paid employment, if at all, in menial and insecure jobs from which they could easily be discharged as and when the needs of the economy so required.

The 1980s: a decade of change?

Recently, vocational education for young people has become rather an anachronism, if it refers to further education for paid employment. Further education is increasingly being used as a *substitute* for employment. Students are being directed into one of two kinds of course: those of a general educational nature and those provided by the Manpower Services Commission which are directed to specific kinds of employment. Neither offers the guarantee of a full-time, permanent paid job at the end of it.

There are fewer and fewer places available on the vocationally-orientated courses such as apprenticeships that used to virtually guarantee paid employment. Employers are withdrawing their support from the traditional types of vocational education. The government is assuming greater and greater control over young people's training, which still maintains the fiction that it is training for paid employment.

This policy is not without precedent. When, in the 1920s and 1930s, youth unemployment, especially for girls, was increasing, further education also acted as a substitute for work. More young women than young men were prepared to enrol on courses to try to enhance their paid employment prospects. When the local economy was in recession, men's evening class enrolments fell since they could neither afford, nor see any advantage in pursuing, further training. In contrast, women's enrolments on both day and evening courses tended to increase during economic recessions. In a booming economy, young women were able to find work immediately — in shops, factories or domestic service — and this obviated the need for continued education. In a recession their labour market prospects were curtailed and young women turned to vocational education as a way of improving their labour market position.

Vocational training also served, as now, to remove them from the labour force altogether. All too often, local authority subsidized courses prepared them only for their assumed future occupations as wives and mothers. It is too early to say whether this will be one of the results of the Youth Training Scheme courses.

Adult occupations in Britain are still characterized by a rigid sexual division of labour (Hakim, 1978) and the further education sector reflects this division. Despite a massive growth in the further education sector since the Second World War and the development of a wide range of new courses, a student's sex still to a large extent determines the course on which she or he will enrol. The difference now is that students 'choose' their courses, rather than being allocated to them according to their sex. Service sector subjects such as office practice, fashion and hairdressing are not accorded the same status within a college as engineering subjects. The former are often, perjoratively, referred to as 'women's subjects'. Indeed, until recently, many of these subjects were to be found in a college's 'department for women and girls'. Engineering and technical subjects enjoy the prestige of being thought to be the more worthy contributors to the national economy. Further education continues to operate on the assumption that women's first duty is to marry, bear and rear children, and that their involvement in paid employment is a temporary phase in their lives for which little training is necessary or desirable. Current policies and trends in women's vocational education suggest that it is unlikely to offer much of a challenge to this assumption in the immediate future.

References

Blackstone, T and Lodge, P (1982) *Educational Policy and Educational Inequality* Martin Robertson: London

Blunden, G (1982) *Women's Place in Non-advanced Further Education: The Early Development of Three Colleges in South West England* PhD University of Bristol (unpublished)

Byrne, E (1978) *Women and Education* Tavistock: London

Department of Education and Science (1978) *Statistics of Education* **5** HMSO: London

Hakim, C (1978) Sexual divisions within the labour force: occupational segregation *Department of Employment Gazette* **86** 11: 1264-68

Malos, E ed (1980) *The Politics of Housework* Allison and Busby: London

13. Lessons from the past: the experience of women teachers in Quebec and Ontario

Marta Danylewycz and Alison Prentice

Summary: This paper focuses on the history of women teachers as an important context for understanding the position of women in teaching today. An outline of recent North American approaches to the topic introduces the authors' own research on nineteenth and twentieth century women teachers who worked in two Canadian provinces: Ontario and Quebec. This research examines the variables of ethnicity, age, household status, class and gender in their regional and economic contexts, showing how they interacted with and affected teachers' experiences. We conclude with a brief examination of women teachers' attempts to organize, connecting both their successes and their failures with the continuing ambiguity of the social conditions under which they have always worked and lived.

The sexual division of labour in teaching

Contemporary debates on the role of women in schools and the social characteristics of teachers have a long history. Their roots can be traced not only to the early days of teacher organizing in the late nineteenth and early twentieth centuries, but to the earlier nineteenth century origins of mass public education when some school promoters called into question the very presence of women in non-domestic schools. To understand the sources and evolution of debates about women teachers is to begin to understand some of the ambiguities and contradictions which affect the role of women in the schools today.

The history of teaching has received considerable attention in North America during the past decade. Looking first at the ideas and politics of mid-nineteenth century school reformers, historians have pointed out the extent to which leading school men and women shared and used the ideology of 'true womanhood' to explain both the increasing involvement of women in elementary education outside of their own homes and their lower status in the occupation compared to that of men (Riley, 1969; Melder, 1972; Sklar, 1973). More recent analyses, on the other hand, have focused on the teachers themselves. Examining teachers' conditions of work and the social characteristics of schoolmistresses and masters in various regions, these studies have attempted to document more closely the actual, as opposed to the ideal or perceived, experience of teachers and the way in which this experience changed over time. Work on the history of teachers and their organizations in North America has begun to suggest that, whether or not teachers accepted the professional ethic promoted by the state, they resisted the state's intervention and attempted to organize around their own needs. This was true not only of those teachers who, convinced of their own special abilities and qualifications, were involved in a quest for status and advancement through the promotion of professional hierarchies, but also of the far greater number who, both individually and collectively, struggled for better conditions of work and wages for the rank and file (Prentice, 1975; Bernard and Vinovskis, 1977; Strober and Tyack, 1980; Tyack and Strober, 1981; Danylewycz and Prentice, 1982; Urban, 1982; Danylewycz, Light and Prentice, 1983).

Partly as a result of these studies, historians interested in teachers have become increasingly aware of the vital importance of the sexual division of labour in any consideration of the occupation. It has become clear that historical discussion of working conditions or social structure within the occupation, or of teachers' individual or collective efforts to improve their situations must take into account the persistence of important historical differences in the treatment and experience of men and women teachers. Indeed, the continuous renewal of such differences, fostered by school administrators, schoolmasters and schoolmistresses alike, as well as by church, state and family, has had a profound impact on the working lives of all teachers. It is true, furthermore, that the development of socially constructed and reinforced gender roles in teaching provides historians and sociologists with not only an early example of the sexual division of labour in capitalist industrializing societies, but also a case study which can illuminate this process in other occupations which have emerged in these societies.

Quebec and Ontario: contrasting cases

The authors' own work explores the ways in which cultural, economic and political factors influenced the sexual division of labour in teaching in Canada during the period of industrialization, the commercialization of agriculture and the expansion of public schooling. It focuses on two central Canadian provinces, Ontario and Quebec. Although they shared many characteristics with each other, and with parts of the United States, these provinces were also unique and in some ways sharply contrasting societies. As a result, they provided interesting case studies for testing prevailing models of the development of sexual divisions of labour in teaching (Danylewycz and Prentice, 1982; Danylewycz, Light and Prentice, 1983; Danylewycz, 1983).

A province chiefly inhabited by the descendants of the original inhabitants of New France, Quebec was an established rural society facing serious land and even food shortages by the middle of the nineteenth century. These conditions were driving farm families to new lands in the northern and eastern parts of the province and also to eastern Ontario and to the industrial towns of New England. At the same time, Quebec's largest city, Montreal, was itself undergoing rapid industrial development and attracting immigrants from Ireland as well as from its own rural hinterland. Finally, resource industries such as lumbering played a growing part in the economy of the province, providing farmers with both additional and alternative sources of employment.

Compared with Quebec, Ontario was a relatively new society. Also predominantly rural in character, the more westerly province was peopled mainly by migrants from the United States and the British Isles. Lumbering flourished in parts of Ontario as it did in Quebec, but the industrial and commercial development of its chief city, Toronto, was not as rapid as that experienced by Montreal. In fact, because of the province's later development and the marketing needs of its wheat economy Ontario boasted quite a number of smaller urban centres, in contrast to Quebec where small towns were proportionally less numerous. If material contrasts between Ontario and Quebec were important, cultural differences were no less significant. The eastern province was predominantly French speaking, the western English. And, by the third quarter of the nineteenth century, it was clear that differences in language were re-inforced by differences in religion, as the Roman Catholicism of Quebec intensified and Ontario became more and more vocally Protestant in outlook.

The sexual division of labour in the two provinces also evolved differently. In contrast to earlier American and Canadian studies which linked the feminization of teaching to the development of hierarchies in urban school systems and emphasized the persistence of male teachers in rural schools (Strober and Tyack, 1980; Strober and Lanford, 1981), we found that in eastern Ontario and most of rural Quebec, as well as in the schools under the control of the Catholic School Board of the city of Montreal, these models did not fit. On the contrary, as Catholic schooling became more centralized and bureaucratized in Montreal, lay male teachers moved from slightly under half to a majority of the lay teachers employed by the Catholic School Commission of the city. In rural Quebec and parts of rural eastern Ontario, in contrast, men disappeared from teachers' ranks remarkably early, well before the introduction of hierarchies, longer school years, or other factors typically associated with feminization (Danylewycz and Prentice, 1982; Danylewycz, Light and Prentice, 1983).

The regional economies of the rural areas we examined seemed to account for the deviations from the earlier models historians had proposed to explain the increasing sexual division of labour in public school teaching. Poverty and the presence, in Quebec and eastern Ontario, of industries such as lumbering, which called young men into the bush rather than the school, combined to produce a majority of female teachers almost from the beginning of public schooling. Another factor which affected the early sexual division of labour in teaching in French Canada, and may have had an impact elsewhere, was the presence of an important tradition of women in teaching prior to the emergence of government-supported schooling. Nuns had been significantly involved in formal education since the founding of New France, and the informal sexual division of labour in eighteenth and early nineteenth century households usually dictated that mothers assume responsibility for the education of their daughters and often of other children as well. These domestic or family 'schools' were at times more formally organized and taught by women in need of independent incomes, such as spinsters or widows. The rapid growth of women's teaching orders and continuing feminization of the rural lay teaching force in the second half of the nineteenth century in Quebec thus merely strengthened an already strong female presence in education.

The atypical expansion of the male lay teaching force in Montreal was not so much related to economic as to political factors. The commissioners who governed the Montreal Catholic state-supported schools promoted the interests of male teachers at the expense of their female counterparts. The emergence of gender-based hierarchies was thwarted, first, by the existence of organizational structures internal to the various religious communities whose members were also employed by the Catholic School Commission and, second, by the progressive development of a two-caste system for lay teachers working for the Commission. Members of this board created a formal structure for men teachers, which not only promoted their professional interests but also defined salary ranges and set educational standards. For women, no such channels for hiring and advancement were put in place. This was in contrast to the approach of the Public School Board of the city of Toronto, which welcomed women teachers into the public school system but, at the same time, confined them to poorly paid positions in the junior grades of the schools (Danylewycz and Prentice, 1982; Danylewycz, 1983).

Yet the social organization of teaching in the past has been even more complex and variable than the existence of these differing patterns would imply. We have examined the changing characteristics of teachers as they are revealed in Canadian manuscript census records, available for the years 1851, 1861, 1871 and 1881, and our explorations of these records not only uncovered further contrasts between the experiences of men and women in teaching but shed considerable light on the ways in which such contrasts developed (Laskin, Light and Prentice, 1982).

Ontario, first of all, seems to have had a larger and more persistent pool of cash-hungry immigrant men looking for teaching jobs than was the case in Quebec. The average ages and household positions of teachers also proved to have explanatory power. Men teachers were older than women, on the average, in both Quebec and Ontario, and were far more likely to be either boarders in the households of others, or heads of their own households, than the women. In Ontario, the growing number of rural schoolmistresses thus meant not only an increase in the proportion of Canadian-born teachers but an increase in the proportion who were dependent young people living in the households of their parents. Evidently as rural school trustees found that they were less and less able to afford the salaries of male teachers or that fewer immigrant men were available for hire, they increasingly turned to the girls of their own communities in their search for teachers. In Quebec, where rural districts adopted this pattern several decades earlier, an even greater need for economy also dictated that some 25 per cent of country schoolmistresses had not only to teach but to live in the frequently inadequate school houses that were the locations of their daily work.

Class backgrounds of teachers, in contrast to age or ethnicity, were more difficult to determine. Within the census returns the only indication of class are the occupations of teachers' relatives living in the same households. If teachers boarded with families that were not their own or were the sole breadwinners in their families, information on class background could not be obtained. And even for the teachers who lived in the households of parents or siblings reporting occupations, the problem of assessing and classifying these occupations still remained. In the rural regions, most teachers came from farming families whose wealth or class position could not be easily identified. Only in the cities, where the economy was more diversified, was some insight into teachers' backgrounds possible. We found that in Toronto and Montreal the female teaching force was divided more or less equally between daughters of workers and daughters of professionals, civil servants and small businessmen, with only a tiny minority coming from the extreme ends of the social spectrum. Women teachers as a group, therefore, cannot be exclusively identified with either one or the other of the great social classes created by nineteenth century capitalist development. They came from both.

The rise of teacher consciousness

These differences in age, ethnicity, household status, and social background, as well as regional differences, posed serious obstacles to the formation of a collective, province-wide consciousness among teachers. A combination of factors over which the employers of teachers had no controi, such as local poverty, rapidly rising enrollments, especially in urban centres, or the hostility of the community to public schooling, and those which their own politics engendered, such as the insistence on rigid hierarchies of control in the larger school systems, or the frequent failure to provide adequate wages or accommodation in both rural and urban settings, merely reinforced the sense of isolation and powerlessness expeienced by many teachers. Equally fragmenting was the perception by teachers of their work as a temporary stop-gap on the way to marriage or other employment. It is not surprising, then, that the first signs of discontent among teachers were individual, sporadic and held little promise of collective improvement.

Like workers in other occupations, many expressed their discontent by simply abandoning teaching as soon as the opportunity presented itself. Women teachers took husbands and embarked on motherhood, or moved into other areas of paid employment, more often than not in the better paying industrial occupations. Some who took these options publicized their decisions to leave teaching in the newspapers in the hope, perhaps, of embarrassing their former employers. Nor were teachers, who persevered in the occupation, necessarily silent or entirely acquiescent. It was not uncommon for Catholic women teachers to join religious orders devoted to educational work and, thus, through conventual life, escape some of the more debilitating aspects of lay teaching (Danylewycz, 1981). Protestant schoolmistressses, or Catholic ones who rejected this alternative, however, also had ways of expressing their grievances. Letters written to the Montreal Catholic School Commission illustrate the extent of their disenchantment. One such protest, voiced in 1881, was the work of several teachers and accused the commissioners of favouring schoolmasters. Was it not time, they asked, that: 'men of the law sought to protect the interests of poor women teachers, which have been sacrificed to the advantage of a handful of men . . .?' (Danylewycz and Prentice, 1982: 20). One year later there was even talk of a strike. The walkout did not materialize but the threat of one and the barrage of complaints that had preceded it led the commissioners to change part of the newly-implemented pension plan, which placed a heavy burden on the poorly paid women (DeCelles, 1882).

Schoolmistresses in Montreal also organized the support of parents and students when the Catholic Commission, because of a shortage of funds, tried to close down their schools. On at least a few occasions, the school that was due for closing remained open as a result and its mistresses employed. Finally, Quebec teachers, both rural and urban, put their case in the press. They accused school commissioners of stinginess and ignorance in educational matters; they demanded higher wages and expressed support for the early teacher unions. The overriding concern was to keep the public informed of the conditions under which teachers worked. 'We are the exploited', one woman teacher wrote in 1902. 'They humiliate us from year to year. They have turned our career into one of disenchantment and misery.' (Institutrice, 1902).

Ontario's teachers registered similar complaints. As early as the 1840s, Elizabeth Ann Inglis wrote to the Chief Superintendent of Schools for the province about her annoyance that the school trustees who employed her, although admitting that her work was superior to that of most men, paid her a significantly lower wage (Prentice, 1975). Others, like John Metcalfe Willson, who taught in the 1860s in Ontario's rural townships, moved almost annually to new communities in search of higher wages or better working conditions (Boyce, 1967).

Isolated and individual though these protests were, they reveal that at least some teachers of both sexes were aware of ways in which they were subject to exploitation, especially if they wished to remain in teaching for any length of time. They were perhaps less aware of the sources of their relative lack of power, however, tending to blame 'cheap' trustees and, if they were men, the infiltration of women into the occupation for their low wages and frequently poor working conditions.

While teachers' perceptions of their problems continued to reflect both the myopia caused by their acceptance of sexual stereotypes, as well as the difficulty of deciphering how these problems were related to the economic, political and social structures in which their work was embedded, some at least saw that collective action might produce more results than individual protest. The first to organize were the men teachers, and one can trace schoolmasters' associations back to the 1840s in parts of Ontario and Quebec. The early organizations were somewhat ephemeral, reflecting the extreme mobility of the teacher population, the difficulties of travel and communication in pioneer communities, and, it would appear, the determination of the state to control any collectivities that teachers might try to create. The more permanent teacher organizations, which began to emerge in the 1850s and 1860s, were elite associations at best, chiefly representing male administrators or would-be administrators – school principals, government school inspectors and the like – rather than the rank and file. It was in the cities that the rank and file teachers first began to recognize the need for alternative organizations of their own. In the city of Toronto in the 1880s these teachers were women. The association they founded eventually became part of a province-wide federation of women teachers' associations which speaks for the women teachers of Ontario to this day (Women Teachers' Association, 1932; Labarrère-Paulé, 1965; French, 1968; Smaller, 1983).

The problems faced by the early organizers of the Toronto Women Teachers' Association were the classic problems of their time, and of other women from their time to our own: they lacked power; they lacked a voice; they even lacked space they could call their own. They recognized that they had special concerns as women: obvious ones such as lower average salaries than the men; a lower status in the schools; and less opportunity for advancement in a school system which was increasingly hierarchical in structure. But there were also subtler problems. School trustees tried to control the clothing that women teachers chose to wear and the modes of transport they used, not just inside but outside of school hours. Inside the schools the women had to contend with the effect of oiled floors on their floor length skirts.

The Toronto Women Teachers' Association won the battle to have the oiling of floors stopped; the Association successfully protested a school trustee's attempt to prevent teachers from wearing bloomers and riding bicycles. It was a longer struggle to win private meeting spaces, both in and outside of the schools, but these were eventually won as well. Members of the Association gained a voice for women teachers when they insisted on speaking directly to the school trustees rather than continuing to allow the male governed Toronto Teachers' Association to speak for them. Eventually they elected their own members to the executive of the Toronto Teachers' Association, as well as women members to the School Board. They also succeeded in reversing the Board's policy of tying salaries to the grade level taught, a policy which had clearly discriminated against the women teachers. But the larger campaigns they eventually shared with the provincial Federation of Women Teachers' Associations, founded in 1918, were less successful. These campaigns, for equal pay and to more effectively organize in larger numbers, were to drag on for decades in fact, perhaps because the women had, along with their battles with the men teachers and school boards, internal battles to fight amongst themselves.

For despite their growing consciousness of their subordinate status and unique condition, women teachers' efforts to organize in Toronto and Ontario were marked by extreme ambivalence. They were ambivalent towards their male colleagues, whose co-operation appeared to be essential if serious fights with school boards over salaries and working conditions were to be won, and yet whose agenda was very different from their own. They were equally ambivalent about the nature of their work and their status as teachers. Affiliation of the Toronto Women Teachers' Association with the Toronto Trades and Labour Council, contemplated in the period just prior to the First World War, for example, appears to have been set aside by the women, chiefly because affiliation was at odds with their quest for professional recognition and feminine respectability (Women Teachers' Association, 1932; Bryans, 1974; Smaller, 1983).

It would be many years after the First World War before the women teachers of Ontario were able to take a more militant stand or to begin to recognize the factors that worked to create their unequal status in the profession, let alone the relationship of their occupation to those of other workers or to the state. But the early organizers of women teachers in Ontario were at least clear that the question of gender was central to their situation and needed to be addressed. And, despite powerful pressure to amalgamate with male teachers' organizations over the years, the Federation of Women Teachers' Associations of Ontario has continued to stress this original insight, insisting on the need to organize separately from the men (French, 1968).

Separate organizations for French Catholic women teachers were not as enduring as their Ontario counterparts. Nor has their history been as extensively explored. We do know that an *Association des Institutrices Catholiques* was formed in Montreal in 1901, chiefly to provide support for women teachers who needed assistance during illness or unemployment. This organization was short-lived however, and, in 1921, was replaced by the women's section of the newly-formed and more enduring *Alliance des Professeurs Catholiques de Montréal*.

It was in the rural areas of Quebec that powerful women teachers' organizations finally emerged. Under the leadership of Lauré Gaudreault, a 44-year-old teacher and journalist, the *Association des Institutrices Rurales* was founded in the district of Malbaie in 1936. Other groupings followed suit and combined forces to create, in the following year, a federation of rural women teachers. Although reluctant to call their organization a union, this federation was distinguished by its early pursuit of labour-oriented goals under the 1924 *Loi des Syndicats Professionnels* which sanctioned collective bargaining (Thivierge, 1983).

Past as present in the experience of women teachers

The creation of strong provincial teacher organizations marked a new stage in the history of women teachers. No longer confined to sporadic, short-lived or locally organized protest, women teachers employed in public schools now had access to somewhat more powerful vehicles to further their interests. Their concerns could be more effectively expressed and, at times, their grievances settled.

Yet the potential strength of these larger and more stable bodies could not be realized as long as the contradictions and tensions created by gender, class and regional differences persisted. The ambivalence which had characterized women teachers' actions in the past persisted as well. Finally, the involvement of the state in teacher training and certification, the strength of gender-defined hierarchies in education, and the expect-ations of parents and school governors that teachers place the interests of the community above their own needs for higher salaries and better working conditions, have continued to place a strain on the collective actions of both schoolmistresses and schoolmasters.

Exploring the history of teachers demonstrates how important it is to go beyond school-related reforms and to question the wider structures of society if we are to create educational systems that are genuinely accept-able to, and accepting of, women teachers. The experiences of nineteenth and early twentieth century Quebec and Ontario schoolmistresses were embedded in the organization of the family, the sexual division of labour and regional economic development. This is no less so today. The study of the history of teaching also demonstrates that the situation of contemp-orary women teachers cannot be understood solely in the context of contemporary social and political structures or economic development. The position of women teachers today reflects this history of tension and ambiguity.

References

Bernard, R N and Vinousksis, M A (1977) The female school teacher in ante-bellum Massachusetts *Journal of Social History* **10** 3: 332-45

Boyce, G E (1967) *Historic Hastings* Hastings County Council: Belleville, Ontario

Bryans, W (1974) Virtuous women at half the price: the feminization of the teaching force and early women teacher organizations in Ontario MA Thesis: University of Toronto

Danylewycz, M (1981) Taking the veil in Montreal: an alternative to marriage, motherhood and spinsterhood PhD Thesis: University of Toronto

Danylewycz, M (1983) Sexes et classes sociales dans l'enseignement: le cas de Montréal à la fin du 19e siècle *in* Fahmy-Eid and Dumont

Danylewycz, M, Light, B and Prentice, A (1983) The evolution of the sexual division of labour in teaching: a nineteenth century Ontario and Quebec case study *Histoire sociale/Social History* 15 30

Danylewycz, M and Prentice, A (1982) Teachers, gender and bureaucratizing school systems in nineteenth century Montreal and Toronto Paper presented at a Conference in Comparative Urban History: Guelph, Ontario

DeCelles, A D (1882) Les maîtresses d'école en grève! *Journal de l'instruction publique* 11 10: 299-300

Fahmy-Eid, N and Dumont, M eds (1983) *Maîtresses de maison, maîtresses d'école: Femmes, famille et éducation dans l'histoire du Québec* Boréal Express: Montréal

French, D (1968) *High Button Bootstraps: Federation of Women Teachers' Association of Ontario, 1918-1968* The Ryerson Press: Toronto

Institutrice (1902) Autour de l'école *La Patrie* October 10

Labarrère-Paulé, A (1965) *Les instituteurs laiques au Canada français, 1836-1900* Les Presses de l'Université de Laval: Québec

Laskin, S, Light, B and Prentice, A (1982) Studying the History of an Occupation: Quantitative Sources on Teachers in the Nineteenth Century *Archivaria* 14: 75-92

Melder, K (1972) Women's high calling: the teaching profession in America, 1830-1860 *American Studies* 13: 19-32

Prentice, A (1975) The feminization of teaching in British North America, 1845-1875 *Histoire sociale/Social History* 8: 5-20

Riley, G (1969) Origin of the argument for improved female education *History of Education Quarterly* 9 4: 455-70

Schmuck, P and Charles, W W eds (1981) *Educational Policy and Management: Sex Differentials* Academic Press: San Diego, California

Sklar, K K (1973) *Catharine Beecher: A Study in American Domesticity* Yale University Press: New Haven, Connecticut

Smaller, H (1983) A room of one's own: the early years of the Women Teachers' Association of Toronto Unpublished paper: Ontario Institute for Studies in Education

Strober, M and Lanford, A G (1981) The percentages of women in public school teaching: a cross sectional analysis, 1850-1880 *Social Science and History Association Annual Meeting* Nashville, Tennessee

Strober, M H and Tyack, D (1980) Why do women teach and men manage *Signs* 5 3: 494-503

Thivierge, M (1983) La syndicalisation des institutrices catholiques, 1900-1959 *in* Fahmy-Eid and Dumont

Tyack, D and Strober, M H (1981) Jobs and gender: a history of the structuring of educational employment by sex *in* Schmuck and Charles

Urban, W J (1982) *Why Teachers Organized* Wayne State University Press: Detroit

Women Teachers' Association (1932) *The Story of the Women Teachers' Association of Toronto* Thomas Nelson: Toronto

Acknowledgements

This paper draws on the research that we have done on Quebec and Ontario teachers, generously sponsored by the Ontario Institute for Studies in Education and the Social Sciences and Humanities Research Council of Canada. Parts of this paper have been excerpted from Danylewycz and Prentice, 1982 and Danylewycz, Light and Prentice, 1983 and we are grateful to the editors of Histoire sociale/Social History and the History of Education Quarterly for permission to reprint these excerpts. Finally we wish to thank John Abbott and Harry Smaller for their very helpful criticisms of early drafts of the chapter.

14. Women's access to higher education in Scotland

Shirley Cunningham

Summary: The access of women to higher education in Scotland is described against an international backcloth, in the light of two contrasting traditions to which Scots girls have fallen heir: the democratic tradition of Scottish education on the one hand and, on the other, the conservative role of women in Western Europe generally. Both traditions have had their effect. As long ago as the mid-1960s Scottish girls had already achieved an equality with boys in the completion of upper secondary schooling and entry into higher education unmatched by the great majority of Western European countries, England included. The historical antecedents and present characteristics of the Scottish educational system which appear to have helped the girls particularly, such as cheap schooling and co-education, are outlined. Women are, however, as elsewhere, still largely found in certain fields of study, notably arts and social science faculties and teacher-training, although there has been some widening of horizons in recent years.

Introduction

How do Scottish girls compare to those in other countries in their chances of higher education? The question has relevance beyond the boundaries of a small country on the windy northern fringes of Europe because, strangely, the Scottish education system has offered greater opportunities for girls than might be expected from a country whose best-known church-man, John Knox, is still remembered for his blast against 'the monstrous regiment of women' and in which a distinguished, well-travelled, twentieth-century author, Naomi Mitchison, detected a 'curious deep anti-feminism'.

Others have commented on this strongly conservative tradition, deeply embedded in West European culture, of the role of Scotswomen in society which places them very firmly in the home. Scotland is: 'a nation of porridge-makers, cleaners, cooks and housekeepers', as one journalist remarked tartly in the early 1970s.

This hardly seems the most congenial climate for a girl's intellectual talents to flourish. Certainly, in the debate of the late 1960s on women's rights (or lack of them) in Britain, there was nothing to suggest that Scotland's women were more 'liberated' than their English counterparts, either in the eyes of the law or the world of work, with all the familiar manifestations of discrimination.

It comes, then, as rather a surprise to find that for years past girls in Scotland have travelled further along the road to higher education than most of their West European sisters, English included, and, as long ago as the mid-1960s, they had already achieved an equality with boys in the completion of upper secondary schooling and entry into higher education, albeit in limited fields. Scottish schools and universities, it could be said, have served the girls better than society has served its womenfolk.

This paradox seems to have arisen because Scots girls have fallen heir not just to the conservative tradition of woman's role but also to the long-standing 'democratic' tradition of Scottish education of which the country has been extremely proud: the academic equivalent of the log-cabin to White House legend that states the road to the top is open to the able, however inferior their social standing, and that schools and universities are not the preserve of a small elite. The reality of the legend has been questioned (Kellas, 1980); it was a road for boys, yet nevertheless it helped to shape the Scottish system in ways which have benefited the girls.

This chapter will look at four aspects of women's higher education in Scotland: firstly, its place in an international perspective; secondly, its historical development; thirdly, features of the system which have proved beneficial to girls; and, finally, other characteristics of the country's educational tradition.

The international perspective

The obscurity of Scottish education in a world context derives from the usual amalgamation, in international statistics, of Scotland with England, Wales and Northern Ireland as 'Great Britain' or the 'United Kingdom', where England, its population of 45 million, nine times that of Scotland, sets the norm. This can be misleading as, despite sharing for centuries a common monarch and parliament with the others, Scotland has retained its own distinctive systems of law, religion and education.

International perspectives have to be painted with a broad brush, since data are bedevilled with problems of definition and different methods of counting students. Yet, thanks to the work by bodies such as UNESCO and OECD, it is possible to trace developments in women's higher education from about 1950. In Britain, higher education is generally defined as that carried on in universities, teacher training colleges and advanced further education colleges, beyond the highest standard of the terminal secondary-school certificates, namely the Advanced level of the General Certificate of Education (GCE) in England, Wales and Northern Ireland and the Higher grade of the Scottish Certificate of Education (SCE), or the technical equivalent. Although rough, a useful international distinction is drawn between 'university-type higher education' and other tertiary-level courses (broadly, degree and sub-degree level standard) (OECD, 1971).

Three clear worldwide trends emerge: the first is a considerable, sometimes spectacular, increase in women's participation in higher education, both in total numbers and as a proportion of all students; the second is that, despite this progress, the number of women continues, almost without exception, to lag behind the number of men, particularly in university-type education; the third is that the flow of new women students has mostly been along channels where women were already well-entrenched. Both in university and non-university education there is a striking difference in the types of study followed by men and women, and women are still congregated in a few fields — in arts and social science faculties of universities and in teacher training.

These trends are found in economically advanced countries too, as was shown by an intensive survey by OECD of developments in their 23 member countries, mostly in Western Europe, from 1950 to 1967 (OECD, 1970; 1971). Table 1 illustrates both the growth and continuing short-fall of women's numbers. In 1965, apart from the USA, only France and Finland had anything approaching a balance of the sexes.

| | 1965 | | 1976 | |
	N (1,000s)	%	N (1,000s)	%
Belgium	11.7	24.0	29.6	34.1
Denmark	9.0	30.2	24.3	36.5
Finland	20.3	49.3	37.0	48.8
France	179.6	41.4	385.4	44.2
Germany	59.8	22.5	249.9	35.8
Ireland	4.5	28.1	9.4	41.4
Italy	134.0	32.5	378.8**	38.6
Holland	11.6	18.0	33.8	26.2
Norway	4.8	24.6	14.8	36.5
Sweden	46.9*	38.1	46.6	41.2
UK	48.2	25.6	119.2	33.7
USA	2607.5*	41.5	3298.1	45.6

* 1970 figures
** 1975 figures
Source: OECD, 1981, Tables 18 and 19

Table 1. *Number (in thousands) of women students in university-type higher education in 1965 and 1976 in selected Western countries, and percentage of full-time students whom they represent*

There are, nevertheless, equally remarkable differences between countries, not only in the position of women but also in the chances of young people of either sex entering higher education (OECD, 1971: Table II-9) — hardly surprising, even between neighbours, since 'each system of education is, at any given time, the product of a set of historical circumstances — social, economic, ethnic, cultural — which are not likely to be duplicated in any other country' (UNESCO, 1966).

So where does Scotland stand in the international scene — especially
that of Western Europe with which, historically and geographically, its
ties are closest? In two of the major trends it has followed suit: the growth
in numbers of women students and their concentration in traditional
fields of study. But in a third trend there is a deviation from the pattern:
while fewer girls than boys still attend Scottish universities, for at least
25 years Scottish girls have entered higher education generally in as great
numbers as the boys. While in colleges of education, where the mid-1960s
were boom years and the mid-1970s the time of swingeing government
cut-backs, actual numbers have fallen, the high proportion of women in
the whole higher education sector is quite striking. As long ago as 1965,
women's share of 48 per cent put Scotland up with Finland and France
as leaders in Western Europe (Table 2).

	Universities		Colleges of Education*		Further education (Advanced courses)		All higher education		
	Men	Women	Men	Women	Men	Women	Men	Women	Women %
1965-6	5,839	2,840	325	2,986	1,331	991	7,495	6,817	47.6
1970-1	6,641	3,687	655	3,265	2,541	1,351	9,837	8,303	45.8
1974-5	6,461	4,482	599	2,717	4,364	2,792	11,424	9,991	46.7
1981-2	6,759	5,122	184	670	6,212	5,041	13,155	10,833	45.2

* non-graduate entrants except for BEd students

Source: Annual *Scottish Abstract of Statistics* and Scottish Education
Department (unpublished data)

Table 2. *New entrants to full-time higher education in Scotland
by type of course and sex in selected years.*

These figures, however, relate to women students in Scotland, who are not
necessarily the same as Scottish women students, and ignore the considerable cross-traffic in the United Kingdom at university level, as about
a quarter of students at Scottish universities come from elsewhere. Nevertheless, evidence that Scottish girls had as good a chance as boys of
entering higher education comes from a special inquiry commissioned
by the Robbins Committee (1963) whose influential report, *Higher
Education*, has been unmatched in its analysis of the British scene. The
report estimated that, as long ago as 1954, 6.9 per cent of Scottish-
domiciled girls compared with 6.2 per cent of boys of the appropriate
age group entered full-time higher education, the equivalent figures for
England and Wales being 5.3 per cent of girls and 6.1 per cent of boys
(Appendix One, Part IV, Tables 31 and 32).

The evidence from Robbins showing that 30 years ago, remarkably,
Scottish girls were rather more likely to continue to higher education

than English boys, gives some cause for national cheer, which must be muted, however, by the fact that the numbers were still small. By 1962, only about one in 30 girls in Scotland entered full-time university level courses, compared to about one in four in the USA. Today, the figure is about one in 10 (Burnhill and McPherson, in press), and they are still to be found largely in arts and social science faculties, though numbers in science and medicine have increased.

It also has to be said that the good fortunes of Scottish girls have come about by accident rather than by deliberate implementation of the principles of sex equality; a brief historical perspective helps to explain their position.

Historical perspective

There are, as mentioned, three main types of establishment in Scotland whose work is classed as 'higher education' — the universities, teacher-training colleges, and some further education colleges, notably those known as Central Institutions, which are regional or national rather than local.

There are eight universities, responsible for the bulk of university-level work. Four of them (St Andrews, Aberdeen, Glasgow and Edinburgh) were founded in the fifteenth or sixteenth century; the other four (Stirling, Heriot-Watt, Strathclyde and Dundee) since 1960, though with the exception of the new university at Stirling, the newcomers to university ranks were experienced in advanced level work.

In the 1960s, there were ten teacher-training colleges in Scotland, now reduced to seven. Since 1958 they have been designated as 'colleges of education' in recognition of their elevation beyond mere professional training centres. In Scotland (indeed, in Britain), unlike many other countries, all teacher-training is considered as higher education, by virtue of work beyond the standard of the SCE Highers, the normal entrance requirement for the three-year diploma in primary education. With a few exceptions, teachers in Scottish secondary schools are required to be university graduates who take a one-year post-graduate college course. However, university-level work has also been carried out in some colleges since the introduction of the BEd teaching degree in the mid-1960s.

Degree courses have also been taught in most of the 14 Central Institutions (CIs) since the establishment in Britain of the degree-awarding Council for National Academic Awards (CNAA) in 1964. In essence, the CIs and other further education colleges are the 'post-school comprehensives' as the level of courses ranges from degree and other advanced work to lower grade vocational training and part-time courses. The CIs have changed in nature since the early 1900s and they now offer a wide range of courses. Indeed, not until the mid-1960s was there an agreed official definition of 'advanced' work, which makes an historical perspective difficult. In the past, of the three sectors of higher education, CIs have in fact been used least by girls, though in recent years their proportion has increased.

Universities

Tracing the fortunes of girls in Scottish universities, however, is relatively easy. Women were admitted as fully recognized students to the four existing universities in 1892 — rather tardily, considering that American state universities had been open to women since the 1860s, New Zealand produced the first Commonwealth graduate in 1877, and London was the first of the then seven British universities (four in Scotland, three in England) to admit women to full degrees in 1878. However, as Peterson (1971: 153) wryly comments, London, 'with its vast number of external students whose only connection with the university was an examination must have seemed the one male university where there could be no reasonable objection to the admission of women'. Yet, in comparison with Oxford and Cambridge who did not grant full degrees to women until after the First World War, the ancient Scottish universities were progressive.

Ironically, it was the battle of an English woman, Sophia Jex-Blake, with Edinburgh University to train as a doctor, that marshalled support for the cause of women's university education in Scotland. That battle, marked with lawsuits and even riots in the capital, did no credit to Edinburgh University as a body, despite unstinting support for the women by some professors, and Miss Jex-Blake eventually qualified abroad, before returning to practise medicine. The interest of this case lies in the revelation of a strongly conservative attitude, not so much to the higher education of women as such but rather to what was considered suitable study, and medicine was not included. Otherwise, Scottish universities had been quite sympathetic to the cause: in 1874 Edinburgh instituted a Certificate of Arts for women who had passed three or more of the seven subjects required of men for the MA degree, and in 1876 St Andrews established the diploma of Lady Literate in Arts which could be sat at various centres in Scotland and proved extremely popular before its discontinuation in 1920.

Since the first 50 or so women graduated in 1896, there have been four main phases of growth (Table 3). The initial sharp upsurge was predictable, but more remarkable was the expansion during the 1920s, with a record 3,679 women in 1927-8 not equalled until after the Second World War. For several years women made up 30 per cent or more of the students, though later the percentage dropped back as the economic recession bit hard. The third period of expansion followed the Second World War, with women's share remaining at a fairly steady 26 or 27 per cent, and the fourth coincided with greatly increased university provision in Great Britain generally, following government acceptance of the Robbins Report (1963). Since then, the number of women students in Scotland has trebled, a faster rate of growth than for men, and their share has crept up to a record 41 per cent in 1980-1.

Number of full-time students	1900-1	1910-1	1920-1	1930-1	1938-9	1950-1	1960-1	1970-1	1980-1
Total	5,151	6,736	11,746	11,150	10,034	16,001	18,529	36,579	44,448
Men	4,432	5,137	8,716	7,614	7,324	12,010	13,483	24,735	26,407
Women	719	1,599	3,030	3,536	2,710	3,991	5,046	11,844	18,041
Women as % of total	14.0	23.7	25.8	31.7	27.0	24.9	27.2	32.4	40.6

Source: UGC Annual *Returns*

Table 3. *Number of full-time students at Scottish universities and proportion of these who are women, 1900-1980.*

This share has been consistently higher than at English universities, yet, in view of the early 'golden years', progress in the subsequent half century has been slow. There seem two main reasons — first, that in a way women in Scotland got off to too good a start to maintain the impetus, and second, that they have increasingly used an alternative avenue of higher education, namely the colleges of education.

Teacher-training colleges

The inclusion of teacher-training colleges in the higher education sector undoubtedly contributes to the equality of opportunity for girls which has marked Scotland out from most of its West European neighbours. Inclusion is justified both by the level of their work (acknowledged by their designation since 1958 as 'colleges of education') and also by the longstanding and relatively high entrance requirements for all would-be teachers in Scotland, including teachers of very young children who elsewhere have often been trained only at the secondary level.

Many Scottish girls, though, have entered colleges of education not from a long-held desire to be primary teachers but because these colleges were regarded as an alternative to university, especially in the 1960s and 1970s (ie before the drastic cut-backs in places), by 'those girls whose qualifications are in the arts but below current university standards', as Flett *et al* (1971) put it. They argue, moreover, that historically the colleges have been 'disproportionately used as an avenue of higher education by relatively disadvantaged groups such as women and school leavers of working-class origin' (Flett *et al*, 1971).

Certainly, before universities were open to women, teacher-training was used as an avenue of 'higher education' (using the term loosely) by girls. By the 1850s, a third of the 500 students in Scotland's training centres were women, many paying their own expenses, and in the rest of the century there are various references to their marked superiority over men. In an era of stiff competition (four applicants to every place) and nowhere for the clever girl to go to, the calibre of women students was very high (Roberts, 1972).

Between the wars, however, the colleges offered little competition to the universities: for abler girls, even those intending to teach, there were positive advantages in first gaining a degree. Universities were open, the prestige of college courses was not particularly high, and teacher unemployment in the 1920s increased the saleability of a degree, especially as it was required of men teachers from 1924.

Since the Second World War, the relationship between universities and training colleges has been different as Flett *et al* (1971) suggest, with the two being regarded as alternative routes. The most probable explanation hinges on selection, with the universities harder to enter but the colleges greatly increasing their teacher-training places in line with government policy. In the late 1960s, more girls actually entered non-graduate college courses than universities in Scotland.

There are many reasons why girls enter teaching but the importance of differing stringency of selection is that pupils (and teachers) have seen the colleges as suitable for girls who are able but not quite able enough for university. Flett *et al* (1972) suggest that the ready availability of college (until the mid-1970s) actually encouraged school girls to under-achieve and to specialize in the arts subjects. In days of plentiful employment there was less advantage in a university degree, which may partly explain why Scottish women have been slower at reaching a position of equality in university than might have been predicted from their flying start.

Teaching has always exerted a pull for girls, whether they entered training straight from school or gained a degree first. Numbers of men graduates entering teaching tend to fluctuate according to the economic climate, but, before the imposition of entry quotas, more than 40 per cent of the total number of Scottish women graduates have regularly trained as teachers, and of the women arts graduates the percentage is even higher.

Features of the Scottish system

The next part of this chapter looks at some characteristics of the Scottish system which, judging by the experience of other countries, may help girls along the road to higher education. It is a long road, for admission to higher education is, as Frank Bowles (1964) pointed out, only the final step in a long series of selections.

The secondary stage

The less developed an educational system, the more likely girls are to lose out. In better developed countries the biggest drop-out of girls occurs during the secondary stage (Chabaud, 1970), but in poor countries girls do not always have an equal chance even of elementary schooling. Yet it is the secondary stage which, in the West, is the most crucial for determining the level of participation in higher education according to the OECD (1970; 1971). This organization concluded that, on the whole, the great expansion of higher education in member countries between 1950 and 1967 owed more to the growing proportion of secondary school 'graduates' than to demographic changes (ie the post-war 'baby boom').

A key to the progress of Scots girls, then, must be the fact that as many girls as boys pass through the series of selections 'culminating in a leaving exam which establishes eligibility for entry into higher education' — and have done so since as long ago as the mid-1960s when elsewhere it was a rare event for girls to keep pace with boys at this stage. In 1965, the OECD found only five Western countries where they did so — the United States and, within the more comparable European tradition, France, Finland, Ireland and Sweden (OECD, 1971: Table III-5). The United Kingdom was not included in these five, the domination of English pupils through sheer numbers concealing a different picture in Scotland where, in 1965, 17.8 per cent of the boys and 18.0 of the girls left school with one or more SCE 'Highers'.

Secondary education for the few, post-primary work for the many, was still quite common European practice in the 1950s and 1960s, but the raising of the school-leaving age after the war to 15 (and to 16 in 1972) ensured that all British children experienced three years of secondary education. Nor were pupils channelled into vocational (including teacher-training) courses, as often happened on the Continent, but followed general secondary courses, which until recently were virtually the only direct route to higher education. But where Scots girls in particular may have had an edge over English girls was in having, firstly, a better chance of entering what UNESCO term 'long secondary courses' leading to an upper school certificate and, secondly, an upper school certificate itself more to their liking.

Before the spread in Britain of non-selective comprehensive education in the 1970s, Scotland was always more generous in its provision of 'certificate' places than England: even if they did not last the pace about a third of Scottish children embarked about the age of 12 on 'grammar-type' courses, in contrast to about one-fifth in England (Osborne, 1968).

How early selection for academic courses might affect girls is an interesting speculation. The large numbers of qualified school leavers, and as many girls as boys, turned out over the years by the USA and the USSR, both with comprehensive systems, together with Chabaud's (1970) finding, internationally, that where secondary places generally were limited girls were penalized, would suggest selectivity might not be in the interests of girls. There is, too, the trend in West Europe to more open comprehensive systems in an avowed attempt to mobilize intellectual talent among groups under-represented in selective systems — the working class, the poor, the rural and the female included (de Wolff and Harnqvist, 1961).

The four Western European countries which produced in the 1960s as
many qualified girls as boys (Finland, France, Ireland and Sweden) did
so, however, under quite rigidly selective systems. And yet again, the
quite rapid spread of comprehensive schooling in Scotland during the late
1960s and 1970s, with the postponement of academic channelling, can
hardly be said to have harmed the girls either: in 1981, 32 per cent of
them left with one or more passes at the SCE Higher grade compared
with 27 per cent of the boys. In the same year English girls came their
nearest to catching up with the boys: 16 per cent left with one or more
GCE A levels, compared to 17 per cent of the boys (Central Statistical
Office, 1982).

This leads to the thought that the actual Scottish examination structure,
which reflects the country's tradition of education in breadth rather than
depth, has, throughout the 1960s and 1970s and whether under selective
or comprehensive umbrella, proved more helpful to girls than the English
system. In both countries the SCE O grade or GCE O level has provided
a modest goal at 16, only one year beyond the end of compulsory
schooling (until the raising of the leaving age), but thereafter the Scottish
Highers require only one year's further study, as opposed to two years
for the GCE A level. The Highers are also easier: Scottish pupils sit more
subjects than their English counterparts. The narrower gap in standard,
as well as in time, may very well provide a more attractive stepping stone
to girls for two reasons — the lack of confidence in their own academic
ability at this age (Maccoby and Jacklin, 1975) and the younger age at
which the examinations are taken — 17, or even 16, compared to the
more usual 18 in England. The closer girls are to adulthood and to facing
the implications of a dual role of work and marriage, the greater the
pressure to leave the formal education system, and on this point it is
perhaps worth noticing that girls enter Scottish universities at a younger
age than they enter English universities.

Two other features of Scottish schooling which have probably helped
the girls are its cheapness and its co-educational practice.

Financial considerations are the most frequently mentioned bar to
the education of girls in other countries, but, at the most basic level
there is, throughout the length and breadth of Scotland, a network of
well-staffed, well-equipped schools providing free secondary education
and near enough for most children to travel to them daily. In the supply,
too, of free books and other equipment, of subsidized travel and meals
and, indeed, of hostel accommodation in sparsely populated areas like
the Highlands, Scotland must be counted very generous by international
standards, with a blunting of financial pincers on families who otherwise
might educate their sons at the expense — almost literally — of their
daughters.

Cheap schooling has long been a Scottish practice: even when schooling
had to be paid for, fees were low and Scotland was many years ahead of
England in its provision of free places. It is an aspect of that 'democratic'

tradition that education was open to all who could benefit, however humble their origins, and it is girls who have benefited.

The standards of achievement in the Highers by rural pupils generally, and country girls in particular, indicate they are clearly not handicapped by that paucity of provision often blamed for low rural performance found elsewhere, even in such educationally conscious countries as France and Russia. Country girls in Scotland, who should on international evidence be doubly disadvantaged, by sex and residence, are among the most highly qualified school leavers (Cunningham, 1978).

As for co-education, the tenor of international opinion is that it helps girls by allowing them easier access to the same academic curriculum, resources and qualified staff as boys. Co-education, as shown in France where single-sex grammar schools are usual, is not a prerequisite for high academic achievement by girls, but, without the tight central curricular control exercised in France, Scotland's practice of educating boys and girls together has probably counteracted the tendency in many countries for girls to be fobbed off with lower grade courses. Single-sex schools in Scotland, unlike in England, have been virtually confined to the small fee-paying sector. In 1970, only two dozen of more than 500 publicly funded secondary schools were single-sex and the number has since fallen. Co-education, however, may have encouraged sex stereotyping of school subjects (Deem, 1978).

Historically, the widespread existence of co-education owes more to population patterns — few places outside the major cities being large enough to sustain more than one school — than to any principle that girls were entitled to the same level of education as boys.

The tertiary stage

So far, the journey through secondary school to the gates of higher education has been highlighted, because it is at this stage in advanced countries that most potential candidates drop out, rather than between school and university; the post-war expansion of higher education owes more to developments in secondary education than to fundamental changes at tertiary level (OECD, 1971). Perhaps more surprisingly, the OECD found no clear link between numbers of qualified leavers, transfer rates (ie the proportion of those eligible who used their 'ticket') and changing university admission policies, though in broad terms open systems of access lead to high numbers of women students, as in the USA.

A 'high number of girls', however, can also mean 'compared with boys', and in the more selective West European tradition there is some evidence, too, that where the path is easier (eg by recognition of the school leaving certificate as sufficient entrance qualification or by fairly unrestricted entry into certain faculties) girls are attracted in greater numbers than if faced with a competitive situation. Again, both their lack of academic confidence and the social pressures of their future role may dissuade them from voluntarily pitting themselves against more hurdles.

The UK system of higher education is doubly selective: not only do candidates have to hold a school certificate of a certain level (number and standard of passes), but pressure on university places especially ensures that faculties impose their own requirements, often well above minimum entrance regulations. Compared to English girls, Scottish girls have benefited in that in the past university selection appears to have been less stringent (Robbins, 1963) and, since then, as universities have become more selective, colleges of education, as mentioned earlier, have increasingly provided an alternative.

The point was also made earlier that the more highly developed any system is, the better are the chances for girls. Compared with England, and elsewhere in Europe, university education was well established in Scotland in the first half of the twentieth century and was quite able to absorb the influx of women. The University Grants Committee (1921/2) spoke of the Scottish 'university habit' and, while 'students per head of population' is a crude measure, it offers some guide: Peddie (1947) estimated that the ratio in Scotland was 1/500, in England 1/1000 and Wales 1/1500.

The long monopoly of Scottish universities in post-school education has not always been a good influence, but the fact that they are more 'universities of the people' than English universities are has probably done much to break down that psychological barrier felt by less advantaged groups. The existence of four (now eight) universities in a country as small as Scotland has meant that many students could live at home and set out each day for university much as they had done for school, a financial benefit to women, especially in the inter-war years. (Surveys in Sweden suggest that there is still an inverse relationship between the distance of universities from their home and women's enrolment (OECD, 1979).) Today, the majority of British students in higher education are extensively supported from public funds, but before a uniform grants system women, too, benefited from the Scottish tradition of help for the needy scholar in the form of bursaries and other awards. Between the wars, a higher proportion of women than men were financially assisted, and tuition fees were relatively low, especially in arts faculties.

Indeed, the non-specialist three-year Ordinary degree in Arts, again in the national tradition of breadth rather than depth of study, may attract girls in particular, in view of women's preference for shorter courses and their lower academic self-confidence and aspirations. Not only has it been a traditional route to teaching, but the course is shorter than, say, medicine and may be seen as less difficult than either the specialized three-year Honours course in England or its four-year Scottish equivalent. Of the Ordinary degrees in Arts awarded by Aberdeen University, for example, between 1956 and 1970, 64 per cent went to women. In contrast only 37 per cent of the Honours degrees in Arts went to women, though now more women are doing Honours.

The concentration of girls in certain spots, such as university arts faculties and teacher-training, is the less progressive aspect of women's higher education in Scotland and, indeed, is an all too familiar picture in Western Europe — leading to 'an illusion of quasi-equality of opportunity' (OECD, 1971: 47). We need only note that the most commonly quoted factors, such as subject bias in secondary school, the compatibility of teaching with family life, 'numerus clausus' policies of selection in certain university faculties, *de facto* if not *de jure* discrimination in some professions, and so on, have all made their appearance in Scotland. Many such practices are now illegal under the Sex Discrimination Act 1975, but habit changes more slowly than law. However, more girls are trickling into 'male' university faculties such as agriculture and engineering.

The academic tradition

Mention of the well-beaten path trodden by Scottish girls, itself a reflection of the conservative role of women, brings us full circle to the starting point of this chapter, and that was the conflicting traditions to which they were heirs.

So far, the broad theme has been that the Scottish education system and, especially, the democratic traditions that have shaped it, have benefited the girls — even though by circumstance rather than any deliberate policy of natural justice for women — and there is little overt indication of that 'curious anti-feminism' that Naomi Mitchison spoke about. But there is another relevant historical strand, and that is the strong academic bias of Scottish schooling. Its over-intellectualism, its over-veneration of university as the most desirable goal for any able pupil, have come under increasing attack not only from well-known critics such as A S Neill, who fled the oppressive yoke of schoolmastering in his native land to set up the international school of Summerhill in southern England, but from within the system itself, with recent proposals for reform (Scottish Education Department, 1983a; 1983b).

Despite concern at the number of pupils who find themselves almost passively swept to higher education (Scottish Education Department, 1973), it may be that the academic straitjacket has actually helped liberate the girls, by counteracting that old and still quite commonly held view that their education should be geared to their future role as homemakers. At least in Scotland the legacy of scholarship has provided a better opportunity for that academic grounding often lacking in countries which are still trying to inject a little more intellectual stiffening into the education of girls, in place of 'finishing school' for the well-off and low-grade 'vocational' (ie domestic) courses for the majority. Hence the pleas for co-education, for access to the same facilities and certificates as boys, because only then can doors be opened to the outside world.

The Scottish academic tradition, though, is to do with more than the virtues of scholarship: there is also concern with the hard practicalities of life and education as an escape road from a poor economy. 'Vocational' courses in secondary schools, for instance, designed to halt the drift from more remote areas to the cities, and often overseas, are not popular with parents who prefer to see their children on the academic conveyor belt, even if it carries them away from home. The rush of women to university in the 1920s, too, was partly to do with earning a living in hard times: 'A degree was useful so far as it was saleable', wrote one Aberdeen woman graduate of the time (Shepherd, 1942).

To what ends Scottish women put their educational qualifications in the dying years of this century will depend to a great extent on economic pressures, on facilities such as creches, flexible hours, refresher training courses and many more such practical matters which enable them to cope with the dual role of paid employment and homemaking — for few foresee the relinquishment of that responsibility. Again, social attitudes are the crux. Some women graduates remain at home, 'captives by choice' (Kelsall *et al*, 1972), others are less willing to invest in years of training if there are no prospects of a satisfying career. The 1975 Sex Discrimination Act has certainly helped to officially open more doors to women, and the education system has given them the keys in a way that might be envied by women elsewhere. How strong the bonds of conservatism are is the crucial question.

References

Acker, S and Warren Piper, D eds (in press) *Is| Higher Education Fair to Women?* SRHE: Guildford

Bowles, F (1964) *Access to Higher Education* Vol 1 UNESCO: Paris

Burnhill, P and McPherson, A (in press) Careers and gender: the expectations of able Scottish school leavers in 1971 and 1981 *in* Acker and Warren Piper

Byrne, E M (1978) *Women and Education* Tavistock: London

Central Statistical Office (CSO) (1982) *Social Trends 13* HMSO: London

Chabaud, J (1970) *The Education and Advancement of Women* UNESCO: Paris

Cunningham, S (1978) The entry of girls to higher education — a Scottish perspective Unpublished PhD thesis University of Aberdeen, Scotland

Deem, R (1978) *Women and Schooling* Routledge and Kegan Paul, London

De Wolff, P and Harnqvist, K (1961) Reserves of ability: size and distribution *in* Halsey

Flett, U, Jones, C and McPherson, A F (1971) *After Highers: Working Paper 7* Department of Sociology, University of Edinburgh

Flett, U, Jones, C and McPherson, A F (1972)| *Women Entrants to University and Colleges of Education — Some Competing Explanations* Department of Sociology, University of Edinburgh

Halsey, A H ed (1961) *Ability and Educational Opportunity* OECD: Paris

Her Majesty's Stationery Office *Scottish Educational Statistics* published annually from 1966 to 1974 HMSO: Edinburgh

Kellas, J G (1980) *Modern Scotland* Allen and Unwin: London

Kelsall, R K, Poole, A and Kuhn, A (1972) *Graduates: the Sociology of an Elite* Methuen: London

Maccoby, E E and Jacklin, C N (1975) *The Psychology of Sex Differences* Oxford University Press; London

Meikle, H W ed (1947) *Scotland* Nelson: Edinburgh

Organization for Economic Co-operation and Development (1970, 1971) *Development of Higher Education 1950-1967: Statistical Survey* and *Analytic Report* OECD: Paris

Organization for Economic Co-operation and Development (1979) *Equal Opportunities for Women* OECD: Paris

Organization for Economic Co-operation and Development (1981) *Educational Statistics in OECD Countries* OECD: Paris

Osborne, G (1968) *Change in Scottish Education* Longmans, Green and Co: London

Peddie, J R (1947) Education *in* Meikle

Peterson, A D C (1971) *A Hundred Years of Education* Duckworth: London

Robbins Committee (1963) *Higher Education. Report*: Appendix One: *The Demand for Places in Higher Education* HMSO: London

Roberts, A F B (1972) Teacher training in the city Unpublished paper Aberdeen College of Education, Scotland

Scotland, J (1969) *The History of Scottish Education Vols 1 and 2* University of London Press: London

Scottish Education Department (1973) *The Transition from School to University* HMSO: Edinburgh

Scottish Education Department (1983a) *Teaching and Learning in the Senior Stages of the Scottish Secondary School* HMSO: Edinburgh

Scottish Education Department (1983b) *16-18s in Scotland: an Action Plan* SED: Edinburgh

Scottish Office *Scottish Abstract of Statistics* Annually from 1971 HMSO: Edinburgh

Shepherd, N (1942) Women in the university *Aberdeen University Review XXIX* 87: 171-81

United Nations Educational Scientific and Cultural Organization (1966) *Access of Girls to Secondary Education* UNESCO: Paris

United Nations Educational Scientific and Cultural Organization (1967) *Access of Girls and Women to Higher Education* UNESCO: Paris

United Nations Educational Scientific and Cultural Organization (1968) *Access to Higher Education in Europe* UNESCO: Paris

United Nations Educational Scientific and Cultural Organization *Statistical Yearbooks* UNESCO: Paris

University Grants Committee (1919ff) *Reports and Returns from Universities and University Colleges in Receipt of Exchequer Grant* Annually except 1939-1946 HMSO: London

Acknowledgement

My thanks to Mr John C Stocks, head of the Education Department, Aberdeen College of Education, for his comments on the draft of this chapter. Thanks, too, to Mr Peter Burnhill, Centre for Educational Sociology, University of Edinburgh and Miss M A Gallagher, Scottish Education Department, for help with statistics.

Part 3:
The education of women in the
context of other social institutions

15. Women, family and education

Miriam David

Summary: This chapter explores women's education as shaped by their experience in families and schools and in the interaction between families and schools. It is argued that girls learn what it is to be a woman through their experiences in families as well as in schools. Motherhood as an activity is qualitatively different from fatherhood; it includes the tasks of care and education. Motherhood is changing. Mothers demand more out-of-home care and education for their children, and yet they are expected to have better educational standards of childrearing than in the past. The schools, too, now expect more of mothers and, at the same time, they are willing to rely on mothers' voluntary involvement in classroom activities. The 'hidden curriculum' requires different activities of mothers and fathers. The school day is not like the working day. In the school curriculum, too, girls are taught that their tasks as parents will be different from boys' parental duties. School-age parents are not acceptable to school authorities. In families, in schools and in family-school interactions, boys and girls learn what is expected of them as adults and that the expectations are not the same for both sexes, despite tremendous efforts to achieve equal opportunities. To achieve sex equality, care and work have to be valued equally.

Women's education is shaped not only by their experiences of formal schooling but also by their experiences and observations within families. Much has been written by feminists, criticizing psychoanalysis but remaining within its traditions, of the ways in which young girls learn and internalize their notions of femininity and motherhood from their very early experiences of being mothered (see especially Chodorow, 1978; Eichenbaum and Orbach, 1982). In this chapter I want to investigate the way in which the process of learning what it means to be a woman is both based upon the structural social relationships in advanced industrial societies and also plays a crucial part in their reproduction. It is not only in intense emotional relationships, particularly the mother-daughter relationship, that women learn about their future roles but also through observation and teaching within families and schools. Most important is the way in which families and schools are structured to interact in particular ways with each other and provide the bedrock of women's work: motherhood.

I am going to explore first the characteristics of mothering, especially within families and their effects on early socialization, second, children's early experiences of care and education and, third, the relationships between mothers and schools in terms of the social expectations of parents and pupils and also the hidden curriculum of schools. I want to argue that girls cannot but learn different roles and relationships from those learned by boys because of women's different position in the family, in caring roles and in schools. The social expectation that motherhood carries with it caring and educational tasks makes motherhood qualitatively different from fatherhood. These social expectations are written into the division of labour within families, within schools and into the social relationships between families and schools, as much as in the economic division of labour. To provide equal opportunities in social and economic life for men and women entails not only removing sex discrimination in education and employment but also changing the relationships between the unpaid work of caring for family members and paid employment, and hence schools' expectations of parental responsibilities. I have explored elsewhere (David, 1980) the ways in which the State has assumed a sexual division of responsibilities and applied that to the structure of family-school relationships.

Socialization for the vast majority of children starts off within families and it is obvious that the central figure in this process is the mother. Not only is the mother central to socialization, but motherhood as an exclusive, home-based activity is held up to be the way socialization ought to be undertaken. This model affects all other forms of socialization, whether they are 'care' or 'education'. Mothering is the model for all workers or unpaid carers who are involved in early childhood relationships. Yet there is no one version of motherhood. Little is known, through research, of what mothers actually do and how they care for and rear their children. Much more is known about the 'alternatives' to mothers, in particular about out-of-home care and education for pre-school children. Most research on pre-school provision has been conducted on the issue of whether out-of-home care harms children and assumes that exclusive mothering at home is the best form of care (Kamerman and Kahn, 1981; Clarke-Stewart, 1982). The converse question — Does mothering harm children? — is seen as absurd. Yet the answer must surely be: it all depends. Once children reach the age of compulsory schooling (which can vary between countries by as much as 20 per cent of a child's life) much more is known about their lives. Schooling is never looked at on the assumption that it might harm children, and that exclusive mothering might actually be preferable. It is assumed, by educational researchers and policy-makers alike, that mothers alone cannot care for and educate their children. Mothers are presumed to need the professional support of teachers. Compulsory schooling is provided precisely to enable children to develop their autonomy from their families, and become independent adults.

Full-time mothering is the official ideology for pre-school child care and, as a result, it is the fact. The most recent figures, in Britain, from the

General Household Survey, show that about 70 per cent of pre-school children are looked after by their mothers at home (Study Commission on the Family, 1983: 27). From the little evidence we have, what these mothers, who care exclusively for their children, do by way of care varies enormously — according to social class and income, whether in a one- or two-parent family, by region and type of locality, by numbers and sex of the children. Perhaps most important is the general fact that the work of mothers caring exclusively for children is isolated and isolating: that it is in the private world of the family insulated from the public.

Motherhood, too, is not a single activity. At very least it combines both the physical care of the children, and the housework involved in maintaining that care — washing and ironing nappies, clothes, etc, and the 'education' of the children. Apart from the work involved in looking after young children, there is general housework involved in maintaining the whole family. Both the Newsons (1964) and Oakley (1974a and b) have shown, in their various studies, how mothers of pre-school children describe themselves first and foremost as housewives rather than mothers. As Oakley (1974a) states most forcefully, child care and housework are not always compatible. 'One unusual aspect of housework as a job is that it is combined with another job: child-rearer . . . The child care/housework combination poses certain problems. But the contradiction is not simply that children are messy creatures who untidy the tidy house and demand to be fed and played with while a meal is being cooked or a room cleaned. The two roles are, in principle, fundamentally opposed. The servicing function is basic to housework: children are people. Child care is "productive"; housework is not' (Oakley, 1974a: 166).

Some of the housework entailed is about caring for men as husbands rather than looking after their children. The standards that many housewives try to maintain may not be imposed directly by their husbands but spring directly from what these women have themselves learnt and from their own friends and neighbours. As Comer (1974) puts it, what gives housework its rationality is the sense of personal fulfilment.

This sense of personal achievement also affects standards of child care. There has certainly been a 'movement' towards more 'educative' standards for mothers in the past couple of decades. Many women now view child care as a specialized activity in which they invest considerable energy. Other mothers seek to share their child care responsibilities and have begun to press for some kind of out-of-home education for their children, seeing it as vital to their children's development. These demands come as much from mothers who are at home as from mothers who are involved in the labour force on a paid basis. It is the 'educational' content that is sought. There is, however, an enormous variety in the kinds of out-of-home education that pre-school children in Britain receive, ranging from mother and toddler groups for the one- to three-year-olds, to playgroups for the three- and four-year-olds which tend to involve mothers in some of the work, to private and State day nurseries and nursery schools and classes. There is the same demand in other countries, but perhaps less variety in facilities since the demand is usually met. A report from the Centre for Educational Research and Innovation (CERI) of the international Organization for Economic Co-operation and Development (OECD) states the demand as follows: 'A new awareness of children, whether it be on the part of the society in general or within the family, is developing . . . this awareness explains the attention given to children's education that is to be found at all levels of society. Nowadays, sending children to school at the age of six no longer seems enough, and there is general acceptance that learning begins long before this age. This belief combined with other factors favouring pre-school (mothers in the workforce, desire for peer relationships) have resulted in an increased nursery attendance . . . today more and more levels of the population are becoming aware of the importance of the education of young children and want appropriate forms of pre-school facilities to be provided for their own' (CERI, 1982: 26).

Britain is unusual, as far as advanced industrial societies go, in the kinds of pre-school education provided. In all other countries in OECD, compulsory schooling starts later than in Britain — at age six or seven, rather than five — but there is now more universal provision of both pre-school education and a more extensive range of non-maternal out-of-home care such as creches. For example, in Belgium 98.9 per cent of three- to six-year-olds attend pre-school education (CERI, 1982: 227).

In Britain about 50 per cent of pre-school children experience some form of 'day-care' before the start of compulsory schooling (Study Commission on the Family, 1983: 25). Most of this is indeed 'educational': either at a playgroup, day nursery or in a nursery class or school. However, the greatest proportion of this group consists of pre-school children attending primary school as 'rising fives', that is, in the year or term before they become five years old. Attendance at nursery or primary school is not affected by the working status of mothers. Similar proportions of children with mothers who work full- or part-time or who stay at home attend school before they are five years old. Nursery schools tend, because of their history, to be located in inner city areas but to take children of the middle classes because of parental demand. Nursery schools are not compulsory and, since the 1980 Education Act, local education authorities (LEAs) in England and Wales are free to choose whether or not to provide any nursery education.

The most 'popular' out-of-home care in Britain is the playgroup, which is a cross between formal schooling and care. It tends to be used most by the children of women who are working only part-time. Mothers who work full-time tend not to rely on playgroups but to use instead care by an 'individual other than parent' such as a childminder, relative or friend. Mothers who stay at home do not use regular care by other individuals, although they may do so on an informal basis. From Oakley's vignettes of housewives, for example, we get a picture of mothers meeting and mixing with relatives, friends and other mothers on an *ad hoc* basis to break down the isolation and boredom they feel as exclusive mothers

(Oakley, 1974b). Dunn and Kendrick (1982) have provided a similar picture of mothers with one pre-school child expecting their second.

The playgroup movement started over 20 years ago as a result of governmental refusal to provide nursery education on a wide scale. A woman wrote to *The Guardian* suggesting that mothers club together to provide their own educational and play facilities for their pre-school children until such time as the Government relented. The playgroup movement has now grown massively and has become partially formalized through the Preschool Playgroups Association (PPA), to which many playgroups now belong. It remains, though, a fundamentally middle-class scheme, sustained and reinforced by self-help values. As Janet Finch (1983) has shown, it is difficult for working-class mothers to set up playgroups and keep them going because of their very different material circumstances and values. The ethos of the playgroup movement has begun to influence styles of motherhood. Not only has self-help, in the form of rotas of mothers for playgroups, become central to the running of playgroups but also the PPA has begun to promote the idea of the positive educational role entailed in motherhood. For instance, the PPA has started mother and toddler groups, for children too young to attend playgroups. The main initiative is a scheme of pre-school home visiting which involves mothers of school-age and older children in visiting mothers of pre-school children in their own homes to give a hand with the children or housework and to instruct them in better methods of parenting (Aplin and Pugh, 1983).

Some mothers have few choices about the ways in which they rear their children. Those who, for a variety of reasons, are deemed by social work agencies not to be coping well or putting their children at risk of physical abuse or neglect may not be allowed to be exclusive mothers. Their children may be taken into care and placed with more suitable parents or given a place in a State day nursery. At the present time, such nurseries are only provided for about 1 per cent of the under-fives. This 'care' is qualitatively different from the educational facilities already mentioned. It is seen as substitute parental care for children of 'inadequate' mothers. The family centre, which is the modern version of the day nursery in deprived areas, run by charitable organizations rather than the State, operates on the same set of assumptions as the PPA's and the State's, that educated women can teach 'inadequate' mothers how best to mother their children.

There is now a curious polarity in styles of motherhood for young children. On the one hand, mothers are being promoted as the 'best' educators of their pre-school children and encouraged, taught or 'helped' with this task. On the other hand, mothers of young children are increasingly involved in the labour force either full- or part-time. In Britain, the proportion of mothers who work full-time is about 7 per cent; that of mothers who work part-time, at least 23 per cent. Many mothers do not regard their bits of paid work — as child-minders for other women's children, as home-workers, in a shop a couple of hours a day in the rush-hour — as a form of employment, though it is real and demanding, especially in terms of juggling child care. So the figures of mothers in paid employment are most likely to be an underestimate.

Despite all this variety, what children have learnt by the time they start compulsory schooling is that mothers are the central figures in their lives — in organizing both their care and education. It is their mothers who decide whom they will play with, who will look after them, where they will go, and how much 'education' they will have. Public agencies build upon this and assume that the mother is in charge. They expect mothers to orchestrate their children's lives. Laura Balbo comments that women act as the family's representative to other agencies. 'Because many goods and services are produced outside the family, by other institutions (firms, schools, hospitals and so on), and because access to them requires time and flexibility on the part of 'clients', someone has to do the work of dealing with these agencies, adapting to their often complex, time-consuming, rigid indeed bureaucratic procedures. It is women who keep in touch with teachers, school staff, who take children to clinics and hospitals, who visit welfare agencies to obtain what the family is entitled to.' (Balbo, 1981: 9).

In the pre-school years, mothers are expected to take their children to health centres and clinics for their check-ups and inoculations. The Professor of Child Health at Bristol University commented on television recently that the mother of one of his patients was a 'good mother' precisely because she had managed to bring her child, on time, to all her clinic appointments.

Mothers are also crucial for children's attendance at pre-school facilities. Although there has been a change in the amount (and kind) of out-of-home facilities available for pre-school children, all provision relies on mothers to ferry the children there and back. Van der Eyken, reviewing pre-school education in Europe, made the point that early childhood education attempted to free men and women from oppressive role stereotyping (Van der Eyken, 1981: 5). But he also showed, through his quotations from fathers, that it is mothers who almost invariably do the fetching of the children. He argued that mothers who can send their children to pre-school facilities are able to choose between housework *tout court* and paid employment. This hardly changes parental sex role stereotyping. No one expects fathers to have to choose between paid employment and housework. Pre-school education has somewhat changed the content of mothering and reduced the extent of mothers' day-to-day responsibility, but it has not eliminated mothers' central role in early childhood care.

Not only are mothers crucial in maintaining their children's attendance at pre-school facilities, whether nursery or infant school or playgroup, but schools are also coming to rely on the unpaid work of mothers to keep going. In recent years there has been positive encouragement to school-teachers to involve mothers in classroom activities. In Britain, for example, the Department of Education and Science (DES) funded a large project to gather information to disseminate to teachers on how best to involve 'parents in nursery and infant schools' (Tizard, Mortimore and Burchell, 1981). The kind of work that mothers are asked to do is helping with listening to young children read, acting as 'monitor' to groups of children on outings, repairing and laminating books, running the library or book-shop, etc. Now, occasionally, fathers are also allowed in to do this. The impetus for the general initiative to involve parents in classroom activities came from ideas about the important links between home and school. Research, used by the Plowden Committee (1967), showed that children thrived when there was agreement in aims between home and school. Nowadays in Britain both working-class and middle-class schools involve 'parents'. Teachers in working-class schools try to help a few mothers learn to be more effective as parents, in the same way as nurseries and playgroups do. Middle-class schools seek voluntary help from mothers with the right previous qualifications and experience — and with the time available. With the cuts in public spending on education, schools have been forced to rely on the unpaid, voluntary work of mothers to enable them to keep up their standards. In many respects, trained mothers are replacing teachers (and nursery nurses) in the classroom and their labour is obtained 'free'.

The whole 'hidden curriculum' of the school points to the different work of mothers and fathers. The school is not organized to fit the needs of working parents. The school day is nothing like the working day. Its hours are much shorter and the school year is shorter than the working year. As a corollary, school holidays or vacations are longer than those experienced by most employed people and more frequent since they include short breaks in the middle of each school term (known in Britain as half-term). Mothers who take paid employment either have to find part-time work to suit school hours or make elaborate arrangements to cover child care before and after the school day and in the holidays. Britain is again unusual in not having developed a system of after-school and holiday play schemes. For instance, it is unlike Denmark or Germany where the school hours are short — the Continental day — but where there are extensive facilities for play after school hours. In some English local education authorities (LEAs), consideration is being given to the Continental Day on the grounds of cost-effectiveness to the LEA, without thought for after-school facilities. This type of day would dispense with the need for a formal system of school meals. The present discretion for LEAs about the provision of school meals has already altered the kinds of work that mothers do. As Glendenning argues, it has increased the unpaid work of some mothers in the making of packed lunches (1983: 51). On the other hand, it has reduced the low paid work of other mothers who were involved in being 'dinner ladies'. Indeed, the main virtue of the changeover was seen as the move towards 'self-help' on the part of mothers and other providers. In one LEA (Lincolnshire) it was suggested that mothers could work together to provide a voluntary service for their children.

The school curriculum has never been seen as fully sufficient in itself for all children's needs. Many parents have seen the necessity to provide extra-curricular activities for their children, in addition to what they are offered at school, such as sports and swimming, varieties of musical instruction, dancing etc. Some LEAs have tried to capitalize on this expectation by charging fees for their provision of extra-curricular facilities. Hereford and Worcester LEA, charging fees for individual music instruction, were taken to court for acting illegally. The LEA was found to be wrong in charging fees for aspects of the supposedly free curriculum of schools (see Bull, 1983). Despite the High Court verdict, the DES, with the encouragement of its present political masters, continues to support LEAs who charge fees. This is seen as a legitimate way of reducing public spending on compulsory education.

Mothers' work is entailed in these extra-curricular activities, both in organizing them and often in acting as unpaid chauffeur to children in order for them to attend these activities. Nowadays, even the ordinary school day involves mothers in more fetching and carrying than was normally the case a couple of generations ago. There is, however, a sex difference to maternal protectiveness. Mothers continue to take their daughters to and from school long after they would have ceased to do this for sons. There are also class differences and urban/suburban/rural differences in whether mothers meet their children at the school gate or wait patiently at home for their arrival. Cutbacks in the provision of school transport in Britain, through the 1980 Education Act, have also intensified mothers' involvement in this aspect of school attendance. Changes in the traffic conditions of cities have also contributed to the greater care taken by mothers of their children's daily arrival at and departure from school.

The curriculum itself provides but a limited part of what children learn about the sexual division of responsibility for care and work. This is not to argue that the curriculum is irrelevant. Much has been written of the ways in which the curriculum channels boys and girls in gender-specific directions towards forms of paid employment and paid caring activities (for example, Deem, 1980). The differential treatment that boys and girls receive within school has also been closely studied (Spender, 1982). What is less often researched is the ways in which the curriculum is presented to pupils by teachers. In an incisive essay about the relations between families and elementary schools in predominantly black areas of Boston, Lightfoot highlights the fact that teachers are mainly women. She comments that, historically, teachers were chosen for their 'maternal attributes'. Now each elementary teacher is, more importantly, 'the other woman' in a young child's daily life (Lightfoot, 1977; Lightfoot, 1978). In their early school days children quickly build up an idea of the work entailed in being mothers and fathers. The picture comes from their observations of their teachers — usually female — as well as their own parents.

This picture is only further detailed by school children's experiences of secondary schooling. Despite extensive legislation in the USA, which the British drew on for the Sex Discrimination Act 1975, the secondary curriculum remains geared to a sexually segregated labour market, whether or not it is an academic labour market. Kelly (1981) and Weinreich-Haste (1981) have shown that science subjects are seen by pupils as masculine, and the arts as feminine. In recent years there has been a growing emphasis on providing curricula that will help children learn about a variety of adult roles — parenthood as well as paid employment. But most of these 'new' courses are provided chiefly for girls, and often replace the 'old' courses in domestic science. These new courses are variously entitled 'preparation for parenthood', 'family responsibility and child development', or 'education for family life'. Boys may be introduced to family responsibility through religious education or moral education, or the odd sex education class. The curriculum, as regards parenthood, is much less intensive for boys than it has become for girls, especially those in lower ability groups.

Parenthood assumes a different place in boys' than in girls' lives. Those girls who take the lessons in parenthood to heart and actually become mothers whilst still at school are still 'punished' for having broken one of the most sacred of school rules — not to have children whilst still being a child. Although mother and baby homes are now a rarity, school-girl mothers are not usually allowed to remain in 'normal' school for fear that they might affect other pupils and influence them to have babies too. Some LEAs provide special educational units with nursery care for their babies. This is now commonly the case in the USA (Zellman, 1981). Other LEAs provide home tuition and yet others help the girls to have abortions and return to school after a 'respectable' leave of absence.

Mothers of adolescents are no less responsible for maintaining their children's school attendance than are the mothers of young children. The ways in which they are expected to do so may be less intensive on a daily basis but they are real all the same. For example, absence is usually condoned only on receipt of a 'mum's note'. Mothers may have to pay out of the housekeeping money for their children's involvement in certain curricular activities. It has been found, for instance, that girls' involvement in domestic science courses is more costly than boys' involvement in their sex-specific subjects such as craftwork and woodwork (Bull, 1980). Providing suitable clothing or school uniform in order to maintain their children's appearance is also expected of mothers in Britain. One adolescent girl in Bristol comprehensive was recently admonished for 'being scruffily dressed' and sent home (a round trip journey of one-and-a-half hours) in the afternoon to clean up her clothes. Her mother subsequently received the following letter from the Deputy Headteacher of the school. 'We have few dress regulations in the Middle School. Appropriate, neat appearance is a main requirement . . . It is not my style to humiliate anyone, quite the contrary, but as a mother myself I would want my daughter challenged if indeed she was dressed in school as Anna was yesterday . . . This is not my sole opinion, but the judgment of several of the staff . . . Anna's education and well-being at the moment are vitally important to her and to the school.' Mothers bear the responsibility for their children's appearance and, indeed, the letter amounted to a reminder that educational achievement and school reputation depend upon mothers' co-operation with school rules.

In various ways — in families, in the relations between families and schools and in schools for both primary and secondary ages — girls (and boys) learn what is expected of them as adults, and especially as mothers and fathers. In particular, they learn that motherhood is, indeed, different from fatherhood and that it too entails 'real' work, albeit unpaid and now sanctioned with the value that it is 'self-help' and therefore morally good. Despite various efforts to change the amount and nature of schooling in ways intended to promote equal opportunities between boys and girls — early childhood education, reducing formal curricular sex differentiation, enabling teachers to combat sexism — schools, like other State agencies, continue to rely on a sexual division of responsibility at home. Although there have been major shifts in the form and content of schooling and in families, the basic structure of a sexual division of labour in which caring is the chief responsibility of women and paid employment the main adult activity for men remains intact. Until the relationships between caring and paid employment are made explicit and each activity is valued on an equal basis, equal opportunities for men and women cannot be achieved. Girls will continue to learn through families and schools and the way they interact that, for at least part of their lives, motherhood is their destiny.

References

Aplin, S and Pugh, G (1983) *Preschool Home Visiting* National Children's Bureau: London

Balbo, L (1981) Crazy quilts: rethinking the Welfare State *Debate from a Woman's Perspective* mimeo

Bull, D (1980) What price 'free' education? *Poverty Pamphlet 48* Child Poverty Action Group: London

Bull, D (1983) Privatisation or exportation? *Where* 188: 8-12

Bull, D and Wilding, P eds (1983) Thatcherism and the poor *Poverty Pamphlet 59* Child Poverty Action Group: London

Central Advisory Council for Education (1967) *Children and their Primary Schools* (Plowden Report) HMSO: London

Centre for Educational Research and Innovation (1982) *Caring for Children* OECD: Paris

Chodorow, N (1978) *The Reproduction of Mothering: Psychoanalysis and the Sociology of Gender* University of California Press: Berkeley, California

Clarke-Stewart, A (1982) *Day Care* Fontana: London

Comer, L (1974) *Wedlocked Women* Feminist Books: Leeds

David, M E (1980) *The State, The Family and Education* Routledge and Kegan Paul: London

Deem, R ed (1980) *Schooling for Women's Work* Routledge and Kegal Paul: London

Dunn, J and Kendrick, J (1983) *Siblings* Cambridge University Press: Cambridge

Eichenbaum, L and Orbach, S (1982) *Inside Out: Outside In* Penguin: Harmondsworth, Middlesex

Finch, J (1983) The deceit of self-help Unpublished paper

Glendenning, C (1983) School meals: privatisation, stigma and local 'autonomy' *in* Bull and Wilding

Kamerman, S and Kahn, A (1981) *Child Care and Working Parents* Columbia University Press: New York

Kelly, A (1981) Science achievement as an aspect of sex roles *in* Kelly

Kelly, A *ed* (1981) *The Missing Half: Girls and Science Education* Manchester University Press: Manchester

Lightfoot, S L (1977) Family-school interactions *Signs: Journal of Women and Culture* 3: 395-408

Lightfoot, S L (1978) *Worlds Apart* Basic Books: New York

Newson, J and E (1964) *Patterns of Infant Care in an Urban Community* Penguin: Harmondsworth, Middlesex

Oakley, A (1974a) *The Sociology of Housework* Martin Robertson: Oxford

Oakley, A (1974b) *Housewife* Penguin: Harmondsworth, Middlesex

Spender, D (1982) *Invisible Women* Writers and Readers Co-operative: London

Study Commission on the Family (1983) Final Report *Families in the Future* 3 Park Row, London NW1 6XN

Tizard, B, Mortimore, J and Burchell, J (1981) *Involving Parents in Infant and Nursery Schools* Grant McIntyre: London

Van der Eyken, W (1981) *Preschool Education in Europe* Longmans: London

Weinreich-Haste, H (1981) The image of science *in* Kelly

Zellman, G (1981) *A Title IX Perspective on the Schools' Response to Teenage Pregnancy and Parenthood* Rand Corporation: Santa Monica, California

16. Women's education and employment in the Soviet Union

Alastair McAuley

Summary: The Soviet government has always placed a high value on education — for women as well as men. Education has been seen as an instrument of economic development and as a vehicle for personal development and cultural growth. This chapter charts the growth in educational attainments of women over the past 40 years or so.

Rising educational standards have not resulted in reductions in occupational segregation or earnings differentials — even if they have opened up new and rewarding careers for women. The chapter argues that these continuing disparities between the sexes in the USSR can be attributed to differences in the types of training they receive and to persisting difficulties faced by women in reconciling their roles as workers and wives or mothers. These can only partly be blamed on the conscious policies of the government, however; they also result from the persistence of traditional attitudes in society at large.

Thus a commitment to education for women is shown to be insufficient for the attainment of sexual equality in employment. Investment in service facilities and a concerted effort to change traditional attitudes is also required.

Introduction

This chapter is devoted to an analysis of Soviet policies related to the education of women and their influence on women's employment over the past 40 years. This is one of the issues explored in my book *Women's Work and Wages in the Soviet Union* (McAuley, 1981), where further evidence in support for the arguments advanced in this chapter will be found. (For additional reading, see Atkinson *et al*, 1977; Lapidus, 1978; Lapidus, 1982; Scott, 1976.)

Soviet policy has always emphasized the importance of education for both men and women. Education and the acquisition of skills have been held to be necessary if women are to achieve economic independence; they are necessary for the enjoyment of a full cultural life; they are a prerequisite for the economic expansion that underpins the building of socialism. And the figures cited below show that this official commitment to education has borne fruit: the average level of education among the Soviet population has risen markedly in the past half century. Also, differences between the educational attainments of men and women have virtually disappeared. But elimination of sex-linked differences in the amount of schooling has not resulted in a reduction of occupational segregation; nor has it brought about any marked fall in earnings differentials.

However, it is not only the amount of education that a person receives that may be presumed to influence his or her employment prospects. *What* a person learns is surely at least as important as *how much*. In any case, analysis of the Soviet evidence reveals clear differences in access to vocational training for boys and girls. It also shows systematic differences in the subjects studied by the two sexes. These variations in the amount and type of vocational training received by men and women in the USSR may well contribute to observed levels of occupational segregation.

These differences in the education and training received by the two sexes cannot be ascribed entirely, or even mainly, to the operation of sexually discriminatory recruitment policies by the Soviet authorities. By the time that they are old enough to make decisions about their future careers, Soviet boys and girls have been exposed to a network of differentiated socialization pressures, from family, school, and society, and they have developed different ideas of what constitutes a suitable career. These differences in attitude interact with differing opportunities in order to maintain — and possibly to reinforce — patterns of occupational segregation and the resultant inequality in earnings.

Evidence relating to these three propositions is given in the rest of the chapter. The first part of the discussion shows how much the levels of education have risen over the last 40 years or so, and also gives impressionistic evidence of the intensification of segregation in employment. Later, differences in the content of the training received by the two sexes and variations in attitudes towards particular jobs among Soviet school leavers are dealt with. Finally, the wider issue of the conflict in women's social roles is considered.

The educational attainments of men and women, 1939-1982

It is customary (at least among economists) to measure the educational attainment of particular groups by the average number of years' schooling they have received. Unfortunately there are no official figures relating to the Soviet population that make use of this indicator; rather, national censuses report the proportion of the population that has attained particular educational standards. For the purposes of this chapter, the most relevant of these is what the Soviets call 'an incomplete secondary education'. In practical terms, this implies attendance at school for seven or eight years.

The first Soviet census to contain data on educational attainment in a form that can be compared with the present was held in 1939. At that date, only 12 per cent of the occupied (ie employed) population had an incomplete secondary education or better. As might have been expected, men were somewhat more educated than women: 14 per cent of occupied men had reached the relevant standard, whereas only 10 per cent of women had. The next Soviet census was held in 1959. At that date, some 43 per cent of the occupied population had an incomplete secondary education or better, and the difference between men and women had been eliminated. In 1970, the proportion of the occupied population with a notional eight or more years of schooling had risen to 65 per cent and at the present time (1982) it is 85 per cent. There is still virtually no difference in the proportion of men and women who have attained this standard. Thus, in the 50 years or so that have elapsed since the introduction of a centrally planned economy, some measure of secondary education has been extended to almost all of the labour force.

In fact, the indicator used in the previous paragraph understates Soviet achievement. It is possible to construct estimates of the average number of years of schooling received by specific groups from a knowledge of the institutional structure of Soviet education and more detailed statistics given in individual censuses. In 1970, for example, urban occupied men had received on average 8.9 years' schooling, while urban women could claim 9.0 years. For the rural occupied population the figures were 6.7 years and 6.5 years respectively. Thus, among the urban population, occupied women had more formal schooling than occupied men. The difference was particularly marked among the younger age groups. Surveys of industrial workers show the same pattern (Kotlyar and Turchaninova, 1975). Indeed even in rural areas, among the youngest age groups in both the 1959 and 1970 censuses, women could claim more formal education than men. But among the older cohorts the traditional pattern reasserted itself.

The educational standards of Soviet women, then, have improved markedly in the last half-century. Among the youngest age groups, a complete secondary education (that is, 10 or 11 years of schooling) is the norm rather than the exception. In terms of formal education, women now surpass men in the USSR, and again this is more marked among the young. But increases in formal schooling have not led to a reduction in occupational segregation. Rather, the reverse has occurred: as women have become more educated they have come, increasingly, to dominate particular occupations or professions. Increasingly women work with other women rather than among both sexes.

The measurement of occupational segregation raises a number of complex statistical problems that cannot be explored here. The evidence for the above assertions must therefore remain impressionistic. Analysis of the occupational returns in the 1939 census showed that some 17.3 per cent of women employed in manual non-agricultural jobs worked in categories that were at least 75 per cent female. For those women in non-manual positions, the relevant proportion was 24.5 per cent. By 1959, about one-quarter of women in manual non-agricultural jobs (and between one-third and two-fifths of those in non-manual positions) worked in segregated occupations. In 1970, some 53.9 per cent of manual non-agricultural women workers and 47.1 per cent of non-manual workers were employed in these segregated occupations. Thus, although the range of jobs done by Soviet women has traditionally been much broader than that of women in western Europe, the extent to which they have been separated from male workers is similar. Despite a substantial commitment to education on the part of the Soviet authorities, it is still possible to talk of women's work in the USSR. Such work differs from that done by men and, the evidence suggests, it is significantly less well paid.

Measuring the earnings of men and women in the Soviet Union raises problems that cannot be discussed adequately here. However, examination of a wide variety of Soviet surveys spanning the years 1956 to 1974 suggests that women earn some 60 to 65 per cent as much as men. Also, there is little to suggest that increases in schooling — either absolutely or relative to men — have had a substantial impact on women's relative earnings. Thus, while at any point in time differences in the amount of schooling among women or among men might provide a significant explanation of earnings differentiation for each sex taken separately, the available evidence is not consistent with the existence of a general relationship between earnings and amounts of education.

Vocational training for men and women

Differences in the amount of schooling received by men and women seem to explain few of the differences in employment prospects enjoyed by the two sexes in the USSR. But the quantity of education is only one dimension of the process whereby a person's character and skills are formed. It might be argued that what and where a person studies are equally, if not more, important. Sex-linked differences in the content or type of courses followed are explored below.

There is much less statistical information available about what subjects are studied by Soviet children and young people than about how much time they spend in school. But there is enough to bring out two significant differences in the experience of the two sexes: boys (and men) enjoy much greater access to vocational training establishments for industrial workers; men also choose disproportionately to enrol on secondary specialist and further training courses, leading to careers in the productive sector of the economy. Each of these is considered in more detail.

On leaving secondary school in the USSR there are five channels through which young people can effect the transition into full-time employment. First, they can proceed to a further educational establishment (university, polytechnic institute etc) for high level training; second (and third) they can enrol in a 'secondary-specialist' institute (at the age of 15 or 18); fourth, they can enrol at a vocational training school (PTU); finally they can enter the labour market with no formal training. Secondary specialist training includes courses in such fields as nursing; PTUs provide courses for those wishing to acquire more explicitly industrial skills.

Statistics on the proportion of Soviet school leavers proceeding via each of these channels are not readily available. However, for the mid-1970s I have managed to construct the following estimates from Soviet sources:

per cent of school leavers that transfer to	Boys	Girls
Further education	8	8
Secondary specialist education	11	14
PTU	57	19
Work	24	58

Thus, while girls are somewhat more likely than boys to acquire a secondary specialist training, boys are three times as likely to go to a PTU.

The reasons for this state of affairs are various: they include the consequences of protective legislation that prohibits the employment of women in certain industrial occupations and also, probably, the prejudices of enterprise managers and PTU directors. In consequence, it becomes very much more difficult for women employed in industry to become skilled workers. One eminent Soviet sociologist has suggested that, in any given town, only four or five per cent of women workers will be highly skilled; two-thirds will be unskilled and 30 per cent semi-skilled. On the other hand, he suggests that almost one-third of the men will be highly skilled and only one-fifth unskilled. Women's failure to acquire the training necessary for promotion into the more highly skilled grades goes a long way toward explaining their lower earnings.

The figures cited above suggest that somewhat more girls than boys go on to obtain formal qualifications from further or secondary specialist educational establishments. The Soviet authorities publish some information about the 'profiles' of the courses attended by the two sexes. This shows that since the early 1960s more than four-fifths of male students at secondary specialist establishments were training for careers in the productive sector of the economy (agriculture, industry, transport, construction); only two-fifths of female students were on such courses. Although not so heavily dominated by 'practical' courses, the same disparity between the sexes is apparent among students in further education.

This concentration of women on particular courses, together with increases in the number of women who have had further education, has resulted in their monopolizing particular occupations. For example, in 1940 more than one-half of the male students in further education establishments were training to be teachers; in 1975, less than one-fifth of male students were enrolled on teacher-training courses. Among women, on the other hand, the proportion of students on teacher-training courses only fell from 67 per cent to 40 per cent in the same period, and the actual number of students doubled. Teaching in the USSR is now largely a female profession; so is general medical practice and to a significant extent, accountancy. The emergence of an educated elite in the female labour force has certainly been accompanied by the growth of occupational segregation, if it has not actually encouraged it. Given the sectoral pattern of earnings relativities, this segregation has resulted in the maintenance of earnings differentials.

The fact that men and women pursue different routes through the educational system has been attributed to the existence of protective legislation and other external constraints. But it would be wrong to conclude that these sex-linked differences in professional and vocational training can be ascribed wholly — or even mainly — to official policy or prejudice. In the past 20 years or so Soviet sociologists have carried out a large number of studies into the career choices of school leavers (see, for example, Konstantinovskii, 1977). In general, these show that by the age of 15 (or 18) young people have developed clear preferences among the various professional opportunities open to them. There is not enough space here to reproduce the detailed statistical results from any of these studies, but they echo the differences in career choice described above. Boys rate careers in the 'productive sphere', and particularly in heavy industry, more highly than girls do. Girls show a definite preference for careers in the 'non-productive sphere'. Sex appears to be a more influential determinant of career choice than does residence: rural boys think like urban boys and not like rural girls. These results suggest that the different patterns of enrolment by men and women reflect individual choices as much as direct government policy.

This is not to say that state and society do not bear a more general responsibility for the attitudes of young people towards different careers. This is not the place to go into the question of socialization and sex-role typing. However, while it must surely be the case that the family and society at large exercise an important influence on the development of the young person's sense of identity and scale of values, it is also true that formal education plays a major role in the inculcation of such values. And there is evidence to suggest that despite a common curriculum until the age of 15, Soviet education does encourage the development of traditional sexual stereotyping.

Education and social role

So far in this chapter I have been concerned with those who are undergoing education or training, with individuals who have not yet become full-time members of the labour force. I now wish to look at a different problem. A number of Soviet analysts have suggested that in modern industrial conditions what is required is not so much a labour force with high levels of education on entry but one in which individual workers are both willing and able to continue studying for several years after embarking on a career or to return to 'school' for re-training on several occasions during the course of their working lives. Whether or not such requirements are genuinely called for by the demands of modern industry there can be little doubt that Soviet institutions call for such a pattern of behaviour. And such a requirement is difficult to reconcile with the other social roles that women are expected to undertake.

Among manual workers, the accepted procedures for career advancement in the Soviet Union operate to the detriment of women as a sex. The initial acquisition of a skill involves attendance at a PTU or secondary specialist establishment, but the number of girls following *industrial* training courses at the latter does not compensate for their under-representation in the former institutions. Women, far more than men, are forced to make do with a general secondary education and on-the-job training when they first enter employment.

Advancement in industry requires the acquisition of higher skill-grades. This involves the worker in demonstrating knowledge as well as practical competence. Too often it also requires attendance at courses 'for the raising of qualifications'. These frequently take place out of working hours. Not only is it the case that the material presented on these courses is assimilated more easily by those who have had the benefit of a PTU training, but, also, the key initial steps in this procedure are taken between the ages of 20 and 30 which, in the words of one Soviet economist '. . . for most women coincides with the time when their children are being born and need to be looked after, when they are involved in setting up home and caring for their families' (Kotlyar, 1973: 398. See also Shishkan, 1976; Kotlyar and Turchaninova, 1975). By the time the children are able to take care of themselves, it is too late; the women have been out-distanced by their male contemporaries. The impact of these procedures is easiest to see in the case of industrial workers but similar processes are at work in the professions and the services sector. And they account, in part, for the male-dominated hierarchies that are to be found in education, in medicine, and in the universities as well as in Soviet industry.

Thus, conventional attitudes towards the sexes, together with a bureaucratic approach towards skill acquisition and significant under-investment in consumer services, result in the continuation of patterns of occupational segregation and the persistence of inequalities in earnings between the sexes, despite enormous investment in education for women. In the USSR, despite substantial advances, women remain prisoners of their traditional social roles.

Conclusion

In this chapter I have shown how in the past half century Soviet authorities have maintained their commitment to education — for women as well as for men. Over this period, the educational attainment of the Soviet population has risen markedly and differences between the sexes in amounts of schooling have been virtually eliminated. This investment in education has undoubtedly meant that many women have been afforded the opportunity of pursuing challenging and rewarding careers, and that the choice of occupation facing all Soviet women has been expanded. Education has also meant, I believe, that Soviet women have been enabled to enjoy a richer and more varied cultural life and this in turn may have broadened their own emotional horizons. But this massive increase in the levels of education attained by Soviet women has not broken down occupational barriers. There is still extensive segregation; indeed there is some evidence to suggest that education has reinforced the tendency for men's work and women's work to differ. Soviet women still earn significantly less than Soviet men.

The persistence of segregation and inequality has been ascribed to the fact that the sexes study different subjects — at least in the upper levels of the formal educational system — and that men are more likely than women to receive vocational training. This in turn has been attributed in part to the existence of legislation that prevents women from undertaking certain well-paid occupations, in part to prejudice, and in part to different career preferences among boys and girls, and young men and women. These differences in attitude are not innate; they are a reflection of differential socialization pressures. But these differential pressures can only partly be attributed to the educational process; home and society must also accept responsibility.

Occupational segregation and earnings inequality can also be attributed to the difficulties experienced by Soviet women in combining the roles of mother or wife and worker. The institutional structure of further training and skill acquisition does not fit the demands that society makes upon the time of young women. And their problems are aggravated by the failure of the authorities to invest in consumer services. Lack of shopping facilities, lack of consumer durables, overcrowded housing and transport, all make the job of running a home more time-consuming. In consequence women may not be able to make use of the education they have — or avail themselves of the opportunities that their society offers them.

Official Soviet policy generates the expectation that women will work outside the home as well as bear responsibility for their families' well-being. To assist them in discharging this double burden the state has provided extensive educational facilities. As pointed out above, education must have had an enriching effect on women's lives — but this is offset to some extent by the psychological stresses caused by the demands of home and job. The falling birth rate and reported increases in the incidence of alcoholism among women testify to the intensity of these stresses.

The Soviet experiment has been instructive. It has shown that a determined government can bring about radical changes in social behaviour — as the Soviet government has managed to reverse the traditional disparity in the educational attainment of men and women. But it has also shown that there are very definite limits to the power of education to improve the position of women. Expanded educational facilities, by themselves, cannot ensure economic independence for women as a sex, whatever may be the case for isolated individuals. If the goal of social equality is to be attained, education for women must be accompanied by investment in service facilities and, most important, by a concerted effort to change traditional attitudes.

References

Atkinson, D, Dallin, A and Lapidus, G eds (1977) *Women in Russia* Stanford University Press: Stanford, California

Konstantinovskii, D L (1977) *Dinamika professionalnykh orientatsii molodezhi Sibiri* Izdatelstvo 'Nauka': Novosibirsk, USSR

Kotlyar, A E (1973) Metodologicheskie voprosy izuchenia struktury zanyatosti popolu v territorialnom razreze *in* Maikov

Kotlyar, A E and Turchaninova, S Ya (1975) *Zaniotost' zhenshchin v proizvodstve* Statistika: Moscow, USSR

Lapidus, G (1978) *Women in Soviet Society* University of California Press: Berkeley, California

Lapidus, G ed (1982) *Women, Work and Family in the Soviet Union* M E Sharpe: Armonk, NY

McAuley, A (1981) *Women's Work and Wages in the Soviet Union* George Allen and Unwin: London

Maikov, A Z ed (1973) *Problemy Ratsionalnogo Ispolzovania Trudovykh Resursov*: Moscow

Rutkevich, M N ed (1969) *The Career Plans of Youth* International Arts and Sciences Press: White Plains, NY

Scott, H (1976) *Women and Socialism* Allison and Busby: London

Shishkan, N M (1976) *Trud zhenshchin v usloviiakh razvitogo Sotsializma* Izdatelstvo 'Shtiintsa': Kishinev, USSR

17. Islamic tradition and women's education in Egypt

Cynthia Nelson

Summary: This chapter tries to answer two basic questions: (i) How does Islam construct the image of women and women's education? and (ii) How has the emergence of secular education for women challenged traditional Islamic conceptions of women's status and the nature of their participation in shaping the social order in which they live?

Within the historical context of Egypt, and from the perspective of an anthropologist, the chapter sketches the different influences of Islamic tradition and Western secularism on women's education. By the mid-twentieth century, secular ideology and education became the main channel through which Egyptian women acquired new rights and status in the public domain. However, more recent political and social crises have forced a re-examination of secular moral values among many educated women and men in Egyptian society, and an alternative Islam is emerging.

The fundamental question facing women in contemporary Egyptian society is whether 'alternative Islam' will continue to provide a viable institutional and moral basis in the face of the continued challenges of the twentieth century.

Introduction

'Islam is facing today, indeed has been at least for the past hundred years, the great challenge of modern civilization and the ethical philosophical, social and economic problems that this civilization has posed to modern man. In no field can the impact be more deeply felt than in the field of education, because it is through education that, in the final analysis, the new generations, who will have to meet this challenge, will be formed. The role of Islam and Islamic tradition in the formation of the generation is being questioned along with the role of religion at large' (Nashabi, 1979: 27-8).

That religious traditions shape aspirations and place constraints on the education that women receive in any given society is a well documented observation in the social sciences. That women can use education to alter their roles as mothers, workers, citizens and improve the quality of their lives is a cherished assumption of feminists in both Western and non-Western developed and developing societies. In making an assessment regarding the role of education in altering women's roles and status, or improving the quality of their lives, we need to examine the ways in which the social, political and economic context of education influences the lives of women in particular.

Without succumbing to the fallacy of religious tradition as fundamentally determining these issues, this chapter will raise the following questions, answers to which constitute the problematic of the essay. First, how does Islam construct women and what relationship does this religious tradition have to ideas about women's education? Second, how has the emergence of women's education challenged traditional Islamic conceptions of women's social status and the nature of their participation in shaping the social order in which they live? To answer the first question we need to clarify our understanding of Islam and the Islamic conception of education. To answer the second we need to examine the changing nature of women's participation in shaping their own social reality, grounding our interpretation within the particular social and historical context of Egyptian society.

As an anthropologist, I assume that any discussion of Islam must be approached from a perspective that recognizes a more complex notion of Islamic tradition than can be extracted primarily from religious texts. As Eickelman has recently noted: '. . . recent studies by anthropologists and social historians of Islam . . . suggest that in almost every studied locale there are opposing conceptions of Islam . . . co-present and in dynamic tension with each other. Some of these ideologies tend to be *universalistic* in that they are explicit in their implications. Others are *particularistic* in that they are largely implicit and tied to particular social contexts.' (1981: 203).

The very richness and variety of religious tradition in the Muslim Middle East has led one Egyptian Muslim anthropologist to suggest replacing the term *Islam* by *islams* in order to emphasize better the vibrancy of the Islamic tradition he seeks to interpret (el-Zein, 1977). It is beyond the scope of this chapter to tackle the enormous variability of Islamic traditions and their impact on women's education that exists on different levels in the Muslim world, such as the national/cultural level (where one might compare the education of Muslim women in China to that in Pakistan or Kuwait); or the juridical level (where one might examine the formulations of various schools and sects of Islam on the education of women); or class-based levels (where one might examine women's access to education in particular social formations). Examples of this type of overview can be found in other recent publications (Beck and Keddie, 1978; Berzigan and Fernea, 1978 and Tucker, 1981).

Instead we will focus our discussion on the dynamic encounter between traditional Islamic and Western secular ideologies and the resulting influence on the structure and process of women's education as this has been unfolding within the particular social historical context of Egypt. As a logical starting point to this discussion we begin with the period following the Napoleonic invasion of Egypt in the late eighteenth century and the subsequent process of secularization that began during the nineteenth century and expanded throughout the contemporary period, and examine women's education as a particular instance of the broader confrontation between Islam and the West (Daniel, 1960; Said, 1979). For it is within the context of this 'colonial encounter' that we can better understand the relationship of religious tradition to women's education, as well as the uses women have made of education to alter traditional religious conceptions of their roles in society. Since Islam cuts across every phase of social life in pre-contact Egyptian society, it is necessary to the discussion that follows to summarize briefly some of the traditional Islamic ideas and images underlying the conception of women and hence, by extension, notions about their education.

Islamic tradition

By Islam we mean an institution that has both a conceptual base and a social structure. The conceptual base of Islamic institutions is the *Quran* (the revealed Word of God to His Prophet Muhammad), *al Sunna* (the tradition and sayings of the Prophet) and the *Sharicah* (the Islamic Laws derived from interpretations of the *Quran*). We will not enter into the debate as to whether Islam is to be blamed or praised for women's status in Muslim societies. Nor do we argue that the particular status of women in any Muslim society can be explained simply by the religious precepts of Islam. Many scholars have claimed that the principles of patriarchal arbitrariness and sexual rigidity in the family expressed in the scripture do not fully reflect the Prophet's teachings. Islamic law, particularly those sections concerned with personal status and the family, was compiled and made final as part of the *Shari-cah* two to three centuries after the death of the Prophet — at a time when the military success of Islamic conquests in many parts of the world had led Muslims to regard women as interchangeable booty (Bellah, 1968: 16). However, we would argue that Islam, as ideology, is significant in the processes of ordering social relations in Muslim societies, particularly in ascribing to women their status and role. Historically, women in Muslim societies, like women in Western societies, have been excluded from the production of the forms of thought, images and symbols through which a great deal of their experience and social relations are expressed and ordered (Smith, 1975). Even apologists for Islam recognize 'To a limited extent the low status of Middle Eastern women is attributable to *the abuses of Islamic law on the part of males*' (Saleh, 1972: 7).

Traditional Islam envisages man's and woman's role as complementary, not as competing. Each has certain privileges and duties in accordance with his or her nature and sphere of influence. The man possesses certain privileges, such as political authority and mobility within the larger society, against which he has to perform certain duties. First of all he bears all economic responsibility for his wife and family, despite the fact that his wife may be economically independent. In the extended family system the man often supports not only his wife, but also his mother, sisters, aunts and in-laws. Accordingly, the woman enjoys certain privileges, indicating that her position was not as subservient as popular Western literature sometimes conveys. The *Quran* recognized the woman's claim to considerate treatment by the husband, and interpreters have enacted that a wife is entitled to be fed and clothed at her husband's expense (Andersen, 1950; Andersen, 1951). The woman does not have to worry about earning a living. There is always the larger family structure in which she can take refuge (that is, be protected).

The woman is allowed to inherit and to maintain complete control over her own property and to dispose of it without mediation of husband or guardian. Discrimination against the woman as heiress is not a consequence of Muslim law (despite the fact that males inherit twice as much as females) but of particular practices allowed to develop (Levy, 1965: 98). The woman's chief responsibility is to provide a home for her family and to bring up her children properly. For the Muslim woman the home and the larger family structure are her world.

Traditionally, and until very recently, the Muslim woman had no right to get a divorce without her husband's consent except if at the time of marriage contract she asked 'to have the *'isma* in her hand.' This phrase refers to the introduction into the marriage contract of the right of the woman to divorce her husband if certain circumstances should arise that make life between them impossible. If the woman did not have the *'isma*, and could prove her husband was either mad, impotent, unable to support her or extremely cruel, she had the right to go to a judge and divorce. On the other hand, a man could divorce his wife with no justification of his action simply by pronouncing the *talaq* ('I divorce thee') three times. The 50 years of debate and controversy that led in 1979 to altering this Personal Status Law of the *Shari⁻ᶜah* is related to the broader struggle for women's education and emancipation that began during the early part of the twentieth century.

By way of summary we can say that traditional Islam envisages the role of men and women in terms of complementarity — not equality (Nelson and Olesen, 1977). A woman was secluded (or protected) from the public world of the man who exercised complete authority within the larger society. The woman affirmed her own definition of self through marriage and bearing children. This social segregation of women is based upon religio-cultural premises that the honour and respectability of men is protected and preserved through their women. And that to protect himself from her polluting powers man must maintain strict authority over her public actions (Mernissi, 1975). Islam watches carefully over the virtue of its respectable women and enforces strict public morality. It is not surprising, therefore, to see that conventions of public decency, or what Antoun has called the 'modesty code', are highly developed in this region of the world (Antoun, 1968; Dodd, 1973).

Traditional Islamic conceptions of education are embedded in the very essence of being Muslim. As Nashabi has pointed out: 'it should be clear that strictly speaking there is no such thing as an Islamic educational philosophy . . . This observation is related to the Islamic view of man's attitude to knowledge in Muslim society. This attitude is primarily defined in the Holy *Quran* where the word *'allama* (to teach, to instruct) is mostly used with reference to God when He chose to instruct man about what he ought to know . . .' (1979: 30).

It is of great significance that the first verse revealed in the *Quran* was a command: 'Read, in the name of Thy Lord who has created . . .' That the first word of the *Quran* to be revealed was 'read', to a man who was unlettered, expresses not only the supreme symbol of revelation in Islam, the book, but also conveys the traditional Islamic attitude to education. It is essentially qualitative, in the sense that the acquisition of knowledge is not the result of the love of knowledge as such; it is a means to know God, who is the ultimate truth. The aim of education is not to produce a good citizen, but to produce a good man. The activity of one who imparts knowledge is not 'educative': it is 'instructive'.

Ideally speaking, in the *Quranic* way of life women as well as men had rights to acquire knowledge, express opinions and participate actively in affairs concerning the survival and well being of the community. That they have not always been encouraged to do so may rest more in the socio-political conditions of particular historical moments than to the precepts of Islam *per se*.

For example, we are told of a fifteenth century three-volume biography of famous Egyptians which lists more than 1,000 women, some of whom played important roles in intellectual circles, as scholars learned in Islamic law and as teachers in schools. The volume also mentions women who were members of Sufi orders, women who ran shops, and women who engaged in a variety of other activities (Smock and Youssef, 1977: 39).

At another time, particularly under the suzerainty of the Ottomans (1517-1798), women appeared to have fewer opportunities than men to be educated. During the Ottoman period, all schools in Egypt were religion-oriented and therefore catered primarily for boys and men. Women were admitted only to the *Kuttabs* (ungraded *Quranic* schools) for the benefit of the general public to learn the *Quran* by rote and some-times the rudiments of reading, writing and arithmetic. The *madrassah* (an ungraded higher school) and *Al-Azhar* (the mosque university) did not accept female students. Although girls from upper class families frequently had private tutors at home and a few women were accomplished reciters of poetry (Said, 1979: 187), the prevailing cultural atmosphere in con-servative eighteenth century Egyptian society dictated that women's education be confined to those subjects that prepared them to be wives and mothers.

That these basic premises were upheld by both men and women as a basic value underlying the Egyptian society at the time of the Napoleonic invasion has been sketched by historians of the period. With the impact of Western colonialism on Egypt during the nineteenth century many traditional Islamic premises were called into question. It is in the sphere of education that we see the dynamics of the struggle between the competing ideologies set in motion by the colonial encounter. In the remaining pages we shall examine the impact of these ideologies on women's education and their changing status in society.

The colonial encounter: Islamic religious tradition confronts modern secular education

The beginnings of the modernization process in Egypt date to the Napoleonic invasion of Egypt in 1798, which revolutionized Egyptian thought and provided leaders with an opportunity to compare and contrast two vastly differing world views: the medieval Muslim and the modern scientific outlook. The old culture was subjected to a severe test and in response Egypt undertook a series of changes to modify its traditional culture. The most important social change brought about by this colonial encounter was the development of modern secular education, introduced during Mohammad Ali's rule (1806-1848), which was vastly different from the already existing religious system of education. The result of this contact was the creation of an educational system, rivalling the traditional religious one but not supplanting it. As one social philosopher has described the process: 'Medieval Egyptian society was deeply uprooted by the impact of Western civilization during the Napoleonic invasion in 1798. The change which followed brought Egypt *a new system of education* which, though conditioned to a great extent by the traditional methods of the old, differed from it in purpose, form and content' (Radwan, 1951: 82).

The ultimate aim of Egypt's national, and hence educational, policy at the beginning of the nineteenth century was to revolutionize a culture which was unaware of 400 years of European development. It was with this in mind that Mohammad Ali designed his new educational system, using France as his model. He saw education as the principal tool in revolutionizing society to bring about social change and to realize his aspirations of 'raising a large army and conquering the world around him' (Radwan, 1951: 113). It is clear from this that the shock of the French occupation, first encountered with incredulity, brought about changes felt by a few clear sighted individuals as a shattering of traditional ways. It did not, however, radically change the Islamic conception of women's participation in the educational structures of society. The embryonic state school system under Mohammad Ali was military in character, organization and purpose, and therefore women were excluded. A traditional Islamic society at that time was literally a male society, except for the School of Midwifery founded in 1827 by Clot Bey, one of two important Frenchmen in the court of Mohammad Ali. Unable to recruit Egyptian girls, because work so close to the processes of nature was considered too crude, Clot Bey had to buy 24 Sudanese and Ethiopian girls at the slave market. He freed them and trained them for several years before entrusting them with deliveries in the *harem*. These young women died of consumption, but not before winning over public opinion. They were replaced by approximately 30 young Egyptians brought by their mothers and to whom an 'alim came to give Arabic lessons. 'An 'alim, a Muslim doctor, teaching women — this is truly a revolution. When one has seen this, it seems insignificant to add that the students . . . were not embarrassed in the least to remain with their faces uncovered even in the presence of Christians. Their head was simply surrounded by a veil of white gauze covering the chin and falling gracefully on the shoulder' (Schoelcher as quoted in Tomiche, 1968: 183).

This brief participation in public life was to stop after Mohammad Ali's reign. The State factories and the schools were closed, and women returned to the seclusion of the harem.

It was not until 1873 that the first State girls' school was opened by the Khedive Ismail's third wife Jashem Afet Hanum. Known as the Suyufiyya Girls' School, it admitted 400 pupils and its curriculum combined fundamental subjects such as arithmetic, geography, history, and religious knowledge with training in practical household crafts such as sewing and weaving. It was not until 1900, though, that the girls attending these institutions were allowed to sit for their final examinations (Abdel Kader, 1973: 18-19).

The legacy of the nineteenth century was to create a dichotomy of cultural outlook produced by the introduction of a State school system modelled on European lines and the expansion of missionary and foreign community schools, superimposed on the religious kuttab system. Each system served a different clientele and performed a different function. The religious schools continued to provide a rudimentary education for the masses in the form of the three Rs (reading, writing and arithmetic), while the modern government schools provided a secular European style education for the existing and aspiring elite. The dual system unquestionably perpetuated differences between social classes by creating an intellectual elite — 'the cultured aristocracy' — who monopolized government positions and high-income professions.

It also perpetuated and deepened the split between two ideological orientations, leading to an internal struggle between Islamic reformists and traditionalists that had considerable influence on the course of political events (Kerr, 1969; Tomiche, 1968; Faksh, 1980). This struggle led, on the one hand, to the increasing gap between the State's desire for industrialization and the Muslim religious leaders' desire to conserve religious tradition. On the other hand, it led to the bitter feelings, frustrations and unrest which would foster the claims of Egyptian women in the twentieth century. Nowhere can we more clearly illustrate the influence that this ideological struggle had on the situation of women's education than the movement towards emancipation that was initiated by Muslim reformists during the first half of the twentieth century in Egypt.

Islamic reform and un-veiling women's education

Muslim Reformists began to advocate that women enter into the modern
education system to prepare them for 'positive citizenship'. Qasim Amin,
follower of Mohammad Abdou, one of the great religious reformers of
the period, wrote a small book with the help of Abdou and Lutfi al-Sayyid,
a prominent nationalist leader, on the *Emancipation of Women*. This
raised a violent controversy, one which provoked no less than 30 books
and pamphlets in answer. It roused the *ulema* (Muslim religious leaders)
of Al-Azhar to such anger that the Khedive, who constantly tried to please
them, would no longer receive Amin at his levees. Amin's book advocated
that women should receive a 'modest degree of education, and that they
should no longer be secluded from society'. The uproar that this book
occasioned caused Amin to write a second one entitled *The New Woman*
to refute the charges made against him. In the second book, which he
wrote on his own, he advocated stronger measures and claimed that a
change in Egypt's mental attitude was necessary — that is, a mental and
intellectual revolution. He said that women were held in bondage by their
ignorance, and could not fulfil the role they ought to play in society.
Hence the moral basis of society had decayed and had caused the whole
of Islam to decay. This bondage of women, he claimed, was not an Islamic
trait, but one introduced to it from the outside and, therefore, one that
needed to be set aside. The heart of the social problem lay in the position
of women in the society, a position which could be improved only by
allowing them to become educated. Towards the end of the book, Amin
wrote: 'We want definite ends and means, and we need to prepare the
young for the new life. No amount of talking from pulpits or orders
from authorities can transform us, nor can magic or intercession from
above. To change, we have to work' (Ahmad, 1960: 51).

What we observe from this examination of Muslim reformist ideas is
that the concern for altering women's status in Egyptian society was still
an almost exclusively male interest. Although Amin's aspirations for the
emancipation of women are, by modern standards, very modest, they do
represent the first public expression of support for women's participation
in secular education; and though they aroused controversy, others picked
up on the idea. By the turn of the twentieth century, the strong feeling
in Egypt for national independence from British rule, which came to the
surface with the Orabi Revolt in 1882 and reached a climax in the 1919
Revolution, gave impetus to the emancipation of women as one of the
tenets of the nationalists (Lutfi al-Sayyed, 1968: 152-53). It was the
wives and daughters of the urban bourgeoisie who, under circumstances
of intense social and political upheaval, ushered in the feminist movement.

On 16 March 1919, word spread over Cairo that a procession of veiled
women planned to march through the streets of the city in protest against
the decision of the occupying British forces to exile four of the Wafd
nationalist leaders. One of the four men sentenced to exile was the
husband of Hoda Sha'rawi and it was she who led the procession of women.

This act was the first step on the road she was destined to travel as a pioneer leader for women's rights, not only in Egypt but in all countries of the Arab world. When people began to get over their initial surprise of seeing this procession of *veiled women*, a number of gallant gentlemen passers-by joined hands around the group of ladies and *formed a cordon for their protection and dignity*. Meanwhile, expressions of encouragement and cheers of admiration rose from the ever-increasing crowds. Soon, however, British soldiers of the Army of Occupation encircled the procession and brought it to a halt. They held up the advance of the women with pointed bayonets (Rasheed, 1973: 8).

A great movement was born and Hoda Sha'rawi was acclaimed a national leader and popular heroine. Within four years, on 16 March 1923, the Egyptian Feminist Union, the first organized women's association of its kind in the Arab world, came into existence under the leadership of Sha'rawi. Her *fille spirituelle*, Ceza Nabarawi, launched in 1925 the first feminist journal *L'Egyptienne* written for women by women. The fact that it was written in French and not Arabic reflects the class and educational background of its founder.

The recognition of the right of women to receive an education came in the constitution of 1923 which included an article (19) that made elementary education a minimum requirement for Egyptian children of both sexes from six to 12 years of age. In 1925 the first high school for girls was opened and by 1929 women were granted equal rights to education at university level. In 1933 the first four women graduated from Cairo University. Primary education became compulsory for both girls and boys in 1933. Although this law was never enforced, and female education remained a very sporadic practice, it did prompt the construction of additional primary schools where girls were taught in the morning and boys in the afternoon (Abu Zeid, 1970). In 1927, only 2.3 per cent of all women were literate, as compared to 11.4 per cent of all males. Moreover, in 1943, 10 years after the enactment of supposedly compulsory primary education, only 6.1 per cent of all women were literate, while the male figure had risen to 23.5 per cent. Of this small group of literate women, only 0.9 per cent had an intermediate or high school certificate (Census Book of Egypt, 1960 2, quoted in Abdel Kader, 1973: 28).

By the mid-twentieth century we find a nation deeply split over reformist and traditionalist orientations, an unreformed Al-Azhar, and a religious class which was desperately trying to defend its crumbling position while refusing to participate in the modernization of Egyptian life and thought (Crecelius, 1966). Despite the earlier trends initiated by Muslim reformists, which not only expanded the possibilities for free education for women to middle and lower classes but also changed the conception of educated women, it was left to the 'Free Officers' who masterminded the 1952 Revolt to attempt to close the gap between the traditional-sacred and modernizing-secular world views.

Socialism and the ascendance of secular education

Until the Revolution, the integrating factor in Egypt had been Islam, which had been a whole way of life covering not just personal conduct and relationships but legal, political, social, economic and educational aspects. But Islam was regarded by Nasser, himself a devout Muslim, as inadequate to deal with problems of Western origin. 'Ours is a scientific socialism based on science not on chaos. It is not at all a material socialism. We have never said that it was, nor have we said that we were opposed to religion. What we have said was that our religion is a socialist one and that in the Middle Ages Islam had successfully applied the first socialist experiment in the world' (Nasser quoted in Baker, 1978: 105).

Sharabi (1966) takes the view that the disintegration of the Islamic hold resulted not only from the decline of Islamic Law but also from the secularization of education which began with the introduction of technical schools and Christian missionary schools. The exact role and function of Islam in the modern Egyptian educational system was an issue to be resolved during the era of Nasser's socialism.

The revolutionary government sought to achieve cultural unity no less than political unity, for it perceived the necessity of social and cultural transformation on the way to political revolution. The efforts to forge national unity were mainly reflected in a considerable educational expansion at all levels of the modern system of education. By 1961, Al-Azhar was converted into a modern style university offering degrees in the full range of scientific and humanistic secular disciplines alongside those of Islamic Law and theology. It totally integrated the religious system of education with the government's modern system. Women were allowed for the first time to matriculate at Al-Azhar.

The goal of the educational system was in line with the revolutionary government's general programme of economic development and industrialization of the country. Hence the main objective of education in the schools and universities of Egypt during this period was to train women (as well as men) for active participation in shaping the life of the new socialist state: 'Woman must be regarded equal to man and she must therefore shed the remaining shackles that impede her free movement so that she may play a constructive and profoundly important part in shaping the life of the country' (Egyptian National Charter, 1962).

The important theme expressed in this statement is that education means education of the masses for work in a revolutionary and progressive society. A new conception of the 'educated woman' was emerging. The image of a woman as a 'constructive force' was a different conception from that of Islamic tradition where the notion of an 'educated working partner' would have seemed absurd to a society that veiled and secluded its women. However, the conception of 'an honourable woman is a secluded woman' was clearly incompatible with the secularist ideas of the revolutionary regime. Nevertheless, the Charter did not envisage that women would abdicate from their traditional responsibilities, for it stipulated:

'The family is the first cell in a society and it must therefore be afforded all means of protection so that it might be better able to preserve the national tradition to rejuvenate its texture, and to carry along the whole society in the direction of the goals set by the national struggle.'

At the same time as women were being actively encouraged to enter the public world of university, industry and government, they were also, as the hubs of their families, being constrained to preserve the national tradition. This ambivalent attitude did not deter women from pursuing education and entering the wage labour force, and certain trends during the period of 1952-1970 point to an increase in the number of Egyptian women in higher education — from 4,749 on the eve of the Nasserite revolution to 47,683 in the year of his death. This represents an increase of the total student enrolment from 10 per cent (1952) to 30 per cent (1970). A similar trend is shown in women's entry into wage labour.

Despite the great expansion of mass education for women, the educational system has remained inadequate, as the absolute number (though not the percentage) of illiterates, particularly women, has continued to increase. In the early 1970s there were still about 80 per cent female illiterates and only 0.3 per cent university educated women (Hyde, 1978: 41). This high illiteracy rate (with its attendant predominance of traditional cultural beliefs and practices), accompanied by the great stress laid on university education, has served to perpetuate the imbalances in the different levels of the educational system and, in effect, to exacerbate the wide cultural cleavage separating the illiterate masses from a highly educated group at the other extreme. This dichotomy in Egyptian society and culture is reflected clearly in the political culture of the educated Egyptians. It is a culture marked by a crisis of identity, ambivalence of attitudes, values and beliefs not only towards the traditional Islamic order of society but also towards the new national order and the elite (Ibrahim, 1979; Smith, 1980).

Certain social and political events of the late 1960s and early 1970s set in motion the conditions for the revival or resurgence of what several scholars have described as 'alternative Islam' (el Guindi, 1981a; 1981b; Ibrahim, 1982; Williams, 1979). This phenomenon is the most recent expression of the continuing ideological struggle between Islamic tradition and Western secularism on women's education in Egypt. It also serves as a final illustration of how Islam is continually reinterpreted by each new generation as it faces the challenges of its own historical conditions.

Islamic alternative: the veiled educated woman

As secular education increasingly became the channel through which Egyptian women sought to acquire new rights and status in the public domain, traditional Islamic beliefs and practices, particularly among urban middle and lower class women, served less and less as a basis for social self identity or legitimizing women's role in society. Women took a more public role in society and laid aside traditional dress. This was especially true among the youth in the university campuses throughout the 1950s and 1960s (Nelson, 1968).

However, with the military and political defeat of Egypt by Israel in 1967, Egyptians were disillusioned and shattered by what many felt was Nasser's great deception. One young Egyptian woman expressed the feeling: 'Until 1967, I accepted the way our country was going. I thought Gamal Abd al-Nasser would lead us to progress. Then the war showed us we had been lied to; nothing was the way it had been represented. I started to question everything we were told. I wanted to do something to find my own way. I prayed more and I tried to see what was expected of me as a Muslim woman' (as quoted in Williams, 1979: 54).

In the aftermath of the 1967 defeat there developed a climate of intense and visible religious revival (Nelson, 1974; el Guindi, 1981b). This revival has been asserting itself as an Islamic alternative in Egypt (Ibrahim, 1982). What concerns us about this particular form of Islamic resurgence is its ideology and the presence of assertive and active young women in the movement. As el Guindi has pointed out: 'The core aspect of the Islamic movement and the one that has the most far-reaching impact, is alternative Islam as it is shaped by today's non-elitist Egyptian college educated men and women. Its message is strong, its symbolism vivid, its ritual visible . . . A phenomenon of such generality, involving all corners of urban society and for the first time in Egyptian modern history involving non-elitist women at a large scale and with strong, assertive presence, is far more profound than a political opposition or a secret militancy. It is . . . the alternative in today's Egypt *par excellence*' (1981b: 21). One dominant expression of this phenomenon on the college campuses of Cairo and Alexandria is the increasing presence of 'veiled women'. However, the veil (or what el Guindi and others prefer to call the Islamic dress) reflects an alternative conceptualization of the Muslim woman to that of previous decades. Instead of being perceived as a symbol of upper class status or of 'oppression', contemporary Islamic veiling conveys a more egalitarian spirit in which those women who wear the veil span the entire stratification system. What unites these women is a re-affirmation of the basic Islamic ideology of sex-role complementarity in which the Islamic dress symbolizes strict avoidance between the sexes. At the same time, more Muslim women are donning the veil, the flow of women into co-educational universities is continuing, and women are increasingly invading specializations previously dominated by men. The number of girls enrolled in primary schools jumped from fewer than 300,000 in 1952 to over 1.6 million in 1976 — a more than five-fold increase. At the university level the rise was even more dramatic — from fewer than 10,000 in 1952 to more than 153,000 in 1976 — an increase of more than 15-fold in one quarter of a century. At the same time the ratio of male to female students has steadily decreased (see Tables 1 and 2).

The educated woman choosing to veil is asserting 'an authentic identity vis-à-vis imitations of Western lifestyles; disapproval of what seem to be

Year	Ratio
1952/53	13.2 : 1
1956/57	7.2 : 1
1960/61	5.2 : 1
1964/65	4.4 : 1
1968/69	2.8 : 1
1972/73	2.2 : 1
1975/76	1.8 : 1

Table 1. *Ratio of male to female students in three major universities (Cairo, Ein-Shams, Alexandria), (el Guindi, 1981b: 479)*

	Medicine, pharmacy and dentistry		Engineering		Veterinary medicine	
	Females	*Males*	*Females*	*Males*	*Females*	*Males*
1952/53	603	5,093	609	5,203	29	5,439
1956/57	932	7,116	35	6,970	30	557
1960/61	1,626	8,221	386	10,920	72	1,055
1964/65	3,855	12,412	1,347	18,576	212	2,048
1968/69	6,768	19,662	2,041	20,451	312	2,701
1972/73	8,364	27,415	2,816	20,144	541	3.647
1975/76	12,171	36,814	5,480	29,555	1,018	4,078

Source: Annuaire Statistique (various years). Imprimerie Nationale, Cairo. Statistical Abstract of the United Arab Republique (various years). CAPMAS, Cairo. al-Kitab al-Ihsa'i al-Thanawi (Annual Statistics Book, 1952-1974; 1977). CAPMAS, Cairo.

Table 2. *Enrolment by sex in five practical colleges*

decadent practices in society, warding off effects of inflation by avoiding conspicuous clothing and establishing good (ie moral) reputations' (Ibrahim, 1982: 19). Veiling and alternative Islam seem to represent one kind of response for the educated woman as she faces a complicated and devastating transformation of her society. Her attitude to secularist education is to take out of it science, technology and commitment to professional careers and to clothe it within Islamic tradition. It is her way of imposing a semblance of order on an otherwise chaotic world.

Conclusion

If higher education constitutes the most potent force stimulating a re-assessment of women's roles, as some scholars have argued (Smock and Youssef, 1977), then the case of Egypt is instructive.

One of the implicit arguments of this essay has been that Egyptian women have been altering their traditional roles and status during those moments when the country itself has been passing through social and political crises — the Napoleonic invasion and the resultant colonial encounter; the 1919 revolution; the 1967 military defeat; the October War of 1973 and the *infitah* (open-door policies) of Sadat. During these moments, individuals and groups previously confined within strictly defined sex, generational and occupational limits are allowed, in fact encouraged, to mobilize their latent resources as well as their ordinary abilities.

Throughout our examination of the historical development of women's education in Egypt we notice that women have utilized secular education as the main conduit for their participation into the public world of government, industry and university. In other words social and political crises have enhanced women's participation in education and have consequently brought about a re-assessment of their role and status, the quality and nature of the man-woman relationship and the grounds for public morality (Nelson, 1968; Nelson, 1976).

However, this very re-assessment has increased the sense of alienation from traditional Islamic values and premises and has led, in the present era, to the reinterpretation of religious tradition in the form of an alternative Islamic structure within institutions of higher education. This structure is characterized by the strict adherence to Islamic notions of morality — avoidance of contact between the sexes, modest Islamic dress codes and the emphasis on all-female solidarity groups within the context of an egalitarian community of believers. These basically Islamic traditions are being defined and expressed within the context of secular institutions of higher education in which women are encouraged to pursue professional careers in medicine, law, engineering etc. Like the women of the early part of the century, this new generation is being encouraged to participate in shaping the life of its society; but unlike their predecessors, the veiled educated women are being called to reform a society which has lost touch with its Islamic roots. What is being questioned by this new generation is not the role of religion in society but the very moral values of secular society.

Some authors foresee considerable difficulty within Egypt 'as women attempt to redefine what specific types of extra-familial activities are appropriate or acceptable for women to pursue even when women are granted the right to be educated' (Smock and Youssef, 1977: 75).

From our discussion we notice that each historical challenge to Islam has been met with a creative response suggesting that within Islam there is a dynamic revitalizing force not only to keep Islam alive but to provide it with generative creativity to re-establish itself as a well defined system with original solutions to current problems.

Alternative Islam may represent just such an institutional arrangement, allowing some particular women (until recently remote from the direct encounter with modernization) gradually to prepare themselves for the contemporary transformations. The fundamental question facing Egyptian women is whether alternative Islam will continue to provide a viable institutional arrangement for Egyptian men and women confronting 'the challenges of modern civilization and the ethical philosophical, social and economic problems that this civilization has posed to modern man.' Only the future holds the answer.

References

Abdel Kader, S (1973) *A Report on the Status of Egyptian Women 1900-1973* The American University in Cairo Social Research Center: Cairo

Abdel Rahman, A (1975) Role of women in the construction of the first Islamic society (mimeo)

Abu Zayd, H (1970) *The Education of Women in the UAR During the 19th and 20th Centuries* National Commission for United Nations Educational Scientific and Cultural Organization: Cairo

Ahmad, J (1960) *The Intellectual Origins of Egyptian Nationalism* Oxford University Press: London

Andersen, J (1950) Recent developments in Shari^{c}a law *The Muslim World* XL 244-56

Andersen, J (1951) Recent developments in Shari^{c}a law *The Muslim World* XLI: 271-88

Antoun, R (1968) On the modesty of women in Arab Muslim villages: a study of the accommodation of traditions *American Anthropologist* 70: 671-97

Baker, R (1978) *Egypt's Uncertain Revolution Under Nasser and Sadat* Harvard University Press: Cambridge, Mass

Beck, L and Keddie, N eds (1978) *Women in the Muslim World* Harvard University Press: Cambridge, Mass

Bellah, R (1968) Islamic tradition and the problems of modernization (mimeo)

Berzigan, B and Fernea, E (1978) *Muslim Women Speak* University of Texas Press: Austin, Texas

Coleman, J ed (1969) *Education and Political Development* Princeton University Press: Princeton, New Jersey

Crecelius, D (1966) Al Azhar in the revolution *Middle East Journal* 20: 31-49

Daniel, N (1960) *Islam and the West: The Making of an Image* University Press: Edinburgh

Dodd, P (1973) Family honor and the forces of change in Arab society *International Journal of Middle East Studies* 4 1: 40-54

Devos, G ed (1976) *Responses to Change* D Van Nostrand and Company: New York

Eickleman, D (1981) *The Middle East: An Anthropological Approach* Prentice Hall Inc: Englewood Cliffs, New Jersey

el Guindi, F (1981a) Veiling infitah with Muslim ethic: Egypt's contemporary Islamic movement *Social Problems* 28 4: 466-85

el Guindi, F (1981b) Is there an Islamic alternative: Egypt's contemporary Islamic movement *International Insight* 1 vi: 75-93

el-Zein, A (1977) Beyond ideology and theology: the search for the anthropology of Islam *Annual Review of Anthropology* 6: 227-54

Faksh, M (1980) The consequences of the introduction and spread of modern education: education and national integration in Egypt *Middle East Studies* 16; 42-55

Giele, J and Smock, A eds (1977) *Women: Roles and Status in Eight Countries* John Wiley and Sons: New York

Heyworth-Dunne, J (1968) *An Introduction to the History of Education in Modern Egypt* Frank Cass and Company: London

Hyde, G (1978) *Education in Modern Egypt: Ideals and Realities* Routledge Kegan and Paul: London

Ibrahim, A (1979) Salama Musa: an essay on cultural alienation *Middle East Studies* 15 3: 346-57

Ibrahim, S (1981) An Islamic alternative in Egypt: the Muslim brotherhood and Sadat *Arab Studies Quarterly* 4 1 and 2: 75-93

Ibrahim, S (1982) *The New Arab Social Order: A Study of the Social Impact of Oil Wealth* Croom Helm: London

Kerr, M (1969) Egypt *in* Coleman

Levy, R (1965) *The Social Structure of Islam* The University Press: Cambridge

Loutfy, K (1982) The problem of illiteracy in Egypt *Population Studies 62* July-Sept: 79-84

Lutfi al Sayyed, A (1968) The beginnings of modernization among the rectors of al Azhar *in* Polk and Chambers

Mernissi, F (1975) *Beyond the Veil: Male and Female Dynamics in a Modern Muslim Society* Halstead Press: New York

Nashabi, H (1979) Islam and the liberal tradition *in* Salem

Nelson, C (1968) Changing roles in a changing society *Anthropological Quarterly* 41 2: 57-77

Nelson, C (1974) Religious experience, sacred symbols and social reality *Humaniora Islamica 11:* 253-66

Nelson, C (1976) Social change and sexual identity in contemporary Egypt *in* Devos (1976)

Nelson, C and Olesen, V (1977) Veil of illusion: critique of the concept equality in Western feminist thought *in* Nelson and Olesen (1977)

Nelson, C and Olesen, V *eds* (1977) Feminist thought Catalyst 10/11 Summer (special issue)

Nelson, C and Koch, K *eds* (1977) *Law and Social Change in Contemporary Egypt* Cairo Papers in Social Science: Cairo

Nowaihi, M (1977) Changing the law on personal status within a liberal interpretation of the shari^ca *in* Nelson and Koch

Polk, W and Chambers, R (1968) *Beginnings of Modernization in the Middle East* University of Chicago Press: Chicago

Radwan, A (1951) *Old and New Forces of Education in Egypt* Teacher's College Columbia University: New York

Rasheed, B (1973) *The Egyptian Feminist Union* Anglo Egyptian Books: Cairo

Saleh, S (1972) Women in Islam: their status in religion and traditional culture *International Journal of Sociology of the Family* 2 1: 1-7

Said, E (1979) *Orientalism* Random House: New York

Salem, E *ed* (1979) *The Liberal Arts and the Future of Higher Education in the Middle East* The American University of Beirut: Beirut

Shaltut, S (1975) *The Quran and Woman* International Islamic Center for Population Studies and Research, Al Azhar: Cairo

Sharabi, H (1966) Islam and modernization in the Arab world *in* Thompson and Reischaaer

Smith, C (1980) The intellectual and modernization: definitions and reconsiderations: the Egyptian experience Society for the Comparative Study of Society and History

Smith, D (1975) An analysis of ideological structure and how women are excluded *Canadian Journal of Sociology and Anthropology* 12 4: 353-69

Smock, A and Youssef, N (1977) Egypt: from seclusion to limited participation *in* Giele and Smock (1977)

Thompson, J and Reischaaer, R *eds* (1966) *Modernization of the Arab World* D van Nostrand Company: New York

Tomiche, N (1968) The situation of Egyptian women in the first half of the nineteenth century *in* Polk and Chambers

Tucker, J *ed* (1981) Introduction: women and work in the Middle East *Merip Reports* 95: 3-5

Williams, J (1979) A return to the veil in Egypt *Middle East Review* Spring: 49-54

18. New technology and women's education in Sweden

Boel Berner

Summary: This chapter discusses women's education against the background of changing occupational and job structures due to the introduction of new information technology. It is argued that women must enter specialized technical education to a much greater extent than today in order to widen their present narrow labour market, to gain basic technological skills, and to influence the type of technology produced. The chances for a dramatic change in selection patterns at school and at the place of work are, however, considered to be limited, given the historically structured sex-typing of skilled technical occupations and the power that men enjoy from the present division of labour.

It is further argued that above all women must struggle against the deskilling of their present jobs which is an effect of the introduction of new technology. This would be a collective, as against an individual, strategy. The role of education and training in understanding, preserving and developing women's skills in this struggle is discussed and exemplified with a case study on the Swedish National Insurance Workers Union.

Introduction

I have in front of me an advertisement recently published in the major Swedish newspapers. In bold, somewhat threatening, letters is written: 'Give Your Child a Chance in Life — Get Your Home Computer Now!', and below is a picture of a child confidently studying a visual display unit while working away at a computer keyboard. This lucky child is — of course — a boy.

The picture is instructive and typical. It plays on the diffuse fear of many parents that *their* child may lose out in the future computerized society. And it takes for granted that those who will make it, who will have the knowledge and confidence gained in early contacts with computers, will be the boys, the men. They will be the masters. The computer is *their* technology.

The microelectronics revolution — as it is sometimes called — will affect our future jobs and most of our everyday activities (Forester, 1980). Much of today's knowledge and skills may become obsolete or eroded. New skills and occupations will be created. For women, traditionally excluded both from technical training and positions of power in society, these changes create a difficult challenge. What can be done to enhance women's knowledge, employment possibilities and working environment? How can we protect women's values and skills despite computerization – and perhaps with its help?

This chapter deals with women's education and microelectronics or information technology. I suggest two things: first, that women must enter specialized technical education to a much larger extent than today and, second, above all, that women must get access to training and influence at their *place of work*. My discussion starts with an account of the gender division of labour in today's labour market and the likely negative effects of the new information technology on women's work. I will then take up what needs to be changed in the educational system in order to counteract these effects and improve women's chances. The chapter ends with a case study of women's action at the workplace to preserve and expand their present skills and influence the introduction of new technology.

Women's work and the division of labour

I would like to underline three important characteristics of the labour market.

Women's work

Since the Second World War, women have entered the labour market in large numbers. In 1950, only 35 per cent of Swedish women worked outside the home. Today, 70 per cent of all women (aged 16 to 64) are in paid employment. Women constitute nearly half (45 per cent) of the Swedish labour force. The pattern is similar in other industrialized countries (Arbetsmarknadsdepartementet, 1979: 37ff; Höglund, 1982).

It is above all married women and women with small children who have entered the labour market in recent years. Instead of leaving their jobs when they have children, women change to part-time work or take evening and night shifts. Half of all women in paid employment work part-time, as against 5 per cent of the men. Eighty six per cent of those who work at night are women.

Women still have the major responsibility for the care of children and other dependants and for routine work at home. Women therefore work *more* than men, despite having only part-time paid employment. State child care is poorly developed in Sweden (only 28 per cent of children three to five years of age are in creches, as against 95 per cent in France and 75 per cent in West Germany – Höglund, 1982). Men take very limited responsibility for everyday work at home, even in families where both partners work full-time. All in all, men do about half as much household work as women. In Sweden, as elsewhere, women's working week is substantially longer than men's (Arbetsmarknadsdepartementet, 1979: 41; Hartmann, 1981).

Women's work is different from men's

Sweden has one of the most segregated labour markets of all industrialized countries, although the pattern is similar elsewhere (Murgatroyd, 1982). Most women work in service-type occupations which can be seen as extensions of their domestic role: health care, education, social work in the public sector, secretarial, retail and cleaning jobs in the private sector. There are very few men in women's occupations and very few women in male dominated occupations. Industrial (apart from textile and food processing), transport and construction jobs are completely dominated by men. Men comprise the engineers and technicians (97 per cent), the skilled machinists (92 per cent), and the computer programmers and systems analysts (85 per cent) (Berner, 1981: 131; Arbetsmarknadsdepartementet, 1979: 43; Datadelegationen, 1981: 75).

Men also work in a wider range of occupations than women (about 300 in all). Three-quarters of all women work in only 30 occupations, and 40 per cent are in four categories: secretaries and typists, nurse assistants, shop assistants and cleaners.

Women's work is subordinate to men's

Everywhere, even in women-dominated occupations, women are subordinate to men. Women take orders from men, service men, are controlled by men. Women are over-represented in routine, unskilled, dead-end jobs with low wages, strenuous working conditions, and they have little influence on working hours, job content and prospects for promotion. Women are under-represented in − or altogether absent from − top jobs, especially in the private sector.

Women's work and new technology

The main thrust of mechanization and the automation of work has been in the production of *things*, which comprises mainly men's work. Until recently, it was deemed neither technically possible nor economically feasible to automate the type of work most women do, that is, *service* and *information handling* work. With the advent of cheap and versatile computing power in the form of microelectronics, things have changed. It is generally considered that due to the division of labour outlined above, women's work will be disproportionately affected by new technology:

☐ The *type of jobs* which will disappear, are women's jobs. None of the quantitative forecasts made − and which predict job losses of between 25 and 70 per cent in office jobs, 40 per cent in sales jobs, etc − are likely to be reliable (Science Policy Research Unit, 1982:

55), but it is noteworthy that *all* forecasters predict substantial job losses in the type of jobs where women predominate, and which constitute a large proportion of women's employment.

☐ The jobs at the *bottom* of the hierarchy will be the first to be affected by new technology. Many routine jobs will disappear; others will become even more controlled and boring (Huws, 1982). Both these developments will affect women more than men.

☐ The higher-level, technical jobs which will be created will most likely be occupied by men. Women will have to make special efforts to break the *stereotypes and discriminatory policies* which have allowed these to become men's jobs only.

☐ Women work part-time and have the main responsibility for house-work and childcare. They therefore have little time and opportunity for union work, for in-house training or for part-time study. The type of work many women do, consisting of tightly controlled and routine tasks, provides little opportunity to gain information about changes at their work-place, gain confidence in their own ability or create solidarity amongst themselves. Male-dominated unions seldom take account of women's special situations and demands (Honkasalo, 1982; Kaul and Lie, 1982; Glenn and Feldberg, 1979). All these factors create vicious circles which militate against women's *chances to influence* the introduction of new technology and take advantage of the promotion possibilities offered.

The wide-scale introduction of the new information technology will create both a new *occupational* structure in society, with a larger proportion of skilled and technical jobs and, presumably, a smaller proportion of un-skilled ones, and a new *job* structure, when existing tasks will be changed and, possibly, deskilled. Women are likely to lose out in both these developments. Entry into the more creative and skilled jobs will almost exclusively be through the educational system. I will first briefly analyse women's position and chances in this system before going on to discuss the changes which will occur within existing jobs.

Women and technical education

As shown in many studies, the existing school and university system reflects and, to a large extent, reinforces the existing class and gender divisions in society (Bisseret, 1974; Deem, 1978; Wernerson, 1977). Women's education prepares for a subordinate position in the work force and for continued domestic responsibility. Women rarely choose technical or scientific courses or education leading to positions of power and influence in the economy (Kelly, 1980; Blackstone and Weinreich-Haste, 1980).

Many theories have been advanced to explain this situation (see Arnot, 1981 for an overview). The theories have different focuses and lead to different strategies for change. There seems, however, to be general agreement that more women should enter technical and computer education. One argument given is the already mentioned narrow and shrinking labour market for women. Jobs in engineering, science and computer technology offer better prospects for girls of average ability than traditional women's jobs. Another argument stresses the need for *all* women to reach at least some mastery and confidence in handling everyday machinery, from cars to computers. Women have been kept ignorant and dependent on men in most technical matters. This male monopoly on technology must be broken. A third argument stresses the contribution women can make to technology. In a limited (and more official) version women are seen as an untapped 'pool of talent' to be used for industrial expansion and technological development along established lines. In a more radical feminist version, it is argued that women — because of their more developed sense of social responsibility — may create a more humane and less destructive technology than men have created until now (Rothschild, 1981).

Formal and informal exclusion

Today, about 5 per cent of those with an engineering or technology diploma in Sweden are women. The figure is higher in Poland and the Soviet Union (11 and 30 per cent respectively), and much lower in the United States (1 per cent) and Great Britain (0.4 per cent) (Girls Into Science and Technology, no date: 3). Thus, social stereotypes, official policy and the structure of selection in the educational system must play a much greater role in occupational choice than the much heralded biological factors (Griffiths and Saraga, 1979).

I suggest that the present —and future — chances for women in technical education should be assessed in the light of a historical analysis of how the sex typing of technical occupations was established and consolidated. The story varies slightly in different countries, but with remarkably similar results (Berner, 1981; 1982; Noble, 1977). Technical and scientific occupations emerged as new bases of power in industrializing Europe and America by the turn of the century. Their antecedents are to be found in three extremely selective and male-dominated areas: the military, the metal crafts and guilds and the university. Their importance increased with the rise of science-based technology and the intensified competition between the major capitalist and imperialist powers. Elite positions in state and private employment were increasingly obtained through advanced training in technical universities, but lower level technical training expanded rapidly, and engineering was depicted as a career open to men of talent and hard work. Women, naturally, were excluded from such careers. This occurred in Sweden at about the same time (the 1870s) as women were admitted to medical schools and university science courses. This exclusion was thought to be more or less natural and was backed up by a bourgeois ideology of natural spheres and different destinations in life for men and women. The world of men was, according to this ideology, the world of achievement, industry, technology and public responsibility. The world of women centered around nurturance, the family and eternal moral values. The two worlds did not meet; the presence of women in industry and technical education was seen as unnatural and a sacrilege. (They were, of course, welcomed into exploited manual jobs in industry.) Women, therefore, lost control over many pre-industrial, now industrialized, processes, such as brewing and textile production, and were not able to gain any knowledge of the new scientific and industrial technology.

The occupational structure evolving in the late nineteenth and early twentieth centuries had its counterpart in a sex- and class-divided school system. Working-class girls received only the most rudimentary education. Middle-class girls were taught skills required for their future domestic role and for certain jobs thought to be fit for women (such as teaching and nursing). The scientific or mathematical training given was normally insufficient for any future intellectual work. Not until the 1920s were women admitted into Swedish State supported secondary schools, and it is only recently that women generally have been given the same formal chances and educational resources as men. Higher technical education was opened to women in 1921, but not until the 1960s did a significant number of women gain the educational credits required for entry.

The formal barriers gone, a dualistic ideology still reigned, which channelled women into relatively marginal positions in technology. Women engineers first entered (and still mainly enter) the schools of chemistry and architecture — fields of technology which were seen as 'close to the home' and women's traditional tasks. Men dominate in mechanical and electrical engineering, the technologies which have been central to Swedish industrial and economic power.

A changing pattern?

Only in times of desperate demand for technical labour were women thought of as a relevant 'reserve army'. The routinization of much engineering, and later also computing, work has opened the doors for women technologists, at least in the lower echelons (Berner, 1981; Kraft, 1979). Acute shortages in the boom years of the late 1950s led to discussions of how women could be induced to enter technology (the same effect as the 'Sputnik shock' had produced in the USA), but little was done until similar problems arose in the 1970s. This time, official demand for more technical specialists was reinforced by the women's movement's claims for equality. The women's movement had, until then, been almost completely silent on the question of technical education and technical influence for women.

Today's labour market is characterized by a complex, horizontal and vertical, division of labour, with complicated educational entry routes, training and retraining possibilities. The educational system is large, diversified and in many ways incomprehensible to less privileged groups in society. Selection today is the responsibility of the individual pupil, not a matter of collective exclusion. It is possible, but by no means common or probable, to make a non-sexist choice of education and career.

Many factors militate against girls' choice of subjects involving technology and science. The ideology of 'natural spheres' has given way to one of 'special interests' and 'special aptitudes', but with the same stereotypical contents, which influence the toys given to children, the contents of school books, the options provided within the school system, and the careers advice given by teachers, parents and professional careers officers. Careers advisers generally have a social science or arts background, and therefore know little of technical jobs, and rarely recommend them to girls. Maths and science teachers are generally men, and girls therefore lack female role models who would counteract group stereotypes which maintain, for example, that it is impossible to be at the same time both a woman and an engineer. Many pupils avoid choices which would make them the only girl (or boy) in the group. It takes strong commitment and belief in one's own ability to make such counter-choices. But much research indicates that it is exactly this confidence in their own intellectual ability that many girls lack — a situation which may have been created by their experiences at school, and which influences their performance in subjects such as maths and physics which have a reputation for being both difficult and unfeminine (Kelly, 1980; Girls Into Science and Technology, 1982; Walden and Walkerdine, 1982).

Most affirmative action programmes have acted on these three levels — of *counteracting stereotypes, providing options*, and *strengthening self-confidence.* Thus women engineers and scientists visit schools to provide role models for girls, or girls are invited to technical universities, industrial and scientific work-places. Efforts have been made to change sexist metaphors and vocabulary in science textbooks and to give examples based on women's experience. Official policy in, for example, Sweden is to make technology a compulsory subject at all levels, to give all children at least a rudimentary training in computing, to limit the possibilities to opt out of maths and science until the age of 16, and to give additional credit points to women choosing a male-dominated career (and the opposite). Finally, in many countries, all-girl workshops have been organized to get interested girls together, and to familiarize others with technology, experimental science and computing. Girls are thus provided, though on a limited scale, with the kind of encouragement, feedback and experience which their brothers have always had in the family, school and occupational settings. Many more examples of efforts to make girls more confident and teachers and parents less conservative and constraining could be cited (see Granstam, 1981; 1982; Girls Into Science and Technology, 1982; Simonis, 1981; Sjöberg, 1982; Tobias, 1978; Smail *et al*, 1981).

Despite positive results from these and other experiments, they are clearly not enough. What has to be changed is perhaps not primarily the girls or the teachers, but the type of science and technology produced today which is regarded as alien by many women. A dramatic reversal of selection processes at school, in a labour market characterized by well-entrenched male power, is hardly to be expected. Moderate changes may take place but will mainly affect individual women and new entrants to the labour market. Women's collective situation in the face of new technology must be improved in other ways. In the next section I will discuss what may happen to women's skills, and the role of education and training, when new technology is introduced.

Women's skills and the new technology

The concept of skills is a difficult one. It may refer to (a) complex competencies developed in work, and with some 'objective' character, or (b) control over the labour process, or (c) conventional definitions of occupational status (Beechey, 1982; 63f). Skills are normally a scarce commodity which provides its owner with a better bargaining position and thus higher wages, better working conditions, etc. This scarcity may be kept up by artificial means, such as the control of entry to the relevant education, certification or trade union — or by ideological means excluding lower-status groups, such as women and minorities (Phillips and Taylor, 1980; Cockburn, 1981; Lindgren, 1982).

Women's jobs are normally considered unskilled in sense (c) above, quite often just because they are held by women. The skills which women bring to, and develop, in work are also often seen as extensions of 'natural' female qualities (patience, dexterity, sociability and empathy). Being invisible and impossible to monopolize, these skills are exploited and undervalued by the employer. Their application nevertheless gives women a sense of satisfaction and contribution in work. What may happen, however, is the destruction or deterioration of these skills with the computerization of many women's jobs.

Later on I discuss one particular example. Many others could have been given on the effects of the computerization of banking, office work, sales work, health care, etc (see Science Policy Research Unit, 1982; and Huws, 1982 for an overview). Often the tone is pessimistic and considerable deskilling (in all the senses outlined above) is predicted (Braverman, 1974; Arnold *et al*, 1981). Other writers stress the contradictory character of the new technology, and argue that it is not the technology *as such* which causes deskilling but the uses to which it is put, and the organization of work which is reinforced or introduced with it (Zimmerman, 1981; Glenn and Feldberg, 1979; Perby, 1981). In some cases, action programmes for education and alternative uses of the new technology have been proposed (Morgall, 1981; Huws, 1982; Menzies, 1982; Hedberg and Mehlmann, 1982; Hedberg *et al*, 1982; Dataeffektutredningen, 1981).

When the new technology is about to be introduced in a particular work environment, education becomes important in at least four ways.

First, analysis of how far there is a *need* for the computer as a tool will increase workers' awareness of their own skills and the impact of computerization on them. This educational work must be done by the potential users themselves, but with ample *information* as to what computerization entails being discussed by the employers, and with the help of trade union counselling and computer specialists. This consultation should be compulsory, and workers should have a right of veto against unwanted computerization.

Second, when computers are being introduced, all potential users should have free *instruction* in their use. Instruction should contain both an element of specialized computer operation skills, and an element of general knowledge about how the computer functions: its limits, possibilities and effects on the work environment. As in the consultation stage above, studies may be most instructive and liberating in women-only courses (Walden and Walkerdine, 1982; Ahrnell, 1983).

Third, nobody should be expected to work with computer terminals (eg wordprocessors) all day. Increased productivity through computerization could allow for shorter working hours for *all* (both men and women) — something which would normally require a *redistribution* of tasks along non-sexist lines. Those in more routine positions (normally women) should get increased opportunity for in-house training, educational leave and promotion opportunities. One positive example is a data-processing centre in Uppsala in Sweden, where women and men share most jobs, and where women have been given training and education in order to move from being computer operators (an unskilled job) to programming, technical operating, computer repair and counselling tasks. Management co-operation, however, seems necessary for such reforms (Kahn, 1983).

Finally, completely *new* tasks could be created with the help of computers which would be more creative and interesting than many present office jobs (Morgall, 1981; Menzies, 1982). Such tasks could build on the skills used in women's work today and supplement them with education in areas such as programming, economics, information analysis or other relevant fields.

The case study presented below is an example of the importance of women's education in the first way mentioned above, which led to suggestions about how education could help in the other three ways. It deals with the computerization of office jobs in the Swedish National Insurance system.

National insurance, women's skills and computer technology

The Swedish National Insurance (ie Social Security) system administers pensions, sick allowances and other social benefits. By the 1970s, it had become very large, complex and expensive to administer, and so introduced a complex electronic data processing (EDP) system to make services more cost-effective. This consists of a large central mainframe installation, connected to about 1,200 terminals in the local social security offices. Plans are now being developed for a new computerized system to be used in the next 10 to 20 years.

To meet this situation, the union which organizes almost all of the 21,000 employees, together with researchers at the Swedish Centre for Working Life, organized a study course for self-study by local union members. About 9,000 members participated in more than 900 study groups and discussed previous computerization and their needs and demands for the future. Their answers to a number of questions were used in drawing up a trade union action programme, which has influenced the official plans for the future computerization of the social insurance system (Boman, 1983; Göranzon et al, 1982). The central administration of the insurance system (ie the 'employers'), and its technical and financial experts, wanted computerization to increase productivity and standardize procedures: there should be a uniform application of social insurance laws across the country. From that point of view, previous computerization had been successful: some 3,000 jobs, which might otherwise have been required, did not have to be filled, despite many new tasks for the offices, and a number of routine tasks, such as calculations of pensions and allowances, were now performed automatically thus producing standardized results.

The local employees — 81 per cent of whom are women — and the trade union, however, were less positive. Their reaction and proposals were based on a different conception of what their job was all about. They stressed the quality of the services provided and a socially oriented professional competence, rather than the quantity and uniformity of output. The skills needed in social insurance work consist of a combination of theoretical knowledge about laws and regulations, and practical experience of the complications which arise when these laws are applied in individual cases. Considerable expertise is needed to cope with complex rules and formal language, on the one hand, and to provide human service, on the other. The women, especially, stress the importance of personal contacts in order to help, listen, explain, refer and take care of the people who come to the offices. These contacts, and the social skills involved therein, are not seen or appreciated by the central administration and are under threat of disappearing with further computerization.

The existing system had already influenced the kind of information given to clients. The system allowed only short and packaged messages, which were incomprehensible to many people. What was alarming was that the insurance employees felt they were losing the competence needed to explain how the computerized decisions had been made, and to translate the formalized computer language into a need-oriented one that their clients could understand. When — as suggested by management — even more advanced knowledge ('the handbook') was to be fed into the computer, the professional vocabulary would lose its meaning for the employees. But the practical skills would also be affected. Without the computer system, the employee has to deal with a great variety of cases.

But with further computer development, these will have to be reduced to 'typical' cases to be fed into the computer. The employee, however, must be able to work manually when confronted with a case outside the standardized one. Many employees felt it would be impossible to retain complete insurance knowledge if only parts of it were used and developed in everyday work.

Already the type of training needed had changed. Competence in insurance regulations, ie in the relevant area of work, had been partially replaced by competence in data processing technology. Today, it was felt, many employees thought more in terms of how to feed information into the computer than in terms of how to understand and help the clients. This tendency would be aggravated if, and when, more advanced tasks were taken over by the computer. All in all, service would deteriorate and work satisfaction disappear.

The demands

The trade union proposals are based upon the insights voiced in the self-study groups. Thus, instead of centralized control, the programme demands a decentralization of future EDP systems, with systems development taking place in the local offices. Local offices should also have the right to veto any changes they do not want. Instead of further automation of tasks, the employees propose an increased efficiency, reliability, availability and flexibility of the existing system, which would restore some control to the local offices. They absolutely oppose the computerization of advanced tasks, and want the computerization of routine tasks to proceed according to case-by-case negotiations. Instead of insurance knowledge giving way to computer knowledge they demand that the EDP system be made so simple that all employees can combine a limited knowledge of the technology involved with a solid knowledge of insurance. And, instead of losing their professional competence to the computers, they want increased education related to the overall features of the laws and regulations involved in work, and some training in the EDP field, in order to influence systems development at the local level. Finally, nobody should have to work only at a computer terminal; professional competence should be evenly distributed allowing for work rotation.

Clearly, therefore, the insurance employees want to consider and use the computer as a tool for their own — and, above all, their clients' — perceived needs. The Swedish Parliament, however, recently decided to postpone the development of a decentralized system along the lines proposed by the union. This set-back does not diminish the importance of the large-scale mobilization of attitudes created by the union, and the knowledge and awareness gained by the women in the study-groups. It remains to be seen how these can be used in further struggle to increase the competence and confidence of employees to take power over technology in the future.

References

Ahrnell, B-M (1983) Tjejkurs självklar — hade aldrig kommit fram till maskinerna annars *Datavärlden* 7.2.83: 39

Arbetsmarknadsdepartementet (1979) *Steg på väg*... SOU 1979: 56: Stockholm

Arnold, E, Birke, L and Faulkner, W (1981) Women and microelectronics: the case of word processors *Women's Studies International Quarterly* 4 3: 321-40

Arnot, M (1981) Culture and political economy: dual perspectives in the sociology of women's education *Educational Analysis* 3 1: 97-116

Beechey, V (1982) The sexual division of labour and the labour process: a critical assessment of Braverman *in* Wood

Berner, B (1981) *Teknikens värld. Teknisk förändring och ingenjörsarbete i svensk industri* Arkiv: Lund

Berner, B (1982) Kvinnor, kunskap och makt i teknikens värld *Kvinnovetenskaplig tidskrift* 3 3: 25-39

Bisseret, N (1974) *Les inégaux ou la sélection universitaire* PUF: Paris

Blackstone, T and Weinreich-Haste, H (1980) Why are there so few women scientists and engineers? *New Society* 21.2.80: 383-85

Boman, A (1983) *Omsorg och solidaritet — ohållbara argument?* Arbetslivscentrum: Stockholm

Braverman, H (1974) *Labour and Monopoly Capital* Monthly Review Press: New York

Cockburn, C (1981) The material of male power *Feminist Review* 9: 41-58

Datadelegationen (1981) *Samordnad datapolitik* Ds B 1981: 20: Stockholm

Dataeffektutredningen (1981) *Kontorens datorisering* Ds A 1981: 16: Stockholm

Deem, R (1978) *Women and Schooling* Routledge and Kegan Paul: London

Forester, T ed (1980) *The Microelectronics Revolution* Basil Blackwell: Oxford

Girls Into Science and Technology (1982) *Options and Careers* Manchester Polytechnic: Manchester

Girls into Science and Technology (no date) *Introductory Booklet* Manchester Polytechnic: Manchester

Glenn, E N and Feldberg, R L (1979) Proletarianizing clerical work: technology and organizational control in the office *in* Zimbalist

Granstam, I (1981) *Kvinnor och teknisk utbildning* Institute of Technology: Linköping

Granstam, I (1982) *Barn och teknik* Linköping University: Linköping

Griffiths, D and Saraga, E (1979) Sex differences and cognitive abilities: a sterile field of enquiry? *in* Hartnett, Boden and Fuller

Göranzon, B et al (1982) *Job Design and Automation in Sweden* Center for Working Life: Stockholm

Hartmann, H (1981) The family as the locus of gender, class, and political struggle: the example of housework *Signs: Journal of Women in Culture and Society* 6 3: 366-94

Hartnett, O, Boden, G and Fuller, M eds (1979) *Sex-role Stereotyping* Tavistock Publications: London

Hedberg, B, Mehlmann, M, Parmsund, M, Stadler, B and Stjernberg, T (1982) *Bra affärer med datorer?* Arbetslivscentrum: Stockholm

Hedberg, B and Mehlmann, M (1982) *Dator i bank* Arbetslivscentrum: Stockholm

Honkasalo, M—L (1982) Dead end — views on career development and life situation of women in the electronics industry *Economic and Industrial Democracy* 3: 445-64

Huws, U (1982) *Your Job in the Eighties. A Woman's Guide to New Technology* Pluto Press; London

Höglünd, E (1982) Svenska kvinnan arbetar mest i världen — men blir fast i samma yrken *Veckans affärer* 4.3.82: 38-41

Kahn, H (1983) Arbetsrotation och internutbildning har gjort kvinnorna kvalificerade *Datavärlden* 21.2.83: 39

Kaul, H and Lie, M (1982) When paths are vicious circles — how women's working conditions limit influence *Economic and Industrial Democracy 3:* 465-81

Kelly, A ed (1980) *The Missing Half* Manchester University Press: Manchester

Kraft, P (1979) The routinizing of computer programming *Sociology of Work and Occupations* 6 2: 139-55

Lindgren, G (1982) Anpassning och protest: om deltidsarbete i det kapitalistiska patriarkatet *Kvinnovetenskaplig tidskrift* 3 2: 33-45

Menzies, H (1982) Women and microelectronics *Canadian Women Studies/Cahiers de la Femme* 3 4: 13-17

Morgall, J (1981) Typing our way to freedom: is it true that new office technology can liberate women? *Feminist Review* 9: 87-101

Murgatroyd, L (1982) Gender and occupational stratification *Sociological Review* 30 4: 575-602

Noble, D (1977) *America by Design* Knopf: New York

Perby, M-L (1981) Kvinnor, datateknologi och arbete *Kvinnovetenskaplig Tidskrift* 2 1-2: 43-50

Phillips, A and Taylor, B (1980) Sex and skill: notes towards a feminist economics *Feminist Review* 6: 79-88

Rothschild, J (1981) A feminist perspective on technology and the future *Women's Studies International Quarterly* 4 1: 65-74

Simonis, D (1981) *Women in Science: A Developing Country* Paper prepared for the GASAT Conference 1981, Eindhoven, The Netherlands November 9-13

Sjöberg, S (1982) Soft girls in hard science? *Tidskrift för Nordisk Förening för Pedagogisk Forskning* 1-2: 55-63

Smail, B, Whyte, J and Kelly, A (1981) *Girls Into Science and Technology: the First Two Years* Paper for the International Conference on Girls and Science and Technology, Eindhoven, Holland, November

Science Policy Research Unit Women and Technology Studies (1982) *Microelectronics and Women's Employment in Britain* SPRU: University of Sussex

Tobias, S (1978) *Overcoming Math Anxiety* W W Norton & Co: New York

Walden, R and Walkerdine, V (1982) *Girls and Mathematics: the Early Years* Bedford Way Papers 8: University of London Institute of Education

Wernerson, I (1977) *Könsdifferentiering i grundskolan* Department of Pedagogics: Göteborg

Wertheimer, B M and Nelson, A H (1982) Education for social change: two routes *Economic and Industrial Democracy* 3: 483-513

Wood, S ed (1982) *The Degradation of Work? Skill, Deskilling and the Labour Process* Hutchinson: London

Zimbalist, A ed (1979) *Case Studies on the Labour Process* Monthly Review Press: New York and London

Zimmerman, J (1981) Technology and the future of women: haven't we met somewhere before? *Women's Studies International Quarterly* 4 3: 355-67

Part 4:
Women, education and social change: policies and strategies

19. Women's education and development in India

Carolyn Elliott

Summary: Social legislation and education were the major strategies to fulfil India's Constitutional commitment to equality between men and women. The 1975 Report of the Committee on the Status of Women in India concluded these had not worked. Development was causing a devaluation of women's status, and poor rural women were invisible to development programmes and educators. The number of adult women illiterates is over 200 million and increasing. Following the recommendations of women's groups, the Indian Planning Commission shifted to a focus on women's employment and eradicating adult illiteracy. Formal education, while not neglected, is seen as catering only for the needs of a minority and unable to address the growing problem of illiteracy. The most interesting educational thinking and experimentation is in adult education and non-formal education where there are many successful programmes run by small private groups. These have many lessons for formal education but the process of transferring ideas to the bureaucratic setting of government is perilous. Formal education needs the same creative energy as the newer programmes lest girls be denied access to modern opportunities and women be trained only for the lowest level field positions in the development system.

Introduction

'Nowadays, in every department and place, corruption is growing. When the due money had to be paid to the labourers, the foreman forged their thumb-print and exploited them once again . . . During the discussions at the literacy center in my village, we have learnt not to put our thumb-print on false papers and to maintain a private copy of our attendance. So, when the turn came for me to put my thumb-print on the false papers I refused to do so and told my colleagues to abstain from doing so, but they were scared that the foreman would strike their name off the master roll, therefore they continued to put their thumb-print wherever the foreman wanted them to' (Women's Development Unit, no date).

This is part of a narrative by a young village woman in Rajasthan, one of the more educationally backward states of India, where traditional patterns of deference and fear continue to govern relations between classes, generations, and men and women. Her narrative conveys a remarkable but not atypical growth in confidence and awareness through

participation in an adult education programme. Literacy and knowledge are only part of what this class meant to her. Equally important were
the friends with whom she endured parental opposition to attending the
class, the teacher who gave sewing lessons and moral support after hours,
and the development workers who helped her to write to the district
authorities protesting about malpractices. It is the social resources
provided by a village community with a strong development programme
that enabled her to make use of her new awareness and skills.

In contrast, the educated women in her village contribute relatively
little to village development. Usually of higher caste, they follow the
traditional mode of demonstrating status by withdrawing from public
view as well as from labour outside the home. Education for these women
is part of their marriage qualification; for many families now think a girl
with some learning will be a more informed mother and suitable partner
for her more educated husband. Their education may be reflected in
private decisions about family planning or health care but, unless the
traditional family ideal is disrupted by circumstance, it does not propel
them into new roles or community leadership.

This contrast between the formally educated women and those who
have enjoyed only a few months of evening classes is a disturbing one, for
it raises fundamental questions about education as a strategy for women
in Third World countries. Who has access to formal education? How can
education accomplish changing traditional roles and perspectives? What
linkages are needed with development programmes? What priority should
be given to formal education? These are among the issues involved. India,
with over 35 years since independence, six five-year plans, and a relatively
strong women's movement provides rich experience for assessment. This
chapter cannot undertake a comprehensive investigation, nor is there
sufficient data available. It offers instead an overview of Indian policy on
women's education and development and a consideration of the responses
of the women's movement. Such a discussion may suggest avenues
deserving more systematic work.

Planning for women and development

Equality between women and men, with liberation from traditional
constraints, has been the cornerstone of Indian policy toward women since
independence in 1947. The foundation for the constitutional commitment to equality was laid by Mahatma Gandhi who, through his writings,
and even more with his success in mobilizing women for civil disobedience,
transformed the views of the national leadership about women's potential
contribution to the nation. In 1931, the Congress Party (which was later
to form the government of independent India) committed itself to universal adult suffrage, and when the Constitution was framed there was no
opposition to the full enfranchisement of women. The Constitution is a
very progressive document, with guarantees of equal rights and privileges

for men and women, and a specific prohibition against discrimination in employment. Constitutional directives were rapidly embodied in social legislation on equal remuneration, property rights, age of marriage, dowry, and a wide range of other problems.

Equality did not preclude, however, special attention to historically deprived groups such as women. India's Planning Commission viewed women as handicapped by social custom and in urgent need of rehabilitative social services because of their family responsibilities. The early five-year development plans emphasized maternal and child health, protection of women workers, nutrition and family planning to meet women's special needs. Allocations for these services declined over successive plans, on the assumption that women also benefited from the general social services programme.

India placed the greatest hope on education as a long-term strategy for guaranteeing equal opportunity to women. The Constitution directed that within 20 years there should be free and compulsory education for all children to the age of 14 — a goal which proved to be impossible because of failure to reach girls, scheduled castes (former untouchables), and the tribal peoples who inhabit remote hill areas. Later development plans therefore increased the attention to education. A review in 1959 of women's education recommended that 'the education of women should be regarded as a major and special problem in education for years to come and that a bold and determined effort be made to face its difficulties and magnitude and to close the existing gap between the education of men and women in as short a time as possible' (Government of India, 1959: 38). Condensed courses for women who had failed to complete schooling and attempts to produce functional literacy for village women were added to the educational effort. In addition, various social services programmes had educational components to convey information about health, nutrition, family planning, and child care through some 53,000 local women's groups (mahila mandals) organized by government extension workers.

By 1975, it was clear that legalistic and educational approaches, supplemented by social welfare services for specially vulnerable women, were not working. Legislated changes in social customs such as dowry were not being implemented, and few women were able to avail themselves of the new provisions for inheritance. Furthermore, there was evidence that the very success of development was exacerbating inequalities between women and men, as shown most dramatically in the declining ratio of women to men in the population. This result, which runs counter to the outlines of development in other parts of the world where the proportion of women has increased, indicates in India an increasing devaluation of women reflected in family nutrition and health care, work burdens, and lack of control over child-bearing (Government of India, Planning Commission, 1980: 423). Development has also brought women declining labour force participation, more unemployment, and increasing migration. These were the alarming discoveries of the Committee

on the Status of Women, which was appointed by the Indian government to prepare a report for International Women's Year (Government
of India, Ministry of Social Welfare, 1975). Their investigations were a
shattering experience for the committee members who, with the sole
exception of one man, were all successful professional women. They
realized how little they (and others) understood the conditions under
which most Indian women live.

The educational profile in 1975 indicated that formal schooling had
failed to reach even modified goals for women and that it had not allevi-
ated inequalities. Though girls' enrolment had grown more rapidly than
boys', only two out of three primary-school-age girls were enrolled.
Among the scheduled caste and tribal girls, enrolment was lower still at
40 per cent. Worse, the drop-out rate was much higher for girls: only
30 per cent of girls enrolled were able to complete primary school, most of
the wastage being in Class One. At higher levels, the proportion of girls
enrolled in each group declined from one in five in middle school, to
one in eight in secondary school. Thus, secondary education for girls is
largely confined to middle and upper class urban girls and well-to-do
rural families. The fact that university education for girls is growing
faster than primary education shows that educational progress is easiest
for the middle classes. The combined result of population growth and
these educational lags is a rise in the absolute number of illiterate women
in India, which now exceeds over 200 million. Sixty-seven per cent of all
women in the prime productive/reproductive age group, 15 to 34, are
illiterate.

These findings aroused a great deal of attention in India, and made a
major impact on both social science research and national planning. In
brief, social scientists 'discovered' poor rural women. Recognizing that
these women had been invisible to research focused on the family or the
organized sector of the labour market, they sought explanations for the
devaluation of women in a series of new investigations. Research on
intra-household inequalities in food and services, on unpaid family
workers, on the 90 per cent of paid workers who are in the unorganized
sector and on women migrants, revealed that inequality is greatest among
the families with the least assets (Jain, 1983). It also revealed the critical
contribution made by women to family incomes: frequently over half,
despite their lower wages and unshared household duties. Women's movement activists, many of whom are social scientists, mobilized to action by
their data, pressed these findings on government and called for changes in
policy (Center for Women's Development Studies, 1983).

The Planning Commission responded with two important shifts in
strategy. For the first time it incorporated a separate chapter on Women
and Development in the 1980-85 Plan. Though this move was largely
symbolic — the recommendations are not reflected in the operational
plans of the various economic sectors — it did focus attention on women
and thus provided a basis for subsequent evaluation. An important substantive shift in strategy was announced. The main thrust for women

would be on employment opportunities to upgrade their economic position. This would include imparting new technological skills, providing credit and marketing services to women entrepreneurs, and enhancing women's control of economic assets by granting them joint title to land and by enforcing wage laws.

On two other fronts, however, the Commission did not agree with the women's recommendations. The Plan continued to view women as members of families, with special vulnerability within the family. It also resisted the ear-marking of resources, with special cells for monitoring, within the sectoral programmes.

Formal education is not neglected in this new framework, but both planners and women activists appear to have lost faith in its capacity to reach poor women or to affect their lives. Support for this view comes from their experience of many innovative rural development programmes run by private (in Indian parlance, 'voluntary') agencies. Those working with the very poor feel they must concentrate on meeting the urgent needs of the currently productive generation, which includes large numbers of illiterate women aged between 15 and 25 with a long working life ahead. These women's needs are economic and political — for employment or credit; for support in demanding fair wages and access to government programmes. The education they require must be closely linked to these needs, and provided when they are available. The formal system is largely unavailable to them or to their girl-children, who are kept at home to look after young siblings and help with household chores, or sent out as child earners. Day-time schedules, failure to adjust vacations to peak agricultural seasons, age bars, and costs of clothing and books are widely acknowledged factors preventing their enrolment. Perhaps equally important is the isolation of the school from the community, such that enrolment yields none of the socio-political resources for development which were so important to the young woman quoted at the beginning.

Even for extension workers, voluntary agencies have found formal education unnecessary or detrimental. In many villages of India, an educated worker is almost by definition an outsider, because there are so few educated village women. This is most true for programmes such as health and family planning where only married middle-aged women are acceptable to the community. Faced with a choice between illiterate local women and educated outsiders, several community health programmes have successfully trained illiterate women in basic diagnostic and monitoring skills, and are finding them very effective. An innovative educational programme teaching girls in night schools has found it easier to train high school drop-outs as teachers than to re-train teachers with MEd degrees for their new curriculum (Naik, 1982). This is supported by an evaluation of village programmes which reports a negative correlation between formal education and teacher effectiveness, as long as teachers are minimally skilled (Shrivastava, 1980).

Aware of the widespread failure of government programmes to reach the very poor, the Planning Commission began earmarking funds for disadvantaged groups in the 1974 plan, India's fifth five-year plan. Designed to meet minimum needs, this programme places universal elementary education and elementary adult literacy as its first priorities for these groups (Shrivastava, 1980). The minimum needs programme has stimulated many innovative efforts in adult and non-formal education, which have lessons for educational planners.

Adult education

The most interesting programme for women's education in India now is adult education. This programme is attempting to reach all illiterate adults in the prime reproductive/productive age range of 15 to 35, some 100 million people. Women are two-thirds of this clientele, which includes large numbers of the hardest-to-reach group: poor rural women. Therefore the programme has had to experiment with all kinds of innovations to attract these women.

A concern for educating adults is not itself new in India, nor is the attempt to link education with development. The initial community development schemes in 1952 visualized development as an integrated process, with social education an important component in it. Village women's organizations were started by government extension workers to teach literacy, nutrition, health, family planning, and crafts for leisure-time earning — reflecting a very middle-class view of women. As India became more concerned with increasing agricultural production, however, it withdrew staff support for social education and progressively reduced funding for adult education while the number of adult illiterates rose (Bordia, 1982). The Education Ministry ran a desultory literacy scheme which made little impact. The one bright spot was a functional literacy programme tied to the Green Revolution, which sought to educate and inform illiterate farmers about new agricultural practices. This programme ran some 100 centres for educating farm women, a minuscule number in India but they were of some significance in introducing a linkage between women and agriculture.

The National Adult Education Program (NAEP), launched in 1978, was a new departure in many ways. First, it signified a change in educational priorities, from a preoccupation with technical and higher education to a new focus on primary and adult education. (Nevertheless, India still continues to spend $30 on each student in higher education for each $1 on a primary student.) Secondly, NAEP recruited more than 600 different non-governmental agencies for running the centres, including a number of local groups who are quite activist in their approach to development. Financial contributions from the NAEP stimulated a major growth in the activities of voluntary agencies, enabling many very innovative groups to grow. Most importantly, the NAEP returned to, and updated, the notion of linking education with development. This was expressed both in the organization, ie decentralization to local development groups, and the curriculum, which was based on the very progressive assumption 'that the illiterate and the poor can rise to their own liberation through literacy, dialogue and action' (Bordia, 1982). The curriculum, which each agency formulated for its own constituency, emphasized functional skills and social awareness equally with literacy.

The experience of women in adult education centres has been encouraging. Over 55 per cent of the participants are women, a much higher proportion of the relevant population than is reached by formal schooling. They have found it more difficult than men to gain literacy through adult education, but have progressed as much as men in functional skills (measured as knowledge of access to co-operatives, banks, and to new agricultural practices) and in social awareness (Hebsur, 1981). It is disappointing, however, that the social awareness curriculum has had relatively little impact on the attitudes of either men or women toward customs which particularly constrain women, eg dowry, age of marriage, or minimum wage. One evaluation reports that the literacy components, which are more concrete and familiar to teachers, tend to dominate teaching in many centres (Hebsur, 1981).

Equally important as these initial results has been the discovery of what makes effective programmes for women. Several successful programmes which made demonstrable impact on women's lives as well as their skills have been the subject of case studies identifying critical determinants for women. One such programme, conducted by a voluntary organization working with tribal people in South India, is called Action for Welfare and Awakening in the Rural Environment (AWARE) (Institute of Social Studies Trust, in press). AWARE places adult education firmly in the context of community development. It approaches villages first through programmes to stimulate awareness ('conscientization') by informing villagers of their rights and organizing them for action. It believes that no amount of literacy or economic schemes will help poor people until they are ready to act as a group to use them. Therefore literacy classes are provided only when the community requests them.

AWARE first entered the tribal area by conducting residential camps for village youth. These camps combined agricultural training with exposure to government officials and to prosperous farms in non-tribal areas. At the end of three months the usually silent tribal boys had become very outspoken about tribal problems, and knew techniques for organizing communities. Many of these youths are now field staff for the AWARE development programme. The programme begins in an area with village surveys to establish needs and facilities, leading to selection of a few villages for intensive work. A village association and a women's group are formed in each village for community education and discussion. The style of conducting these groups is crucial. Villagers are encouraged to quiz the extension workers lecturing to them and to unite in approaching the government to demand the services to which they are entitled. AWARE has also established community education centres in tribal and scheduled caste localities in 80 villages. These centres have a very flexible programme depending on the village needs. Some conduct classes for students who have dropped out of school or want help with school work, some emphasize community education through discussions and dramas, and some have instituted literacy centres in response to community demand.

This programme has made a perceptible impact on tribal women. They have taken the lead in a campaign against alcoholism, and have eliminated alcohol from the whole region. They have also had a very successful strike for minimum wages, and are planning collective economic projects. Those interested in literacy were planning to devote their leisure time to a concentrated effort during the slack agricultural season.

Quite different models have also been effective in adult education. Two urban programmes, one in Delhi and another in Madras, show that literacy classes can succeed without an elaborate conscientization programme preceding them (Institute of Social Studies Trust, in press). The Delhi programme was conducted by the government in a poor Muslim locality where the girls work long hours in home-based sweat shops. Women in the community are seldom allowed to go out of the house, and then only in veil. The girls had a strong incentive for literacy, however, because most had literate brothers and knew enough of the urban environment to feel disabled by illiteracy. Furthermore, the literacy classes provided one of the few opportunities to get away from their repressive home environments and enjoy friendships.

Classes in the Delhi programme followed standard, routine methods of teaching. Instructors had no initial training in adult education, though some in-service training was provided. Their salaries were low and payment irregular. In brief, there was little contributing to success except a dedicated director who was herself a member of the community. Yet the project did keep its students and make them literate. At its conclusion, most expressed their intention to continue learning and prepare for a Board examination.

The YWCA conducted another relatively successful urban project in the south Indian city of Madras. They organized adult education classes in 15 centres — purposely a small number to enable good supervision. These centres were unrelated to development programmes, and at first concentrated only on literacy. Faltering attendance led the YWCA to add training in marketable skills, for example, the production of plastic shower caps for hotels. This improved attendance, and a high proportion of women completed the course. Afterwards a number of participants joined together in co-operative societies for other income-generating activities, an indication of their new capabilities.

Several conclusions emerge from this variety of experiences. All point to the crucial role of the teacher. Most importantly, the teacher must hold the class throughout the 10-month duration, not leave for another job, migrate to the city, or become too absorbed in family obligations to attend regularly. A major reason for failure in most adult education programmes is loss of teachers. Above this minimum requirement is the teacher's personality, a stronger factor for success than education or skill. Well-liked teachers with strong community roots are able to motivate students even when the programme does not otherwise appear strong.

What makes an effective teacher for adult women? Virginia Shrivastava (1980) did a systematic evaluation of teachers in 40 centres, examining student learning as well as their reports. She found that local persons recruited in consultation with the community were more effective and less likely to leave than outsiders. Best among these were teachers from the same caste status as the learners, enabling peer group learning. Young male teachers were as effective as women, provided they were of respectable families and younger than the married women so as to avoid social restrictions on women mixing with potential partners. Better a local enthusiastic male, she argues, than a female outsider, or a woman motivated only by need of a job. As previously discussed, a high level of formal education is, if anything, a disadvantage.

Among the most interesting of her findings is that motivated teachers are made, not born. She found no difference in motivation between effective and ineffective teachers at the beginning of the adult education programmes, nor did pre-service training make much difference. But by the end of their teaching the good teachers had changed greatly. They were more involved with the community and were dedicated to adult education as a movement for development. All such teachers worked in organizations with committed leadership that gave frequent and positive supervisory attention to their teachers. The routinized, dispirited teachers were found in organizations which gave little or no supervision, failed to pay teachers on time, and ignored their problems. These teachers reflected the marginal view of adult education and of women that their organizations conveyed to them.

A question of much concern has been to find the best way of giving over-burdened adult women access to education. The case studies suggest there is no general answer other than the prescription that programmes should meet needs perceived by the community. AWARE's systematic surveys identified community problems which provided it with an entrée, whereas the Delhi programme fortuitously, without research, matched the urban community's interest in literacy. For rural women, many organizations have concluded that economic incentives – organizing income-generating projects or teaching marketable skills – are the most effective approaches. Such incentives are ineffective without an associated development programme to create an economic pay-off. In the YWCA programme, none of the women were able to continue to make shower caps after the course finished because there was no continuing organization to market them, and the co-operatives they formed independently used none of the new technical skills they had learned.

Another problem is the scatter of small economic programmes across the landscape, with little co-ordination or linkage to higher levels of the economy. All too often they teach low-level skills, such as tailoring, that cannot survive labour market competition, or promote craft industries that are no longer economically feasible. Therefore some planners have proposed embedding all adult education programmes in economic agencies: factories, development agencies, co-operatives, etc. There is a danger that educational goals and teaching skills will be subordinated, however, which has been the experience of literacy classes taught by health workers in India's integrated Child Development Scheme (ICDS) (Koshy *et al*, 1976).

Strategy should follow from the basic question of goals for adult education. If the goal is to teach women to analyse their own life-situation and develop alternatives, as feminist educators propose, then learning is not an end in itself. The goal is for women to transform their lives (Bernard and Gayfer, 1983). Programmes which successfully teach literacy without challenging traditional attitudes to issues such as dowry, like the Delhi programme, have only a marginal impact on this larger goal. Similarly, training in marketable skills, even if resulting in higher income, may not transform women's lives if unchanged family structures leave women with no control over their income. Women's education must not be a marginal or second-rate system of learning but a long-term mainstream programme to develop the attitudes, capacities and support systems of women to enable them to participate fully in development.

Universalization of primary education

In contrast to adult education, there is little momentum behind primary education for girls. India remains committed to the ever-receding goal of universalizing primary education — now projected for 1990 — and recognizes this is primarily a problem of reaching and retaining girls. But there is as yet no sustained plan for enrolling girls, nor even targets for reducing their drop-out rate from primary school, which has remained steadily high for decades. Therefore a leading educational planner has concluded that India cannot achieve universal literacy through the formal educational system (Bordia, 1982). Nor have women and development activists pressed the case. They too see the formal system as catering only for a minority while the problem of illiteracy grows. Therefore they have emphasized adult education in order to raise the status of women who are already adults, and these comprise the largest group of women (Government of India, Ministry of Social Welfare, 1975).

The need for special attention to girls' education has been widely accepted. In 1958, a National Committee on Women's Education was established to address the problems of wastage, lapsing literacy and vocational education. Even before their report, special schemes were introduced to promote girls' education: attendance scholarships for students, appointment of school mothers to assist girls in school, and measures to increase the number of women teachers in rural areas. This list was subsequently expanded to a vast choice of incentives including free uniforms, free books, mid-day meals, and reimbursement of fees.

The current five-year plan has added more ideas to the list: adjustment of school hours for working children, remedial coaching, crèches to relieve students of child care responsibilities, and non-formal education. Most of these ideas have won a warm response from parents wherever they have been tried. There is no dearth of useful ideas.

But primary education of girls has suffered from the problem of primary education in general. Under the pressure of investments in infrastructure and production, funding for social services has declined over the five-year plans, to 14.7 per cent in the current one. In the last plan, over half the funds available for primary education were left unspent (Government of India, Planning Commission, 1980), a further indication of its low priority. The special schemes for girls have been very meagrely funded and allowed to lapse once central incentives to state governments for girls' education ran out. In this context, one wonders how India will spend the much larger amount — almost double — made available for primary education under the sixth plan. One bright spot is a recent set of commitments by state governments to the politically popular mid-day meals schemes for school children. While seen primarily as a nutrition programme, this may have some impact on attendance.

The most interesting new thinking is on non-formal education. There is a very successful experiment in the western India state of Maharashtra which demonstrates that parents will allow pre-adolescent daughters to attend night classes if the project is well integrated into the community. This has been a major obstacle with many programmes. The project team, a group of educationists from a research centre in Puna, adopted a number of stratagems to build community involvement (Naik, 1982). They appointed local people as project assistants to arouse village concern about the state of schooling available to them, and to collect local material which could be used in formulating a curriculum. The project team met with villagers to discuss the relationship between formal and non-formal education, and made it clear that the community would have to assume responsibility for the non-formal education after the initial five-year experimental phase. Community traders participated in surveying out-of-school children, selecting teachers, securing rent-free accommodation and mobilizing public support. The project has been unable, however, to involve local school teachers in the formal system.

The teachers are locally recruited and of the same class background as the students. As discussed earlier, this project has preferred to take untrained teachers because it has an entirely new curriculum closely linked to rural life. They are trained in a well-designed programme which is one of the most important innovations of the project. Training is carried out at six-week intervals in the project area, not at the city headquarters, while classes continue at night. This enables the training staff to visit classes and draw on classroom experiences in the training seasons. Above all, it provides teachers with strong supportive supervision. The conduct of the training sessions is planned as a model for teachers to conduct their classes, with an emphasis on peer group interaction and lack of hierarchy.

They are called 'bhai', meaning elder brother, rather than 'guru', in order to establish a family relationship with pupils, transcending caste barriers. One measure of the enthusiasm aroused in the teachers is their decision not to honour the long and ill-timed vacations of the formal school. The evening classes run continuously throughout the year, just like the day-time chores of the working children.

This project has demolished a number of the myths about the demand for primary education that have all too often led planners to comfortable despair. Seventy per cent of the project's 1,300 students are girls, many of them first daughters of families where boys and younger children are already in school. Economic and work pressures were the reasons why they had been kept out of school, not social taboos or early marriage (Government of India, Planning Commission, 1978). This should make girls' education a much easier problem to address than cultural stereotypes suggest. The reason the girls give for attending school is to gain skills for adult life — keep accounts, write letters, read documents, and manage daily transactions — not to marry an educated husband. This indicates they are much more open to development than the education-for-marriage myth suggests. One of the current problems for the project is to generate development activities for its graduates, a need for follow-up action which few educational projects are prepared to undertake.

Conclusions

These experiments in adult education and non-formal education are very promising. They show how community involvement, teacher training and support, rescheduling, and relevant curricula create schools which attract poor women and children even without financial incentives. Many poor families prefer these classes even for their daughters who go to school, despite the fact that they offer only minimal education and no certification.

Unfortunately these models are very hard to duplicate in either the private or public sectors. The NAEP experience with voluntary agencies was a mixed one, with exemplary projects handicapped by sham agencies set up only to capture government funding. Government also found it difficult to tolerate financial support to agencies which challenged local party supporters, either by promoting development activism among the poor or by directly political activities. Therefore, it has withdrawn funding from many voluntary groups — not including the four reported above, which have other resources — and the programme has lost much of its momentum.

Even where they are successful and sustainable, voluntary efforts cannot reach more than a small proportion of disadvantaged women in a country the size of India. Nor are most equipped to provide the follow-through to economic programmes and post-literacy education to make a lasting transformation in women's skills and status. Only the government has the geographic reach and comprehensive approach required for national impact. Yet the transfer of learning to government from small, committed private groups is a perilous process in India. Many of the techniques voluntary agencies have found successful depend on modes of building staff morale and community participation which would be difficult to duplicate in a bureaucratic organization. One of the most challenging jobs for educational planners is to discern what is transferable.

Financial incentives and support services, while less potent for learners, may be a more viable route for government. Making these available to the most needy, however, requires a co-ordinated plan aimed at the hardest-to-reach women in poor and isolated communities. Until this is done, inequalities will continue to grow among women, and between women and men. This is not to suggest that government can, or should, take responsibility for changing women's lives. Women, individually and collectively, must build their own futures, using government programmes as a resource for change.

For women engaged in mobilizing women for this goal, the concern is a different one. While no one would deny the urgency of addressing the income needs of adult women, the problems of schooling for girls must not be neglected. Formal schooling is essential to give large numbers of girls in poor communities access to technical jobs of the modern sector which their brothers are beginning to enter. Similarly, emphasis on training illiterate women for the lowest level of development work may displace a concern for preparing women to enter decision-making levels. One fears that a system well-staffed with women field workers but without women in superior positions would make little basic change. For women to participate fully in development at all levels, the formal school system urgently requires the same investment of energy and creative thinking that the women's movement has devoted to community development.

References

Bernard, A and Gayfer, M (1983) *Women Hold Up More than Half the Sky: A Third World Perspective on Women and Non-formal Education for Development* International Council for Adult Education: Toronto

Bordia, A (1982) *Planning and Administration of National Literacy Programs: Indian Experience* International Institute of Educational Planning, UNESCO: Paris

Centre for Women's Development Studies (1983) *Women's Work and Employment: Struggle for a Policy: Selections from Indian Documents* Centre for Women's Development Studies: Delhi

Government of India (1959) *Report of the National Committee on Women's Education* Government of India Press: New Delhi

Government of India, Ministry of Social Welfare (1975) *Towards Equality: Report of the Committee on the Status of Women in India* Government of India Press: New Delhi

Government of India, Planning Commission (1978) *Study of the Special Programmes for Girls' Education* Government of India Press: New Delhi

Government of India, Planning Commission (1980) *Sixth Five Year Plan 1980-1985* Government of India Press: New Delhi

Hebsur, R K *et al* (1981) *National Adult Education Program in Maharashtra: An Evaluation* Tata Institute of Social Sciences: Bombay

Institute of Social Studies Trust (in press) *Adult Education for Women* Vikas

Jain, D (1983) Development as if women mattered: can women build a new paradigm? Lecture at OECD/DAC meeting, 26 January mimeo

Kelly, G and Elliott, C eds (1982) *Women's Education in the Third World: Comparative Perspectives* State University of New York Press: Albany

Koshy, J A *et al* (1976) *The Mahbubnagar Experiment: Non-formal Education for Rural Women* Council for Social Development: New Delhi

Naik, C (1982) An action-research project on universal primary education: the plan and the process *in* Kelly and Elliott

Shrivastava, V (1980) *Non-formal Education Programmes for Women in Indian Colleges: A Study of Social Change and Leadership Patterns* Unpublished PhD dissertation, University of Toronto

20. Sweden's efforts to achieve sex role equality in education

Hilda Scott

Summary: In 1968 Sweden became the first country in the world to frame a government policy of achieving equality between the sexes by changing the role of men as well as that of women. Since then, one of the explicit goals of the school system has been to break down stereotyped attitudes in young people about what is appropriate behaviour for men and women, and to encourage non-traditional choices in their further study and occupations. Steps taken to strengthen the curriculum of the nine-year comprehensive school in this direction are examined against the background of the Swedish sex role equality programme. Findings of a five-year study undertaken by the National Board of Education to determine how schools can influence pupils' decisions more effectively are reported. The article documents the absence of significant change in students' choices at the secondary school level. Changes in university level education are described and women's enrolment figures given. Three obstacles to realizing sex role equality in Swedish education are identified, arising out of the conflicting priorities of the schools, the structure of the labour market, and the sex role concept itself.

Introduction

Optimism and pessimism struggle for precedence in the perception of any observer of Swedish efforts to use the country's educational system to break down sex role stereotyping in the schools and, through the development of new attitudes in young people, in society at large. Optimism is in order because the Swedish experience has shown that it is possible not only to win widespread acceptance for the goals of sex role equality in what is, by definition, a bureaucratic and conservative public entity — state-supported education — but to turn this acceptance into concrete measures of a sweeping nature. Pessimism follows like a cold shower, because these changes, spanning 20 years, have had no measurable effect on the traditional study and career choices of the vast majority of compulsory school leavers, nor have they altered the heavily male dominated character of the school structure.

Perhaps two decades is too short a period in which to make serious inroads on the discrimination against women which dates back to the very beginnings of general education. Nevertheless, the Swedish experience asks us to think deeply (although surely not for the first time) about the extent to which the school can achieve autonomy in the system in which it is embedded, the extent to which it can actually influence that system, inadequacies in our understanding of how sex roles are learned and reinforced, and the self-perpetuating nature of male power.

The school system

The comprehensive school

The present nine-year compulsory comprehensive school in Sweden was established in 1962. It begins the year the child turns seven, and takes pupils through a uniform course until they are 16. At the start, sex education (introduced into the Swedish schools in 1956), domestic science and child care were taught to both girls and boys; handicrafts, however, were divided along traditional lines, with sewing for girls and manual training for boys.

Following government decisions in the late 1960s, the equality aspects were substantially reinforced by a revised curriculum that took effect in the 1970-71 school year. Since then, both girls and boys have had handwork in textiles, wood and metals up to the sixth class. In the last three years, pupils choose an optional course in a technical subject, a foreign language, economics or the arts, and may decide whether they want to continue in textile handicrafts or in the workshop. This curriculum made domestic science compulsory for both sexes in the eighth and ninth years, with child care included in the last year. Vocational education was introduced, with each child paying a visit to three different types of workplace in the eighth year and a period of practice at an actual job in the ninth.

After extensive research and discussion, which is described below, the present curriculum was introduced in 1980-81 and took full effect in 1982. It goes further in imposing on both sexes experience of non-traditional activities from the time they enter school. Domestic science has been pushed back so that it is now part of class schedules at the junior and middle levels (years 1 to 3 and 4 to 6), and child care includes new material on marriage and the family. Children are exposed to technical topics from the earliest years, and technology has been made compulsory for senior level students (years 7 to 9). Course content is being expanded to provide some basic acquaintance with economic problems. Physical training has been made co-educational.

An important change is the amount of time to be devoted to vocational guidance, which has gradually been substantially increased as will be seen below. A potentially significant alteration eliminates the element of choice. Formerly, girls and boys could select, from among the fields available, the one in which they took their practical training, with the predictable result that girls wanted to work in service jobs and boys in technical occupations. Now it will be possible, in so far as facilities permit, to guide them to try out less conventional jobs — girls handling tools, or boys in child care, for instance.

In addition to preparing pupils of both sexes to assume the same roles in adult life, the school is expected to instil a questioning attitude towards existing relationships between women and men through the content of the teaching at all levels in a variety of subjects, including history, geography, civics, biology and language. Textbooks and teaching aids have been under continuous supervision since the late 1960s to eliminate gender role bias. As the 1970-71 curriculum put it: 'The reasons for and consequences of differences in the status of men and women on the labour market, in the family, and in public life should be discussed in a manner that will make pupils experience the question of sexual roles as one that is exciting and can engage them, by virtue of its importance both for the individual and society at large' (National Swedish Board of Education, 1969: 46).

The integrated upper secondary school

A school leaving certificate qualifies students for admission to the integrated upper secondary school, which is actually attended by about 80 per cent of the age cohort. Established in 1971 by act of parliament, the integrated secondary school combined the previous vocational, continuation, and upper secondary schools (the 'gymnasium' in the European sense) into a single system. This move was intended to democratize education, to break down artificial barriers between theoretical and practical learning, and, at the same time, to deploy educational resources more effectively. It offers a choice of three lines: scientific and technical, economic, or the humanities. There are more than 20 course combinations possible, planned for two, three or four years. Most of these are considered preparation for university level education.

It should be added that there are no privately operated schools in Sweden. Education is tuition-free at all levels. Children in the compulsory school receive free textbooks, lunches, and transportation. Older students receive study grants and may apply for further financial aid.

The sex role equality debate

Report to the United Nations

Developments in the Swedish school system during the 1960s and 1970s must be seen not only against the background of the general Western drive to achieve greater equality of opportunity through education but in the context of a specifically Swedish sex role equality programme — the first comprehensive government sponsored drive outside the socialist countries to break down traditional gender roles, and the first ever to incorporate a determination to change the position of men as well as that of women.

In 1968, the Swedish government submitted to the United Nations a detailed document, *The Status of Women in Sweden*, in which it discussed the proposition that if roles in society are socially rather than biologically determined there is no reason why they cannot be shared equally by women and men, and that men as well as women would benefit from this change. The job of government, it was said, was to design policies that would move society in this direction.

The Social Democratic Party programme

At this time, the Swedish 'sex role debate' had been under way for six or seven years, a product of the social unrest of the 1960s. The women's movement was part of the wave of protest against alienation, the dead hand of the 'consumer society', in favour of a more human environment and more participation by individuals in the decisions that affected their lives. It coincided with a tremendous demand for women workers in an expanding economy.

While in other countries women's demands were pushed to the periphery, in Sweden they were caught up by the ruling Social Democratic Party and became part of a general 'equality' platform that in 1968 carried the Social Democrats to their greatest post-Second World War victory. The aim was to restore the balance for all underprivileged groups — the young, the old, the handicapped, the unemployed, low-income groups and rural dwellers, as well as women.

A crucial role in convincing the party that it must incorporate the goal of equality between the sexes in its programme was played by the Social Democratic women's organization which, as early as 1960, had urged the party to form a study group on the subject. All the basic aims that were later to be implemented in legislation and social, educational, and labour market policy were suggested by this committee of prominent Social Democratic women in 'The Erlander Report', adopted by the party in 1964. They appeared again in the policy declaration drawn up by a working group on equality questions, chaired by one of Sweden's leading social scientists and most respected political figures, Alva Myrdal. Its recommendations were adopted as guidelines for policy at the Social Democratic Party congress in 1969. This document stated that government powers over industry were to be used to eliminate sex discrimination, that labour market and educational policies must counteract sex determined choices of occupation, and that expanded services, especially day care and public transportation, were essential for an effective equality policy.

Early measures

The new comprehensive school curriculum was one of the earliest legislative fruits of this programme, which also included a tax reform providing for individual tax returns (eliminating the disadvantage to working wives inherent in the former compulsory joint return for couples), reforms in the family law (1971), and the now famous parental benefits to replace maternity benefits, permitting leave on the birth of a child to be divided by the parents as they saw fit (1974). An Advisory Council on Equality between Men and Women, appointed by the government, began work in 1973 on measures intended to help women to take advantage of their right to work on the same basis as men (Scott, 1982).

The 'sex role project'

Hardly had the major school reorganization been launched when the National Board of Education undertook a five-year 'Sex Role Project' to determine what the school could do to influence young men and women to make less traditional study and vocational choices (Vestin, no date).

Part of the project was a review of Swedish and foreign literature on sex role differentiation. Various sub-projects were set up to study the content and teaching of Swedish language and literature, and the way science teaching, especially physics, turned girls away from the study of technical subjects. Attitudes of parents, teachers and pupils were surveyed. Models of in-service training for teachers on sex role questions were tested. A study package for parents' organizations was produced and evaluated.

Stronger vocational guidance, combined with experiments in instruction and including some ideas suggested by teachers themselves, were tried out in individual schools. Commenting on the results of one such concentrated effort in 1975, the last years of the Sex Role Project, a vocational guidance officer said: '*Every* girl now thinks in terms of a job. This *is* progress. They want children, but they don't pin their hopes on marriage. They don't intend to be housewives for some future husband. But there has been no change in their vocational choices'.

This was the central conclusion of the 800-page report summing up the findings of the Sex Role Project, later published in a shortened paperback version for the use of Swedish educators as *ett friare val (A Freer Choice)* (National Swedish Board of Education, 1975). The project director, Margareta Vestin, told me: 'We have found that there is no correlation between giving instruction and the final choice of a vocation. We have had model schools where they have given lots of sex role instruction and had co-educational gymnastics and so on, and there is no difference at all — in attitudes, of course, but in their choices, no'. Vestin pin-pointed four major changes that were needed:

1. The curriculum should require every girl and boy to try fields in which their sex is at present in the minority.
2. The heavily masculine climate in teaching science and technology has to be altered.
3. Vocational guidance should be intensified.
4. The school environment, which mirrors male domination in society as a whole, must be changed.

A host of other recommendations related to teacher training, voluntary parent education, co-operation with the community, closer scrutiny of teaching materials, special measures to combat science fears and lack of technical skills in girls, and the need for more research and pilot projects.

The report on the Sex Role Project was submitted to educational authorities and other organizations for comment and became the basis for the National Board of Education's Action Programme in 1977 (National Swedish Board of Education, 1977). Some of its recommendations were incorporated in the new 1980 curriculum, discussed above. Others are still in the incubation stage. These include the important issues of teacher training, which in the opinion of critics does not sufficiently stress equality problems, and the basically male character of the school system. In 1980, less than 9 per cent of school principals, and only 3 per cent of local school superintendents, were female, while women were 99 per cent of junior level teachers (classes 1 to 3) (Wistrand, 1981: 44).

Trends in study choices

Conventional division in secondary schools

There has been no significant change in the conventional choices made by girls and boys entering the upper secondary school since the integrated school was launched in 1971. As Table 1 (see p 263) shows, an increase in girls choosing the four-year technical line, which rose from 5 per cent in 1973 to a peak of 12 per cent in 1977, appears to have levelled off. Boys are concentrated in technical subjects and the traditional male industries. Girls overwhelmingly favour nursing and caretaking, the clothing and consumer industries, sales and office work along vocational lines, and the liberal arts and social sciences at the theoretical level. The larger share of girls in secondary school education (now 50 per cent) has only intensified this division.

Job segregation continues

This means that, for the great majority of young women whose formal education ends at 15 or 18, the future has changed in the sense that they are likely to be employed for most of their lives (in 1980, 75 per cent of all women aged 16 to 64 were in the labour force). We know from the figures that they go into typically female occupations. In 1980, 60 per cent of all gainfully employed women were either in health care, clerical work or the services; 12 per cent were in manufacturing, transport or communications. An increasing number of women work part-time — 46 per cent of all those in the labour force — which suggests that the division of labour in the home continues along conventional lines (National Labour Market Board, Sweden, 1980). Indeed, Ylva Ericsson, Political Adviser to the Minister on Equality between Men and Women in the Swedish Ministry of Labour, reported to a conference on Women and Labour Market

	1971	1975	1978	1981
Two-year lines				
Clothing industry	87	99	97	94
Consumer studies	97	97	98	97
Workshop	0	2	1	3
Electro-technical	0	2	2	2
Nursing, caretaking	98	97	95	93
Distribution, clerical	66	80	80	80
Three-year lines				
Liberal arts	80	81	84	85
Economics	46	53	53	63
Natural sciences	41	42	44	47
Social sciences	70	68	70	73
Four-year technical line	7	8	11	11

Source: National Central Bureau of Statistics, Sweden

Table 1. *Girls as percentage of first-year enrolment
in the Swedish upper secondary school
by selected study lines, 1971-1981*

Policy at Cornell University in the Autumn of 1983 that Swedish men on average spend seven hours a week on housework, while women devote 35 hours to home chores. She added that although only 2 to 3 per cent of new fathers take advantage of Sweden's paid parental leave in the first six months of the child's life, one quarter of all fathers now take some time off from their jobs to stay at home with the baby during its first year.

Changes at the university level

A reform of higher education carried out in 1977 makes university level education available to new categories of students (work experience and public activity now count towards admission requirements). Simultaneously, a number of professional schools have been upgraded to university level. These are primarily the heavily female programmes for teaching, nursing and laboratory assistants. One result is to raise the standing of these occupations; another has been to increase the share of women in the university population to 58 per cent (Kim, 1980).

As a consequence of the reform, the average age of the student body has increased and the percentage gaining admission directly from secondary school has decreased. Hence comparisons with pre-reform years are not particularly meaningful. Women are now a substantial proportion of first-year students in law, medicine, architecture and theology (see Table 2, p 264), but these are a small percentage of the total number. Their share in the scientific and technical branches has increased overall from 12 per

	1978-79	1980-81
Technical professions	17	18
Architecture	44	44
Physics	13	17
Mathematics	25	25
Mechanical engineering	6	8
Chemical engineering	35	43
Social work, administration, economics	46	48
Economics and business	30	36
Law	49	47
Data processing	29	29
Social work	73	75
Medical, paramedical professions	82	83
Medicine	43	44
Nursing	87	89
Laboratory assistant	89	90
Teacher training	69	72
Preschool education	89	93
Mathematics, sciences	36	33
Languages	81	79
Industrial trades	5	5
Humanities, information, communication	55	58
Journalism	44	49
Divinity	38	45
Librarianship	76	76
Women as percentage of total	57	58

Source: National Central Bureau of Statistics, Sweden

Table 2. *Women as percentage of first-year students
in Swedish university level education
by sector and selected specializations, 1978-1981*

cent in 1973 (a pre-reform year) to 18 per cent in 1980-81. Medical and
paramedical studies and teacher training are the fields favoured by women
and there is heavy competition for the limited places in these programmes,
which account for two-thirds of all women in higher education.

Barriers to change

Obstacles in the way of realising sex role equality in the field of education are of three kinds: those resulting from conflicting priorities in the
school system; those arising out of the structure of the economy; and
those inherent in the sex role concept itself.

Schools expected to fight unemployment

The Swedish school system has, since 1978, had vastly increased responsibility for free-time activities and for the vocational preparation of its students. The purpose of a major reorganization of the nine-year comprehensive school in that year was to combat youth unemployment and the educational failures alleged to have contributed to it.

Unemployment rates have been kept low in Sweden, even in the worst recession years (about 2 per cent, although the rate is twice as high for women as for men), thanks to government training programmes, work relief projects and subsidies to companies to avoid cutbacks. Youth unemployment rates run much higher, however, and peak in the 16- to 19-year-old group: 10.2 per cent for women and 7.2 per cent for men in 1981 (Jangenäs, 1981; Magnusson, 1981).

The job of the comprehensive school, in this situation, is defined as seeing to it that youngsters have a better idea of the world of work that awaits them. Participation in teaching by people with first-hand knowledge of various occupations is to intensify contact between the school and the labour market. Six to ten weeks of on-the-job experience are to be arranged for every pupil during her or his nine years at school. Municipal planning councils help to organize these programmes.

At the secondary school level, the school has been made fully responsible for seeing that all 16- and 17-year-olds are either in school or in jobs. Because the problems of this age group (primarily a lack of marketable skills) cannot be treated effectively by temporary relief work — the main method used until recently — the schools are expected to find a way to make education attractive to those who dropped out at 16, and to provide them with training that will, in turn, make them attractive to employers (Magnusson, 1981).

All this has an equality dimension, at least theoretically, especially in view of the higher rate of unemployment among young women. In practice the new programmes place so many demands on staff and the need to deal with unemployment in a realistic way is so urgent that equality issues are pushed into the background. The first priority is to fit young people for working life as it is.

Decentralization of government, which has been stressed in Swedish public life in recent years, has meanwhile weakened the ability of the National Board of Education (NBE) to exert pressure. It no longer has its own sex role projects, and impulses do not come from the centre but from the regional authorities. The most the NBE can do is to keep the subject alive by supplying information.

The demands of the market

There is built into the structure of the economy a fundamental obstacle to reducing occupational segregation. Although the total labour force has increased substantially since 1965, the number of people employed in industrial jobs in Sweden has been dropping steadily, as it has in almost all of Western Europe and the US, as a result of rationalization and the export of manufacturing to cheap labour areas in Asia and Africa. In addition, consumer industries, which favour women workers, have been shrinking faster than those making capital goods. Net additions to the labour force have been made and will continue to be made in the services and the public sector; it was to fill these poorly paid jobs that so many women were hired in the first place.

The demand in industry will be for highly skilled workers, and these are rarely women. In fact, as the microchip reduces the number of semi-skilled industrial jobs, men who cannot upgrade their capabilities will be competing with women at the bottom of the labour market. The question is to what extent women will be able to hold the gains in employment they have made.

If most of the new jobs are in traditional female fields, routine arguments about the value of technical training for girls are not likely to be convincing unless girls and women can be persuaded to aim for top skills. It appears that a more vigorous and innovative approach to job equality is needed, one which will include a reassessment of the value of 'women's' work (and of the unpaid work that women continue to do).

Contradictions in the sex role approach

Since the beginning of the 1980s, criticism has been directed at the basic thinking underlying the sex role approach to equality. According to sex role learning theory, women and men develop 'female' and 'male' personalities by internalizing as children the appropriate stereotyped behaviour they see given approval in the world around them. Thus a change in socialization can be expected to change attitudes and behaviour in a radical way. The Swedish model assumed that men as well as women were oppressed and limited by their traditional roles, and that they would welcome a more equal division if legislation and social policy created a favourable atmosphere.

When it launched its sex role equality programme, the Social Democratic Party did not envisage a power clash between the sexes but a 'trade-off', with men doing more in the home and women more in production. The experience of the past 15 years has revealed, however, that equality is indeed about power sharing, and that sex roles are more firmly anchored in people's sense of self than previously had been believed.

The bland, conflict-free model of sex role evolution stressed in Sweden holds out promises of change that it cannot fulfil; it has produced formal equality but it cannot produce full equality. This is the view of women leaders who, disappointed with the results to date, talk about the need for women to seize their share of the power (Scott, 1982; Wistrand, 1981). So far, they say, work for equality has been conducted on male terms. It is no coincidence that the least progress in advancing equality in education has been made in the promotion of women within the school structure.

A case in point

A case study from the Volvo plant in Gothenburg points up both the potential in some of the methods Sweden has been using and the reluctance of men in power to take advantage of this potential.

When in 1977 the Swedish white collar labour confederation and the national employers' association signed an agreement to work for equality between men and women on the job, Volvo Gothenburg became the first company to serve as an experimental workplace. As reported by Margaret Flitch (1981), all women white collar workers were contacted, invited to attend seminars, a three-day personal development course, and six-month apprenticeship courses in 'men's' jobs, with a guarantee of their old job back if they wanted it. In the construction department: 'One of the women was an engineer and she ran classes in car mechanics for all the girls. They loved it so much that they didn't even want to go home. Seven o'clock at night found them still turning bolts. Siv's course runs for six weeks and there are only 12 girls per time. Consequently it will be some time before everyone gets a chance to take the course but the women feel that Siv is the only one qualified to teach the course. They haven't dared to try another teacher, like a man perhaps' (1981: 2).

What are the real prospects for women at Volvo? Today, all top managers are men. Of third-level managers, 4 per cent are women. Of all women employed at the plant, 96 per cent are in bottom level jobs compared with 16 per cent of men. The president of Volvo believes that managers' attitudes must be changed, but 'he was not prepared to tell them to change'. One capable woman executive left to become president of her own company because, she said, to work in a male dominated company like Volvo is to work with the wind in your face. She felt that 'only a few women of promise would be given a fair chance at Volvo in our lifetimes' (1981: 14).

References

Flitch, M (1981) Women at Volvo *Equal Opportunities International* 1 2: 12-14

Jangenäs, B (1981) Employment and labor market policy in Sweden during the recession of the late 1970s *Current Sweden* 266 (The Swedish Institute)

Kim, L (1980) New rules for admission to higher education in Sweden *Current Sweden* 252

Magnusson, B (1981) What is being done in Sweden for unemployed 16- and 17-year olds? *Current Sweden* 275

National Committee on Equality between Men and Women (1979) *Step by Step: National Plan of Action for Equality* Liber Förlag: Stockholm

National Labour Market Board (Sweden) (1980) *Jämställdhet på arbetsmarknaden* (Equality in the Labour Market — Statistics 1980)

National Swedish Board of Education (1977) The sex roles at school photocopy

National Swedish Board of Education (1969) *Curriculum for the Comprehensive School Lgr 69* (photocopy)

National Swedish Board of Education (1975) *ett friare val (A Freer Choice)* Liber Läromedel: Stockholm

Scott, Hilda (1982) *Sweden's Right to be Human. Sex Role Equality: The Goal and the Reality* Allison & Busby: London

Vestin, M (no date) School, instruction, and sex role questions (photocopy) The National Swedish Board of Education

Wistrand Birgitta (1981) *Swedish Women on the Move* The Swedish Institute: Stockholm

21. Strategies for the emancipation of women in Third World socialist societies

Maxine Molyneux

Summary: The newly established socialist states of the South have made considerable progress in a relatively short period of time in improving the formal position of women. They have introduced a range of policies aimed at restructuring the family along more egalitarian lines, drawing women into employment and expanding female educational opportunities. Although these measures are said to be aimed at promoting women's emancipation, they also fulfil other goals of a more general, practical, kind. In this sense, an improvement in the position of women forms a necessary part of the overall process of social transformation and economic development. Women's emancipation, for these governments, is not a goal *per se*, but is only pursued insofar as it is compatible with these wider objectives. An understanding of the priorities of these states is indispensable for understanding why, despite the progress made, full equality between the sexes is far from having been realized.

Introduction

The countries which claim an allegiance to revolutionary socialist principles have always been those with the greatest official commitment to women's emancipation. They have the most sustained record in implementing policies which have sought to remove the more obvious and formal inequalities between the sexes, and, in this respect, they have achieved more and sooner than Western liberal democracies. Long before the governments of Europe or the United States gave women equal rights, equal pay and the vote, or began to introduce state-provided nurseries and paid maternity leave, states committed to a socialist path of development were able to claim that many of these policies were either already implemented or were in the process of being so.

For various reasons, including the pressure exerted by women's liberation movements, advanced capitalist countries have now nearly all caught up with their socialist counterparts, at least in the legislative sphere. However, they lag behind in nursery provision, as they do in public welfare generally, and their record on women's employment conditions and opportunities is poorer. The practice of the developed socialist states not only goes some way further than that of comparable capitalist ones, but an even greater gulf separates the two systems in the Third World with respect to women's overall social and economic position. Compared with capitalist countries with similar cultural conditions and levels of development, it is generally the case that the socialist states in the Third World have a far better record on improving women's legal, economic and social position. They have also attempted to discourage customary practices which are oppressive of women, such as footbinding in China or veiling in Democratic Yemen. In short, women in China, Cuba, Democratic Yemen or Soviet Central Asia, suffer far less discrimination on the basis of gender than do those in Guatemala, Iran, Pakistan or Nigeria, even though they have still not attained full equality with men. This chapter attempts to explain why this is so and discusses the main policies which have been adopted as well as the practical and theoretical considerations which have influenced Third World socialist states on this issue.

Socialist policies: theories and practice

The self-proclaimed socialist states which have done most to improve the position of women are those which combine the following features: they officially endorse Marxist theory and, to varying degrees, model themselves on the USSR; they have sought to abolish private ownership of productive property; and are characterized by a commitment to planned economic development and by a comparatively high level of social welfare. Although for the sake of brevity we shall here refer to these countries as 'socialist', it is clear that while they are not capitalist, they are not, properly speaking, socialist either. Their economies are not fully socialized and they have not implemented the principle of socialist democracy. Most of the recently established socialist states in the Southern hemisphere have, for obvious reasons, achieved even less in this regard than their more industrialized counterparts in the North.

The policies which these socialist states have formulated in order to solve 'the women question' are, with minor differences, strikingly uniform in their essentials across a range of very diverse countries. The USSR, China, Democratic Yemen, Vietnam, Cuba, the GDR, Albania and Mozambique have all introduced sweeping reforms regarding the position of women in areas such as education, the family, legal reform and employment (Molyneux, 1981). These reforms have much in common with both the official theory and practice of the USSR, and draw on Marxism for their theoretical and moral justification. Most of these states are, or have been, allies of the USSR and the influence of the Soviet model is evident from the policies they pursue.

Those which relate to women have remained broadly in line with the resolutions of the second congress of the Comintern, which, in 1920, laid down the following guidelines. Socialist states should attempt to bring women out of the home and into the economy by expanding employment opportunities; reorganize peasant households that 'keep women in subservient positions'; develop communal services to alleviate domestic work and childcare; provide equal opportunities for women; mobilize women into political work and into government administration, and provide protective legislation 'to safeguard women's reproductive activities' (Jancar, 1981).

These policies also claim a common inspiration in the classic Marxist theory of women's subordination contained in Engels' *Origin of the Family, Private Property and the State.* This, and Lenin's *On the Emancipation of Women* are widely available in translation in such countries as China, Vietnam or Mozambique, and extracts or echoes of their main themes appear in policy documents as explanations or validations of the strategies pursued. The core of the official analysis is Engels' theory that women's oppression is linked to the division of labour and family form which accompany the rise of class society and private property. In this process, women are marginalized from productive work and subordinated through marriage and the family to men and property relations. Women's emancipation can only be achieved, according to this theory, by abolishing private property, the inegalitarian 'bourgeois' family, and the division of labour which relegates women to the role of housewife and mother. For Engels, and for socialist policy makers inspired by his theory, this has implied reforming the family and socializing women's work in the domestic sphere, thus enabling women to acquire financial independence by working for a wage. This is the theoretical underpinning to the 1920 resolutions.

Although many of the measures adopted by socialist states are similar to those demanded by feminists since the nineteenth century, there is an important point which needs to be made in relation to socialist thinking on this question. For socialist states, the emancipation of women is not so much a goal *in itself* but is, rather, pursued chiefly insofar as it contributes to the achievement of the wider goals of economic development and socialist reconstruction. The strategies which socialist states pursue in relation to women and the family, must therefore be understood not just in terms of socialist theory or principles but also in terms of the practical exigencies of socialist planning.

Most socialist revolutions, including that which convulsed Russia in the early decades of this century, have occurred in the poorer regions of the world, many of them characterized by an extreme scarcity of resources, low *per capita* income, low literacy, marked regional inequalities, a large peasantry and a limited industrial base. Moreover, these revolutions have all faced military threats after the overthrow of the old regime. Post-revolutionary planning has therefore stressed the urgency of promoting rapid economic development to improve the standard of living and meet welfare and defence commitments. For most of these countries this has meant that the state assumes a leading role in economic life; that principal productive and financial resources are nationalized and industrialization is given maximum support. At the same time, the agrarian sector is transformed through the expropriation of the larger holdings, production is rationalized and, where possible, state farms and co-operatives are established. In broad outline these policies amount to the establishment of a planned economy with a strong state sector, considerable intervention at the level of prices, wages and production, and an emphasis on re-distribution in the form of free or heavily subsidized housing, health, education and public welfare.

Women's emancipation and socialist reconstruction

In the context of underdeveloped societies, such policies imply not only economic but also social changes of a major kind. The pre-revolutionary social order is seen by socialist states as an obstacle to economic develop-ment and social reform. What they term traditional or feudal social relations must therefore be dismantled, and the old order must be pro-gressively displaced by a new, centralized, secular and egalitarian society more suited to the demands of economic development. In most socialist societies, particularly those of the Third World, this has involved an attempt to bring about a comparatively rapid transformation of previous social relations and ideologies, and of the existing legal, political, and religious systems.

This radical development strategy has a number of implications for women, both in terms of its immediate or long-term effects on their lives, and in terms of how government planners perceive the part they are to play in the process. Revolutionary governments see women's importance in the period of social and economic transformation as helping to accomplish at least three goals: to extend the government's political support; to increase the active labour force; and to help 'modernize' the family and harness it more directly to state goals.

The first of these considerations is to consolidate the power of the state by drawing women into political activity in such organizations as the women's unions, the party, neighbourhood associations and other mass organizations (Lenin, 1970). In those countries which experienced a protracted revolutionary war, such as China or Vietnam, many women had already taken an active part in political and military activities. There-fore, it was more a question of maintaining and extending that support than of creating it *ex nihilo*. In general, there is a fear that unless women are politicized they may not co-operate in the process of social trans-formation, and may even enter the ranks of the opposition. More positively, in some contexts, women have been seen as crucial agents of revolutionary change whose politicization challenges ancient customs and privileges, carrying the revolution into the very heart of the old order: the family. In Soviet Central Asia in the 1920s, for example, where there was no industrial proletariat, the Bolsheviks designated women the vanguard force for socialism. As they saw it, women were the most oppressed group and would therefore be the most sympathetic to the revolutionary transformations they were attempting to introduce (Massell, 1974).

The second way in which the mobilization of women is regarded as important is more directly relevant to the economy. The education of women and their entry into employment increases and improves the available labour supply, a process which is a necessary concomitant of any successful development programme. In most underdeveloped countries, women form only a small percentage of the economically active population (usually well under 20 per cent). The average non-industrial female employment rate is even lower and has been calculated for the Middle East at less than 4 per cent, and for Latin America at approximately 20 per cent (Yousseff, 1974). While the figures conceal the real extent of women's involvement by registering mainly formal rather than informal activities, the work they do is frequently unpaid, and confined to family concerns in workshops, trade or in the fields.

With the socialization of many areas of production and distribution, the pattern and nature of employment changes. Some of the jobs women previously did disappear and new ones are created. Socialist governments regard women as a large reserve of potential employees or voluntary workers who could participate in collective projects once satisfactory alternatives to their existing conditions are provided, and the familial constraints which might otherwise prevent them from doing so are erased.

This latter point helps to explain the third objective. Post-revolutionary governments regard women as important levers in reconstructing the family: this they consider a matter of principle, as well as of necessity, in that it can help to promote wider social and economic changes. If women are to become politically active and enter wage employment they must be freed from traditional familial and cultural constraints. In many countries it is not only a question of the social stigma attached to women taking up paid work or leading an independent life: their male kin can legally prevent them from doing so.

However, there is a further consideration which lies behind family reform, namely the attempt to hasten the transformation of the economy by eroding pre-existing social relations and practices. This applies in those countries which were not greatly transformed by the impact of capitalism and where pre-capitalist relations retained some effectiveness. Women's subordination is an integral part of the reproduction of many forms of peasant or tribal property and production systems. The strict control of marriage alliances by kin groups, and systems of inheritance which discriminate against women frequently do so in order to preserve the integrity of the social system concerned. Thus, when revolutionary governments outlaw institutions such as polygyny, the brideprice, child marriage, and discrimination against women in property settlements, they are not doing so only to emancipate women, but also to hasten the disappearance of the pre-existing social order as a whole.

Priority areas: the family and education

In order to fulfil these three objectives and secure the conditions which will enable women to participate in the process of social transformation, post-revolutionary governments emphasize two main policy initiatives. The first is, not surprisingly, family reform, and the second is to expand female educational opportunities. As far as reforming the family is concerned, we have seen how it is perceived as part of the overall development strategy, as well as a means of securing some of the conditions whereby women can participate more fully in social life. For this latter aim to be achieved, it is necessary both to restructure relations within the family (between men and women, parents and children), and to alleviate some of its previous responsibilities through greater state support in the areas of education and childcare.

All post-revolutionary socialist governments use legal reform as an instrument to promote social change in this area, and the underdeveloped countries have passed legislation designed to undermine traditional customs, transform the family structure along more egalitarian lines, and bring the institution more directly under the influence of the state. These 'family laws' (China's of 1950; Cuba's of 1975; Democratic Yemen's of 1974), differ to the extent that they respond to the conditions prevailing in the countries in which they are formulated. But they all share common objectives in undermining traditional male privileges, freeing women for a greater role in public life and creating a more stable and effective family form. Where the gender inequalities are greater, as in pre-revolutionary China and many parts of the Muslim world, the laws are more far reaching in their implications for social change. In Democratic Yemen, China, Vietnam and Mozambique, the measures introduced to alter family relations have involved major changes in the former marriage and religious practices of the people (Molyneux, 1982). Where they previously existed, child and arranged marriages, polygyny, and divorce by repudiation have been outlawed, and women acquire rights they were previously denied, in the realm of property or over children. At the same time the hold of religion and of religious authorities is weakened and secular arrangements under the aegis of the state are encouraged.

In countries where such practices did not exist at the time of the revolution, as for example in Cuba or in Nicaragua, post-revolutionary legal reform has involved the abolition of men's privileges enshrined within the earlier codes. These gave men almost unchallenged authority within the family, to the extent of denying women custody rights to their children on divorce (Pescatello, 1976). The Cuban Family Law is also one of only three in the world (Sweden and the GDR have the others) which state that husbands and wives should share the responsibility for housekeeping and childcare, albeit only in cases where the wife is in paid employment (Murray, 1979; Griffiths and Griffiths 1979).

In promoting greater equality between the sexes, the family reforms are seen as laying the basis for a new socialist family which will not only be stronger and more harmonious, but also better equipped to perform the roles assigned to it by the state. Socialist countries emulate the Soviet Union in seeing the family as 'the basic cell of society', and once it has been 'modernized', it is charged with responsibility for helping to socialize the next generation into accepting the values of the new society (Liegle, 1970).

Women's role in this process is regarded as crucial, an attitude which is summed up in the following statement from the Chinese weekly *Beijing Review*, 'The future of the revolution and the hopes of the motherland rest with the children . . . the bringing up of such a mammoth new force is a great undertaking for the whole of society and primarily for the woman' (*Beijing Review*, 1978). In theory, some of this work is to be shared by the state since working mothers acquire the services of nurseries and daycare centres, in order that they may fulfil their dual roles as mothers and wage workers. Indeed, this is a pledge written into the constitutions of these countries. Family reform is therefore seen simultaneously as an indispensable adjunct of both economic change and social stability, and as a pre-condition for mobilizing women into economic and political activity. The realization of these two latter goals is also dependent upon the provision of a widespread educational process and the integration of girls and women into it.

As with family reform, education is seen as an important means of securing the conditions for building a new socialist society. On coming to power, most revolutionary governments, especially those in the poorer countries of the Third World, inherited low educational levels, high illiteracy (90 per cent in both China and Democratic Yemen), and an elite educational system concentrated in the urban areas and insufficiently responsive to the needs of economic development. Their educational policy is therefore geared to remedying this as rapidly as possible and is based on two main assumptions: that education is a necessary concomitant of economic development and that it, like the family, plays a vital part in shaping the attitudes of what these countries call the 'new socialist man' (Williamson, 1979).

Post-revolutionary governments have therefore allocated substantial resources to expanding the educational infrastructure; they have doubled or trebled previous allocations, while curricula have been changed in accordance with offical guidelines. A first step has been to launch mass literacy campaigns and this is accompanied by expanding the number of schools to meet the increased intake, especially at primary level. The provision of technical training is a priority along with the restructuring of higher education to bring its concerns more in line with those of government planning. Given the scarcity of resources the results are impressive. By 1978, Cuba, North Korea, China and Vietnam claimed to have achieved universal primary education, and had made substantial progress in other areas (World Bank Report, 1981).

Education is also seen as a crucial step in the process of emancipating women and preparing them for a greater role in public life. In addition, women are expected to be responsible for the early education of their children; 'educate the mother — educate the child' is a common theme in the justification of female schooling programmes. In underdeveloped societies, rural women are the most educationally disadvantaged group and they have been major beneficiaries of educational reform. The extreme disparities between male and female participation which characterize most of these countries have been significantly reduced in the socialist bloc.

Yet despite the progress that has been made in family reform and education, it has been both limited and uneven. Legal and family reform have eroded some of the worst formal inequalities between the sexes in a relatively short period of time, and have helped to provide the basis for further transformations in the future. But these formal gains are still far from having been realized in practice. Kin control, brideprice and dowry systems, arranged and child marriages, continue to survive in many countries despite the new laws and official disapproval. In China, with greater prosperity in some areas, and increased tolerance of family enterprises, there has been a marked rise in the expenditure on marriages, including inflated brideprices and dowry costs (Croll, 1983).

In general, although substantially changed, the family remains a locus of inequality between the sexes, albeit of a more informal kind. Women continue to be those responsible for housework and childcare, while also being expected to participate fully in wage employment and political life. Comparatively little is done through official channels to encourage men to accept greater domestic responsibility and adapt to the new situation in the ways that women have had to do. For many women, wage employment has therefore been double-edged. While some have been able to acquire greater leverage in their families and some financial independence, these gains have often been at the expense of an increased overall workload. In the underdeveloped countries, this is made worse by the fact that housework remains onerous, and maternity leave, nurseries and|childcare facilities are only available to a very small minority.

Only North Korea which, significantly, suffers from an acute labour shortage seems to have made significant progress in this area. It claims to have established 60,000 childcare centres accommodating three-and-a-half million children (Cauldwell, 1978). Other countries are more modest in their achievements: Democratic Yemen by 1977, despite a labour shortage, had established only 17 nurseries catering for less than 2,000 children (Molyneux, 1982), while Cuba by 1975 had created 654, catering for 48,000 families (Griffiths and Griffiths, 1979).

In education too, progress has been uneven. The more developed socialist countries of Eastern Europe have succeeded in virtually eliminating the discrepancy between the sexes in terms of access to education. However, in the poorer countries, despite some improvement, the asymmetry remains, particularly in the rural areas. Although female participation has increased, absenteeism and high dropout rates reflect continuing family pressure on girls to work in the households or on the land, especially where private production persists (Molyneux, 1981; Croll, 1983). In higher education, too, there is a marked sex-difference in the participation rates with female enrolment often less than one-quarter that of the male. In China, a country where the revolutionary government has enjoyed a longer period of rule than most other underdeveloped socialist states, the discrepancies remain pronounced. Figures for 1981 show that women made up only one-quarter of both students and teachers in higher education, with similar figures for middle school (secondary), and 'specialized', that is, technical schools (*Shongguo Tongji Nianjian*, 1982). There is evidence that women are officially discouraged from entering certain areas of study on the grounds that these are more suitable for men (Croll, 1983).

In all socialist countries, to varying degrees, forms of gender typing still operate: the majority of women continue to be assigned to, or elect to do, courses which will train them for occupations associated with the nurturing role, such as home economics, primary education, secretarial work, sewing and health. Nonetheless, far more progress has been made in encouraging girls to enter areas previously restricted to boys, than in channelling men towards training in areas traditionally regarded as appropriate for women.

The combined effects of lower educational levels and gender typing tend to confine women's employment prospects to the lower paid and less rewarding jobs, and this pattern is reinforced by the continuing burden of domestic responsibilities which women have to bear. The socialist states of the South have given even less support than their counterparts in the North to eroding gender differences, and biological or essentialist explanations of a traditional kind are often used to justify the sexual division of labour, even in those countries where women have proved themselves capable of crossing the gender boundaries as guerilla fighters and army leaders.

On the basis of an analysis of the record of these societies so far, some initial conclusions can be drawn. Perhaps the most important general observation is that state intervention and the implementation of a series of radical reforms have done much to improve the position of women in these transitional 'socialist' countries, but they have not brought about gender equality. However, an evaluation of this record has to take two major constraints into account. The first is that these countries have, until very recently, been socially conservative, and attitudes will take a considerable time to change; legal reforms and Party proclamations will not, in themselves, suffice to enable women to attain equality with men. The second constraint is the extreme scarcity of resources. Most of these countries lack the necessary material means required to alleviate some of the most basic problems in such areas as welfare provision, pay or education.

Yet state policy is not just a matter of allocating resources; it also involves establishing priorities, and it would seem that, even within the constraints identified, further initiatives could be taken to improve the position of women. Greater official support could be given for self-help community childcare schemes, for households to share domestic responsibilities, and for changing stereotypical attitudes about men's and women's roles both inside and outside the home. Even more could be achieved if these countries allowed their women's unions a degree of autonomy from the ruling parties and a greater say in the formulation of government policies. As it is, they act more like a mild pressure group, a role which does not detract from their official function as 'transmission belts' of party policy.

It is clear that what has taken place so far is gradual incremental development along the lines dictated by existing priorities; but this is inadequate if these governments are to go beyond an instrumental mobilization of women into the development process and instead try to realize the socialist goal of social emancipation. There is little evidence that full gender equality is a goal which is seriously striven for in these countries, and there is considerable hostility to feminist perspectives on how this could be brought about. Feminism is regarded as a Western phenomenon, which is divisive and individualistic, deflecting attention away from the more important issues of class struggle and the construction of socialism. The persistence of notions of male/female complementarity rather than undifferentiated roles, the rejection of the principle of reproductive freedom, the support given to the nuclear family form, the existence of a sexual division of labour in the public and private spheres, to say nothing of the virtual absence of discussion of issues such as male violence against women and sexuality — all these sharply distinguish socialist from Western feminist concerns about women.

It is too early in the development of these countries to draw up an overall balance sheet, but the likelihood of their achieving their stated aim of 'emancipating women' is dependent on this aim assuming greater importance in the system of priorities than it has to date. Women's position in these underdeveloped socialist countries has certainly improved, both relative to the previous situation and to comparable states at similar levels of development and with similar cultural backgrounds. But it has been an emancipation which has taken place as part of the process of realizing some of the wider goals which these states have set themselves, and it therefore remains an emancipation of a rather limited kind.

References

Beijing Review (1978) 29 October

Cauldwell, M (1978) North Korea — aspects of a new society *Contemporary Review* 1355 London

Croll, E (1983) *Women in Post Mao China* Zed Press: London

Engels, F *Origin of the Family, Private Property and the State* in Marx, K and Engels, F *Selected Works* (1970) Lawrence and Wishart: London

Griffiths, J and Griffiths, P (1979) *Cuba, the Second Decade* Writers and Readers: London

Jancar, B Woolf (1981) *Women Under Communism* Johns Hopkins: Baltimore

Lenin, V (1970) *On the Emancipation of Women* Progress: Moscow

Liegle, (1970) *The Family's Role in Soviet Education* Springer: New York

Marx, K and Engels, F (1970) *Selected Works* Lawrence and Wishart: London

Massell, G (1974) *The Surrogate Proletariat* Princeton University Press

Molyneux, M (1981) Women's emancipation under socialism: a model for the Third World? *World Development* 9 9/10

Molyneux, M (1982) *State Policies and the Position of Women Workers in the People's Democratic Republic of Yemen: 1967-1977* ILO: Geneva

Murray, N (1979) Socialism and Feminism: Women and the Cuban Revolution Part I *in Feminist Review* 1 2 Part II *in Feminist Review* 1 3 London

Pescatello, A (1976) *Power and Pawn: The Female in Iberian Families, Societies, and Cultures* Greenwood Press: Connecticut and London

Shongguo Tongji Nianjian: 1981 (1982) Hong Kong

Williamson, B (1979) *Education, Social Structure and Development* Macmillan: London

World Bank Report: 1981 (1982) World Bank: Oxford

Youssef, N Haggag (1974) *Women and Work in Developing Societies* Population Monograph Series No 15 University of California: Berkeley

22. Counter-sexist strategies in Australian schools

Lyn Yates

Summary: This chapter discusses the range of counter-sexist strategies in Australian schools, some tensions within them, and some questions to be faced given the difficulty of succeeding in producing change in this area.

First, it is suggested that conceptions of what constitutes sexism vary. Political values and technical understandings about schooling processes play a part in this, but there is also an important distinction within the counter-sexist work between the concern with equal opportunity (or selection/allocation) and the concern with sexist teaching (or consciousness-formation). Varied conceptions of the relationship between counter-sexist and multi-cultural strategies are also noted.

Secondly, types of strategies being undertaken are identified. Within the equal opportunity concern there are legal and other checks on provision for girls and boys, and attempts to reform school careers counselling. In the area of the teaching process, there is attention to 'democratic' negotiated relationships; to language and interaction discriminations and ways to remedy these; and to sexual harassment. In curriculum, the developing recognition of deeper issues is noted, and work on women's studies, on health and human relationships, on mathematics and on the 'sexually inclusive curriculum' is discussed.

Types of broader and narrower perspectives are noted, and a final question concerning the influence of technological change and unemployment is raised.

Introduction

If sexism were a simple and straightforward issue and if there were close links between the rhetoric and the reality, or the adoption of a strategy and the achievement of its ends, then Australia, contrary to the popular stereotype, might be considered a benchmark of enlightenment in its attempts to eliminate sexism in schools. From the report by a study group to the Australian Schools Commission in 1975 which proclaimed that 'Sexist education is a contradiction in terms' (*Girls, School and Society*, 1975), to a recommendation such as that of the Victorian Education Department to principals of schools in February 1983 which reminded them that 'Combating discrimination based on a person's sex is an Education Department priority' (and which went on to outline a host of steps schools might be expected to take in regard to this), there has been a considerable increase in official recognition of sexism as an issue and the granting of resources to do something about it. At grassroots level, too, teachers concerned about sexism attempt to develop new ways of teaching and organizing in schools, hold conferences, staff resources centres, and put the issue as a continuing and prominent feature of the work of their unions. Even in the fields of research which feed on and help direct education, it is now almost mandatory for any academic conference to have at least one section devoted to work on sexism, and for bodies funding and promoting school-based developments to self-consciously employ workers to make sure the area of discrimination on the basis of gender is not overlooked. And yet, despite all this, evidence of achievements in terms of outcomes is rather more difficult to point to, and it seems reasonable to continue to ask whether this flurry of activities has really permeated the structures and processes which constitute Australian schooling.

To attempt to give an account of counter-sexist strategies in Australian schools in one short chapter entails a great deal of selection and compression, since there are complexities to be dealt with on at least three levels. First, as suggested already, there is the sheer quantity of specific initiatives taken. Secondly, there is the difficulty of discussing education in Australia as a whole, where the education systems operate on a state rather than federal basis, and when, within at least some of these states, decentralization is taken much further. There is always some central policy direction and funding of schools, but in some states schools have a very large degree of autonomy in specific curriculum matters. 'Counter-sexist strategies' then involve both policies and practices initiated and disseminated from the centre, and practices initiated by individual teachers and disseminated through both official and unofficial channels. Finally, there are questions of the levels of analysis and range of questions which might be applied to a discussion of such strategies. What follows, then, will not be a comprehensive and detailed account of the strategies and the ways in which practices differ among the states, but an attempt to give something of an overview of the types of procedures and different contexts in which they are attempting to operate, and to raise some questions regarding the directions along which various initiatives have been taken.

No comprehensive review of developments here is readily available, but information on them can be obtained through reports put out by Equal Opportunity Units of the various Education Departments in each state. For convenience, the discussion in this chapter is divided into a number of headings to make clearer some distinct issues which arise. However, it should be noted that, within a particular school or the work of a particular teacher, the strategies may draw on a number of the approaches outlined below. Finally, as will be discussed later, there are differences as to what different groups would count as a counter-sexist strategy. Strategies referred to in this chapter are those whose protagonists identify them as such, rather than ones which a particular analysis would necessarily support as contributing to counter-sexist ends. All the initiatives below are taken within the broad framework of a concern about girls and what happens to them, but the specific assumptions and directions of the various activities are not always in harmony with each other.

What is sexism?

A first major issue that might be identified in the work related to sexism over the last decade is the variety of conceptions of what constitutes sexism. For example, a poster issued by the Victorian Council of School Organizations (VICCSO) and the Victorian Federation of State School Parents' Clubs (VFSSPC) lists the following range of definitions:

What is it?

1. Making assumptions, having expectations and attitudes based purely on someone's sex.
2. When everyone's lives is defined as a member of one or another sex, and every kind of thinking is stamped with the brand of 'masculine' or 'feminine'.
3. A social system and practice in which benefits and disadvantages are meted out on the basis of sex.
4. A belief that the human sexes have a distinctive make-up that determines their respective lives, usually involving the idea that one sex is superior and has the right to rule the other.
5. A process through which females and males progressively learn that different things are required of them because of their sex.
6. The predetermination of a person's choice without regard to individual differences.
7. Any arbitrary stereotyping of males and females on the basis of their gender.

It is Sexism! (*It Kit*, no date)

The various definitions here in fact point to a number of different ways in which the sources of sexism might be conceptualized and, by implication, to a range of teaching and other strategies which might be required to combat it.

What sorts of things might be at issue here with regard to the differing definitions of the problem? First, political values are involved, as is clear from the fact that strategies relating to sexism often form the subject of debate in newspapers, and have resulted in organized bodies such as the Association of Concerned Parents and the group Women Who Want to be Women, specifically devoted to opposing them. What is a programme of information dissemination for one group is a programme of propaganda for another. Here too, questions might be raised about why many of the policies outlined below have been supported both by conservative governments concerned with stability and social cohesion and by individuals and groups explicitly concerned with producing social change.

Secondly, as will be discussed further below, definitions of sexism change according to the understanding people have of how the processes of schooling and learning work. A good example here is some of the more recent debates about segregated, as compared with mixed education: the Victorian Education Department's policy on Equal Opportunity specifically mentions the promotion of co-education as a means to this end, whereas other work concentrating on the processes whereby girls are disadvantaged has recommended or experimented with single-sex grouping as a means of overcoming this (for example: BRUSEC 1982-3; Sarah, Scott and Spender, 1980, and reports in the South Australian *Women's Studies Resource Centre Newsletter*, May 1983 and Victorian teachers' union counter-sexist newsletter *Ms Muffet* 8 February 1981).

Thirdly, however, beyond all these particular differences, there are two distinct themes running through all the work on sexism. These might be characterized as, on the one hand, a concern with equal opportunity (or with the allocation and selection that takes place through schools) and, on the other, a concern with sexist teaching (or with what is learnt in schools). These themes are sometimes closely related, but are sometimes moving to somewhat different ends.

The great bulk of the funding of strategies related to schooling, both by governments and by teachers' unions, has been raised on the basis of identified gross *inequalities* of treatment and of achievement of girls as compared with boys in the course of schooling. Indeed, in some states 'Equal Opportunity' has been treated as a synonym for 'counter-sexist': so-called Equal Opportunity Resource Centres and appointees did not, and were not intended to, concern themselves with the inequalities related to class or ethnic origin (except as these were intermingled in discriminations on the basis of gender). On the other hand, although the original report from which much of the subsequent work has stemmed also used the evidence of inequality of treatment to make its case, the central definition was a somewhat different one which concerned the *messages* which were learnt in school. 'Sexism is a process through which females and males not only progressively learn that different things are required and expected of them because of their sex, but learn those things in an unexamined way. Good education is incompatible with such a process; central to it is the examination of assumptions and the rational consideration of alternatives. Hence 'sexist education' is a contradiction in terms; good education is necessarily non-sexist, it makes no assumptions about sex differences.' (*Girls, School and Society*, 1975: 2.30.)

A lot of the work which has attempted to reform textbooks and readers (for example, the 'Sugar and Snails' series of books for primary children which are produced by the Women's Movement Children's Literature Co-operative) or to have the subject of 'sex roles' raised as an item for consideration in the curriculum (especially by the various resource centres, see note on p 289), has had a concern that schooling has been passing on and reinforcing a *distorted* picture of the world. (For example, books for young children have portrayed almost all women as full-time housewives, though the majority of women in fact are in the paid workforce; and history books have characterized the nature of a particular society by reference to only a few of its activities which show only what men did.)

These two ways of characterizing the issue (sexism as inequality and sexism as ideology) correspond to two roles with which the system of education is centrally concerned: on the one hand the selection and allocation of talent to jobs and other positions in the society, and on the other the cultural selection and transmission which identifies what society values and what is to be the basis of shared understandings for the future society. What the experience of Australian schools in recent years seems to show is that the first of these roles is a much more amenable field of approach for policy change than the latter, in that, in this democratic pluralist society, 'equality' and 'equality of opportunity' are still part of the shared rhetoric under which schooling operates, whereas more specific elements of what is to be valued (at least where change is foreshadowed) are not.

Finally, a note should be made here of a parallel area of concern in Australia over the past decade, namely 'multiculturalism' (Galbally Report, 1978; Allen, 1978). The way in which this policy (and practice) initiative has been related to the counter-sexist project has taken a number of forms. At one extreme, a common one, there appears to be a naive assumption that values and modes of life of different ethnic groups can be valued and promoted in the curriculum with no implications or conflicts concerning what is being valued in the mainstream curriculum or the counter-sexist projects. At the other, less common extreme, is a belief that in counter-sexist concerns there are absolute standards for behaviour which we must try to impose on everybody. Finally, there are beginning to be some attempts to work out in both principle and practice what we are trying to value in both instances and ways to put the concerns together (Berberich, 1979; Sobski, 1979; *Ms Muffett* 18, March 1983; Migrant Girls Report, 1982).

'Equal opportunity' initiatives

The strategies I want to discuss in this section are those specifically concerned with equalizing resources and provisions for girls in school and trying to change patterns of different subject choice and subsequent job entry for girls as compared with boys.

Provision

At the most obvious levels of inequality, such as the amount of money spent on girls compared with boys, the existence of subjects open only to one sex and the dominance of the senior levels of the teaching hierarchy by men, there has been much official concern expressed (*Girls, School and Society*, 1975; *Report of the Victorian Committee on Equal Opportunity*,

1977). With regard to the first two issues, if inequalities or unequal subject availability is demonstrated, at least some schools in the state system are now legally required to right the situation. Nevertheless, patterns of subject choice and post-school career patterns remain strongly gender-typed (Equal Opportunity Unit, 1981; Game and Pringle, 1983; Owen, 1982; Sweet, 1980a; Sweet, 1980b). Equality of provision or offering may be important in terms of simple justice, but by itself it seems that it will have little effect in changing subtle, deeply entrenched patterns of social-ization and structures of discrimination (see Ashton and Maguire, 1980; Coleman, 1968; Bourdieu and Passeron, 1977). Moreover, although the great majority of Australian children attend the government-provided state schools, of the 23 per cent who do not, a quite disproportionate number are those who will fill the positions of power and authority in the society. These children attend fee-charging 'independent' schools, which although government supported, are not bound by Education Department policies on counter-sexism. While there is some evidence that some of the single-sex girls' independent schools offer opportunities for combating some gender stereotypes (Connell, Ashenden, Kessler and Dowsett, 1982; Sarah, Scott and Spender, 1980), 'independent' schools also include religious fundamentalist schools committed to promoting extreme gender stereotypes, which is the case with the majority of boys' schools which remain little touched by the issues of concern here. With the latter, insofar as there is change towards mixed-sex teaching, it may be a change dis-advantageous to the girls involved (Walford, 1983; Connell, Ashenden, Kessler and Dowsett, 1982).

With regard to teachers and the 'role-models' they are thought to provide, procedures of appointment vary considerably in the different states. However, despite considerable publicity given to this issue, the situation here seems actually to have deteriorated (*Ms Muffett* 19, 1983). Again, while there is a willingness to recognize that something is wrong in terms of the lack of women in senior positions, there is far less willingness to acknowledge that it is due to any of the procedures currently operating. Affirmative action is still generally treated with great suspicion as a proposal to force institutions to take on less suitable women in place of well qualified men, rather than as a procedure to prevent suitable and well qualified women being overlooked. For example, use of the common apparently neutral criterion of seniority (defined as years of teaching service) discriminates against women who take time out to raise children, yet in only one state, New South Wales, is there accreditation for time spent in childrearing.

Careers counselling

A great deal of money and energy has been devoted to producing kits, videotapes and registers of speakers, to attempt to change patterns of subject and job choice among girls. This campaign has focused on having girls 'broaden their options' through (a) trying to prevent girls from dropping mathematics and (b) trying to encourage them to take on 'non-traditional' careers, especially apprenticeships in trades such as electronics, carpentry, plumbing (Jennings, 1982). The context of this strategy is a situation where most women now work in the paid workforce for a considerable part of their lives, and most girls in the past have entered an extremely restricted range of jobs. Such areas of 'traditional' girls' jobs (especially sales, clerical and typing) are among those most under attack by developments in technology (*Girls, School and Society*, 1975; Sweet, 1980a; Sweet, 1980b; Jennings, 1982; Owen, 1982), and current (February 1983) unemployment among teenage girls is 30.2 per cent as compared with a national average of 9.6 per cent. To date, as the employment figures and statistics on apprenticeships (Jennings, 1982) indicate, the results of these strategies have been somewhat disappointing. This seems to be partly due to the inadequacy of the strategies (taken as means in themselves) and partly to the state of the economy as a whole, where the over-supply of labour has encouraged employers to avoid taking on those seen as involving any risk. However, more recent initiatives here have begun to acknowledge the importance of structural and process issues if change is to occur. For example, there are moves in the Hunter Valley to encourage group apprenticeships so that girls do not have to| brave change as lone pioneers; there are attempts to work with employers rather than just the potential applicants; and there are moves by women's groups to seek affirmative action policies and legislation.

Teaching process

Again a great variety of types of interest and attempts at change are evident here. There are various networks operating by which teachers share their own ideas; Australian academics are involved in research projects based on a range of theoretical premises (the sociological theories of sex-role theory, the social-psychological analysis of self-esteem and its components, the sociological/neo-Marxist assumptions about schooling as social reproduction); and work done in other countries is noted and disseminated. The following are three examples of approaches to this area with an attempt to indicate some of their sources and directions.

1. One approach, which is used particularly by teachers whose interest in counter-sexism is allied to concerns about feminism rather than drawn primarily from the Equal Opportunity policies of the Education Departments, has been to try to overcome the sexist oppression seen to be involved in hierarchical competitive teaching arrangements. These teachers are allied with other progressive teachers who draw on other sources in attempting to institute 'democratic' teaching. In Victoria, for example, they support and promote the non-externally examined group of courses available in sixth forms, whose content and process are negotiated with students rather than simply imposed on them.

2. A second area of much interest recently has been in the classroom

processes of mixed-sex interaction, drawing particularly on Dale Spender's work (especially through the widely circulated review article, Conversational Politics, Ramsay 1981; see also Spender and Sarah, 1980; Spender, 1980; Spender, 1982). Her work suggested, for example, that teachers are likely to give two-thirds of their attention to males and to be concerned with the questions of interest to them, even when they as teachers are specifically concerned about the treatment of girls. The discussion of this and other similar research (for example, Galton, 1981; Samuel, 1981) has been one of the sources of experiments at reviving some single-sex grouping for the teaching of mathematics in some schools. An alternative response to the 'conversational politics' issue, which has been given somewhat less attention, is to take up the *Girls, School and Society* position quoted earlier, and to treat interaction biases as a subject for students to examine.

3. A third area of concern with the teaching process is sexual harassment. Sexual harassment is interpreted fairly broadly in this chapter: at an extreme it refers to pressure on girls or women to be sexually compliant to men who have power (either physical or institutional) over them; at another level it encompasses the various ways in which girls and women are treated as sex objects and are expected to act in a way which focuses on their sexual status and thereby trivializes them (and which, if they reject the 'compliments' and affectionate man-handling, is likely to make them seem aggressive, humourless, and so on).

The issue of sexual harassment is a good example of how the issues being discussed in different parts of this chapter interrelate, and how a concern with issues of equal opportunity may lead to quite detailed attention to process and context. At one level, in relation to schools, the issue of sexual harassment has been raised as affecting female teachers, and thereby the atmosphere in which the whole school operates. At another level, with particular school projects which started from a concern with equal opportunity, a move to give girls a chance to discuss the pressures on them soon led to a focus on sexual harassment as an important issue for them. The strategies in relation to this have included the running of conferences, publicity in newsletters, the setting up of groups to develop resource materials, enabling speakers to be available to talk to a school staff as a whole, and the establishment of 'equal opportunity' committees in schools. Nevertheless, the attempt to change or even to raise the issue of changing deeply ingrained ways of acting is clearly of a different order of difficulty than actions concerning resource-allocation.

Curriculum

In the last decade, strategies related to counter-sexist curricula have taken a number of forms in Australia, but overall the type of gradual development is some indication of a growing recognition of the breadth and depth of the issues to be confronted.

In the earlier stages, as suggested above, there was concern that the curriculum treated women and girls badly, both by omission and by distortion in the ways they were portrayed. Action both by centrally sponsored bodies like the national Curriculum Development Centre, and by teachers spontaneously concerned about these issues, took two main forms. One was an attempt to correct the distortions in existing textbooks by producing, for example, 'non-sexist' reading materials for primary levels and units on women in history. The other was an attempt to develop units of work specifically dealing with issues of gender. It should be said here that although a lot of work has been done in these areas, and although a host of material is available from bodies like the Equal Opportunity Units and the union appointees in this area in the various states, a visitor walking into any classroom or school library would still be very likely to find a huge amount of sexist material. There is also evidence that in some situations attempts to use units on gender issues lead to resistance or to marginalization, that is, the treatment of the area as a non-serious, non-integral part of the curriculum (Waugh and Foster, 1978; Yates, 1982).

One line of further development of strategies in this area has been to extend the initiatives mentioned above so that subjects dealing with issues of women and gender are more generally available, and are part of the regular channels of accreditation. For example, in Victoria a course on Women's Studies has recently been accredited at sixth-form level (as units on Women and Literature and Women in Australian History were earlier included as part of the existing courses in English Literature and Australian History). Further, a Women's Studies Association dedicated to the promotion and dissemination of information and materials relevant to such teaching has recently been formed. These developments still run some risk of being marginalized, and used as a way of containing this area without its affecting the rest of the curriculum, but they are undoubtedly a means by which teachers and students can reduce the sense of alienation produced by sexist curricular materials.

A second area where there has been an attempt to redefine what schools hold to be important knowledge is in the moves to include and promote the teaching of 'health and human relationships'. There is some question here as to whether this should be listed as a 'counter-sexist' strategy. On the one hand, the initial Victorian Committee of Inquiry into this area (1977) proposed the move as a means of combating some general forces of social disintegration. On the other hand, many teachers who initially began teaching these courses, and the Education Department itself, include teaching in the area under the rubric of strategies against sexism.

A development of a different kind can be seen in mathematics. This is an area that has always been a staple part of the curriculum. An early enthusiasm in the counter-sexist work for relatively simple explanations of sexism (such as the lack of illustrations of girls in textbooks, or the amount of encouragement given to girls) proved inadequate. Now, in some projects at least, there is a type of qualitative change in the questions being asked, a turning to issues of content, to questioning the nature and presentation of mathematics and whether this could be put together differently (Shelley, 1982; Barnes, 1982; Carss, 1980).

There are also, at a very preliminary stage of conception, approaches which attempt to analyse the whole picture and to change more fundamentally what school offers *overall* to *all* students. For example, some people in South Australia and in Victoria are taking up Jean Blackburn's ideas on the 'sexually inclusive curriculum' (Blackburn, 1981): a curriculum in which the balance of subjects will allow both boys and girls to reflect better on the processes at work in creating our current society, and in which issues of domestic work and reproduction and the bringing up of children are given greater weight without being either trivialized or treated as propaganda.

Finally, in curriculum as in other areas, tensions between different strategies can be seen. There are tensions between those who wish to stress negotiation and democracy in decisions about content to be covered and those who want to argue for the reintroduction of some compulsions (for example, of mathematics, or of a whole common curriculum up to Year 9). There are differences of focus, according to whether the concern is to help a particular group of girls to develop or whether the concern is to regulate what the system does to everyone. There are strategies which are reactive to existing problems and those which are based on complex analyses. And there are questions of long-term compared with short-term interests to be faced, and of how to balance these.

The processes of change

This chapter has not attempted to put together a particular argument about the nature of change in this area, but rather, by reviewing activities, to give something of the flavour of a movement in progress and to suggest some of the concerns and issues which might be relevant for appreciating and assisting it.

The type of issues that have been raised here are set out below:

The aims of the strategies. Are the concerns about changed shares of the cake, or of the sort of cake we want to share in? Some of the developments of particular practices suggest that defining aims in terms of the first question, the equal opportunity concern, is of strategic value, but trying to work on that issue soon leads to attempts to 'change the cake', in that forms of relationship between girls and boys and men and women may need to be changed if girls are to be treated as of equal concern by the system of schooling.

How schooling works. Practices draw on a range of views about how schooling and learning operate: from a naive faith in equally available offerings and resources, to a fairly simple view of the hidden curriculum and role models, to more subtle concerns about the nature of the embedding of schooling in social and cultural processes. Practices themselves have begun to change in recognition that the simpler assumptions have limited value. Propaganda about job choices is not enough; questions need to be raised about what really connects with students' minds, and about the structures of job entry that can undercut the credentials that schooling provides.

Institutional arrangements and possibilities for action. Understanding the modes of centralization and decentralization in the systems of schooling, and exploiting them appropriately, has been an important concern of those working in this area. A question which has received less overt discussion is the issue of concern for the group as compared with concern for the whole. To date, the emphasis in the Australian context has been more heavily on the first issue outlined above, and has dealt with the second in negative rather than positive ways (moves to counter discrimination and distortion rather than positive rearrangements to non-sexist ends).

Schooling in context. Finally, in the current Australian scene, an overview might suggest that technological change and widespread unemployment have been a main source of the questioning of past contents and modes of schooling. They have made us re-examine the way we lead our lives and educate our students. They are also, however, a current and potential means of undercutting the advances already being made. Future researchers and reformers will need to learn to cope with the problems as well as to take advantage of the possibilities raised by rapid social change.

Note

Because of the local nature of much of the material referred to in this chapter, no attempt has been made to list sources comprehensively. A general annotated bibliography of Australian resources, including people, institutions, literature and other media, is *Girls' Own* (1981). For further, more up-to-date, detailed information on projects and sources of information, readers could write to the Victorian Equal Opportunity Resource Centre, 29 Dawson Street, Brunswick, Victoria, 3057, Australia.

References

Allen, L (1983) A bibliography of multiculturalism *Social Alternatives* **3** 3
Ashton, D and Maguire, M (1980) Young women in the labour market: stability and change *in* Deem
Barnes, M (1980) Using the history of mathematics in classroom teaching Australian Association of Mathematics Teachers Conference Papers: Sydney
Berberich, L (1979) *Non-sexist Multi-cultural Education? A Bibliography of Non-sexist Inter-cultural Books K-6* Centre for Non-sexist Resources: Sydney
Blackburn, J (1981) Address to Australian Women's Education Coalition Conference: Canberra: unpublished

Bourdieu, P and Passeron, J-P (1977) *Reproduction in Education, Society and Culture* Sage: London

Brunswick Secondary Education Committee (BRUSEC) (1982-3) *Equal Opportunity Project Annual Report* Melbourne

Carss, M (1980) Girls, mathematics and language: some observations for classrooms Paper presented at a Conference on Increasing the Participation of Girls in Mathematics: Raywood, South Australia

Coleman, J (1971) The concept of equality of educational opportunity *in* Open University

Connell, R W, Ashenden, D J, Kessler, S and Dowsett, G W (1982) *Making the Difference: Schools, Families and Social Divisions* George Allen and Unwin: Sydney

Deem, R ed (1980) *Schooling for Women's Work* Routledge and Kegan Paul: London

Equal Opportunity Unit of the Victorian Education Department (1981) Equal opportunity in Victorian schools questionnaire report: unpublished

Galbally Report (1978) *Migrant Services and Programs* Australian Government Printing Service (AGPS): Canberra

Galton, M (1981) Differential treatment of boy and girl pupils during science lessons *in* Kelly

Game, A and Pringle, R (1983) *Gender at Work* Allen and Unwin: Sydney

Girls' Own (1981) Campaign to Encourage Non-sexist Education (CENSE) and Equal Opportunity Resource Centre (EORC): Melbourne

Girls, School and Society (1975) Report by a Study Group to the Schools Commission: Canberra

It Kit (no date) Victorian Council of School Organizations (VICCSO) and Victorian Federation of State Schools Parents Clubs (VFSSPC): Melbourne

Jennings, B (1982) The girls' apprenticeship programme in Victoria: some observations Third Women and Labour Conference Papers: Adelaide

Kelly, A ed (1981) *The Missing Half: Girls and Science Education* Manchester University Press: Manchester

Ms Muffet Newsletter of the Joint Technical Teachers Union of Victoria (TTUV), Victorian Association of Secondary Teachers (VSTA) and Victorian Teachers Union (VTU) Counter-sexism Project

Migrant Girls Employment/Unemployment Conference Report (1982) Brunswick-Coburg Migrant Youth Action Group: Melbourne

Migrant Services and Programs (Galbally Report) (1978) Australian Government Printing Service (AGPS): Canberra

Open University (1971) *School and Society* Routledge and Kegan Paul: London

Owen, M (1982) Women's employment: past and future Third Women and Labour Conference Papers: Adelaide

Ramsay, E (1981) Conversational Politics *South Australian Institute of Teachers Contact Network Newsletter* 22

Report of the Advisory Committee on Health and Human Relations Education in Schools (1980) Victorian Education Department: Melbourne

Report of the Victorian Committee on Equal Opportunity in Schools (1977) Government Printer: Melbourne

Samuel, J (1981) Feminism and science teaching; some classroom observations *in* Kelly

Sarah, E, Scott, M and Spender, D (1980) The education of feminists: the case for single-sex schools *in* Spender and Sarah

Shelley, N (1982) An alternative pathway to mathematical understanding Australian Association of Mathematics Teachers Conference Papers: Sydney

Sobski, J (1979) Growing up in a multicultural society: Social Development Unit Paper Paper delivered to Australian Women's Education Coalition Conference: unpublished

Spender, D and Sarah, E (1980) *Learning to Lose* The Women's Press: London

Spender, D (1980) *Man Made Language* Routledge and Kegan Paul: London

Spender, D (1982) *Invisible Women* Writers and Readers: London

Sweet, R (1980a) An analysis of trends in the teenage labour market in NSW 1971-1976 *New South Wales Department of Technical and Further Education Research Report*: Sydney

Sweet, R (1980b) The new marginal workers: teenage part-time employment in Australia in the 1970s *New South Wales Department of Technical and Further Education Research Report*: Sydney

Sweet, R (1982) Hidden unemployment among teenagers: a comparison of in-school and out-of-school indicators *New South Wales Department of Technical and Further Education Research Report*: Sydney

Walford, G (1983) Girls in boys' public schools: a prelude to further research *British Journal of Sociology of Education* 4 1: 39-54

Waugh, P and Foster, V (1978) Education and the 'down-girl' principle *Refactory Girl 16*

Women's Studies Seminar Report (1982) Victorian Institute of Secondary Education (VISE): Melbourne

Yates, L (1982) Women's studies in the framework of the secondary school curriculum *in* Women's Studies Seminar Report

Acknowledgement

Helen Clarke, Curriculum Consultant at the Victorian Equal Opportunity Resource Centre provided assistance for the writing of this chapter.

23. Women's Studies: the challenge to man-made education

Renate Duelli Klein

Summary: This paper is an overview of the origins, development and guiding principles in Women's Studies, that is, its theories about organizational structure, subject matter, and teaching and research principles. In addition, it briefly mentions the practice of Women's Studies internationally and focuses specifically on developments in the USA, the UK and West Germany.

Women's Studies emerged in response to increased worldwide feminist activities in the late 1960s. It posits that knowledge and the educational system that transmits it are man-made, serve the interests of dominant groups, and thus take part in the continued oppression of women. In thousands of courses, hundreds of degree-granting programmes (especially in the USA), and on all educational levels, feminist teachers and students worldwide challenge such male-biased learning, and feminist scholarship has seen a remarkable proliferation in the last decade.

Women's Studies encourages the creation of knowledge in which subjective life experiences are recognized as integral to all intellectual activity. Thus, every issue is material for Women's Studies and it is investigated across the boundaries of traditional academic disciplines: Women's Studies is not just another academic discipline but part of a social movement openly orientated towards changing the *status quo*. In their teaching and research, Women's Studies practitioners investigate the world from women-centred perspectives in which women are valid in their own right and not only through their relations to men and male institutions. Curricular content as much as teaching and research methodology are geared towards reflecting and exploring non-oppressive and non-hierarchical relationships between people.

Such theoretical aims are put into practice in a variety of forms. However, there is consensus among Women's Studies practitioners internationally that one of their most important goals is to encourage women to become assertive and autonomous human beings who are critical of men's dominance. Not surprisingly, such radical intentions meet with resistance from the conventional educational establishment. It remains to be seen if Women's Studies will continue to be radical and to function as the educational arm of the Women's Liberation Movement.

Theories of Women's Studies

Origins and development

It was in the wake of the revitalized Women's Liberation Movement of the late 1960s that Women's Studies (WS) came into existence. Students and teachers worldwide brought their anger and concern about the continuing exploitation and oppression of women from the streets into their classrooms and began asking questions: Why were there so few women professors? Why were there so few women writers, artists, scientists on their curriculum? Why was it that philosophy concerned itself with 'great men'; that history seemed to consist of men's wars and negotiations; that science seemed all man-made and that where women were mentioned their contributions were seen as minor only? Why was women's productive and reproductive work trivialized? Why were their experiences distorted? Why were there no positive descriptions of the work of our foremothers? Why no role-models for female students? Why was is that education for women taught them little about their own and other women's lives? In sum, why were women only viewed in relation to men as 'other' with 'man-as-the-norm' (Acker, 1980: 88) and rarely as self-determining autonomous human beings?

Such recognition that what had been presented as human knowledge was in fact knowledge produced by, about, and for (white) men, marked the beginning of the WS movement. Now in its second decade, it has been called the educational success story of the 1970s and 'a phenomenon that is impossible to cover completely . . . because it is everywhere' (Boxer, 1982: 662). Indeed, as some of its pioneers state (Howe and Ahlum, 1973; Tobias, 1978) the international expansion of WS courses, feminist research centres and scholarship, WS-journals, books, organizations and conferences has dramatically outgrown in scope, variety and sheer numbers their early expectations: there are now thousands of courses worldwide and the growth continues.

This expansion in teaching feminist courses and doing feminist research — the two intrinsically linked components of WS — has been largest in the USA, where it is highly institutionalized and 'visible'. But the UK, Canada and some European countries have seen a remarkable proliferation of WS too. Neither is it restricted to Western countries. India, for example, has a steadily expanding WS movement (Mazumdar, 1980). Nor is WS confined to any one educational level. There are WS courses at institutions of higher learning, in adult education and in further and secondary education. And outside formal education there is a worldwide growth of what has been called 'street Women's Studies' (Tobias, 1978). Individual courses and programmes of study vary greatly in content and structure according to the cultural specificity of women's conditions in their respective countries. However, the PhD programme at a research university in the USA, the New Horizons course within Further Education in the UK, the Women and Health Seminar in India, the feminist 150-hour course offered by the Trade Unions in Italy, or the *Volkshochschulkurs* on women's work in Germany all came into existence in the same spirit: to provide women with a positive educational experience and to create and distribute knowledge in which women's varying and differing needs and interests are the focal point.

Thus, some joint *guiding principles* underlying the theories and practices of WS internationally have emerged. This development is well documented and, in the following pages, I shall draw on the work of scholars from a number of countries. For the United States I rely on papers by Lerner (1972); Salzmann-Webb (1972); Howe and Ahlum (1973); Stimpson (1973, 1978); Gordon (1975); Zangrando (1975); Howe (1977); Slavin Schramm (1978); Tobias (1978); Thorne (1978); Register (1979); Westkott (1981); Minnich (1982); Boxer (1982); for Canada on overviews by Salper (1971); Colby (1978); and Staton (1980). British overview essays and reports on WS include texts by Mack (1974); Rendel (1974, 1980); Whiting (1974); Hartnett and Rendel (1975); Spender (1978); Murgatroyd (1979); Bradshaw, Davies and De Wolfe (1981); Callaway (1981); Evans (1982); Hughes and Kennedy (1983) and Battel, Duelli Klein, Moorhouse and Zmroczek (1983). German papers on WS are by Schöpp-Schilling (1979, 1982); Levin (1979); Holzkamp and Steppke (1979); Metz-Göckel (1979, 1982, 1983); Müller (1979); Planungsgruppe für Frauenstudien Berlin (1980); Sauter-Bailliet (1980); Metz-Göckel/Sauter-Bailliet (1982); Duelli Klein/Nerad (1982); Clemens (1983) and Bock, Braszeit and Schmerl (1983). The development of WS in Italy is documented by Balbo and Ergas (1982). There is a comprehensive annotated bibliography of articles on WS in Bowles and Duelli Klein (1983).

Guiding principles

As said before, WS is part of a social movement and has been called 'the educational arm of the women's movement' (Howe, 1977). Its research and teaching activities are aimed at changing the *status quo*, that is 'to challenge the male monopoly of intellectual thought' (Mack, 1974: 162). WS takes issue with the separation of knowledge and politics, theory and practice, mind and body, public and private, and other dichotomies. By endorsing the feminist principle that 'the personal is political' WS declares itself as an overtly political alternative to man-made education and is determined to produce and transmit knowledge in which women's intellectual activities are given as much legitimization and recognition by society as are men's. This validation, it is hoped, will lead to a redistribution of power between women and men worldwide.

Working for such 'a new reality' (Roberts, 1976) necessitates perceiving the world from a feminist perspective. Put differently, WS teachers and students are feminists. However, as within feminism itself, which in the last decade has developed a diversified body of knowledge, they subscribe to many different 'kinds' of feminism.

WS 'practitioners' (Howe and Ahlum's term to describe WS teachers and students, 1973) also conceptualize WS in a variety of forms. For some, every question is a WS question; WS/feminist research cannot be restricted to 'women's issues' such as female biology, health, reproduction or women's paid and unpaid participation in the labour market and the family. They expect WS to look critically at and evaluate every facet of life from interpersonal relationships to politics, from language to law, from the (ab)use of natural resources to the social construction of reality, from nuclear power to men's wars — but to look at it from *women's* points of view.

Such a broad approach to WS posits that 'WS is not just another subject but more a way of life' (Spender, 1978: 256). In the 15 years of its existence, an enormous qualitative and quantitative wealth of feminist scholarship has been produced. The first years saw a proliferation of research on the lives and achievements of 'great women': 'adding women on' to male knowledge was the main intent and also the most urgently needed task given the dearth of existing teaching materials on women. The focus was on compensatory research, on the *deconstruction* of knowledge (Stimpson, 1973). The aim was to incorporate the results of 'the study of women' into 'the study of men' and make up for women's omission from knowledge by producing a balanced curriculum.

However, integrating research on women led many WS practitioners to the recognition that the so-called 'add-women-and-stir' method (Bunch, 1979) was not enough: the *nature* of all knowledge, they stated, needed a fundamental re-evaluation, investigation and examination not only of cases where women had been omitted, but also of cases where knowledge had been generated which pretended to include women when in fact it included only male views and interests, and was produced from within the realities of men. Such insights led to the *construction* of women-centred knowledge within the conventional disciplines. It also led to the development of new theoretical inter-, multi-, and trans-disciplinary frameworks. 'Research as re-vision' (Callaway, 1981), which scrutinized existing theories and exposed their patriarchal myths, began to be complemented by 'research as vision' — theories of WS — the construction of alternative 'envisioning knowledge' (Rich, 1980: 18). Based on women's past and present contributions to all facets of human life — from the biological to the cultural, and from the material to the spiritual — it aims at developing new concepts for a future free of dominance and oppression.

Such an approach to knowledge-making necessitates the crossing of the boundaries of the established academic disciplines. Its proponents speak of WS 'as a new discipline' (Bowles, 1980; Coyner, 1980) and make the case for WS as a study in its own right: they work towards the institutionalization of autonomous WS as degree-granting courses of study anchored in the institutions as are other academic discplines, eg history or biology. They contend that women-defined spheres are an intellectual necessity, a prerequisite for women to control feminist research and teaching. They conceive of autonomous WS as a (potential) feminist power-base from within which on the one hand to create and transmit knowledge and on the other to continue the critique and encourage the change of androcentric 'men's studies' — that is, the other academic disciplines (Spender, 1981).

The courses that are based on a definition of WS as a study in its own right draw on the diversity of feminist theory. They often combine issue-oriented course topics (such as violence against women; women's

exploitation in the development of 'new technology'; the increasing
worldwide feminization of poverty and women's positions in capitalist
and socialist states) with theoretical discussions (such as the role of dominant groups; the ways knowledge gets encoded and selected; the means by
which knowledge produced by non-dominant groups — women, economically disadvantaged, older, and disabled people — is rendered invisible).
The focus is on developing alternative knowledge for the benefit of these
groups and on strategies of how to put the theory into practice.

Another group of WS practitioners see as their main aim the integration
of feminist research into existing disciplines. They believe in the possibility
of forming fruitful alliances between feminists and academics of the
traditional kind whom, they argue, it must be possible to convince of the
necessity to include feminist insights in their teaching and research. While
a certain amount of interdisciplinary co-operation between scholars from
different fields is seen as important in reaching this goal, the main
allegiances of 'integrationists' remain to the original disciplines. An 'integrationist' WS course in literature, for example, remains 'in literature'
by incorporating feminist literary research rather than (as the 'autonomous'
course would) discussing the specific problem studied (for example, female
writers in nineteenth century England) within the broader context of
investigating the conditions of female writers by drawing on interdisciplinary feminist scholarship. Another example might be that integrationist WS courses start with an examination of theories by progressive
male scholars coming from a marxist or psychoanalytic tradition and
then proceed to develop a feminist critique of these works, whereas
'autonomous' WS practitioners would compare — and develop further —
different *feminist* theories. It must be noted, however, that the above
described autonomous and integrationist approaches to WS in this form
apply to WS in the USA only. Two main developments are presently
taking place — in many institutions simultaneously:

1. a trend towards more autonomy in terms of budget and faculty
   hiring procedures, and the image of Women's Studies as a discipline
   in its own right, often in connection with the establishment of
   independent MA and PhD programmes (Bowles and Duelli Klein,
   1983: 1-26); and
2. a trend towards the transformation of the curriculum of the
   traditional disciplines and a move towards a balanced curriculum
   by integrating feminist scholarship into the existing disciplines
   (Spanier, 1982; Dinnerstein *et al*, 1982).

There is, however, a strong determination among WS practitioners to keep
WS from being rigid, dogmatic and monolithic. Between the 'autonomous'
and 'integrationist' position lie many possible 'varieties' and combinations
(McIntosh and Minnich, 1984). Advocates of different viewpoints may be
present in the same WS classroom or co-operate on the same research
project. Ideally, they prevent each other from imposing 'the one and
only' correct 'type' of WS: there are many, and all of them are needed.

Often it is the nature of a specific educational institution that makes one approach more feasible than the other.

The aim to remain flexible and open to new input (for instance, from groups of women who so far have been under-represented in WS such as women of colour, working class women and lesbians) and hence change, is also exemplified by the many different 'types' of what is called *feminist research* and by the various forms its *teaching practices* take.

Feminist research aims at going beyond being 'an academic exercise'. Its intent is, in one way or another, to be useful in improving the conditions of women's lives. Wherever possible, the researcher begins her research by drawing on her own subjective experiences as a female and expands them to include similar and differing experiences of other women. She thus becomes an integral part of her research project and in many instances the categories of 'researcher' and 'researched', and of 'subject' and 'object' merge. Thus as a woman and a researcher, the feminist scholar brings to her work the advantage of having a 'double consciousness' (Mies, 1978: 45). To document the research process (including 'failed' attempts to assemble facts in some conclusive way) is as important as the research product itself. Some research methods seem better suited than others — for example, qualitative rather than quantitative, personal rather than impersonal, situation-embedded rather than context-stripped (Reinharz, 1981: 75-6). Feminist researchers are eclectic in their choice of research methods and adapt them to the specific demands of their research project. Collaborative research, in general, is preferred to one-woman projects and in empirical research a co-operative relationship is sought with those that are studied in order to minimize hierarchies of power. Whatever research findings emerge, it is hoped that they will reach as broad an audience as possible, especially among feminists who choose as their priority the involvement in campaigns and actions of the women's movement (Duelli Klein, 1980).

Many of the same principles mentioned for feminist research are applicable to the *feminist classroom.* 'Teaching' WS starts with the premise that all, teachers as well as students, are learners. They bring specific resources to the classroom, eg in general the 'teacher' brings her 'academic' expertise, the 'student' her professional skills and both their life experiences as women and their various degrees and forms of involvement with feminism and the Women's Liberation Movement. (The high proportion of older 're-entry women' in WS adds significantly to the breadth of viewpoints among class members.) Again, in many instances the categories of student and teacher overlap and merge. Seminars alternate with lectures but at least part of the time should be reserved for discussions. Knowledge is jointly 'created' rather than handed 'down' from the 'expert' to the 'ignorant'; vertical hierarchies are whenever possible exchanged for horizontal networks among the members of a WS group. As women, the WS practitioners share a lot of commonalities. (The presence of men as practitioners alters things significantly; the 'men-problem' is discussed by Duelli Klein, 1983.) The differences among them resulting from varying ethnicity, sexual orientation, age, physical ability, class, religious and cultural background ideally can inform their discussions and prevent over-generalizations on behalf of 'all' women. Practitioners seek to avoid power differences between teachers and students. However, external constraints, such as the teacher's responsibility to assess coursework and represent WS *vis à vis* the administration, places considerable strain on students and teachers in any attempt to work towards the abolition of hierarchies. Internal constraints such as women's own internalized needs for 'authority' and competitive rather than co-operative behaviour are a source of conflict in WS. They open up areas of discrepancy between the theories of WS and its practices. It depends on the WS practitioners' personalities, interpersonal dynamics and the degree of commitment to the principles of WS and feminism whether they successfully invent solutions to subvert the interfering demands of patriarchy, for example by forming joint teacher/student advisory boards for assessing papers, writing course syllabuses and dealing with administrative requests. The alternative is to remain within the confines of hierarchical 'men's studies'.

Women's studies in practice

International growth

So far, this chapter has emphasized the *diversity* of WS. No one scholar, teacher, type of course or research project can be seen as the sole representative or model of WS. This holds especially true when investigating its growth and present state in an international context. WS evolved in a variety of forms and within a diversity of formal and informal educational levels (Rendel, 1982) and it is important to perceive the worldwide development of WS as an example of horizontal rather than vertical growth. WS has been defined as an 'umbrella concept' (Colby, 1978: 4): the 'mushrooming' of courses and feminist scholarship rather than a linear progressive evolution towards 'one' type of WS. WS, in its first decade, has indeed seen an international 'mushrooming', and feminist courses abound from South America to Canada, from Japan and Korea to India, Africa and all the European countries — albeit under different names and in a variety of forms. There exists now an international network among WS practitioners worldwide: Women's Studies International (Howe, 1981) which assists in the distribution of information about courses, journals, books and international WS conferences.

There are many problems that occur in the international development of a movement that aims at improving the condition of women worldwide. The idea of 'improvement' itself is conceived of differently by women from different cultures, and at the International WS Forum at Copenhagen in 1980 South American and African women cautioned against any one nation wanting to impose its imprint on WS International. However, there was agreement among the participants that there was an urgent need for 'global' feminism (Bunch, 1980) and WS, even in countries where (many would say) there are higher priorities than feminist education, for example, saving women from starvation or malnutrition, giving them access to literacy or freeing them from debilitating diseases. There was consensus that research and education can play a significant part in improving women's conditions. In an African woman's words: 'Research is part of the process of liberation' (Steady, 1980).

The international growth of WS/feminist research may contribute to the growing recognition among feminists that the production and interchange of feminist knowledge that defies male-centred viewpoints will benefit women internationally. There is indeed a lot that women worldwide can learn from each other in order to 'defy patriarchy' (Rueben, 1978).

In the following section, I shall provide summaries of WS in the USA, the UK and West Germany, where WS has become most visible, and I wish to illustrate the previous theoretical section with some practical information. (The sources used are the same as listed on p 294.)

Women's Studies in the USA, the UK, and West Germany

THE USA

Since the first few WS courses in the late 1960s, WS has undergone a remarkable proliferation. The figures for 1982 list over 30,000 individual courses; there are over 430 institutions of higher education which offer WS in some coherent form, more than 130 of which grant a BA, 45 an MA, and ten a PhD degree, most of these in association with another discipline, for example, history or philosophy (Howe, 1982). In addition 28 WS research centres exist, and over 50 projects which aim at integrating WS into the existing disciplines (McIntosh, 1982). When this chapter was written, the annual 1982 survey of US programmes was in progress and it seems that the programmes have continued to increase; research centres are up to 39 (Howe, 1983: 2).

Since 1977, WS has had its own professional organization: the NWSA (National Women's Studies Association) with annual conferences and its own publication (the *Women's Studies Quarterly*, now the *NWSA Newsletter*). The development of WS in the United States is well documented in ten volumes of *Female Studies* (1970-1976) and various publications of the National Institute of Education. Textbooks in WS abound (eg Freeman, 1979; Ruth, 1980; Hull *et al*, 1982; Cruikshank, 1982; Bowles and Duelli Klein, 1983) and a number of scholarly journals distribute the growing body of feminist scholarship, eg *Women's Studies, Women's Studies Quarterly, Feminist Studies, Quest, Frontiers* and *Signs*.

After a mere 15 years of existence, the enormous expansion of WS as a field in its own right in US higher education must be acknowledged. Because of the flexible nature of higher education in the United States, which frequently allows 'special programmes' to be introduced without difficulty, feminists in academe had options to start a coherent course of study in WS which do not exist for the British and European colleagues. Most of the WS programmes are interdisciplinary, that is, the students choose an emphasis in social science or the humanities (rarely the natural sciences) and combine WS courses from various departments with some compulsory courses from the WS programme for their degree in WS. However, WS is still marginal and often on a temporary basis. Thus the questions remain of whether or not the authorities of institutions of higher learning will continue to tolerate feminist intellectuals' quest for women-centred knowledge, and whether (and how) the current political climate and the substantial budget cuts in higher education in general will influence the further development of WS.

THE UK

WS in higher education in the UK is varied and extensive but, as yet, there are very few institutionalized or WS degree courses. In contrast with the USA, the few that exist are all on the postgraduate level: MA courses at Kent University, Bradford University and Sheffield Polytechnic. In addition, a number of MA courses offer an option in WS and at these and other universities it is also possible to do research degrees (MPhil and PhD) with a focus on WS. At the undergraduate level there have been many individual courses since the early 1970s at a large number of universities, some of which count towards the requirement of another discipline-based degree. At several colleges and polytechnics it is possible to receive a diploma in WS, and many university extramural departments list a wide range of WS courses under the umbrella of adult education (Hughes and Kennedy, 1983). The Workers' Educational Association (WEA) has been pioneering the field of WS courses outside formal education.

Despite the existence of these many courses and the growing number of feminist teachers and students, there is no official nationwide British WS network. There are numerous feminist activities in discipline-based women's organizations (for example, WedG — Women in Education Group — and the Women's Caucus of the British Sociological Association) and the London-based WRRC (The Women's Research and Resource Centre) lists available WS courses in its newsletter, maintains a research index of on-going feminist research, has a lending library with useful books for WS courses and has produced an updated version of Hartnett and Rendel's (1975) *Women's Studies in the UK* (Bradshaw, Davies and de Wolfe, 1981). There are four British feminist journals (*Feminist Review; M/F; Women's Studies International Forum* and *Trouble and Strife*) and a remarkable number of textbooks (for example, by the Brighton, Bristol and Cambridge WS Groups; Spender, 1981; Oakley, 1981; Evans, 1982; The Open University course team, 1982).

So far, there has been little dialogue between feminist educators and students from various educational institutions and levels throughout the country on the question of building a nationwide 'trans-disciplinary' WS movement. Unlike the USA with its flexible and diversified educational

system, in Britain it is extremely difficult to overcome the institutionalized disciplinary divisions of academic departments. In many ways,
WS in the UK has never left the traditional disciplines. Rather, (and
with the exception of the few mentioned interdisciplinary degree courses),
feminist faculty at best are able to offer one (or a few) specific feminist
courses within their particular school or department (often sociology).
However, after two national WS conferences in 1981 and 1982 organized
by WS practitioners from the MA courses in WS, plans were made for a
British Women's Studies Association. If it comes to fruition, such an
organization could provide a network for feminists interested in working
towards a WS movement which institutionalizes WS as a study in its
own right.

WEST GERMANY
The development of WS in West Germany is not unlike that in the UK.
Faced with a similarly compartmentalized (and elitist) system of higher
education, so far the number of 'formal' WS courses remains very low.
WS as a degree-granting course of study does not yet exist, although
many feminist academics concern themselves with this question. What has
existed since the early 1970s is a substantial and growing number of
feminist courses within the conventional disciplines as well as interdisciplinary seminars (*Ringvorlesungen*). Only the Free University in
Berlin and Dortmund University have official co-ordinating groups which
make visible the WS courses within the university and provide a network
for the feminists on campus.

However, there are strong interdisciplinary *national* networks among
feminist academics. The *Arbeitskreis der Wissenschaftlerinnen an den
Hochschulen von NW* (The Association of Female Scholars at NW institutions of Higher Education, comprising 12 universities in Nordrhein-
Westfalen) is a multidisciplinary group of female scholars who work
towards the institutionalization of WS specifically, and the improvement
of conditions for female faculty and students in general. The *Inter-
disziplinäre Forschungsgruppe Frauenforschung (IFF)* (Interdisciplinary
Group for Research on Women) at Bielefeld University is the first official
Women's Research Centre at an institution of higher education in West
Germany. In addition, outside formal education, the *Frauenforschungs-
Bildungs-und Informations-Zentrum (FFBIZ)* (Women's Research Edu-
cation and Information Centre) at Berlin has offered many WS courses
since 1978, and has been involved in organizing the annual Summer
University for Women which each year draws thousands of women to
Berlin. There are WS groups in all major towns (eg *Frauenstudien* in
München), and adult education (the *Volkshochschule*) offers WS
courses too.

The *Verein Sozialwissenschaftliche Forschung und Praxis für Frauen*
(Social Science Research and Praxis for Women) and the *Sektion Frauen-
forschung in der Deutschen Gesellschaft für Soziologie* (the Women's
Caucus of the German Sociological Society) both issue a newsletter and

organize national conferences. The journal of the 'Verein', the *Beiträge zur feministischen Theorie und Praxis* (Contributions to Feminist Theory and Praxis), together with *Feministische Studien* (Feminist Studies), a WS journal founded in 1983, provide important interdisciplinary resources for WS courses.

These various networks contribute significantly to the visibility of WS/feminist research in Germany. They are, however, the fruits of year-long insistent labour of a group of academic feminists who are determined to face up to the increasing resistance to feminism from conservative-patriarchal bodies in Germany. Many 'academic' feminists are active in women's movement organizations too and are concerned to maintain the alliances between WS inside formal education and 'street WS' which they see as crucial if 'academic' WS is to keep its radical nature.

'A revolution the extent of which is not yet clear.?

From these three examples, it becomes evident that the guiding principles of WS are put into practice in a variety of forms. But WS practitioners internationally seem to agree that maybe the most important aim of WS consists of encouraging women to take responsibility for their own education and lives, and to become assertive, autonomous, independent, caring and compassionate human beings. WS aims to help women become human beings who not only think critically, and analyse and synthesize 'facts and figures', but also express feelings and emotions in their thoughts and actions.

There could be few more radical goals for education! WS is truly 'a revolution the extent of which is not yet clear' (Howe, 1982: 12). WS has set itself an enormous agenda, for such an overt challenge to male power is bound to meet with considerable opposition. Not surprisingly, traditional academics may consider WS as a 'fad', 'non-academic', and label feminist scholarship 'unscientific' and 'political'. It is the missing recognition that the male-centred frame of reference is no less 'political' and no less 'biased' than the feminist one which accounts for these value judgements. Given the differing access to economic resources and positions of power, WS practitioners will need to continue to be insistent, stubborn, determined and committed. As Elizabeth Minnich suggests (1982: 8): 'We will have to be philosophers and poets and scientists . . . drawing on analysis, observation, empathy and imagination in all that we do'.

WS practitioners will also have to be astutely *political*. Despite the apparently rising number of women who gain access to formerly male-dominated spheres, whether in education or other professions, women of all ages and in all cultures get poorer and poorer and the 'feminization of poverty' has become a recognized sociological concept (Ehrenreich and Stallard, 1982: 217-24).

WS practitioners of the 1980s grew up in a different world from the women who started WS 15 years ago and they are faced with differing economic and psychological realities. It remains to be seen how they will continue to develop, implement and expand WS. The immense wealth in both quality and quantity of WS research and teaching is a promising outlook for the future. However, 'it is a long way to turn knowledge into power' (Metz-Göckel, 1982: 11): WS is evolving and struggling and in this struggle diversifying and changing. In O'Connor Blumhagen and Johnson's words (1978: 120): 'It is an exciting and dynamic area of study, complete with its own controversies and dialogues, and it is accomplishing important work needed for the humanization of academia and society as a whole. Its future is very much open and dependent upon all our contributions'.

References

Acker, Sandra (1980) Women, the other academics *British Journal of Sociology of Education* **1** 1: 81-91

Balbo, Laura and Yasmine, Ergas (1982) *Women's Studies in Italy* The Feminist Press: Old Westbury, NY

Battel, Roisin, Duelli Klein, Renate, Moorhouse, Catherine and Zmroczek, Christine eds (1983) So far, so good — so what: women's studies in the UK *Women's Studies International Forum* **6** 3 (Special Issue)

Boxer, Marilyn (1982) For and about women: the theory and practice of women's studies in the United States *Signs* **7** 3: 661-95

Bock, Ulla, Braszeit, Anne and Schmerl, Christiane (1983) *Frauen im Wissenschaftsbetrieb* Beltz Verlag: Weinheim

Bowles, Gloria (1980) Is women's studies an academic discipline? *in* Bowles and Duelli Klein: 1-11

Bowles, Gloria and Duelli Klein, Renate eds (1980) *Theories of Women's Studies I* Women's Studies Program University of California: Berkeley

Bowles, Gloria and Duelli Klein, Renate eds (1981) *Theories of Women's Studies II* Women's Studies Program University of California: Berkeley

Bowles, Gloria and Duelli Klein, Renate eds (1983) *Theories of Women's Studies* Routledge and Kegan Paul: London and Boston

Bradshaw, Jan, Davies, Wendy and De Wolfe, Patricia (1981) *Women's Studies Courses in the UK* Women's Research and Resources Centre: London

Brighton Women and Science Group (1980) *Alice Through the Microscope: The Power of Science over Women's Lives* Virago: London

Bristol Women's Studies Group (1979) *Half the Sky: An Introduction to Women's Studies* Virago: London

Bunch, Charlotte (1979) Visions and revisions: women and the power to change Panel at NWSA Convention: Lawrence, Kansas, June!

Bunch, Charlotte (1980) Global Feminism. Talk delivered at Women's Studies Forum at Copenhagen, July

Callaway, Helen (1981) Women's perspectives: research as re-vision *in* Reason and Rowan: 457-71

Cambridge Women's Studies Group (1981) *Women in Society* Virago: London

Clemens, Bärbel (1983) Institutionalisierung von Frauenforschung und Frauenstudien — ein Weg zur Förderung von Frauen an der Hochschule? Paper delivered at Kassel University, 28 January

Colby, Marion (1978) Women's Studies: an inclusive concept for an inclusive field *Canadian Women's Studies* **1** 1: 4-6

Coyner, Sandra (1980) Women's Studies as an academic discipline: why and how to do it *in* Bowles and Duelli Klein: 18-40

Cruikshank, Margaret ed (1982) *Lesbian Studies Present and Future* The Feminist Press: Old Westbury, NY

Dinnerstein, Myra, O'Donnell, Sheryl and MacCorquodale, Patricia (1982) Integrating women's studies into the curriculum *Women's Studies Quarterly* **10** 1: 20-23

Duelli Klein, Renate (1980) How to do what we want to do: thoughts about feminist methodology *in* Bowles and Duelli Klein: 48-64

Duelli Klein, Renate (1983) The 'men problem' in women's studies: 'the expert', 'the ignoramus' and 'the poor dear' *Women Studies International Forum* **6** 4

Duelli Klein, Renate, Nerad, Maresi and Metz-Göckel, Sigrid *eds* (1982) *Feministiche Wissenschaft und Frauenstudium* AHD: Hamburg

Ehrenreich, Barbara and Stallard, Karin (1982) The noveau poor *Ms Magazine* **11** 1/2: 217-24

Evans, Mary (1982) In praise of theory: the case for women's studies *Feminist Review* **10**: 61-74

Evans, Mary (1982) *The Woman Question: Readings on the Subordination of Women* Fontana Paperbacks: London

Freeman, Jo *ed* (1979) *Women: A Feminist Perspective* Mayfield: Palo Alto

Gordon, Linda (1975) A socialist view of women's studies *Signs* **1** 2: 559-66

Hartnett, Oonagh and Rendel, Margherita *eds* (1975) *Women's Studies in the UK* London Seminars: London

Holzkamp, Christine and Steppke, Gisela (1979) Lernen, lieben, leiden . . . über unsere Hoffnungen, Ettäuschungen und Lernprozesse als Dozentinnen in Frauenseminaren *in* Metz-Göckel: 81-98

Howe, Florence (1977) *Seven Years Later: Women's Studies Programs in 1976* Report of the National Advisory Council on Women's Educational Programs, Washington

Howe, Florence (1981) Women's Studies International at Copenhagen: from idea to network *Women's Studies Quarterly* **9** 1: 7-11

Howe, Florence (1982) Women's studies program list *Women's Studies Quarterly* **10** 3: 21-31

Howe, Florence (1982) Feminist scholarship – the extent of the revolution *Change Magazine* **14** 3: 12-20

Howe, Florence (1983) Editorial *Women's Studies Quarterly* **11** 2: 2¦

Howe, Florence and Ahlum, Carol (1973) Women's studies and social change *in* Rossi and Calderwood: 393-423

Hughes, Mary and Kennedy, Mary (1983) Breaking out – women in adult education *Women's Studies International Forum* **6** 3: 261-70

Hull, Gloria, Scott, Patricia and Smith, Barbara *eds* (1982) *All the Women Are White, All the Blacks Are Men, But Some of Us Are Brave: Black Women's Studies* The Feminist Press: Old Westbury, NY

Lerner, Gerda (1972) On the teaching and organization of feminist studies *Female Studies* **5**: 34-37

Levin, Tobe (1979) Women's studies in West Germany: community vs academy *Women's Studies Newsletter* **7** 1: 20-22

Mack, Joanna (1974) Women's studies in Cambridge *The New Era* **55** 6: 162-64

Mazumdar, Vina (1980) Women's studies in India Paper delivered at NGO Forum Women's Studies International, Copenhagen

McIntosh, Peggy (1982) Transformations within the academy: reconstructing the liberal arts curriculum Paper presented at NWSA meetings: Arcata, California

McIntosh, Peggy and Minnich, Elizabeth K (in press) Varieties of women's studies forthcoming in *Women's Studies International Forum*

Metz-Göckel, Sigrid *ed* (1979) *Frauenstudium Zur Alternativen Wissenschaftsaneignung von Frauen* AHD: Hamburg

Metz-Göckel, Sigrid (1982) The women's movement and WS in Germany Paper presented to the Women's Caucus, Department of German, University of California, September

Metz-Göckel, Sigrid (1983) Feministische Wissenschaft und Frauenstudien in und ausserhalb der Bildungs- und Wissenschafts-einrichtungen in der BRD forthcoming in *Psychologie Heute*

Metz-Göckel, Sigrid and Sauter-Bailliet, Theresia (1982) Frauenstudien in den USA und die Frauenbildungsbewegung in der Bundesrepublik *in* Duelli Klein, Nerad and Metz-Göckel

Mies, Maria (1978) Methodische Postulate zur Frauenforschung — dargestellt am Beispiel der Gewalt gegen Frauen *Beiträge zur Feministischen Theorie und Praxis* 1 1: 41-63

Minnich, Elizabeth K (1982) A devastating conceptual error: how can we *not* be feminist scholars? *Change Magazine* 14 3: 7-9

Müller, Petra (1979) Frauenforschung und Frauenstudien — women's studies: Ein Beispiel für die Bundesrepublik? *in* Metz-Göckel: 133-49

Murgatroyd, Linda (1979) Notes on the development of women's studies. New questions, new discipline? Unpublished paper delivered at WRRC seminar: London

Oakley, Ann (1981) *Subject Women* Martin Robertson: Oxford

O'Connor Blumhagen, Johnson, Kathleen and Johnson, Walter *eds* (1978) *Women's Studies* Greenwood Press: Westport, Connecticut

Open University Course Team (1982) *The Changing Experience of Women* Martin Robertson: Oxford

Planungsgruppe für Frauenstudien Berlin *eds* (1980) *Ziele, Inhalte und Institutionalisierung von Frauenstudien und Frauenforschung* Free University: Berlin

Reason, Peter and Rowan, John (1981) *Human Inquiry* Wiley: London

Register, Cheri (1979) Brief a-mazing movements *Women's Studies Newsletter* 7 4: 7-10

Reinharz, Shulamit (1981) Experiential Analysis: a contribution to feminist research *in* Bowles and Duelli Klein: 68-97

Rendel, Margherita (1974) Primary sources of oppression *Times Educational Supplement* 29 March

Rendel, Margherita (1980) Women and women's studies in higher education in Britain *in* Planungsgruppe für Frauenstudien Berlin: 59-63

Rendel, Margherita (1982) *Women's Studies — The Study of Women* UNESCO: Paris

Reuben, Elaine (1978) In defiance of the evidence: notes on feminist scholarship *Women's Studies International Quarterly* 1 3: 215-18

Rich, Adrienne (1980) *On Lies, Secrets and Silence* Norton and Co: New York

Roberts, Joan (1976) *Beyond Intellectual Sexism* David McKay: New York

Rossi, Alice and Calderwood, Ann *eds* (1973) *Academic Women on the Move* Russell Sage: New York

Ruth, Sheila *ed* (1980) *Issues in Feminism: A First Course on Women's Studies* Houghton Mifflin: New York

Salzmann-Webb, Marilyn (1972) Feminist studies: frill or necessity? *Female Studies* 5: 64-76

Salper, Roberta (1971) The theory and practice of women's studies *Edcentrics* 3 7: 4-8

Sauter-Bailliet, Theresia (1980) Vom Studium für Frauen zu Frauenstudien: Women's studies in den USA *Englisch Amerikanische Studien* 2 2: 168-82

Schöpp-Schilling, Hanna Beate (1979) Women's studies, women's research and women's research centres: recent developments in the USA and the FRG *Women's Studies International Quarterly* 2 1: 103-16

Schöpp-Schilling, Hanna Beate (1982) Frauenforschung in den USA und der Bundesrepublik *Mitteilungsblatt des Deutschen Akademikerinnenbundes* 61: 8-22

Slavin Schramm, Sarah (1978) Women's studies: its focus, idea power and promise *in* O'Connor Blumhagen and Johnson: 3-12

Spanier, Bonnie (1982) Toward a balanced curriculum: the study of women at Wheaton College *Change Magazine* 14 3: 31-37

Spender, Dale (1978) Notes on the organisation of women's studies *Women's Studies International Quarterly* 1 3: 255-76

Spender, Dale *ed* (1981) *Men's Studies Modified: The Impact of Feminism on the Academic Disciplines* Pergamon: Oxford and New York

Staton, Pat (1980) A decade of women's studies *Canadian Women's Studies* 2 4: 58-9

Steady, Filomela (1980) The need for intra- and inter-national feminist networks. Talk delivered at Women's Studies Forum at Copenhagen, July

Stimpson, Catharine (1973) What matter mind: a theory about the practice of women's studies *Women's Studies* 1: 293-314

Stimpson, Catharine (1978) Women's studies: an overview *Ann Arbor Papers in Women's Studies* University of Michigan Women's Studies Program, Ann Arbor: 14-26

Thorne, Barrie (1978) Contradictions, and a glimpse of utopia: daily life in a university women's studies program *Women's Studies International Quarterly* 1 2: 201-206

Tobias, Sheila (1978) Women's studies: its origins, its organisation, and its prospects *Women's Studies International Quarterly* 1 1: 85-97

Westkott, Marcia (1981) Women's studies as a strategy for change: between criticism and vision *in* Bowles and Duelli Klein

Whiting, Pat (1974) A course in feminist studies *Women Speaking* October-December 1974: 15-16

Zangrando, Joanna (1975) Women's studies in the United States: approaching reality *American Studies International* 14 1: 15-36

Part 5:
Bibliography and biographical notes

Bibliography

Sheila Riddell

The bibliography is divided into four sections; The first covers published chapters and articles in books, including whole books and booklets, by individual authors, the second lists publications (books and documents) issued by official and corporate bodies, and the third includes articles, periodicals and working papers. These three sections include nearly all of the references cited in individual chapters; unpublished manuscripts and a few specialized references have been omitted.

In section IV a number of key references from sections I, II and III and some other important recent publications have been annotated. An asterisk (*) beside a particular entry in the first three parts of the bibliography indicates that it is among those annotated in section IV.

Section I: Books and pamphlets

Abdel Kader, S (1973) *A Report on the Status of Egyptian Women 1900-1973* The American University in Cairo Social Research Center: Cairo

Abu Zayd, H (1970) *The Education of Women in the UAR during the 19th and 20th Centuries* National Commission for United Nations Educational Scientific and Cultural Organization: Cairo

Acker, S (1982) Women and education *in* Hartnett (1982)

Acker, S (1983) Women and teaching: a semi-detached sociology of a semi-profession *in* Walker and Barton (1983)

Acker, S and Warren Piper, D *eds* (in press) *Is Higher Education Fair to Women?* Society for Research into Higher Education: Guildford

Acker, S (in press) Women and higher education: what's the problem? *in* Acker and Warren Piper (in press)

Ahmad, J (1960) *The Intellectual Origins of Egyptian Nationalism* Oxford University Press: London

Allen, W R (1981) Correlates of Black student adjustment, achievement and aspirations at a predominantly white southern university *in* Thomas (1981a)

Altbach, P G, Arnove, R A and Kelly, G P *eds* (1982) *Comparative Education* Macmillan: New York

Anderson, C A and Bowman, M J *eds* (1965) *Education and Economic Development* Frank Cass and Company: London

Anyon, J (1983) Intersections of gender and class: accommodation and resistance by working-class and affluent females to contradictory sex-role ideologies *in* Walker and Barton (1983)

Aplin, S and Pugh, G (1983) *Preschool Home Visiting* National Children's Bureau: London

Apple, M ed (1982) *Cultural and Economic Reproduction in Education* Routledge and Kegan Paul: London

Arce, C H (1978) Minorities in higher education: recent advances and current problems *in* Smith (1978)

*Archer, J and Lloyd, B (1982) *Sex and Gender* Penguin: Harmondsworth

Ashton, D and Maguire, M (1980) Young women in the labour market: stability and change *in* Deem (1980)

Astin, A (1975) *Preventing Students from Dropping Out* Jossey-Bass: San Francisco, California

Astin, A (1978) *Four Critical Years* Jossey-Bass: San Francisco, California

Astin, A *et al* (1981) *The American Freshman: National Norms for Fall 1981* Higher Education Research Institute and American Council on Education: Los Angeles, California

Astin, A (1982a) *The American Freshman, 1966-1981: Some Implications for Educational Policy and Practice* National Commission on Excellence in Education, Department of Education: Washington, DC

Astin, A (1982b) *Final Report of the Commission on the Higher Education of Minorities* Higher Education Research Institute Inc: Los Angeles, California

Atkinson, D, Dallin, A and Lapidus, G eds (1977) *Women in Russia* Stanford University Press: Stanford, California

Atkinson, J M and Drew, P (1979) *Order in Court: The Organisation of Verbal Interaction in Judicial Settings* MacMillan: London

Atkinson, J M and Heritage, J C (in press) Conversation analysis *in* Atkinson and Heritage (in press)

Atkinson, J M and Heritage, J C eds (in press) *Structures of Social Action* Cambridge University Press: Cambridge

Austin, J L (1976) How to do things with words *in* Urmson and Sbisà (1976)

Bailey, R L (1978) *Minority Admissions* D C Heath and Company: Lexington, Massachusetts

Baker, R (1978) *Egypt's Uncertain Revolution under Nasser and Sadat* Harvard University Press: Cambridge, Massachusetts

Balbo, L and Ergas, Y (1982) *Women's Studies in Italy* The Feminist Press: Old Westbury, New York

Banks, O (1981) *Faces of Feminism* Martin Robertson: Oxford

Banks, O (1982) Sociology of education *in* Cohen *et al* (1982)

Barker, D L and Allen, S eds (1976) *Dependence and Exploitation in Work and Marriage* Longman: London

Barrett, M *et al* eds (1979) *Ideology and Cultural Reproduction* Croom Helm: London

Barrett, M (1980) *Women's Oppression Today: Problems in Marxist Feminist Analysis* Verso: London

Barron, R D and Norris, G M (1976) Sexual divisions and the dual labour market *in* Barker and Allen (1976)

Barton, L and Meighan, R eds (1979) *Schools, Pupils and Deviance* Nafferton: Driffield

Barton, L and Walker, S eds (1981) *Schools, Teachers and Teaching* Falmer: Lewes

Beardsley, E (1977) Traits and genderization *in* Vetterling-Braggin *et al* (1977)

*Beck, L and Keddie, N eds (1978) *Women in the Muslim World* Harvard University Press: Cambridge, Massachusetts

Beecher, C (1977) *A Treatise on Domestic Economy* Schocken: New York

Beechey, V (1982) The sexual division of labour and the labour process: a critical assessment of Braverman *in* Wood (1982)

Bell, D A (1980) *Race, Racism and American Law* Little, Brown and Company: Boston, Massachusetts

Berberich, L (1979) *Non-sexist Multi-cultural Education? A Bibliography of Non-sexist Inter-cultural Books K-6* Centre for Non-sexist Resources: Sydney

Bernard, A and Gayfer, M (1983) *Women Hold Up More Than Half the Sky: A Third World Perspective on Women and Non-formal Education for Development* International Council for Adult Education: Toronto

Bernard, J (1972) *The Sex Game* Atheneum: New York

Berner, B (1981) *Teknikens värld. Teknisk förändring och ingenjörsarbete i svensk industri* Arkiv: Lund

Berzigan, B and Fernea, E (1978) *Muslim Women Speak* University of Texas Press: Austin, Texas

Bissert, N (1974) *Les Inégaux ou la Sélection Universitaire* PUF: Paris

Bisseret, N (1979) *Education, Class Language and Ideology* Routledge and Kegan Paul: London

Blackstone, T and Lodge, P (1982) *Educational Policy and Educational Inequality* Martin Robertson: London

Blake, J H (1982) *Demographic Change and Curriculum: 'New' Students in Higher Education* National Commission on Excellence in Education Department of Education: Washington, DC

*Bock, U, Braszeit, A and Schmerl, C (1983) *Frauen im Wissenschaftsbetrieb* Beltz Verlag: Weinheim

Bloom, L Z, Coborn, K and Pearlman, J (1975) *The New Assertive Woman* Delacourte: New York

Boman, A (1983) *Omsorg och solidaritet − ohållbara argument?* Arbetslivscentrum: Stockholm

Bone, A (1980) *The Effect on Women's Opportunities of Teacher Training Cuts* Equal Opportunities Commission: London

Bordia, A (1982) *Planning and Administration of National Literacy Programs: Indian Experience* International Institute of Educational Planning, United Nations Educational, Scientific and Cultural Organization: Paris

Boserup, E (1969) *Women's Role in Economic Development* St Martin's Press: New York

Bourdieu, P (1976) The school as a conservative force *in* Dale *et al* (1976)

Bourdieu, P (1977) Cultural reproduction and social reproduction *in* Karabel and Halsey (1977)

Bourdieu, P and Passeron, J-P (1977) *Reproduction in Education, Society and Culture* Sage: London

Bowles, F (1964) *Access to Higher Education Vol 1* United Nations Educational Scientific and Cultural Organization: Paris (quoted in UNESCO, 1968: 39-40)

Bowles, G (1980) Is women's studies an academic discipline? *in* Bowles and Duelli Klein *eds* (1980)

Bowles, G and Duelli Klein, R *eds* (1980) *Theories of Women's Studies* I and II Women's Studies Program University of California: Berkeley

Bowles, G and Duelli Klein, R (1983) Introduction: theories of women's studies and the autonomy/integration debate *in* Bowles and Duelli Klein (1983)

Bowles, G and Duelli Klein, R *eds* (1983) *Theories of Women's Studies* Routledge and Kegan Paul: London

Bowles, S and Gintis, H (1976) *Schooling in Capitalist America* Routledge and Kegan Paul: London

Bowman, M J and Anderson, C A (1982) The participation of women in education in the Third World *in* Kelly and Elliott (1982)

Boyce, G F (1967) *Historic Hastings* Hastings County Council: Belleville, Ontario

Bradshaw, J, Davies, W and de Wolfe, P (1981) *Women's Studies Courses in the UK* Women's Research and Resources Centre: London

Branson, J and Miller, D B (1979) *Class, Sex and Education in Capitalist Society: Culture, Ideology and the Reproduction of Inequality in Australia* Sorrett: Melbourne

Braverman, H (1974) *Labour and Monopoly Capital* Monthly Review Press: New York

Brend, R M (1975) Male-female intonation patterns in American English *in* Thorne and Henlev (1975)

Brighton Women and Science Group (1980) *Alice Through the Microscope: The Power of Science Over Women's Lives* Virago: London

Bristol Women's Studies Group (1979) *Half the Sky: An Introduction to Women's Studies* Virago: London

Brooks Gardner, C (1980) Street remarks, address rights and the urban female *in* Zimmerman and West (1980)

Brophy, J and Good, T (1974) *Teacher-Student Relationships* Holt Rinehart and Winston: New York

Brown, P and Jordanova, L (1981) Oppressive dichotomies: the nature/culture debate *in* Cambridge Women's Studies Group (1981)

Brumbaugh, R S and Lawrence, N M (1963) *Philosophers on Education: Six Essays on the Foundation of Western Thought* Houghton Mifflin: Boston

Brunswick Secondary Education Committee (BRUSEC) (1982-3) *Equal Opportunity Project Annual Report* Melbourne

Bull, D (1980) *What Price 'Free' Education?* Poverty Pamphlet 48 Child Poverty Action Group: London

Bull, D and Wilding, P *eds* (1983) *Thatcherism and the Poor* Poverty Pamphlet 59 Child Poverty Action Group: London

Burnhill, P and McPherson, A (in press) Careers and gender: the expectations of able Scottish school leavers in 1971 and 1981 *in* Acker and Warren Piper (in press)

Byrne, E (1978) *Women and Education* Tavistock Publications: London

Cahn, S M *ed* (1970) *The Philosophical Foundations of Education* Harper and Row: New York

Callaway, H (1981) Women's perspectives: research as re-vision *in* Reason and Rowan (1981): 457-71

Cambridge Women's Studies Group (1981) *Women in Society* Virago: London

Centre for Women's Development Studies (1983) *Women's Work and Employment: Struggle for a Policy: Selections from Indian Documents* Centre for Women's Development Studies: Delhi

Chabaud, J (1970) *The Education and Advancement of Women* United Nations Educational Scientific and Cultural Organization: Paris

Chesler, P (1971) Marriage and psychotherapy *in* Radical Therapist Collective (1971)

Chetwynd, J and Hartnett, O *eds* (1978) *The Sex Role System* Routledge and Kegan Paul: London

*Chodorow, N (1978) *The Reproduction of Mothering* University of California Press: Berkeley

Chodorow, N (1979) Mothering, male dominance and capitalism *in* Eisenstein (1979)

Clark, B R (1960) *The Open Door College: A Case Study* McGraw Hill: New York, New York

Clark, L (1976) The rights of women: the theory and practice of the ideology of male supremacy *in* Shea and King-Farlow (1976)

Clarke-Stewart, A (1982) *Day Care* Fontana: London

Clarricoates, K (1980) The importance of being Ernest . . . Emma . . . Tom . . . Jane. The perception and categorization of gender conformity and gender deviation in primary schools *in* Deem (1980)

Cohen, L *et al eds* (1982) *Educational Research and Development in Britain 1970-1980* NFER/Nelson: Windsor

Coleman, J (1968) The concept of equality of educational opportunity *in* Open University (1971)

Coleman, J *ed* (1969) *Education and Political Development* Princeton University Press: Princeton, New Jersey

Comber, L C and Keeves, J P (1973) *Science Education in Nineteen Countries* Almqvist and Wiksell: Stockholm

Comer, L (1974) *Wedlocked Women* Feminist Books: Leeds

*Connell, R W, Ashenden, D J, Kessler, S and Dowsett, G W (1982) *Making the Difference: Schools, Families and Social Divisions* George Allen and Unwin: Sydney

*Coote, A and Campbell, B (1982) *Sweet Freedom: the Struggle for Women's Liberation* Picador: London

Coyner, S (1980) Women's Studies as an academic discipline: why and how to do it *in* Bowles and Duelli Klein (1980)

Croll, E (1975) *Women in Post Mao China* Zed Press: London

Cross, P H and Astin, H S (1981) Factors affecting Black students' persistence in college *in* Thomas (1981a)

Cruickshank, M (1970) *History of the Training of Teachers in Scotland* University of London Press: London

Cruickshank, M ed (1982) *Lesbian Studies Present and Future* The Feminist Press: Old Westbury, New York

CSP Ltd (1980) *Information Technology in the Office: The Impact on Women's Jobs* Equal Opportunities Commission: Manchester

Dale, R, Esland, G, Fergusson, R and MacDonald, M eds (1981) *Education and the State: Politics, Patriarchy and Practice* 2 Falmer: Lewes

Dale, R *et al* eds (1976) *Schooling and Capitalism* Routledge and Kegal Paul: London

Dale, R *et al* eds (1981) *Schooling and the National Interest* Falmer Press: Montreal

Damon, W (1977) *The Social World of the Child* Jossey-Bass: San Francisco

Daniel, N (1960) *Islam and the West: The Making of an Image* University Press: Edinburgh

Danylewycz, M (1983) Sexes et classes sociales dans l'enseignement: le cas de Montréal à la fin du 19e siècle *in* Fahmy-Eid and Dumont eds (1983)

David, M E (1980) *The State, the Family and Education* Routledge and Kegan Paul: London

Davies, L (1979) Deadlier than the male? Girls' conformity and deviance in school *in* Barton and Meighan (1979)

Davies, L (1983) Gender, resistance and power *in* Walker and Barton (1983)

de Beauvoir, S (1949 and 1972) *The Second Sex* Penguin: Harmondsworth

*Deble, I (1980) *The School Education of Girls* United Nations Educational Scientific and Cultural Organization: Paris

Deem, R (1978) *Women and Schooling* Routledge and Kegan Paul: London

*Deem, R ed (1980) *Schooling for Women's Work* Routledge and Kegan Paul: London

Delamont, S (1980a) *The Sociology of Women* Allen and Unwin: London

Delamont, S (1980b) *Sex Roles and the School* Methuen: London

Delamont, S (1983) The conservative school? Sex roles at home, at work and at school *in* Walker and Barton (1983)

Devos, G ed (1976) *Responses to Change* D Van Nostrand and Company: New York

De Wolff, P and Harnqvist, K (1961) Reserves of ability: size and distribution *in* Halsey (1961)

Dittmar, N (1976) *Socio-linguistics: A Critical Survey of Theory and Application* Arnold: London

Dixson, M (1976) *The Real Matilda: Women and Identity in Australia 1788-1975* Penguin: Ringwood

Dressler, W U ed (1977) *Current Trends in Textlinguistics* de Gruyter: Berlin

Dubois, B L and Crouch, I eds (1976) *The Sociology of the Languages of American Women* PISE Papers IV Trinity University: San Antonio, Texas

Duelli Klein, R (1980) How to do what we want to do: thoughts about feminist methodology *in* Bowles and Duelli Klein (1980): 48-64

Duelli Klein, R (in press) Women's studies: an intellectual necessity *in* Acker and Warren Piper (in press)

Duelli Klein, R, Nerad, M and Metz-Göckel, S eds (1982) *Feministische Wissenschaft und Frauenstudium* AHD: Hamburg
Dunn, J and Kendrick, J (1983) *Siblings* Cambridge University Press: Cambridge
Dweck, C S (1978) Achievement *in* Lamb (1978)

Edwards, R (1975) *Labour Market Segmentation* Lexington: Massachusetts
Eichenbaum, L and Orbach, S (1982) *Inside Out: Outside In* Penguin: Harmondsworth
Eickleman, D (1981) *The Middle East: An Anthropological Approach* Prentice Hall Inc: Englewood Cliffs, New Jersey
Eisenstein, Z ed (1979) *Capitalist Patriarchy and the Case for Socialist Feminism* Monthly Review Press: New York
Elshtain, J B (1981) *Public Man, Private Woman* Martin Robertson: Oxford
Engels, F (1970) *Origin of the Family, Private Property and the State in* Marx and Engels (1970)
Epstein Jayaratne, T (1983) The value of quantitative methodology for feminist research *in* Bowles and Duelli Klein (1983)
Evans, M (1982) *The Woman Question: Readings on the Subordination of Women* Fontana Paperbacks: London
Evans, T D (1983) Gender, class and education: a teaching bibliography of Australian and New Zealand studies *in* Walker and Barton (1983)

Fahmy-Eid, N and Dumont, M eds (1983) *Maîtresses de Maison, Maîtresses d'ecole: Femmes, Famille et Education dans l'Histoire du Québec* Boreal Express: Montréal
Farb, P (1973) *Word Play: What Happens when People Talk* Knopf: New York
Fennema, E (1980) Sex-related differences in mathematics achievement: where and why *in* Fox *et al* (1980)
Figueroa, P (1976) Values and academic achievement among high school boys in Kingston, Jamaica *in* Figueroa and Persaud (1976)
Figueroa, P and Persaud, O eds (1976) *Sociology of Education — A Caribbean Reader* Oxford University Press: London
Findlay, I R (1973) *Education in Scotland* David and Charles: Newton Abbot, England; Archon Books: Hamden, Connecticut
Firestone, S (1970) *The Dialectic of Sex* Morrow: New York
Forester, T ed (1980) *The Microelectronics Revolution* Basil Blackwell: Oxford
Foster, P (1965) The vocational school fallacy in development planning *in* Anderson and Bowman (1965)
Fox, L H, Brody, L and Tobin, D eds (1980) *Women and the Mathematical Mystique* Johns Hopkins University Press: Baltimore
Freeman, J ed (1979) *Women: A Feminist Perspective* Mayfield: Palo Alto
French, D (1968) *High Button Bootstraps: Federation of Women Teachers' Associations of Ontario, 1918-1968* The Ryerson Press: Toronto
French, P and MacLure, M eds (1981) *Adult-Child Conversation* Croom Helm: London
Freud, S (1916-17) *Introductory Lectures on Psycho-Analysis* Penguin: Harmondsworth
Freud, S (1924) The dissolution of the Oedipus Complex *in On Sexuality* (1977) Penguin: Harmondsworth
Freud, S (1931) Female sexuality *in On Sexuality* (1977) Penguin: Harmondsworth
Freud, S (1977) *On Sexuality* Penguin: Harmondsworth
Friedan, B (1963 and 1965) *The Feminine Mystique* Penguin: Harmondsworth
Friedman, R C, Richart, R M and Van de Wiele, R L eds (1974) *Sex Differences in Behaviour* Wiley: New York
Fuller, M (1980) Black girls in a London comprehensive school *in* Deem (1980)

Galton, M (1981) Differential treatment of boy and girl pupils during science lessons *in* Kelly, A (1981)

Galton, M, Simon, B and Croll, S (1980) *Inside the Primary Classroom* Routledge and Kegan Paul: London

Game, A and Pringle, R (1983) *Gender at Work* Allen and Unwin: Sydney

Garfinkel, H (1967) *Studies in Ethnomethodology* Prentice Hall: Englewood Cliffs, New Jersey

*Giele, J and Smock, A eds (1977) *Women: Roles and Status in Eight Countries* John Wiley and Sons: New York

Giles, H and Powesland, P (1975) *Speech Style and Social Evaluation* Academic Press: London

Giles, H, Bouris, R Y and Davies, A (1975) Prestige speech styles: the imposed norm and inherent value hypotheses *in* McCormack and Wurm (1975)

Gilligan, C (1982) *In a Different Voice: Psychological Theory and Women's Development* Harvard University Press: Cambridge, Massachusetts

Girls' Own (1981) Campaign to Encourage Non-Sexist Education (CENSE) and Equal Opportunities Resources Centre (EORC): Melbourne

Girls into Science and Technology (GIST) (1982) *Options and Careers* Manchester Polytechnic: Manchester

Girls into Science and Technology (GIST) *Introductory Booklet*

Glendenning, C (1983) School meals: privatisation, stigma and local 'autonomy' *in* Bull and Wilding (1983)

Glenn, E N and Feldberg, R L (1979) Proletarianising clerical work: technology and organizational work in the office *in* Zimbalist (1979)

Goldberg, S (1977) *The Inevitability of Patriarchy* Temple Smith: London

Göranzon, B *et al* (1982) *Job Design and Automation in Sweden* Center for Working Life: Sweden

Granstam, I (1981) *Kvinnor och teknisk utbildning* Institute of Technology: Linköping

Granstam, I (1982) *Barn och teknik* Linköping University, Linköping

Gray, J A (1981) A biological basis for the sex differences in achievement in science? *in* Kelly (1981)

Griffiths, D and Saraga, E (1979) Sex differences and cognitive abilities: a sterile field of enquiry? *in* Hartnett, Boden and Fuller (1979)

Griffiths, J and Griffiths, P (1979) *Cuba: the Second Decade* Writers and Readers: London

Halsey, A H ed (1961) *Ability and Educational Opportunity* Organization for Economic Co-operation and Development: Paris

Halsey, A H, Floud, J and Anderson, C A eds (1961) *Education, Economy and Society* The Free Press: New York

Hamilton, C V (1978) Public responsibility or equality and justice *in* Smith (1978)

Hargreaves, D H (1981) Schooling for delinquency *in* Barton and Walker (1981)

Hartman, M (1976) A descriptive study of the language of men and women born in Maine around 1900 as it reflects the Lakoff hypothesis *in* Dubois and Crouch (1976)

Hartmann, H (1979) Capitalism, patriarchy and job segregation by sex *in* Eisenstein (1979)

Hartnett, A ed (1982) *The Social Sciences in Educational Studies* Heinemann: London

Hartnett, O and Rendel, M eds (1975) *Women's Studies in the UK* London Seminars: London

Hartnett, O *et al eds* (1979) *Sex Role Stereotyping* Tavistock: London

Healy, P and Ryan, P (1975) Sex stereotyping in children's books *in* Mercer (1975)

Hebsur, R K *et al* (1981) *National Adult Education Program in Maharashtra: An Evaluation* Tata Institute of Social Sciences: Bombay

Hedberg, B, Mehlmann, M, Parmsund, M, Stadler, B and Stjernberg, T (1982) *Bra affärer med datorer?* Arbetslivscentrum: Stockholm

Hedberg, B and Mehlmann, M (1982) *Dator i bank* Arbetslivscentrum: Stockholm

Heyworth-Dunne, J (1968) *An Introduction to the History of Education in Modern Egypt* Frank Cass and Company: London

Hill, S T *Participation of Black Students in Higher Education: A Statistical Profile from 1970-71 to 1980-81* National Center for Education Statistics Department of Education: Washington, DC

Holmes, B and Scanlon, D G eds (1971) *World Yearbook of Education 1971/2: Higher Education in a Changing World* Evans: London

Holzkamp, C and Steppke, G (1979) Lernen, lieben, leiden . . . über unsere Hoffnungen, Ettäuschungen and Lernprozesse als Dozentinnen in Frauenseminaren *in* Metz-Göckel (1979): 81-98

Hooper, R (1983) *The Computer as a Medium for Distance Education in* Megarry *et al* (1983)

Howe, F (1977) *Seven Years Later: Women's Studies Programs in 1976* Report of the National Advisory Council on Women's Educational Programs: Washington

Howe, F and Ahlum, C (1973) Women's studies and social change *in* Rossi and Calderwood (1973): 393-423

Hudson, R A (1980) *Socio-Linguistics* Cambridge University Press: Cambridge

Hull, G, Scott, P and Smith, B eds (1982) *All the Women Are White, All the Blacks Are Men, But Some of Us Are Brave: Black Women's Studies* The Feminist Press: Old Westbury, New York

Hunt, P (1980) *Gender and Class Consciousness* MacMillan: London

Huws, U (1982) *Your Job in the Eighties. A Woman's Guide to New Technology* Pluto Press: London

Hyde, G (1978) *Education in Modern Egypt: Ideals and Realities* Routledge and Kegan Paul: London

Ibrahim, S (1982) *The New Arab Social Order: A Study of the Social Impact of Oil Wealth* Croom Helm: London

Institute of Social Studies Trust (in press) *Adult Education for Women:* Vikas

It Kit (no date) Victorian Council of School Organisations (VICCSO) and Victorian Federation of State Schools Parents Clubs (VFSSPC): Melbourne

Jacklin, C N (1979) Epilogue *in* Wittig and Petersen (1974)

Jackson, B and Marsden, D (1962) *Education and the Working Class* Routledge and Kegan Paul: London

Jancar, B W (1981) *Women under Communism* Johns Hopkins: Baltimore

Jespersen, O (1922) *Language: Its Nature, Development and Origin* Allen and Unwin: London

Johns-Lewis, C ed (in press) *Intonation and Discourse* Croom Helm: London

Jones, M T (1982) Educating girls in Tunisia: issues generated by the drive for universal enrollment *in* Kelly and Elliott (1982)

Kamerman, S and Kahn, A (1981) *Child Care and Working Parents* Columbia University Press: New York

Karabel, J and Halsey, A H eds (1977) *Power and Ideology in Education* Oxford University Press: New York

Kellas, J G (1980) *Modern Scotland* Allen and Unwin: London

Kelly, A (1981) Science achievement as an aspect of sex roles *in* Kelly (1981)

*Kelly, A ed (1981) *The Missing Half: Girls and Science Education* Manchester University Press: Manchester

*Kelly, G P and Elliott, C M eds (1982) *Women's Education in the Third World: Comparative Perspectives* State University of New York Press: Albany

Kelly, G P and Nihlen, A (1982) Schooling and the reproduction of patriarchy: unequal workloads, unequal rewards *in* Apple (1982)

Kelsall, R K, Poole, A and Kuhn, A (1972) *Graduates: The Sociology of an Elite* Methuen: London

Kerr, M (1969) Egypt *in* Coleman (1969)

Kiger, J A ed (1972) *The Biology of Behaviour* Oregon University Press: Corvallis, Oregon

Kline, S ed (1984 in press) *Achieving Sex Equity through Education* The John Hopkins University Press: Baltimore, Maryland

Kohlberg, L (1966) A cognitive-developmental analysis of children's sex-role concepts and attitudes *in* Maccoby (1966)

Kohlberg, L and Ullian, D (1974) Stages in the developmet of psychosexual concepts and attitudes *in* Friedman *et al* (1974)

Konstantinovskii, D L (1977) *Dinamika Professionalnykh Orientatsii Molodezhi Sibiri* Izdatelstvo 'Nauka': Novosibirsk

Koshy, [J A *et al* (1976) *The Mahbubnagar Experiment: Non-formal Education for Rural Women* Council for Social Development: New Delhi

Kotlyar, A E (1973) Metodologicheskie voprosy izuchenia struktury zanyatosti: popolu v territorialnom razreze *in* Maikov (1973)

Kotlyar, A E and Turchaninova, S Ya (1973) *Zaniatost' zbenshchin v Proizvodstve* Statistika: Moscow

Kotwal, M (1975) Inequalities in the distribution of education between countries, sexes, generations and individuals *in* Organization for Economic Cooperation and Development (1975)

Kramer, C (1975) Women's speech: separate but unequal? *in* Thorne and Henley (1975)

Kuhn, A and Wolpe, A M *eds* (1978) *Feminism and Materialism* Routledge and Kegan Paul: London

Labarrère-Paulé, A (1965) *Les Instituteurs Laiques au Canada Français, 1836-1900* Les Presses de l'Université de Laval: Québec

Labov, W (1966) *The Social Stratification of Speech in New York City* Centre for Applied Linguistics: Washington, DC

Labov, W (1972) *Sociolinguistic Patterns* University of Pennsylvania Press: Philadelphia

Lakoff, R (1975) *Language and Woman's Place* Harper and Row: New York

Lamb, M E ed (1978) *Social and Personality Development* Holt, Rinehart and Winston: New York

Lapidus, G (1978) *Women in Soviet Society* University of California Press: Berkeley, California

*Lapidus, G W ed (1982) *Women, Work and Family in the Soviet Union* M E Sharpe: Armonk, New York

Lenin, V (1970) *On the Emancipation of Women* Progress: Moscow

Leo-Rhynie, E A and Hamilton, M A (1982) Some data on professional women in the Caribbean *in* Women and Development Unit (1982)

Levine, L and Crockett, H J Jr (1966) Speech variation in a Piedmont community: postvocalic r *in* Lieberson (1966)

Levy, J (1972) Lateral specialization of the human brain: behavioural manifestations and possibly evolutionary basis *in* Kiger (1972)

Levy, R (1965) *The Social Structure of Islam* The University Press: Cambridge

Lewis,\M and Brooks-Gun, J (1979) *Social Cognition and the Acquisition of Self* Plenum: New York

Lewis S *et al* (in press) Achieving sex equity for minority women *in* Kline (in press)

Liegle, L (1970) *The Family's Role in Soviet Education* Springer;: New York

Lightfoot, S L (1978) *Worlds Apart* Basic Books: New York

Lindsay, B ed (1980 and 1983) *Comparative Perspectives of Third World Women: the Impact of Race, Sex and Class* Praeger: New York

Llewellyn, M (1980) Studying girls at school: the implications of confusion *in* Deem (1980)

Lloyd, B and Archer, J eds (1976) *Exploring Sex Differences* Academic Press: London

Lobban, G (1978) The influence of the school on sex-role stereotyping *in* Chetwynd and Hartnett (1978)

Local, J K (in press) Patterns and problems in a study of Tyneside intonation *in* Johns-Lewis (in press)

Lutfi al Sayyed, A (1968) The beginnings of modernization among the rectors of al Azhar *in* Polk and Chambers (1968)

Macauley, C (1974) *Letters on Education* Luria ed Garland: New York

Maccoby, E E ed (1966) *The Development of Sex Differences* Stanford University Press: Stanford

*Maccoby, E E and Jacklin, C N (1974) *The Psychology of Sex Differences* Stanford University Press: Stanford

*McAuley, A (1981) *Women's Work and Wages in the Soviet Union* George Allen and Unwin: London

MacCormack, C (1980) Nature, culture and gender: a critique *in* MacCormack and Strathern (1980)

MacCormack, C and Strathern, M eds (1980) *Nature, Culture and Gender* Cambridge University Press: Cambridge

MacCormack, W C and Wurm, S eds (1975) *Language in Anthropology IV: Language in Many Ways* Mouton: The Hague

MacDonald, M (1980) Socio-cultural reproduction and women's education *in* Deem (1980)

*MacDonald, M (1981a) *Class, Gender and Education* Open University Course E 353, Block 4, Units 10-11 The Open University Press: Milton Keynes

MacDonald, M (1981b) Schooling and the reproduction of class and gender relations *in* Dale (1981)

McSweeney, B G and Freedman, M (1982) Lack of time as an obstacle to women's education: the case of Upper Volta *in* Kelly and Elliott (1982)

Maikov, A Z ed (1973) *Problemy Ratsionalnogo Ispalzovania Trudovykh Resursov:* Moscow

*Malos, E ed (1980) *The Politics of Housework* Allison and Busby: London

Martin, J (1978) *The Migrant Presence* Allen and Unwin: Sydney

Martin, J R (1982b) Sex equality and education: a case study *in* Vetterling-Braggin (1982)

Martin, J R (in press) *Ideals of the Educated Woman* Rowman and Allenheld: Totowa, New Jersey

Marx, K and Engels, F (1970) *Selected Works* Lawrence and Wishart: London

Massell, G (1974) *The Surrogate Proletariat* Princeton University Press: Princeton

Mblinyi, M (1969) *The Education of Girls in Tanzania* University College: Dar Es Salaam

Mead, M (1950) *Male and Female* Penguin: Harmondsworth

Megarry, J (1981) *Sex, Gender and Education* Jordanhill College of Education: Glasgow

Megarry, J (1981) *Preface in* Megarry, Nisbet and Hoyle, 1981

Megarry, J, Nisbet, S and Hoyle, E eds (1981) *World Yearbook of Education 1981: Education of Minorities* Kogan Page: London

Megarry, J, Walker, D R F, Nisbet, S and Hoyle, E (1983) *World Yearbook of Education 1982/83: Computers and Education* Kogan Page: London

Meikle, H W ed (1947) *Scotland* Nelson: Edinburgh

*Mercer, J ed (1975) *The Other Half: Women in Australian Society* Penguin: Ringwood, Victoria

Mernissi, F (1975) *Beyond the Veil: Male and Female Dynamics in a Modern Muslim Society* Halstead Press: New York

Metz-Göckel, S ed (1979) *Frauenstudium zur Alternativen Wissenschaftsaneignung von Frauen* AHD: Hamburg

Metz-Göckel, S and Sauter-Bailliet, T (1982) Frauenstudien in den USA und die Frauenbildungsbewegung in der Bundesrepublik *in* Duelli Klein *et al* (1982)

Meyer, J W and Hannan, M T eds (1979) *National Development and the World System* University of Chicago Press: Chicago

Middleton, C (1974) Sexual inequality and stratification theory *in* Parkin (1974)

Migrant Girls Employment/Unemployment Conference Report (1982) Brunswick-Coburg Migrant Youth Action Group: Melbourne

Miller, C and Swift, K (1977) *Words and Women* Gollancz: London

Milroy, L (1980) *Language and Social Networks* Blackwell: Oxford

Mischel, W (1966) A social-learning view of sex differences in behaviour *in* Maccoby (1966)

Mitchell, J (1971) *Woman's Estate* Penguin: Harmondsworth

Mitchell, J (1974) *Psychoanalysis and Feminism* Allen Lane: London

Molyneux, M (1981) *State Policies and the Position of Women Workers in the People's Republic of Yemen: 1967-1977* ILO: Geneva

Moore, W and Wagstaff, L H (1974) *Black Educators in White Colleges* Jossey-Bass: San Francisco, California

Morgan, D (1981) Men, Masculinity and the process of sociological enquiry *in* Roberts (1981)

Moss, J (1982) *Towards Equality: Progress by Girls in Mathematics in Australian Secondary Schools* Australian Council for Educational Research: Melbourne

Müller, P (1979) Frauenforschung und Frauenstudien — women's studies: Ein Beispiel für die Bundesrepublik? *in* Metz-Göckel (1979)

Naik, C (1982) An action-research project on universal primary education: the plan and the process *in* Kelly and Elliott (1982)

Nash, P (1968) *Models of Man: Exploration in the Western Educational Tradition* Wiley: New York

Nash, P, Kazemias, A M and Perkinson, H J eds (1965) *The Educated Man: Studies in the History of Educational Thought* Wiley: New York

Nashabi, H (1979) Islam and the liberal tradition *in* Salem ed (1979)

National Union of Teachers (1980) *Promotion and the Woman Teacher* National Union of Teachers/Equal Opportunities Commission: Manchester

Nelson, C (1976) Social change and sexual identity in contemporary Egypt *in* Devos (1976)

Nelson, C and Koch, K eds (1977) *Law and Social Change in Contemporary Egypt* Cairo Papers in Social Science: Cairo

Nelson, C and Oleson, V (1977) Veil of illusion: critique of the concept equality in Western feminist thought *in* Nelson and Oleson (1977)

Newson, J and E (1964) *Patterns of Infant Care in an Urban Community* Penguin: Harmondsworth

Noble, D (1977) *America by Design* Knopf: New York

Nowaihi, M (1977) Changing the law on personal status within a liberal interpretation of the Sharica *in* Nelson and Koch (1977)

Oakley, A (1974a) *The Sociology of Housework* Martin Robertson: Oxford

Oakley, A (1974b) *Housewife* Penguin: Harmondsworth

Oakley, A (1981) *Subject Women* Martin Robertson: Oxford

O'Connor, B, Johnson, K and Johnson, W eds (1978) *Women's Studies* Greenwood Press: Westport, Connecticut

Olivas, M (1979) *The Dilemma of Access: Minorities in Two Year Colleges* Howard University Press: Washington, DC

Open University (1971) *School and Society* Routledge and Kegan Paul: London
Osborne, G (1968) *Change in Scottish Education* Longmans, Green and Co: London
Ottinger, C (1982) *Student Loan Options: What is Happening?* American Council on Education Policy Brief: Washington, DC

Parkin, F (1974) *The Social Analysis of Class Structure* Tavistock: London
Parsons, T (1942) Age and sex in the social structure of the United States *in* Parsons (1954)
Parsons, T (1954) *Essays in Sociological Theory* The Free Press: Glencoe, Illinois
Parsons, T (1961) The school class as a social system: some of its functions in American society *in* Halsey, Floud and Anderson (1961)
Parsons, T and Bales, R F eds (1955) *Family Socialization and Interaction Process* The Free Press: Glencoe, Illinois
Peddie, J R (1947) Education *in* Meikle (1947)
Perkins, T (1979) Rethinking stereotypes *in* Barrett (1979)
Pescatello, A (1976) *Power and Pawn: The Female in Iberian Families, Societies, and Cultures* Greenwood Press: Connecticut and London
Pestalozzi, T H (1885) *Leonard and Gertrude trans* E Channing Heath: Boston
Peterson, A D C (1971) *A Hundred Years of Education* Duckworth: London
Piaget, J (1932) *The Moral Judgement of the Child* Routledge and Kegan Paul: London
Planungsgruppe für Frauenstudien Berlin eds (1980) *Ziele, Inhalte und Instituional-isierung von Frauenstudien und Frauenforschung* Free University: Berlin
Plato (1974) *Republic trans* Hackett G M A Grube: Indianapolis
Polk, W and Chambers, R eds (1968) *Beginnings of Modernization in the Middle East* University of Chicago Press: Chicago
Price, K ed (1967) *Education and Philosophical Thought* Allyn and Bacon: Boston

Radical Therapist Collective eds (1971) *The Radical Therapist* Ballantyne: New York
Radwan, A (1951) *Old and New Forces of Education in Egypt* Teachers' College Columbia University: New York
Raffel, N R (1979) Federal laws and regulations prohibiting sex discrimination *in* Snyder (1979)
Ram, R (1982) Sex differences in the labour market outcomes of education *in* Kelly and Elliott (1982)
Ramirez, F O and Boli-Bennett, J (1982) Global patterns of educational institution-alization *in* Altbach, Arnove and Kelly (1982)
Rasheed, B (1973) *The Egyptian Feminist Union* Anglo Egyptian Books: Cairo
Reason, P and Rowan, J (1981) *Human Inquiry* Wiley: London
Reinharz, S (1981) Experiential analysis: a contribution to feminist research *in* Bowles and Duelli Klein eds (1983): 68-97
Reiter, R R ed (1975) *Toward an Anthropology of Women* Monthly Review Press: New York
Rendel, M (1980) Women and women's studies in higher education in Britain *in* Planunsgruppe für Frauenstudien Berlin (1980)
Rendel, M (1982) *Women's Studies — The Study of Women* UNESCO: Paris
Rich, A (1980) *On Lies, Secrets and Silence* Norton and Co: New York
Roberts, H ed (1981) *Doing Feminist Research* Routledge and Kegan Paul: London
Roberts, J (1976) *Beyond Intellectual Sexism* David McKay: New York
Rogers, B (1980) *The Domestication of Women* Tavistock: London and New York
Rose, H (1982) Making science feminist *in* Whitelegg et al (1982)
Rossi, A and Calderwood, A eds (1973) *Academic Women on the Move* Russell Sage: New York
Rousseau, J-J (1979) *Emile trans* A Bloom Basic Books: New York
Rowbotham, S (1973) *Woman's Consciousness, Man's World* Penguin: Harmondsworth

Rubin, G (1975) The traffic in women: notes on the 'political economy' of sex *in* Reiter (1975)

Rusk, R R *ed* (1965) *The Doctrines of the Great Educators* St Martins: New York

Ruth, S *ed* (1980) *Issues in Feminism: A First Course on Women's Studies* Houghton Mifflin: New York

Rutkevich, M N *ed* (1969) *The Career Plans of Youth* International Arts and Sciences Press: White Plains: New York

Sacks, H (1974) On the analysability of stories by children *in* Turner (1974)

*Said, E (1979) *Orientalism* Random House: New York

Salem, E *ed* (1979) *The Liberal Arts and the Future of Higher Education in the Middle East* The American University of Beirut: Beirut

Samuel, J (1981) Feminism and science teaching: some classroom observations *in* Kelly (1981)

Saraga, E and Griffiths, D (1981) Biological inevitabilities or political choices? The future for girls in science *in* Kelly (1981)

Sarah, E, Scott, M and Spender, D (1980) The education of feminists: the case for single-sex schools *in* Spender and Sarah (1980)

*Sayers, J (1982) *Biological Politics: Feminist and Anti-Feminist Perspectives* Tavistock: London

Schegloff, E A (1977) On some questions and ambiguities in conversation *in* Dressler (1977)

Shiefelbein, E and Farrell, J P (1982) Women, schooling and work in Chile: evidence from a longitudinal study *in* Kelly and Elliott (1982)

Schmuck, P and Charles, W W *eds* (1981) *Educational Policy and Management: Sex Differentials* Academic Press: San Diego, California

*Schools Commission (1975) *Girls, School and Society* Australian Government Publishing Service: Canberra

Schuller, T and Megarry, J *eds* (1979) *World Yearbook of Education 1979: Recurrent Education and Lifelong Learning* Kogan Page: London

Schulz, M (1975) The semantic derogation of women *in* Thorne and Henley (1975)

Science Policy and Research Unit Women and Technology Studies (1982) *Micro-electronics and Women's Employment in Britain* SPRU: University of Sussex

Scotland, J (1969) *The History of Scottish Education Vols 1 and 2* University of London Press: London

*Scott, H (1976) *Women and Socialism* Allison and Busby: London

Scott, H (1982) *Sweden's Right to be Human. Sex Role Equality: The Goal and the Reality* Allison and Busby: London

Scott, M (1980) Teach her a lesson: sexist curriculum in patriarchal education *in* Spender and Sarah (1980)

Sexton, P (1969) *The Feminized Male: Classrooms, White Collars and the Decline of Manliness* Vintage: New York

Shaltut, S (1975) *The Quran and Woman* International Islamic Center for Population Studies and Research: Al Azhar, Cairo

Sharabi, H (1966) Islam and modernization in the Arab World *in* Thompson and Reischaar (1966)

Sharpe, S (1976) *Just Like a Girl* Penguin: Harmondsworth

Shaw, J (1980) Education and the individual: schooling for girls, or mixed schooling – a mixed blessing? *in* Deem (1980)

Shea, W R and King-Farlow, J *eds* (1976) *Contemporary Issues in Political Philosophy* Science History Publications: New York

Shishkan, N M (1976) *Trud zhenshchin v usloviiakh razvitogo* sotsializma Izdatelstvo 'Shtiintsa' Kishinev

Shuy, R, Wolfram, W and Riley, W K (1967) *A Study of Social Dialects in Detroit* Final report on Project 6-1347, Office of Education, Washington, DC

Sims-Wood, J (1980) *The Progress of Afro-American Women: A Selected Bibliography and Resources Guide* Greenwood Press: Westport, Connecticut

Sklar, K K (1973) *Catharine Beecher: A Study in American Domesticity* Yale University Press: New Haven, Connecticut

Slavin Schramm, S (1978) Women's studies: its focus, idea power and promise *in* O'Connor and Johnson (1978)

Slocum, S (1975) Woman the gatherer: male bias in anthropology *in* Reiter (1975)

Smith, C ed (1978) *Advancing Equality of Opportunity: A Matter of Justice* Howard University Press: Washington, DC

Smith, C (1980) The intellectual and modernization: definitions and reconsiderations; the Egyptian experience *in Society for the Comparative Study of Society and History* (1980)

Smith, P C and Cheung, P P L (1982) Social origins and sex differential schooling in the Philippines *in* Kelly and Elliott (1982)

Smock, A and Youssef, N (1977) Egypt: from exclusion to limited participation *in* Giele and Smock (1977)

Smock, A C (1981) *Women's Education in Developing Countries: Opportunities and Outcomes* Praeger: New York

Smock, A C (1982) Sex differences in educational opportunities and labour force participation in six countries *in* Altbach, Arnove and Kelly (1982)

Snyder, E ed (1979) *The Study of Women: Enlarging Perspectives of Social Reality* Harper and Row: New York, New York

Spender, D (1980) *Man Made Language* Routledge and Kegan Paul: London

Spencer, D (1982) *Invisible Women: The Schooling Scandal* Writers and Readers: London

Spender, D ed (1981) *Men's Studies Modified: The Impact of Feminism on the Academic Disciplines* Pergamon: Oxford

Spender, D and Sarah, E eds (1980) *Learning to Lose: Sexism and Education* The Women's Press: London

Stanley, L and Wise, S (1983) *Breaking Out: Feminist Consciousness and Feminist Research* Routledge and Kegan Paul: London

Stanworth, M (1981) *Gender and Schooling: A Study of Sexual Divisions in the Classroom* Women's Research and Resources Centre: London

Summers, A (1975) *Damned Whores and God's Police: The Colonization of Women in Australia* Penguin: Ringwood, Victoria

*Sutherland, M B (1981) *Sex Bias in Education* Blackwell: Oxford

Swacker, M (1975) The sex of the speaker as a sociolinguistic variable *in* Thorne and Henley (1975)

Sweet, R (1980a) An analysis of trends in the teenage labour market in NSW 1971-1976 *New South Wales Department of Technical and Further Education Report*: Sydney

Sweet, R (1980b) The new marginal workers: teenage part-time employment in Australia in the 1970s *New South Wales Department of Technical and Further Education Research Report*: Sydney

Sweet, R (1982) Hidden unemployment among teenagers: a comparison of in-school and out-of-school indicators *New South Wales Department of Technical and Further Education Research Report*: Sydney

Swift, M (1963) Men and women in Malay society *in* Ward, B (1963)

Swinton, D (1978) Affirmative action in a declining economy *in* Smith (1978)

Thivierge, M (1983) La syndicalisation des institutrices catholiques, 1900-1959 *in* Fahmy-Eid and Dumont (1983)

Thomas, G E ed (1981a) *Black Students in Higher Education: Conditions and Experiences in the 1970s* Greenwood Press: Westport,|Connecticut

Thompson, J and Reischaaer, R eds (1966) *Modernization of the Arab World* D van Nostrand Company: New York

Thorne, B and Henley, N (1975) Difference and dominance: an overview of language, gender and society *in* Thorne and Henley (1975)

*Thorne, B and Henley, N eds (1975) *Language and Sex: Difference and Dominance* Newbury House: Rowley, Massachusetts

Tizard, B, Mortimore, J and Burchell, J (1981) *Involving Parents in Infant and Nursery Schools* Grant McIntyre: London

Tobias, S (1978) *Overcoming Math Anxiety* W W Norton and Co: New York

Tomiche, N (1968) The situation of Egyptian women in the first half of the nineteenth century *in* Polk and Chambers (1968)

*Trudgill, P (1974) *Sociolinguistics: An Introduction* Penguin: Harmondsworth

Trudgill, P (1975a) Sex, covert prestige and linguistic change in the urban British English of Norwich *in* Thorne and Henley (1975)

Trudgill, P (1975b) *Accent, Dialect and the School* Arnold: London

Turner, R (1974) Words, utterances and activities *in* Turner (1974)

Turner, R ed (1974) *Ethnomethodology* Penguin: Harmondsworth

Tyack, D and Strober, M H (1981) Jobs and gender: a history of the structuring of educational employment by sex *in* Schmuck and Charles (1981)

Ullian, D Z (1976) The development of conceptions of masculinity and femininity *in* Lloyd and Archer (1976)

Ulich, R (1945) *History of Educational Thought* American Book: New York

Ulich, R ed (1948) *Three Thousand Years of Educational Wisdom* Harvard University Press: Cambridge, Massachusetts

Urban, W J (1982) *Why Teachers Organized* Wayne State University Press: Detroit

Urmson, J O and Sbisà, M eds (1976) *How to do Things with Words* Second Edition Oxford University Press: Oxford

Van der Eyken, W (1981) *Preschool Education in Europe* Longmans: London

Vestin, M (no date) School, instruction and sex role questions The National Swedish Board of Education: Stockholm

Vetterling-Braggin, M ed (1982) *'Femininity', 'Masculinity' and 'Androgyny'* Littlefield, Adams: Totowa, New Jersey

Vetterling-Braggin, M, Elliston, F A and English, J eds (1977) *Feminism and Philosophy* Littlefield, Adams: Totowa, New Jersey

Viaene, N (1979) Sex differences in explanations of success and failure *in* Hartnett (1979)

Walden, R and Walkerdine, V (1982) *Girls and Mathematics: The Early Years* Bedford Way Paper 8 University of London Institute of Education: London

*Walker, S and Barton, L eds (1983) *Gender, Class and Education* Falmer Press:

Wang, B C (1982) Sex and ethnic differences in educational investment in Malaysia: the effect of reward structures *in* Kelly and Elliott (1982)

Ward, B ed (1963) *Women in New Asia: The Changing Roles of Men and Women in South and Southeast Asia* United Nations Educational Scientific and Cultural Organisation (UNESCO): Paris

Weinreich-Haste, H (1981) The image of science *in* Kelly (1981)

Weir, D and Nolan, F (1977) *Glad to be Out: a Study of School-Leavers* Scottish Council for Research in Education: Edinburgh

Wernerson, I (1977) *Könsdifferentiering i grundskolan* Department of Pedagogics: Göteborg

West, J ed (1982) *Work, Women and the Labour Market* Routledge and Kegan Paul: London

Westkott, M (1981) Women's studies as a strategy for change: between criticism and vision *in* Bowles and Duelli Klein (1983)

Whitelegg, E *et al eds* (1982) *The Changing Experience of Women* Martin Robertson: Oxford

Williamson, B (1979) *Education, Social Structure and Development* Macmillan: London

Willis, P (1977) *Learning to Labour* Saxon House: Farnborough

Wilson, E O (1978) *On Human Nature* Harvard University Press: Cambridge

Wistrand, Brigitta (1981) *Swedish Women on the Move* The Swedish Institute: Stockholm

Wittig, M A and Petersen, A C eds (1979) *Sex-Related Differences in Cognitive Functioning* Academic Press: New York

Wollstonecraft, M (1967) *A Vindication of the Rights of Woman* Norton: New York

Wolpe, A M (1978) Education and the sexual division of labour *in* Kuhn and Wolpe (1978)

Women's Studies Seminar Report (1982) Victorian Institute of Secondary Education (VISE): Melbourne

Women Teachers' Association (1932) *The Story of the Women Teachers' Association of Toronto* Thomas Nelson: Toronto

Wood, S ed (1982) *The Degradation of Work? Skill, Deskilling and the Labour Process* Hutchinson: London

Wooton, A (1981a) Conversation and analysis *in* French and MacLure (1981)

Wooton, A (1981b) Children's use of address terms *in* French and Maclure (1981)

Yates, L (1982) Women's studies in the framework of the secondary school curriculum *in* Women's Studies Seminar Report (1982)

Youssef, N H (1974) *Women and Work in Developing Societies* Population Monograph Series 15 University of California: Berkeley

Zelditch, M (1955) Role differentiation in the nuclear family: a comparative study *in* Parsons and Bales (1955)

Zellman, G (1981) *A Title IX Perspective on the Schools' Response to Teenage Pregnancy and Parenthood* Rand Corporation: Santa Monica, California

Zimbalist, A ed (1979) *Case Studies on the Labour Process* Monthly Review Press: New York and London

Zimmerman, D H and West, C (1975) Sex roles, interruptions and silences *in* Thorne and Henley (1975)

Section II: Official and corporate publications

Central Advisory Council for Education (1967) *Children and their Primary schools* (Plowden Report) HMSO: London

Central Statistical Office (1982) *Social Trends 13* HMSO: London

Centre for Educational Research and Innovation (1982) *Caring for Children* OECD: Paris

Committee on Higher Education (1963) *Higher Education: Report* (Robbins Report) Appendix One: The Demand for Places in Higher Education HMSO: London

Datadelegationen (1981) *Samordnad datapolitik* Ds B 1981: 20: Stockholm

Dataeffektutredningen (1981) *Kontorens datorisering* Ds A 1981: 16: Stockholm

Department of Education and Science (1978) *Statistics of Education 5* HMSO: London

Galbally Report (1978) *Migrant Services and Programs* Australian Government Printing Service (AGPS): Canberra

Government of India (1959) *Report of the National Committee on Women's Education* Government of India Press: New Delhi

Government of India, Ministry of Social Welfare (1975) *Towards Equality: Report of the Committee on the Status of Women in India* Government of India Press: New Delhi

Government of India, Planning Commission (1978) *Study of the Special Programmes for Girls' Education* Government of India Press: New Delhi

Government of India, Planning Commission (1980) *Sixth Five Year Plan 1980-85* Government of India Press: New Delhi

Government of Malaysia (1981) *The Fourth Malaysia Plan 1981-1985* Government Printers: Kuala Lumpur

Malaysia (1980) *Population and Households Census* Department of Statistics: Kuala Lumpur

Malaysia (1983) *Preliminary 1980 Census Returns* Department of Statistics: Kuala Lumpur

Ministry of Education (1973) *The Dropout Study* Government Printers: Kuala Lumpur

Ministry of Education (1980) *Education in Malaysia* Government Printers: Kuala Lumpur

Ministry of Education (1982) *Educational Statistics of Malaysia: 1976-1979* Government Printers: Kuala Lumpur

National Central Bureau of Statistics (Sweden) Högskolan (1980/81) *Statistika meddelanden U 1982: 5*: Stockholm

National Central Bureau of Statistics Gymnasieskolan 1981/82 *Statistika meddelanden U 1982: 11*: Stockholm

National Committee on Equality between Men and Women (1979) *Step by Step: National Plan of Action for Equality* Liber Förlag: Stockholm

National Labour Market Board, Sweden (1980) Jämställdhet på arbetsmarknaden (Equality in the Labour Market — Statistics)

National Swedish Board of Education (1975) *ett friare val (A Freer Choice)* Liber Läromedal: Stockholm

Organization for Economic Co-operation and Development (1979) *Equal Opportunities for Women* OECD: Paris

Organization for Economic Co-operation and Development (1970, 1971) *Development of Higher Education 1950-1967: Statistical Survey and Analytical Report* OECD: Paris

Organization for Economic Co-operation and Development (1975) *Education, Inequality and Life Chances* OECD: Paris

Organization for Economic Co-operation and Development (1981) *Educational Statistics in OECD Countries* OECD: Paris

Report of the Advisory Committee on Health and Human Relations Education in Schools (1980) Victorian Education Department: Melbourne

Robbins Committee (1963) Higher education Report; *Appendix One: The Demand for Places in Higher Education* HMSO: London

Sampson, S N (1977) Chairperson Victorian Committee on Equal Opportunity *Report to the Premier of Victoria* Government Printer: Melbourne

Schools Commission (1975) *Girls School and Society* Australian Government Publishing Service: Canberra

Scottish Education Department (1973) *The Transition from School to University* HMSO: Edinburgh

Scottish Education Department (1975) *Differences of Provision for Boys and Girls in Scottish Secondary Schools* HMSO: Edinburgh

Scottish Education Department (1983a) *Teaching and Learning in the Senior Stages of the Scottish Secondary School* HMSO: Edinburgh

Scottish Education Department (1983b) *16-18s in Scotland: An Action Plan* SED: Edinburgh

Scottish Educational Statistics published annually from 1966 to 1974 HMSO: Edinburgh

Scottish Office *Scottish Abstract of Statistics* Annually from 1971 HMSO: Edinburgh

Study Commission on the Family (1983) Final Report *Families in the Future* 3 Park Row, London NW1 6XN

United Nations Educational Scientific and Cultural Organization (1966) *Access of Girls to Secondary Education* UNESCO: Paris

United Nations Educational Scientific and Cultural Organization (1966) *Technical Seminar on Educational Wastage and School Dropout* Report of Malaysia: Bangkok

United Nations Educational Scientific and Cultural Organization (1967) *Access of Girls and Women to Higher Education* UNESCO: Paris

United Nations Educational. Scientific and Cultural Organization (1968) *Access to Higher Education in Europe* UNESCO: Paris

United Nations Educational Scientific and Cultural Organization *Statistical Yearbooks* UNESCO: Paris,

United Nations Educational Scientific and Cultural Organization (1978) *A Study on Curricula and Standards of Education and Training for Boys and Girls in Secondary Schools and Teacher Colleges in Jamaica* document ED-78/WS/112 Research conducted by Jennings-Wray, Z, Persaud, G and Turner, T, of the Caribbean Society of Educational Administrators (CARSEA) for Jamaica National Commission for UNESCO November

United States Commission on Civil Rights (1981) *Affirmative Action in the 1980s: Dismantling the Process of Discrimination* United States Commission on Civil Rights Clearing House Publication 70: Washington, DC

University Grants Committee (1919ff) *Reports* and *Returns from Universities and University Colleges in Receipt of Exchequer Grant* Annually except 1939-1946 HMSO: London

World Bank Report: 1981 (1982) World Bank: Oxford

Section III: Articles, periodicals and working papers

Acker, S (1980) Women, the other academics *British Journal of Sociology of Education* **1** 1: 81-91

Acker, S (1981) No-woman's-land: British sociology of education 1960-1979 *Sociological Review* **29** 1: 77-104

Ahrnell, B-M (1983) Tjejkurs självklav — hade aldrig kommit fram till maskinerna annars *Datavärlden* 7 2 83: 39

Alba, R D and Lavin, D E (1981) Community colleges and tracking in higher education *Sociology of Education* **54** 4: 223-37

Albert, A A and Porter, J R (1983) Age patterns in the development of children's gender-role stereotypes *Sex Roles* **9**: 59-67

Alexander, K and Eckland, B F (1974) Sex differences in the educational attainment process *American Sociological Review* **39**: 668-82

Allen, L (1983) A bibliography of multiculturalism *Social Alternatives* **3** 3

Andersen, J (1950) Recent developments in Shari^ca law *The Muslim World* **XL**: 244-56

Andersen, J (1951) Recent developments in Shari^ca law *The Muslim World* **XLI**: 271-88

Antoun, R (1968) On the modesty of women in Arab Muslim villages: a study of the accommodation of traditions *American Anthropologist* **70**: 671-97

Arbetsmarknadsdepartementet (1979) Steg på väg . . . SOU 1979: 56: Stockholm

Arnold, E, Birke, L and Faulkner, W (1981) Women and microelectronics: the case of word processors *Women's Studies International Quarterly* **4** 3: 321-40

Arnot, M (1981) Culture and political economy: dual perspectives in the sociology of women's education *Educational Analysis* **3** 1: 97-116

Ashton, E (1983) Measures of play behaviour: the influence of sex-role stereotyped children's books *Sex Roles* **9**: 43-7

Barnes, M (1980) Using the history of mathematics in classroom teaching *Australian Association of Mathematics Teachers Conference Papers*: Sydney

*Battel, R, Duelli Klein, R, Moorhouse, C and Zmroczek, C eds (1983) So far so good . . . so what? Women's studies in the UK *Women's Studies International Forum* **6** 3 (special issue)

Beijing Review (1978) 29 October

Bem, S L (1981) Gender schema theory: a cognitive account of sex typing *Psychological Review* **88**: 354-64

Bernard, R N and Vinousksis, M A (1977) The female school teacher *in* Ante-Bellum Massachusetts *Journal of Social History* **10** 3: 332-45

Berner, B (1982) Kvinnor, kunskap och makt i teknikens värld *Kvinnovetenskaplig tidskrift* **3** 3: 25-39

Blackstone, T and Weinreich-Haste, H (1980) Why are there so few women scientists and engineers? *New Society*|21 2 80: 383-85

Bonacich, E (1979) The past, present and future of split labour market theory *Research in Race and Ethnic Relations: A Research Annual* **1**: 17-64

*Boxer, M (1982) For and about women: the theory and practice of women's studies in the United States *Signs* **7** 3: 661-95

Bradley, D and Mortimer, M (1973) Sex role stereotyping in children's picture books *Refractory Girl* 1

Brophy, J E and Good, T L (1970) Teachers' communications of differential expectations for children's classroom performance: some behavioural data *Journal of Educational Psychology* **61** 5: 365-74

Brouwer, D, Gerritsen, M and De Haan, D (1979) Speech differences between women and men: on the wrong track? *Language in Society* **8**: 33-50

Bruegel, I (1979) Women as a reserve army of labour: a note on recent British experience *Feminist Review* **3**: 12-23

Bull, D (1983) Privatisation or exportation? *Where* **188**: 8-12

Bunch, C (1979) Visions and revisions: women and the power to change Panel at NWSA Convention: Lawrence, Kansas, June 1979

Bunch, C (1980) Global feminism. Talk delivered at Women's Studies Forum, Copenhagen, July 1980

Buswell, C (1981) Sexism in school routines and classroom practices *Durham and Newcastle Research Review* **9** 46: 195-200

Carss, M (1980) Girls, mathematics and language: some observations for classrooms Paper presented at Conference on Increasing the Participation of Girls in Mathematics: Raywood, South Australia

Cauldwell, M (1978) North Korea — aspects of a new society *Contemporary Review* **1355**: London

Churchill, W D and Iwai, S (1981) College attrition, students' use of campus facilities, and a consideration of self-reported personal problems *Research in Higher Education* **14** 4: 355-62

Clarricoates, K (1978) Dinosaurs in the classroom — a re-examination of some aspects of the hidden curriculum in primary schools *Women's Studies International Quarterly* **1** 4: 353-64

Clemens, B (1983) Institutionalisierung von Frauenforschung und Frauenstudien — ein weg zur Förderung von Frauen an der Hochschule? Paper delivered at Kassel University January 28

Cockburn, C (1981) The material of male power *Feminist Review* **9**: 41-58

Colby, M (1978) Women's Studies: an inclusive concept for an inclusive field *Canadian Women's Studies* **1** 1: 4-6

Constantinople, A (1979) Sex-role acquisition: in search of the elephant *Sex Roles* **5**: 121-33

Crecelius, D (1966) al Azhar in the revolution *Middle East Journal* **20**: 31-49

Cross, D (1983) *The Issue of Equity: Current Realities and the Task Ahead* Paper presented at the American Educational Research Association annual conference in Montreal, Canada AERA office: Washington, DC

Danylewycz, M, Light, B and Prentice, A (1983) The evolution of the sexual division of labour in teaching: a nineteenth century Ontario and Quebec case study *Histoire sociale/Social History* **15** 30

Danylewycz, M and Prentice, A (1982) Teachers, gender and bureaucratizing school systems in nineteenth century Montreal and Toronto *Conference in Comparative Urban History* Guelph, Ontario

Davis, J S and Johns, K (1982) Law and family income: a continuing barrier to college enrollment *The Journal of Student Financial Aid* **12** 1: 5-10

DeCelles, A D (1882) Les maîtresses d'école en grève! *Journal de l'instruction publique* **11** 10: 299-300

de Lacoste-Utamsing, C and Holloway, R L (1982) Sexual dimorphism in the human corpus callosum *Science* **216**: 1431-32

Dinnerstein, M, O'Donnell, S and MacCorquodale, P (1982) Integrating women's studies into the curriculum *Women's Studies Quarterly* **10** 1: 20-23

Dodd, P (1973) Family honour and the forces of change in Arab society *International Journal of Middle East Studies* **4** 1: 40-54

Dubois, B L and Crouch, I (1975) The question of tag questions in women's speech: they don't really use more of them, do they? *Language in Society* **4**: 289-94

Duelli Klein, R (1983) The 'men-problem' in women's studies: 'the expert', 'the ignoramus' and 'the poor dear' *Women's Studies International Forum* **6** 4

Edelsky, C (1979) Question intonation and sex roles *Language in Society* **8** 15-32

Edelsky, C (1981) Who's got the floor? *Language in Society* **10** 383-421

Ehrenreich, B and Stallard, K (1982) The nouveau poor *Ms Magazine* **11** 1/2: 217-24

Ehrensaft, P and Armstrong, W (1978) Dominion capitalism: a first statement *Australian and New Zealand Journal of Sociology* **14** 3: 352-63

el Guindi, F (1981a) Veiling infitah with Muslim ethic: Egypt's contemporary Islamic movement *Social Problems* **28** 4: 466-85

el Guindi, F (1981b) Is there an Islamic alternative: Egypt's contemporary Islamic movement *International Insight* **1** vi: 75-93

Eliou, M (1973) The education and advancement of women in Africa: Ivory Coast, Upper Volta, Senegal *International Review of Education* **19**: 30-46

el-Zein, A (1977) Beyond ideology and theology: the search for the anthropology of Islam *Annual Review of Anthropology* **6**: 227-54

Emmerich, W, Goldman, S, Kirsh, B and Sharabany, R (1977) Evidence for a transitional phase in the development of gender constancy *Child Development* **48** 930-36

Etaugh, C and Hadley, T (1977) Causal attributions of male and female performance by young children *Psychology of Women Quarterly* **2** 16-23

Evans, M (1982) In praise of theory: the case for women's studies *Feminist Review* **10**: 61-74

Evans, T D (1979) Creativity, sex-role socialisation and pupil-teacher interaction in early schooling *Sociological Review* **27** 1: 139-55

Evans, T D (1980) Pre-school and primary teachers' interaction with their most and least creative pupils *Research in Education* **24**: 31-43

Evans, T D (1982) Being and becoming: teachers' perceptions of sex-roles and actions towards their male and female pupils *British Journal of Sociology of Education* **3** 2: 127-43

Faksh, M (1980) The consequences of the introduction and spread of modern education: education and national integration in Egypt *Middle East Studies* **16**: 42-55

Finn, J D, Dulberg, L and Reis, J (1979) Sex differences in educational attainment: a cross national perspective *Harvard Educational Review* **49** 477-503

Fischer, J L (1958) Social influences on the choice of a linguistic variant *Word* **14**: 47-56

Fishman, P (1978) Interaction: the work women do *Social Problems* **25** 4: 397-406

Fleming, J (1981) Stress and satisfaction in college years of Black students *Journal of Negro Education* **50** 3: 307-18

Flett, U, Jones, C and McPherson, A F (1971) *After Highers: Working Paper 7* Department of Sociology, University of Edinburgh

Flett, U, Jones, C and McPherson, A F (1972) *Women Entrants to University and College of Education — Some Competing Explanations* Department of Sociology, University of Edinburgh

Flitch, M (1981) Women at Volvo *Equal Opportunities International* **1** 2: 12-14

Foster, P (1971) Education, economy, equality *Interchange* **2** 1: 51-61

Foster, P (1977) Education and social differentiation in less developed countries *Comparative Education Review* **21**: 211-29

Frieze, I H, Whiteley, B E, Hanusa, B H and McHugh, M C (1982) Assessing the theoretical models for sex differences in causal attributions for success and failure *Sex Roles* **8**: 333: 43

Galton, M, Simon, B and Croll, P (1980) *Inside the Primary Classroom* Routledge and Kegan Paul: London

Garnsey, E (1978) Women's work and theories of class stratification *Sociology* **12** 2: 224-43

Garrett, C S, Ein, P L and Tremaine, L (1977) The development of gender stereotyping of adult occupations by elementary school children *Child Development* **48**: 507-12

Gist (Girls Into Science and Technology) (1982) *Options and Careers* Manchester Polytechnic: Manchester

Gist (Girls Into Science and Technology) *Introductory Booklet* Manchester Polytechnic: Manchester

Goldblatt, P (1983)Progress in schooling in Mexican *Municipos* Paper presented at the Annual Meeting of the Comparative and International Education Society, Atlanta, Georgia, March

Gordon, L (1975) A socialist view of women's studies *Signs* **1** 2: 559-66

Haas, M R (1944) Men's and women's speech in Koasati *Language* **20**: 142-49

Hakim, C (1978) Sexual divisions within the labour force: occupational segregation *Department of Employment Gazette* **86** 11: 1264-68

Hamilton, M A (1981) The prediction of academic success — an interim report *Caribbean Journal of Education* **8** 1: 43-58

Hamilton, M A (1982a) Sex differences in the qualitative performance of Jamaican adolescents in the circles test of creativity *Caribbean Journal of Education* **9** 2: 124-34

Hamilton, M A (1982b) Jamaican students' attitude to science as it relates to achievement in external examinations *Science Education* **66** 2: 155-69

Hamilton, M A (in press) The evidence of sex-typed behaviours in professional Jamaican men and women accepted for publication in *Sex Roles* Summer 1985

Hamilton, M A and Leo-Rhynie, E A (1979-80) Sex-role stereotyping and education: the Jamaican perspective *Interchange* **10** 2: 46-56

Hartmann, H (1981) The family as a locus of gender, class and political struggle: the example of housework *Signs: Journal of Women in Culture and Society* **6** 3: 366-94

Healey, T (1976) Can quality coexist with equality in a just community? *The College Board* **102**: 8-11

Heritage, J C (1978) Aspects of the flexibilities of natural language use *Sociology* **12** 79-103

Heritage, J C (in press) Recent developments in conversation analysis *Sociolinguistics Newsletter* special issue edited by Thomas Luckmann (in press)

Heyneman, S P (1976) Influences on academic achievement: a comparison of results from Uganda and more industrialized societies *Sociology of Education* **49** 200-10

Hirschman, L (1974) *Analysis of Supportive and Assertive Behaviour in Conversations* Paper delivered to meeting of Linguistics Society of America, July

Hirschman, L (1979) Political independence and educational opportunity in peninsular Malaysia *Sociology of Education* **52** 2: 67-83

Hoffman, L (1972) Early childhood experiences and women's achievement motives *Journal of Social Issues* **28** 129-56

Höglund, E (1982) Svenska kvinnan arbetar mest i världen — men blir fast i samma yrken *Veckans affärer* 4 3 82: 38-41

Honkasalo, M-L (1982) Dead end — views on career development and life situation of women in the electronics industry *Economic and Industrial Democracy* **3**: 445-64

Horner, M (1972) Toward an understanding of achievement related conflicts in women *Journal of Social Issues* **28** 2: 157-75

Howard-Merriam, K (1979) Women, education and the professions in Egypt *Comparative Education Review* **23** 256-70

Howe, F (1981) Women's Studies International at Copenhagen: from idea to network *Women's Studies Quarterly* **9** 1: 7-11

Howe, F (1982) Feminist scholarship — the extent of the revolution *Change Magazine* **14** 3: 12-20

Howe, F (1982) Women's studies program list *Women's Studies Quarterly* **10** 3: 21-31

Howe, F (1983) Editorial *Women's Studies Quarterly* **11** 2: 2

Hughes, M and Kennedy, M (1983) Breaking out — women in adult education *Women's Studies International Forum* **6** 3: 261-70

Ibrahim, A (1979) Salama Musa: an essay on cultural alienation *Middle East Studies* **15** 3: 346-57

Ibrahim, S (1981) An Islamic alternative in Egypt: the Muslim brotherhood and Sadat *Arab Studies Quarterly* 4 1 and 2: 75-93

Ingleby, D (1981) The politics of psychology: review of a decade *Psychology and Social Issues* **2**: 4-18

Institutrice (1902) Autour de l'école *La Patrie* October 10

Jain, D (1983) Development as if women mattered: can women build a new paradigm? Lecture at OECD/DAC meeting, 26 January 1983, mimeo

Jangenas, B (1981) Employment and labor market policy in Sweden during the recession of the late 1970s *Current Sweden* 266 (The Swedish Institute)

Jennings, B (1982) *The Girls' Apprenticeship Programme in Victoria: Some Observations* Third Women and Labour Conference Papers: Adelaide

Jensen, A (1969) How much can we boost IQ and scholastic achievement? *Harvard Educational Review* 39: 1-123

Jones, B and Anuza, T (1982) Sex differences in cerebral lateralisation in 3 and 4 year old children *Neuropsychologia* 20: 347-50

Journal of Social and Behavioural Sciences (1981) 27 3: 68-201 Special issue on education, socialisation and traditional versus non-traditional career paths of Black females: theoretical and empirical evidence

Kahn, H (1983) Arbetsrotation och internutbildning har gjort kvinnorna kvalificerade *Datavärlden* 21 2 83: 39

Kaluzynska, E (1980) Wiping the floor with theory: a survey of writings on housework *Feminist Review* 6 27-54

Kaul, H and Lie, M (1982) When paths are vicious circles — how women's working conditions limit influence *Economic and Industrial Democracy* 3: 465-81

Kelly, A (1978) *Girls and Science* IEA Monograph No 9 Almqvist and Wiksell: Stockholm

Kelly, D H and Kelly, G P (1982) Education of women in developing countries *Educational Documentation and Information* 56 222 (1st quarter) International Bureau of Education: Geneva

Key, M R (1972) Linguistic behaviour of male and female *Linguistics* 88: 15-31

Kim, L (1980) New rules for admission to higher education in Sweden *Current Sweden* 252

King, R (1971) Unequal access in education — sex and social class *Social and Economic Administration* 5 3: 167-75

Kohlberg, L and Zigler, E (1967) The impact of cognitive maturity on the development of sex role attitudes in the years four to eight *Genetic Psychology Monographs* 75 89-165

Komarovsky, M (1946) Cultural contradictions and sex roles *American Journal of Sociology* 52: 184-89

Kraft, P (1979) The routinizing of computer programming *Sociology of Work and Occupations* 6 2: 139-55

Kramer, C (1977) Perceptions of female and male speech *Language and Speech* 20 2: 151-61

Kuhn, D, Nash, S C and Bruehen, L (1978) Sex role concepts of two- and three-year-olds *Child Development* 49: 445-51

Labov, W, Yaeger, M and Steiner, R (1972) *A Quantitative Study of Sound Change in Progress* Final report on National Science Foundation contract NSF-GS-3287: Philadelphia

Land, H (1975) The myth of the male breadwinner *New Society* 9 10 75: 71-73

Laskin, S, Light, B and Prentice, A (1982) Studying the History of an Occupation: Quantitative Sources on Teachers in the Nineteenth century *Archivaria* 14: 75-92

Leder, G C (1974) Sex differences in mathematics problem appeal as a function of problem context *Journal of Educational Research* 67 8: 351-53

Lee, P C (1973) Male and female teachers in elementary schools: an ecological analysis *Teachers College Record* 75 1: 79-98

Leo-Rhynie, E A (1982) Educational research of some graduate students of UWI — a commentary *Caribbean Journal of Education* 9 2: 135-51

Leo-Rhynie, E A (1983) Approaches to 'A' level work and study used by a sample of Jamaican sixth formers *Caribbean Journal of Education* 102

Lerner, G (1972) On the teaching and organization of feminist studies *Female Studies* **5**: 34-37

Levin, T (1979) Women's studies in West Germany: community vs academy *Women's Studies Newsletter* **7** 1: 20-22

Lewis, M and Weinraub, M (1979) Origins of early sex-role development *Sex Roles* **5** 135-53

Lieberson, S ed (1966) Explorations in sociolinguistics, special issue of *Sociological Inquiry* **36** 2

Lindgren, G (1982) Anpassning och protest: om deltidsarbete i det kapitalistika patriarkatet *Kvinnovetenskaplig tidskrift* **3** 2: 33-45

Lobban, G Sex-roles in reading schemes *Forum for the Discussion of New Trends in Education* **16** 2

Loutfy, K (1982) The problem of illiteracy in Egypt *Population Studies* **62** July-Sept: 79-84

Macaulay, R K S (1978) The myth of female superiority in language *Journal of Child Language* **5**: 353-63

McGhee, P E and Frueh, T (1980) Television viewing and the learning of sex-role stereotypes *Sex Roles* **6**: 179-88

McIntosh, P (1982) Transformations within the academy: reconstructing the liberal arts curriculum Paper delivered at NWSA meetings, Arcata, California

McIntosh, P and Minnich, E K (in press) Varieties of women's studies *in Women's Studies International Forum* (in press)

Mack, J (1974) Women's studies in Cambridge *The New Era* **55** 6: 162-64

MacKinnon, L A (1982) Feminism, marxism, method and the state: an agenda for theory *Signs* **7** 3: 515-44

Magnusson, B (1981) What is being done in Sweden for unemployed 16- and 17-year olds? *Current Sweden* 275

Marcus, D E and Overton, W F (1978) The development of cognitive gender constancy and sex role preference *Child Development* **49** 434-44

Martin, C L and Halverson, C F (1981) A schematic processing model of sex typing and stereotyping in children *Child Development* **52** 1119-34

Martin, J R (1981a) Sophie and Emile: a case study of sex bias in the history of educational thought *Harvard Educational Review* **51**: 357-72

Martin, J R (1981b) The ideal of the educated person *Educational Theory* **31** 97-109

Martin, J R (1982a) Excluding women from the educational realm *Harvard Educational Review* **52**: 133-48

Mazumdar, V (1980) Women's studies in India Paper delivered at NGO Forum Women's Studies International, Copenhagen

Melder, K (1972) Women's high calling: the teaching profession in America, 1830-1860 *American Studies* **13**: 19-32

Meleis, A I, El-Sanabary, N and Beeson, D (1979) Women, modernization and education in Kuwait *Comparative Education Review* **23**: 115-24

Menzies, H (1982) Women and microelectronics *Canadian Women's Studies/Cahiers de la Femme* **3** 4: 13-17

Metz-Göckel, S (1982) The women's movement and WS in Germany Paper presented to the Women's Caucus, Department of German, University of California: Berkeley September 1982

Metz-Göckel, S (1983) Feministische Wissenschaft und Frauenstudien in und ausserhalb der Bildungs — und Wissenshafts — einrichtungen in der BRD *Psychologie Heute* (1983)

Meyer, B (1980) The development of girls' sex-role attitudes *Child Development* **51**: 508-14

Meyer, J W, Ramirez, F O, Rubinson, R and Boli-Bennett, T (1977) The world educational revolution, 1950-1970 *Sociology of Education* **50**: 242-58

Mies, M (1978) Methodische Postulate zur Frauenforschung − dargestellt am Beispiel der Gewalt gegen Frauen *Beiträge zur Feministischen Theorie und Praxis* **1** 1: 41-63

Minnich, E K (1982) A devastating conceptual error: how can we *not* be feminist scholars? *Change Magazine* **14** 3: 7-9

Molyneux, M (1981) Women's emancipation under socialism: a model for the Third World? *World Development* **9**: 9 and 10

Morgall, J (1981) Typing our way to freedom: is it true that new office technology can liberate women? *Feminist Review* **9**: 87-101

Moss, H A (1967) Sex, age and state as determinants of mother-infant interaction *Merrill-Palmer Quarterly* **13** 19-36

Ms Muffet Newsletter of the Joint Technical Teachers Union of Victoria, Victorian Association of Secondary Teachers and Victorian Teachers Union Counter-sexism Project

Murgatroyd, L (1982) Gender and occupational stratification *Sociological Review* **30** 4: 575-602

Murray, N (1979) Socialism and feminism: women and the Cuban revolution Parts 1 and 2 *Feminist Review* **1**: 2 and 3

Mustaffa-Kedah, O (1975/76) The education of women in the Arab states *Literacy Discussions* **4** 4: 119-39

Nelson, C (1968) Changing roles in a changing society *Anthropological Quarterly* **41** 2: 57-77

Nelson, C (1974) Religious experience, sacred symbols and social reality *Humaniora Islamica* **11**: 253-66

Nelson, C and Oleson, V eds (1977) Feminist thought *Catalyst* **10/11** Summer (special issue)

Orsini, A, Schiappa, O, Chiacchio, L and Grossi, D (1982) Sex differences in a children's spatial serial-learning task *Journal of Psychology* **III**: 67-71

O'Shaugnessey, T J (1978) Growth of educational opportunity for Muslim women, 1950 to 1973 *Anthropos* **73** 5-6: 887-901

Owen, M (1982) Women's employment: past and future Third Women and Labour Conference Papers: Adelaide

Parsons, J E, Adler, T F and Kaczala, C M (1982) Socialization of achievement attitudes and beliefs: parental influences *Child Development* **53**: 310-21

Perby, M-L (1981) Kvinnor, datateknologi och arbete *Kvinnovetenskaplig Tidskrift* **2** 1-2: 43-50

Phillips, A and Taylor, B (1980) Sex and skill: notes towards a feminist economics *Feminist Review* **6**: 79-88

Pierce, C (1973) Equality: *Republic v The Monist* **57**: 1-11

Plank, D (1983) *Regional and Age Differences in Brazilian Enrollment Roles, 1970* Paper presented at the Annual Meeting of the Comparative and International Education Society, Atlanta, Georgia March

Prentice, A (1975) The feminization of teaching in British North America, 1845-1875 *Histoire Sociale/Social History* **8**: 5-20

Ram, R (1980) Sex differences in the labour market outcomes of education *Comparative Education Review* **24** 2: S53-77

Ramsay, E (1981) Conversational politics *South Australian Institute of Teachers Contact Network Newsletter* **22**

Raskin, P and Israel, A (1981) Sex role imitation in children. Effects of sex of child, sex of model, and sex-role appropriateness of modeled behaviour *Sex Roles* **7**: 1067-77

Register, C (1979) Brief a-mazing movements *Women's Studies Newsletter* **7** 4: 7-10

Rendel, M (1974) Primary sources of oppression *Times Educational Supplement* March 29

Reuben, E (1978) In defiance of the evidence: notes on feminist scholarship *Women's Studies International Quarterly* **1** 3: 215-18

Riley, G (1969) Origin of the argument for improved female education *History of Education Quarterly* **94**: 455-70

Robinson, E (1980) Address to SRHE/EOC Conference in Manchester Polytechnic 6 March 1980

Rossi, A (1977) A biosocial perspective on parenting *Daedalus* **106**: 1-32

Rothschild, J (1981) A feminist perspective on technology and the future *Women's Studies International Quarterly* **4** 1: 65-74

Sacks, H, Schegloff, E A and Jefferson, G (1974) A simplest systematics for the organisation of turn-taking for conversation *Language* **50**: 696-735

Saleh, S (1972) Women in Islam: their status in religion and traditional culture *International Journal of Sociology of the Family* **2** 1: 1-7

Salper, R (1971) The theory and practice of women's studies *Edcentrics* **3** 7: 4-8

Salzmann-Webb, M (1972) Feminist studies: frill or necessity? *Female Studies* **5**: 64-76

Sampson, S N (1975) Sex role enculturation in schools *in Education News* **15** 4 and 5: 34-39

Sangster, A W (1982) Looking at the common entrance exams *The Sunday Gleaner* 10 October

Sauter-Bailliet, T (1980) Vom Studium für Frauen zu Frauenstudien: Women's Studies in den USA *Enslisch Amerikanische Studien* **2** 2: 168-82

Sayers, J (1983) Is the personal political? Psychoanalysis and feminism revisited *International Journal of Women's Studies* **6**: 71-86

Schegloff, E A (1968) Sequencing in conversational openings *American Anthropologist* **70**: 1075-95

Schneider, J W and Hacker, S L (1972) Sex role imagery and the use of the generic 'man' in introductory texts *Paper presented at the American Sociological Annual Meeting in New Orleans*

Schofield, H (1981) Grade level and the relationship between mathematics attitude and achievement in children *Journal of Educational Research* **75**

Schöpp-Schilling, H B (1982) Frauenforschung in den USA und der Bundesrepublik *Mitteilungsblatt des Deutschen Akademikerinnenbundes* **61**: 8-22

Schöpp-Schilling, H B (1979) Women's studies, women's research and women's research centres: recent developments in the USA and the FRG *Women's Studies International Quarterly* **2** 1: 103-16

Shelley, N (1982) *An Alternative Pathway to Mathematical Understanding* Australian Association of Mathematics Teachers Conference Papers: Sydney

Shepherd, N (1942) Women in the university *Aberdeen University Review* **XXIX** 87: 171-81

Shongguo Tongji Nianjian: 1981 (1982) Hong Kong

Signs: Journal of Women in Culture and Society (1982) Special issue on feminist theory **7** 3 Spring

Simons, D (1981) *Women in Science: A Developing Country* Paper prepared for the GASAT Conference 1981, Eindhoven, The Netherlands November 9-13

Sjöberg, S (1982) Soft girls in hard science *Tidskrift för Nordisk Förening för Pedagogisk Forskning* **1-2**: 55-63

Smail, B, Whyte, J and Kelly, A (1981) *Girls into science and technology: the first two years* Paper for the International Conference on Girls and Science and Technology Eindhoven, Holland November

Smith, C and Lloyd, B B (1978) Maternal behaviour and perceived sex of infant *Child Development* **49**: 1263-65

Smith, D (1975) An analysis of ideological structure and how women are excluded *Canadian Journal of Sociology and Anthropology* **12** 4: 353-69

Smith, D H (1981) Social and academic environment of black students on white campuses *Journal of Negro Education* **50** 3: 299-306

Spanier, B (1982) Toward a balanced curriculum: the study of women at Wheaton College *Change Magazine* **14** 3: 31-7

Spender, D (1978) Notes on the organisation of women's studies *Women's Studies International Quarterly* **1** 3: 255-76

Staton, P (1980) A decade of women's studies *Canadian Women's Studies* **2** 4: 58-9

Steady, F (1980) The need for intra- and inter-national feminist networks. Talk delivered at Women's Studies Forum at Copenhagen July 1980

Stimpson, C (1973) What matter mind: a theory about the practice of women's studies *Women's Studies* **1**: 293-314

Stimpson, C (1978) Women's studies: an overview *Ann Arbor Papers in Women's Studies* University of Michigan Women's Studies Program Ann Arbor: 14-26

Strober, M and Lanford, A G (1981) The percentages of women in public school teaching: a cross sectional analysis, 1850-1880 *Social Science and History Association Annual Meeting* Nashville, Tennessee

Strober, M H and Tyack, D (1980) Why do women teach and men manage? *Signs* **5** 3: 494-503

Thomas, G E (1981b) College characteristics and Black students' four-year college graduation *Journal of Negro Education* **50** 3: 328-45

Thomas, G E and Hargett, S L (1981) Socialisation effects and Black college women: educational and occupational orientations *Journal of Social and Behavioural Sciences* **27** 3: 65-72

Thompson, S K (1975) Gender labels and early sex role development *Child Development* **46**: 339-47

Thorne, B (1978) Contradictions, and a glimpse of Utopia: daily life in a university women's studies program *Women's Studies International Quarterly* **1** 2: 201-06

Tieger, T (1980) On the biological basis of sex differences in aggression *Child Development* **51**: 143 963

Tobias, S (1978) Women's studies: its origins, its organisation, and its prospects *Women's Studies International Quarterly* **1** 1: 85-97

Trent, W T (1983) *Race and Sex Differences in Degree Attainment and Major Field Distributions from 1975-76 to 1980-81* The Johns Hopkins University Center for Social Organization of Schools Report Number 339: Baltimore, Maryland

*Tucker, J ed (1981) Women and work in the Middle East *Merip Reports* **95** March-April

Urberg, K A (1982) The development of the concepts of masculinity and femininity in young children *Sex Roles* **8**: 659-68

Walden, R and Walkerdine, V (1982) *Girls and Mathematics: The Early Years* Bedford Way Papers **8** University of London Institute of Education: London

Walford, G (1983) Girls in boys' public schools: a prelude to further research *British Journal of Sociology of Education* **4** 1: 39-54

Walkerdine, V (1982) *Gender and the Production of Rationality in the Family and at School* Paper given in Manchester at the British Sociological Association Annual Conference 'Gender and Society'

Waugh, P and Foster, V (1978) Education and the 'down-girl' principle *Refractory Girl* **16**

Weis, L (1980) Women and education in Ghana: some problems in assessing change *International Journal of Women's Studies* **3** 5: 431-53

Weitzman, L J, Eifler, D, Hokada, E and Ross, C (1972) Sex-role socialisation in picture books for pre-school children *American Journal of Sociology* **77**: 1125-50

Wentworth, R D (1979) A comparison of the career aspirations of men and women trainee teachers *South Pacific Journal of Teacher Education* **7** 3 and 4: 85-91

Wertheimer, B M and Nelson, A H (1982) Education for social change: two routes *Economic and Industrial Democracy* **3**: 483-513
Whiting, P (1974) A course in feminist studies *Women Speaking* October-December 1974: 15-16
Wickramsinghe, S and Radcliffe, D (1979) Women and education in South Asia *Canadian and International Journal of Education* **8** 2: 117-25
Williams, J (1979) A return to the veil in Egypt *Middle East Review* Spring: 49-54
Wood, M (1966) The influence of sex and knowledge of communication effectiveness on speech *Word* **22**: 112-37
Woodhall, M (1973) Investment in women: a reappraisal of the concept of human capital *International Review of Education* **19** 1: 9-92

Youssef, N H (1976/77) Education and female modernization in the Muslim world *Journal of International Affairs* **30**: 191-209

Zangrando, J (1975) Women's studies in the United States: approaching reality *American Studies International* **14** 1: 15-36
Zimmerman, D H and West, C eds (1980) Language and social interaction special issue of *Sociological Inquiry* **50**: 3-4
Zimmerman, J (1981) Technology and the future of women: haven't we met somewhere before? *Women's Studies International Quarterly* **4** 3: 355-67

Section IV: Annotated bibliography

Archer, J and Lloyd, B (1982) *Sex and Gender* Penguin: Harmondsworth
This book provides a well-written, clear, and cheap introduction to recent theoretical perspectives and research findings on the psychological aspects of current sexual divisions in the USA and England. It includes chapters on physical sex differences; sexuality; aggression, violence and power; fear, anxiety and mental health; the family; work, intelligence and achievement; and on growing up male or female.

Battel, Riosin, Duelli Klein, Renate, Moorhouse, Catherine and Zmroczek, Christine eds (1983) So far so good . . . so what? Women's Studies in the UK *Women's Studies International Forum* **6** 3 (Special Issue)
'So far, so good . . . so what?' is a first collection of Women's Studies in the UK. It documents the presence of Women's Studies in adult higher and secondary education, and includes papers by teachers and students on the theory and practice of WS. Issues discussed are that Women's Studies is marginal, innovative and challenging to the *status quo*, and therefore especially vulnerable to the current economic constraints on education. The collection also questions whether the relationship between Women's Studies and the Women's Liberation Movement will continue to develop, whether Women's Studies will remain feminist, or whether it will swing towards 'legitimate' respectability and away from radical innovative knowledge-making.

Beck, L and Keddie, N eds (1978) *Women in the Muslim World* Harvard University Press: Cambridge, Massachusetts
An anthology of 33 essays, demonstrating the enormous variability and differentiation that exists in the Muslim world, it is organized into four parts: 'General Perspectives on Legal and Socio-Economic Change'; 'Historical Perspectives'; 'Case Studies'; 'Ideology, Religion and Ritual'. Theoretical questions raised include: Did male dominance increase when society became city-centred and class divided? To what extent is male dominance in the Islamic Middle East similar to many other parts of the world? How is it unique? This volume is a timely contribution to the necessary decolonization of the literature on Islamic societies in general and Muslim women in particular.

Bock, Ulla, Braszeit, Anne, and Schmerl, Christiane (1983) Frauenspezifische Aktivitäten und Einrichtungen zur Öffnung der Wissenschaft für Frauen *in Frauen im Wissenschaftsbetrieb* Beltz Verlag: Weinheim
This chapter provides an overview of Women's Studies/feminist research activities in West Germany. It lists initiatives by teachers and students inside and outside formal education. While drawing attention to the enormous growth of feminist educational projects, the authors caution that much of this feminist activity is only possible because of the enormous commitment and dedication, as well as the voluntary work of the feminist faculty and students. Projects listed include feminist research centres, libraries, summer universities, and some of the Women's Studies activities at German universities. The chapter also provides the names of interdisciplinary feminist associations and introduces their publications.

Boxer, Marilyn (1982) For and about women: the theory and practice of women's studies in the United States *Signs* 7 3: 661-95
Boxer's article is a survey of the literature about Women's Studies as a field in American higher education: its history, political issues, theories and structures. She documents not only Women's Studies' unifying vision of a society free of all oppression, but examines the conflicts which arise from Women's Studies' struggle to survive as a radical alternative to the very university system within which it exists. Boxer delineates the tenuous balance between scholarship and politics which academic feminism must maintain. Other major issues which she considers include the adaptation of feminist principles in the classroom, the feminist attempt to transform academic structures and curricula, the struggles against racism and homophobia inside and outside of Women's Studies, the accountability of academic feminism to the larger Women's Liberation Movement, the difficulties of interdisciplinarity in a discipline-based university, the current autonomy versus integration debate, and the formation of feminist methodologies appropriate to Women's Studies as an autonomous discipline and as a force for social change.

Byrne, E (1978) *Women and Education* Tavistock Publications: London
This is one of the most comprehensive books on the position of girls in the British educational system to be produced over recent years. Eileen Byrne addresses the problem of the unequal representation of male and female students at all levels and in all kinds of educational institutions. She also examines the way in which female students become increasingly segregated within certain areas of the curriculum as they progress through the system. Unlike many other writers, she does not neglect the further education sector where the problem of women's segregation in a very narrow part of the curriculum is particularly acute.

As well as stressing the structural nature of discrimination against girls in the education system, Byrne also shows how certain girls are victims of what she calls 'the compound interest of inequality'. She suggests that there are five main indices of inequality: sex, lower social class, lower range of intelligence, residence in certain areas with a history of under-achievement and residence in rural areas. Where two or more of these factors are aggregated, a cumulative cycle of under-achievement is created. This cycle can only be overcome by positive, affirmative intervention programmes aimed at increasing resources, countering cultural and social barriers and adding to skills and experiences.

Chodorow, N (1978) *The Reproduction of Mothering* University of California Press: Berkeley
This book has been enormously influential on current feminist thinking about gender divisions. It is also having a growing influence on developments within child and clinical psychology. Chodorow's thesis, summarized in the chapter 'Psychology and gender divisions', is that women identify on grounds of sex with their daughters and hence foster in them a continuing sense of mergence and fusion in personal relations, whereas they tend to relate to their sons in terms of difference and accordingly foster in them a sense of separateness in personal relations. Chodorow argues that the

differing relational capacities of girls and boys, resulting from their mothering by women in infancy, fit them differently for existing sexual divisions in society.

Connell, R W, Ashenden, D J, Kessler, S and Dowsett, G W (1982) *Making the Difference: Schools, Families and Social Division* George, Allen and Unwin: Sydney
This text is a readable and concise account of a study by the authors of ruling class and working class families and education in two Australian cities. The relationships between gender and class are clearly presented and Connell, Ashenden, Kessler and Dowsett begin the difficult task of developing a sociological account of the construction and reproduction of these relationships. The book contains useful discussions of inequality and education, together with suggestions for 'what to do about it'.

Coote, A and Campbell, B (1982) *Sweet Freedom: The Struggle for Women's Liberation* Picador: London
This is a very readable account by two journalists of the way the family-household system, in which women are expected to be primarily wives and mothers dependent on a male breadwinner, structures union activity, sexual divisions at work (and its classification as skilled or unskilled), education and the media. The book also considers legislation and political activity and their effectiveness in improving women's lot in England.

Deblé, I (1980) *The School Education of Girls* UNESCO: Paris
The aim of this study is to look at the conditions under which girls obtain primary and secondary education in different parts of the world. It also aims to reach an improved understanding of female wastage from the educational system in different countries. Three particular questions are addressed: Are the same number of girls and boys admitted to school? Does their schooling follow the same pattern? Are these two aspects related? The final section looks at the steps taken by various countries to reduce wastage in the education of girls, bearing in mind that each state has its own system of education operating within a particular economic, cultural and social context.

Deem, R ed (1980) *Schooling for Women's Work* Routledge and Kegan Paul: London
This volume is an edited collection of 12 contributions plus introduction and concluding chapter by the editor. Most of the chapters report original empirical research on women and education in Britain, the linking theme being the relationship of women's education to their roles in family and work. Many of the chapters raise theoretical issues as well as report empirical findings. The editor argues that the combined message of the chapters is that the reproduction through schooling of class and gender categories and the sexual division of labour plays a significant part in the perpetuation of the subordinate position of women.

Giele, J and Smock, A eds (1977) *Women: Roles and Status in Eight Countries* John Wiley and Sons: New York
The purpose of this book is to increase our knowledge about women's status and role in eight countries: Egypt, Bangladesh, Mexico, Ghana, Japan, France, the United States and Poland. Each chapter begins with a discussion of the historical and cultural background of the particular country and then examines women's roles and status in the context of the family, education system, family planning facilities and political system prevailing in that society. Through the use of this comparative method the book identifies some common standards by which women's status can be measured across societies, despite vast differences in government, economy and family.

Kelly, A (1981) *The Missing Half: Girls and Science Education* Manchester University Press: Manchester
This is a collection of essays which attempts to explain girls' under-achievement in science and suggests ways to improve their performance. The book is divided into three sections: theoretical interpretations, reports of research studies, and pupils'

and teachers' accounts of personal experience in the classroom. The authors adopt a variety of feminist and non-feminist perspectives. Different socialization models are suggested to account for girls' under-achievement in science. One view expressed is that there is no easy solution to the 'problem' of girls and science, and that change will only occur through a political challenge to the structural bases of their inequality. Another view expressed by one of the authors is that girls' lower level of achievement in science relative to boys is due to their innately inferior visuo-spatial ability. The final section of the book provides useful ideas for countering sexism in the classroom.

Kelly, G P and Elliott, C M eds (1982) *Women's Education in the Third World: Comparative Perspectives* State University of New York Press: Albany
This study focuses on the under-education of women in Africa, Asia, Latin America and the Middle East. The authors ask how education affects women and how it can be made to improve women's lives, while recognizing that schooling throughout the Third World functions in the context of social systems that oppress women. They argue that schools need not merely reflect or reinforce such systems but rather that they can be made into instruments of social transformation.
Part 1 attempts to identify the factors which predict whether a woman will or will not attend school. Part II focuses on the kind of education girls receive once in school and suggests that equality in access to education cannot be meaningful without changes in the content of education, teaching methods and the structure of everyday life in schools. In Parts III and IV, the authors' focus is on the outcomes of female education. They ask whether education enables women to mediate the impact of the family on their economic and social lives and whether education substantially affects women's lives in the family.

Lapidus, G W ed (1982) *Women, Work, and the Family in the Soviet Union* M E Sharpe: Armonk, New York
This volume is designed to offer an overview of current Soviet concerns by presenting a selection of the best recent Soviet writings on these subjects in English translation. The materials have been selected with three objects in mind: to illuminate the problems which stand at the centre of current discussions; to present the findings of some of the more recent Soviet research on women's employment and demographic trends; and to give some insight into current policy debates by including articles which express diverse points of view. A selected bibliography of both Russian and English language books and articles is included.

McAuley, A (1981) *Women's Work and Wages in the Soviet Union* George Allen and Unwin: London
This is the most recent book-length study by a Western author of the role of women in the Soviety economy. It provides a comprehensive assessment of Soviet evidence relating to the influence of education on the social and economic roles of women in a socialist state society. In his conclusion the author maintains that Soviet policy on women has tended to be informed by a rather narrow economic determinism which has failed to take into account men's resistance to changes in the distribution of domestic responsibilities. He suggests that women will not achieve complete equality in Soviet society until an autonomous women's movement emerges.

Maccoby, E E and Jacklin, C N (1974) *The Psychology of Sex Differences* Stanford University Press: Stanford
This book provides an extremely comprehensive review of research on psychological sex differences. In chapters 2 to 7 the authors attempt to establish precisely what the differences are that need to be explained.. They then explore the three main psychological theories that purport to explain these differences. The theories are that psychological sex differentiation occurs in children through imitation, through praise or discouragement and through self-socialization. Each theory is examined in turn to see how well it explains the data on psychological sex-differentiation. The authors conclude that societies have the options of minimizing rather than maximizing sex differences through socialization practices. The authors argue that a variety

of social institutions are viable within the framework set by biology, and that it is up to human beings to select those that foster the life styles they most value.

MacDonald, M (1981a) *Class, Gender and Education* (Open University Course E 353 Block 4 Units 10-11) The Open University Press: Milton Keynes
This is a block prepared for an Open University Course on 'Society, Education and the State' but it also serves as an extensive and recent introduction to issues of gender and education in Britain. The prime concern expressed by the author is 'to investigate the role of educational institutions in constructing and teaching specific definitions of gender to each new generation in preparation for both working and family life' (p3). She is also concerned with the links between class and education under both capitalist and socialist societies and the part played by the hierarchy of male over female in class systems. The volume includes short excerpts from articles by others on women and education and numerous statistical tables and references that will build up a picture of sex-differentiated educational outcomes mostly in Britain but in a cross-cultural context.

Malos, E *ed* (1980) *The Politics of Housework* Allison and Busby: London
This is a collection of readings on housework, mainly produced during the 1960s and 1970s. The readings reflect the development of feminist thinking in this area. In her introduction, Ellen Malos suggests that the writing which came out of the American women's movement in the 1960s tended to stress the psychological and ideological functions of women's role in the home. Subsequently, British and American women started to explore the historical roots of housework and to emphasize that women in the home are not just passive consumers but perform vital and unpaid work for capitalism by reproducing the labour force. Various papers suggest different ways in which women might respond to this recognition of their domestic exploitation. Some writers suggest that women should campaign for wages for housework so that they would have more economic power and could at least withdraw their labour like other workers. Other writers argue that the way forward is through the socialization of housework so that it is no longer assumed to be primarily women's responsibility. A major theme of the book is that women cannot achieve true equality in work or education until there are fundamental changes in the domestic division of labour.

Megarry, J (1981) *Sex, Gender and Education* Jordanhill College of Education: Glasgow
This 40-page booklet was produced at Jordanhill College as a study pack to support an integral part of the Education Department's course for all primary and secondary student teachers. Its main sections are on Sex, intellect and society; Sex, gender and education; Sex and school subjects; Appendices including Glossary, notes on the legal position and the role of the Equal Opportunities Commission, controversial quotations and bibliography.

The booklet was produced as part of a wider study on sexism in Scottish education, funded by the Equal Opportunities Commission; much of the data it presents had not previously been published. Although designed as stimulus material for group seminars, it has since been used elsewhere as independent study material.

Mercer, J (1975) *The Other Half: Women in Australian Society* Penguin: Ringwood, Victoria
This is a collection of essays on the position of women in Australia today, a society which Jan Mercer describes as 'bedevilled by oppression which is both blatant and subtle but never acknowledged'. The book is divided into four sections: Human behaviour and society; The status of women in Australia today; Women labelled as deviants; and The politics of change. Several essays raise the question of whether equality is possible within the present economic system, or whether we need a different basis to build a society where equality in social relations really exists and is not an empty political slogan. There are chapters on the position of migrant and Aboriginal women, and Chapters 6 and 12 deal specifically with the Australian educational system.

Said, E (1979) *Orientalism* Random House: New York
This publication is perhaps one of the most significant, penetrating and critical analyses of European scholarship on the East to be published in recent years. The major thesis is that the greatest Western scholars, despite their sympathy with oriental people, have reduced the East, with all its pulsating life, diversity and individual humanity, to abstract stereotypes invented by Western minds. It highlights the theme of the 'colonial encounter' dealt with in Nelson's paper.

Sayers, J (1982) *Biological Politics: Feminist and Anti-Feminist Perspectives* Tavistock: London
Janet Sayers' chapter, 'Psychology and gender divisions', is based on *Biological Politics* in which she explores in greater detail the place of biology in feminist and anti-feminist explanations of sexual divisions in social and educational institutions. Among topics considered are nineteenth century arguments about the supposed harmfulness of education to women's health; biological determinism, social Darwinism and sociobiology; physical strength, aggression, and male dominance; the social construction of female biology; and psychoanalytic perspectives on gender development and mothering.

Schools Commission (1975) *Girls, School and Society* Australian Government Publishing Service: Canberra, Australia
This work was a major report on empirical and theoretical evidence relevant to a consideration of sexism and counter-sexist strategies in Australian schools. It is important for the quality, succinctness and clarity of its treatment of the issues, for its role as a catalyst for policy and practice initiatives, and because it set a starting-point and framework for the discussion which has been widely used by subsequent state reports, teacher education institutions, etc. The Report covers evidence of demographic changes and statistics concerning the progress and treatment of girls and boys in schools; arguments concerning the nature of the overt and the hidden curriculum, of sex-role learning, of self-perceptions and self-confidence; and discussion on the treatment of sexuality and human relations and vocational counselling in schools. It also looks at 'groups with special needs': migrant, Aboriginal and country girls and women. *Girls, School and Society* makes a wide range of specific recommendations within a general principle that 'action should be designed to extend the capacity of both girls and boys to make considered choices on the basis of relevant knowledge and within a considered value framework'.

Scott, H (1976) *Women and Socialism* Allison and Busby: London
Hilda Scott explores the position of women in East European socialist countries, with particular reference to Czechoslovakia where she lived for many years. She begins by pointing out that, despite the belief that women's liberation would automatically ensue from the socialization of the means of production and the mass entry of women to the labour market, it is still possible to talk of 'men's' and 'women's' work in these countries. Scott examines the thinking of Marx, Engels and Lenin on the 'woman question', and, while acknowledging that there is much that is useful in these ideas, she is critical of the stagnation of socialist thinking on the position of women. She looks at various official policies which particularly affect women including restrictive industrial legislation and concludes that traditionally there has been too great a tendency to manipulate women's position in the labour market. After the Second World War in Czechoslovakia, for instance, when women's labour was desperately required, nurseries were built and there was a strong propaganda campaign to get women into the work force. In the 1960s, however, when there was concern about decline in population growth, abortion and contraception were made difficult to obtain and the building of nurseries was reduced. Scott recognizes the advances that socialist countries have made in working towards equal educational opportunities for boys and girls and encouraging girls to enter occupations like engineering and medicine which are regarded as non-traditional in Western European countries. However, the fundamental problem which remains unsolved is that women still have to fulfil the dual role of wife and

mother. This often causes a great deal of tension. Socialist theory must seriously address the problem of the family and its role in socialist industrialized society, and not assume that the impending scientific and technological revolution will provide all the answers. What Engels called 'the conflict of the sexes' will only be resolved through major social upheaval.

Signs: Journal of Women in Culture and Society (1982) special issue on feminist theory **7** 3 Spring
This collection includes seven substantial chapters on aspects of feminist theory, drawing mostly but not exclusively on American scholarship. Topics include an analysis of varieties of feminist and marxist theories, feminism and science, feminist discourse, and the sexual politics of the American New Right. There is also an extended review-essay on Women's Studies in the United States and some book reviews.

Sutherland, M B (1981) *Sex Bias in Education* Basil Blackwell: Oxford
This book provides a good general overview of the education of girls in Britain (with some reference to Scotland). Professor Margaret Sutherland considers different educational provision and experiences of boys and girls and the evidence on differences in aptitudes and abilities. The effects of social influences, the hidden curriculum, employment prospects and marriage and motherhood on careers are examined in relation to compulsory, further and higher education. Although coverage of each topic is of necessity brief, the book provides a valuable introduction to the topic of sex bias in education, backed by a most useful guide to further reading. Passing reference, too, is made to developments abroad, which gives an additional perspective.

Thorne, B and Henley, N eds (1975) *Language and Sex: Difference and Dominance* Newbury House: Rowley, Massachusetts
This is probably the most important collection of papers on language and gender to be published to date. The contributions cover a wide range of formal and interactional differences between women's and men's language. The editors provide an excellent comprehensive annotated bibliography of studies in this area.

Trudgill, P (1974) *Sociolinguistics: An Introduction* Penguin: Harmondsworth
This is a very readable introduction to sociolinguistic work of the form-based type. Theoretical points are explained with the aid of readily comprehensible examples. Chapter 4 deals specifically with language and gender, and draws its data from a fairly wide range of languages and dialects. The book is cheap and widely available.

Tucker, J ed (1981) Women and work in the Middle East *Merip Reports 95:* March-April
This volume of essays represents the emergent literature on studies of the position of women in the Middle East which recognizes them to be integral members of society, and as important participants in vital activities of production and reproduction. It represents one of the few collections reflecting a materialist approach to the study of women in the Middle East. In brief, it provides good empirical case studies that expand the field of inquiry beyond wage labour to encompass the subjects of reproduction, sexuality, social control, household work and casual labour. Although it does not directly focus on women's education it provides the broader socio-economic and historical context in which to understand issues of women's education in the Middle East.

Walker, S and Barton, L eds (1983) *Gender, Class and Education* Falmer: Lewes
This volume brings together papers presented at the fifth annual Westhill Sociology of Education Conference in Birmingham. Additionally, it contains three teaching bibliographies on gender and education, using materials from North America, Europe, and Australia/New Zealand respectively. The theme of the conference was 'Race, Class and Gender' (the papers on race having been published separately) and the contributions in *Gender, Class and Education* reflect the conference's concern with integrating class and gender approaches. According to the editors, the three major

themes are first, a call for an increase in emphasis in the analysis of gender and education upon the active response made by individuals to their social surroundings, especially when it takes the form of 'resistance' to conditions; second, a concern that the ways in which schools reproduce class and gender relations be better understood by continued exploration of specific historical, situational and institutional processes; third, a belief that it is important to make links between educational theory and educational policy on gender. There are 10 chapters, mostly about education in Britain but in several cases about education in the United States, and they represent the most comprehensive and recent work on gender by sociologists of education in Britain.

Biographical notes on contributors and editors

Sandra Acker (Guest Editor and Chapter 5) is an American who has lived and worked in Britain since 1971. After receiving a BA and teaching certificate from Wayne State University (Detroit), she taught briefly and then enrolled for a higher degree in the Department of Education of the University of Chicago, where she received her MA in 1968 and PhD in 1978. Early experiences in the women's movement in Chicago stimulated an intellectual and practical interest in the education of women. Most of her publications are in this area. She has recently co-edited (with David Warren Piper) *Is Higher Education Fair to Women?* for the Society for Research into Higher Education (in press). Since 1972 she has taught in the School of Education of the University of Bristol where, in addition to courses on the sociology of education, she has developed a study group for teachers in training on 'Women, Society and Education' and an MEd course entitled 'Education and Social Divisions: Class, Sex and Race'. She is founder and convenor of the Centre for the Study of Women and Education at the School of Education. She is currently writing about the sexual division of labour in teaching, and following her seven-year-old daughter's school career with a mixture of interest and apprehension.

Boel Berner (Chapter 18) is a Research Associate and Lecturer in Sociology at the University of Lund in Sweden. She has also worked and studied in London and Paris before gaining her PhD in Lund in 1981. She is the author of numerous articles in the fields of education, science policy, women and technology and technical change. She is co-editor of *Schooling, Ideology and Society* (1977) and *Education and the Division of Labour* (1979) (in Swedish and Danish), and the author of *The World of Technics* (1981) (in Swedish). She has been the editor of *Acta Sociologica* and several other Scandinavian political and scientific journals, including the women's studies journal, *Kvinnovetenskaplig Tidskrift.* Her present research concerns men's schooling for technical work and the knowledge ideology involved in different types of technological education.

Gillian Blunden (Chapter 12) lectures at the South Bristol Technical College, England, teaching both adolescents and adults. She teaches Sociology and Public and Social Administration at both GCE O and A levels.

The author completed her doctorate at the University of Bristol, School of Applied Social Studies, in 1982. She had previously taught full-time at Boston College of Further Education, Lincolnshire, for over two years.

Her publications include 'Typing in the Tech: Domesticity, Ideology and Women's Place in Further Education' in Denis Gleeson (ed) *Youth Training and the Search for Work* (1983) and 'Our Women are Expected to Become . . . Women and Girls in Further Education in England at the Turn of the Century' in London Feminist History Group *The Sexual Dynamics of History: Men's Power, Women's Resistance* (1983).

Carol Buswell (Chapter 8) is Senior Lecturer in Sociology at Newcastle upon Tyne Polytechnic, England. In 1979 she did full-time fieldwork in a comprehensive secondary school in the north of England. 'Sexism in School Routines and Class-room Practices' *Durham and Newcastle Research Review*, IX, 46 (1981) was a discussion of sexist practices and younger pupils in the school, and the paper 'Ped-agogic Change and Social Change' *British Journal of Sociology of Education*, I, 3 (1980) argued that curriculum 'packages' which were becoming widespread would serve to 'de-skill' teachers, particularly women. She continued part-time fieldwork in the school until mid-1982, and the present chapter is based on evidence from that period. The position of women in work, and the changes that are necessary at higher levels of education to alleviate the earlier lack of opportunities and qualifications, is discussed in 'Women, Work and Education' *Social Policy and Administration*, (Summer, 1983).

Shirley Cunningham (Chapter 14) is a Lecturer in Education at Aberdeen College of Education. She has experience of both the English and Scottish educational systems, attending primary and secondary school in Wolverhampton, England, before moving to Scotland to study history at Aberdeen University. She was for several years a journ-alist on Scottish provincial newspapers before returning to Aberdeen University for a postgraduate degree in Education.

Marta Danylewycz (Chapter 13), following her undergraduate degree at Ohio State University, moved to Montreal, where she did a master's degree in History at McGill University and taught in a secondary school for two years. She completed her doctoral studies in French Canadian educational and women's history at the University of Toronto in 1981. Publications by Dr Danylewycz include articles on the relationship between nuns and feminism in nineteenth and early twentieth century Montreal and on women and teaching in Quebec. She has taught at Atkinson College at York University, and at the University of Western Ontario, and held a post-doctoral fellowship at the Ontario Institute for Studies in Edu-cation. She is currently Assistant Professor in the history department, Atkinson College. With her co-author Alison Prentice, she plans to write a book on the history of teachers in Canada.

Miriam David (Chapter 15) is a Lecturer in Social Administration at the University of Bristol. Her main teaching and research interests are in educational policy and child care. She is interested in the ways in which the State in Britain and the USA structures family relationships and responsibilities through its social, economic and educational policies. She teaches courses on education, the family and social policy, the political economy of social policy, social policy in the USA and Women's Studies, both intra- and extra-murally. Her publications include the following books: *School Rule in the USA* (1975); *The State, the Family and Education* (1980) and articles on the New Right's family policies and their implications for women's Education in Jane Lewis (ed) (1983) *Women's Welfare, Women's Rights*; and S Walker and L Barton (eds) (1983) *Gender, Class and Education*

She was a member of the Bristol Women's Studies Group which edited *Half the Sky: an introduction to women's studies* (1979). She is currently writing a book, with Caroline Freeman, to be published by Penguin in 1984, on child care. She is the mother of two children. She has been active in the women's movement since 1970, teaching women's studies and more recently in the feminist-inspired National Child Care Campaign.

Renate Duelli Klein (Chapter 23) is a Swiss neurobiologist with an MSc from Zurich University who did research on ants' orientation behaviour and taught biology and chemistry at college level in Switzerland. After some time in South America and Australia she then got her second education in Women's Studies at Berkeley, USA, where she studied and taught for three years. She is currently finishing her PhD on the dynamics between the theory and practice of Women's Studies in higher education at London University. With Maresi Nerad and Sigrid Metz-Göckel she has edited *Feministische Wissenshaft und Frauenstudium* (1982) and with Gloria Bowles *Theories of Women's Studies* (1983). She is also the European editor of the *Women's Studies International Forum* and one of the editors of the *Athene Series* (both Pergamon Press). Her forthcoming collection (with Rita Arditti and Shelley Minden, in press) on the implications of reproductive technologies for women's lives and the future of motherhood combines her interests from her past as a biologist and her present as a feminist in Women's Studies.

Carolyn M Elliott (Chapter 19) is the Program Officer for Education and Culture in the New Delhi office of the Ford Foundation which has an active programme support for women's studies. Previously, she was the Director of the Wellesley College Center for Research on Women, and Associate Professor of Political Science at the University of California at Santa Cruz. Her publications include Kelly and Elliott (eds) *Women's Education in the Third World* and Thories of Development: An Assessment, in *Women and National Development: Complexities of Change*.

She has spent a total of more than six years in India over a 20-year period, beginning with her dissertation research on Indian politics in 1962.

Terry Evans (Chapter 7) is a Lecturer in Sociology in the School of Education at Gippsland Institute of Advanced Education. He has taught in school, college and university settings over the past 11 years. His current research interests are concerned with the process of gender construction and reproduction in educational settings, and also with the gender relationships which surround women who enter non-traditional work. Dr Evans has completed research in pre-schools, primary schools, high and technical schools, as well as with recent school leavers. The results of his research have been published and presented to conferences in Britain and Australia. Recently, he published a bibliography of Australian and New Zealand studies in the area of gender, class and education.

Jane French (Chapter 4) recently spent a year carrying out ethnographic research on gender and primary schooling in the School of Education at Bristol University. This was followed by two years' research work on the social organization of secondary school science lessons in the Department of Sociology at Manchester University. She is currently a Lecturer in Sociology in the Faculty of Education at New College, Durham. She continues to pursue the research interests initiated at Bristol and Manchester.

Peter French (Chapter 4) spent three years researching infant classroom interaction in a project entitled 'Language at Home and School' at Bristol University. He has lectured in education, sociology and linguistics, and is currently a Senior Lecturer in Language Studies at the College of Ripon and York St John. At present, he is involved with research projects on phonetics in communication and language skills for primary teaching.

Fatimah Hamid Don (Chapter 9) is Professor of Curriculum Development at the University of Malaya in Kuala Lumpur, Malaysia, and Distinguished Professor of the Tun Abdul Razak Chair for Southeast Asian Studies in Ohio University, Athens, United States of America, for the 1983-84 academic year. She has been an educator for almost 20 years. Her research and publications have focused on teacher education, educational planning and development, curriculum, language education, geography education, early childhood education and women's issues. She has worked as educational consultant to the Ministry of Education, the Sabah Foundation, UNESCO, Ministry of Welfare Services and the Manpower and Modernization Unit of the Prime Minister's Department. Currently, she is a research adviser of the National Council for the Integration of Women in Development.

Throughout her career, Professor Fatimah has remained active in women's voluntary organizations. She was Vice President of the National Council of Women's Organizations for two terms. She also belongs to several professional bodies: at present she is a member of the Board of Directors of the International Council on Education for Teaching (ICET). She is also the President of the UNESCO National Association of Malaysia (UNAM).

Professor Fatimah was dean of the Faculty of Education, University of Malaya from 1975 to 1980. She received her training in Malaysia, London, and Los Angeles and has travelled extensively.

Marlene Hamilton (Chapter 10) has been employed at the School of Education (Teaching Section), University of the West Indies, since 1973. She holds the post of Senior Lecturer and teaches Educational Psychology at the undergraduate and post-graduate levels. She has also acted as a UNESCO Consultant, and has conducted a number of studies for this organization in Jamaica and the West Indies. Her research interests span several areas, including creativity, attitudes and achievement levels in the sciences, and sex-role stereotyping. She has published in Caribbean as well as international journals. She is a Jamaican.

Eric Hoyle (Consultant Editor) has been Professor of Education at the University of Bristol since 1971. His previous posts included teaching in two secondary schools, a college of education and a university. His interests and published works are in the areas of educational administration, the process of innovation, the professional development of teachers and the relationship between research and policy.

He is also interested in the sociology of knowledge and the sociological study of organizations and of the professions. He was founding co-editor of *Research in Education* and is on the editorial boards of a number of other journals including the *British Journal of Teacher Education*. He was research consultant to the Donnison Commission on direct grant schools, vice-chairman of the Educational Research Board of the Social Science Research Council and is currently a member of the Executive Committee of the Universities Council for the Education of Teachers, and a co-opted member of Avon Education Committee. He has lectured in various colleges and universities in Africa, Australia, North America and Malaysia.

Gail P Kelly (Chapter 6) is Professor in the Faculty of Educational Studies at the State University of New York at Buffalo. She has co-authored several books on women, including *Women's Education in the Third World: Comparative Perspectives* (1982) (with Carolyn M Elliott) and *Feminism and the Disciplines: Challenge, Discovery and Impact* (in press) (with Ellen DuBois, Elizabeth Kennedy, Carolyn Korsmeyer and Lillian Robinson). Gail Kelly is currently Associate Editor of the *Comparative Education Review* and has written extensively about the field of education. She is also a scholar of French colonial schooling in Southeast Asia and West Africa, and has published articles and monographs on this topic. She has travelled extensively in Western Europe and in the Third World. She directs a staff development project, in conjunction with UNESCO, at the Alvan Ikoku College of Education in Owerri, Imo Stage, Nigeria.

Elsa Leo-Rhynie (Chapter 10) is a Jamaican who has been Research Fellow in Educational Psychology at the School of Education, University of the West Indies, since 1977. Her research interests centre around the prediction of academic performance, particularly in the GCE A level examinations, sex differences and sex role development. She has also done work in teacher education, has carried out evaluations of educational programmes, and has acted as consultant in early childhood development for UNESCO and the Van Leer Foundation. Her work has been published in Caribbean and international journals.

Beverly Lindsay (Chapter 11) is at present a Senior Researcher and Manager for the National Institute of Education in Washington, DC. She was formerly Assistant Professor of Education Policy Studies at the Pennsylvania State University, University

Park, Pennsylvania. She holds EdB, MEd and MA degrees from the University of Massachusetts, Amherst. Her BA (Magna Cum Laude) was awarded from St Mary's University in San Antonio, Texas. Her major areas of research and publication focus on sociocultural and educational issues influencing Third World people. She has received grants from the Ford Foundation, the National Fellowship Fund, and the Pennsylvania State University to conduct research in Africa, the Caribbean, the People's Republic of China and the United States. She is the editor of *Comparative Perspectives of Third World Women: The Impact of Race, Sex, and Class* and the forthcoming anthology, *Migration and National Development in Africa*. Her publications have appeared in the *International Journal of Contemporary Sociology, Higher Education: The International Journal of Higher Education and Educational Planning*, the *International Education Journal*, the *Journal of Modern African Studies*, the *Comparative Education Review*, the *Journal of Negro Education* and the *International Encyclopaedia of Education: Research and Studies*.

Alastair McAuley (Chapter 16) is Senior Lecturer in Economics at the University of Essex. He has been working on the broader topic of inequalities and welfare in the Soviet Union for a number of years and is an expert on Soviet social security. He is the author of *Economic Welfare in the Soviet Union* (1979) and *Women's Work and Wages in the Soviet Union* (1981) as well as several articles on related topics. He lives in Colchester with his wife and three children.

Jane Roland Martin (Chapter 2) is a Professor of Philosophy at the University of Massachusetts, Boston. A past President of the Philosophy of Education Society, she is the author of numerous articles on philosophy and education. In addition, she is the author of *Explaining, Understanding, and Teaching* (1970) and the editor of *Readings in the Philosophy of Education: A Study of Curriculum* (1970). Her current research on the place of women in educational thought took shape during the year she spent as a fellow at the Bunting Institute of Radcliffe College (1980-81). She has since published several essays on the topic, and her book on philosophical ideals of the educated woman is scheduled for publication in 1984 by Roman & Allanheld.

Jacquetta Megarry (Series Editor and Chapter 1) is a freelance author, editor and journalist. After a first degree in Maths and Psychology at Cambridge University she trained and practised as a teacher in Glasgow. She took a Master of Education degree at Glasgow University, where she became Lecturer in Education in 1971 under Stanley Nisbet. She moved to Jordanhill College of Education in 1973, where she worked on general educational topics and also produced distance learning materials in educational technology.

From 1979 to 1980 she had a small grant from the Equal Opportunities Commission to investigate sex-typing in Scottish schools. During this time she produced *Sex, Gender and Education* (1981) — see annotated bibliography — and also several shorter publications on sexism including a report (*Racism and Sexism in Children's Books*) for the Educational Institute of Scotland (the teachers' union).

After leaving Jordanhill, she was briefly Deputy Director of the Scottish Microelectronics Development Programme. Since 1981, when her son Alexander was born, she has worked freelance from home, specializing in computers. She writes regularly for newspapers such as *The Times, Scotsman* and *The Times Educational Supplement*, as well as for specialist computing and academic periodicals. In 1983, *Computer World* (her illustrated introductory book for males and females) was published by Pan as a Piccolo Factbook.

Maxine Molyneux (Chapter 21) is Lecturer in Comparative Sociology at the University of Essex and specializes in developing countries. She is the author of numerous articles on women, socialist revolution and development, and has written two books: an ILO study of female employment in Democratic Yemen, and, with

Fred Halliday, *The Ethiopian Revolution*. She is currently preparing a comparative study of the state policies and the position of women in post-revolutionary societies, for which she has done research in Nicaragua, Afghanistan, Cuba, Ethiopia and Democratic Yemen. She is a founding editor of *Feminist Review*.

Cynthia Nelson (Chapter 17) is a New Englander — born and raised in Maine and educated in the public school system of Massachusetts — of Swedish immigrant parentage. Her higher education included a BA in Sociology/History from the University of Maine in 1955, an MA degree in Human Development from the University of Chicago in 1957 and a PhD degree in Anthropology from the University of California, Berkeley in 1963. For the past 20 years she has been living, learning and teaching in Egypt. Fieldwork experiences include a study of a Tarascan fishing community and a mestizo agricultural village of Lake Patzcuaro, Michoacan Mexico during her doctoral studies. While in Egypt she has conducted research among settled Bedouins of the Western desert, rural Nile delta peasants and various social groups of urban Cairo. Major research areas include: the impact of social and economic change on traditional values and social structure; the relationship of women to the development process; energy and rural development; comparative health and healing systems and epistemological issues in fieldwork. In addition to teaching and administrative responsibilities at the American University in Cairo, she has served as consultant to the World Health Organization on projects related to Primary Health Care in the Sudan and Egypt. Publications include: *The Waiting Village: Social Change in Rural Mexico* (1971); *The Desert and the Sown: Nomads in the Greater Society* Institute of International Studies Monograph Series (eds) (1973); 'Private and Public Politics: Women in the Middle Eastern World' *American Ethnologist* 1 2 (1974); *Women, Health and Development* (1977); 'Energy Technologies and Village Development' co-authored with Salah Arafa *Proceedings of Second International Conference on Technology for Development* (1982).

Stanley Nisbet (Associate Editor) retired from the Chair of Education at the University of Glasgow in 1978. Starting his professional life as a classics teacher he was caught up in the vigorous psychometric activity at Moray House in Edinburgh under Godfrey Thomson, and his early work was in this field. After five years of war-time service in the RAF, part of the time in its Training Research Branch, and a short spell in the University of Manchester, he became professor of education in Queen's University, Belfast and was involved in some of the post-war educational developments in Northern Ireland. From 1951 to 1978 he was professor of education in the University of Glasgow, holding various administrative posts in the University (eg Dean of the Faculty of Arts, 1965-67) and serving on many bodies outside the University (eg the Scottish Council for Research in Education). His teaching was mainly on educational theory, curriculum study (in 1957 he wrote one of the earliest books in this field) and comparative education (with a special interest in Germany and the USSR). Much of his writing has consisted of contributions to official publications. Since his retirement he has participated in projects on a number of subjects, including home-school co-operation in the EEC countries and the monitoring of in-service courses for primary school teachers.

Alison Prentice (Chapter 13) is now a Full Professor in the Department of History and Philosophy of Education at the Ontario Institute for Studies in Education. She has previously taught in a private girls' school, in a public secondary school and at Atkinson College, York University, all in Toronto. Her special interests include the history of educational ideology and the history of women and education, and she has developed courses and published books and articles in these areas. The director, since 1975, of an Ontario Institute project devoted to research in Canadian women's history and the development of documentary studies, bibliographies and other materials for teachers in the women's history field, she has also recently become head of a new Women's Studies Centre at the Ontario Institute for Studies in

Education. She and Marta Danylewycz, her co-author, are planning a book on the subject of their chapter in this volume, the history of women teachers in Canada.

Sheila Riddell (Bibliography) is currently working for an MEd degree by research at Bristol University. Her research is being carried out in Dorset secondary schools where she is looking at the various processes which affect boys' and girls' option choices in the third year. Before this she taught for six years in a comprehensive school. She is active in the women's movement and the peace movement. She has a four-year-old daughter.

Janet Sayers (Chapter 3) has worked as a clinical and educational psychologist, and has been active in the women's movement since 1970. She now teaches Developmental and Abnormal Psychology at the University of Kent where she also convenes the Women's Studies MA degree course. She has written about psychological sex differences, and about the place of biology in explanations of sexual divisions in society. Her current work is on psychoanalysis and feminism. Janet Sayers is married and has two school-age sons.

Hilda Scott (Chapter 20) is a writer specializing in social policy questions as they affect women. Her work has appeared in journals in Europe and the United States. Background material for her article in this volume is drawn from her book *Sweden's Right to be Human, Sex Role Equality: The Goal and the Reality* (1982), based on three study trips to Sweden in 1968, 1975 and 1979. She is also the author of *Does Socialism Liberate Women? Experiences from Eastern Europe*. She now lives in Cambridge, Massachusetts, and is writing a book about women and poverty.

Margaret B Sutherland (Preface) has been Professor of Education in the University of Leeds since 1973. Originally, having taken a degree in French and German at Glasgow University, she taught these languages in Glasgow schools. She also studied Education and Psychology for the degree of MEd of Glasgow University. Her PhD work was done in Queen's University, Belfast, where she was consecutively Lecturer, Senior Lecturer and Reader in Education. A past Chairman of the Education Section of the British Psychological Society and of the British Comparative Education Society, she is currently President of the World Association for Educational Research and a member of the Education Sub-committee of the University Grants Committee. She has written a number of articles in various educational journals, including 'Donna Britannica: University Women Teachers in Great Britain' (*Journal of Educational Thought*, August 1983); her books are *Everyday Imagining and Education* (1971) and *Sex Bias in Education* (1981).

Lyn Yates (Chapter 22) is a Lecturer in Education in the Centre for the Study of Innovation in Education at La Trobe University. Her current writings and research interests are in the areas of curriculum theory, non-sexist education and feminist social theory. She is actively involved in movements concerned with girls, women and education at both school and tertiary levels.

Index

WIDENER UNIVERSITY
WOLFGRAM
LIBRARY
CHESTER, PA.

DATE DUE

APR 0 3 1985			

DEMCO 38-297